LIBERATION SOCIOLOGY

DATE DUE

			PRINTED IN U.S.A.

LIBERATION SOCIOLOGY

3RD EDITION

by

Joe R. Feagin
TEXAS A&M UNIVERSITY

Hernán Vera
UNIVERSITY OF FLORIDA

AND

Kimberley Ducey
UNIVERSITY OF WINNIPEG

Routledge
Taylor & Francis Group

LONDON AND NEW YORK

First published 2015 by Paradigm Publishers

Published 2016 by Routledge
2 Park Square, Milton Park, Abingdon, Oxon OX14 4RN
711 Third Avenue, New York, NY 10017, USA

Routledge is an imprint of the Taylor & Francis Group, an informa business

Library of Congress Cataloging-in-Publication Data

Feagin, Joe R.
   Liberation sociology / by Joe R. Feagin, Texas A&M University, Hernán Vera, University of Florida, Kimberley Ducey, University of Winnipeg. — 3rd edition.
       p. cm.
   Includes bibliographical references and index.
   ISBN 978-1-61205-724-8 (pbk. : alk. paper) — ISBN 978-1-61205-725-5 (consumer ebook)
 1. Social justice. 2. Social ethics. 3. Sociology—Moral and ethical aspects.
4. Sociology—Political aspects. 5. Applied sociology. 6. Critical theory. I. Vera, Hernán, 1937– II. Ducey, Kimberley. III. Title.
   HM671.F43 2014
   303.3'72—dc23

                                                                    2014012162

Designed and Typeset by Straight Creek Bookmakers.

ISBN 13: 978-1-61205-724-8 (pbk)
ISBN 13: 978-1-61205-723-1 (hbk)

CONTENTS

Preface and Acknowledgments

Liberation Sociology has a distinctive history, following developments in liberation-oriented social science as well as the world through three editions. Not long after the first edition of this book, the New York City and Washington, DC, events of September 11, 2001, changed the world in which we live. Soon thereafter, President George W. Bush began aggressive preemptive military invasions against the governments of Afghanistan and Iraq. Rather quickly, the myths of US innocence and moral superiority were no longer tenable in the face of revelations about torture by US soldiers in Iraqi prisons, about rendition episodes in which agencies of the US government secretly moved US prisoners abroad to places where torture was less visible or was politically acceptable, and about the US president and other high-government officials supporting extreme torture tactics banned by international agreements.

One US television network soon began a popular and propagandistic television series called *24*, whose plot line usually involved "terrorists" who, when tortured, at the last minute provided accurate information needed to avert terrible events that would involve many deaths. Under this worst-case scenario set by the television producers, average viewers likely found it hard to think of constitutional alternatives to the aggressive torture applied before their eyes. Yet, these media-contrived events do not reveal that such torture is usually counterproductive, because most people admit to anything under torture. Such programs clearly desensitize the public to the horrors of torture and thereby subvert the protections against totalitarianism theoretically provided by the US constitutional tradition.

Soon after our first edition of this book, a media "feeding frenzy" was generated by 9/11 and the subsequent Iraqi invasion, and the media often provided the world with haunting images of a sharpened racial divide in the United States. Americans of color, especially those with Middle Eastern backgrounds, were routinely stereotyped and mocked in the mainstream media, discriminated against in the workplace and malls, and violently attacked on the streets. Moreover, travelers within the United States have been constantly reminded that the US government views itself as "at war with terrorism" when they are forced to dispose of their mouthwash and hand lotion bottles in passing through security searches at airports. Such extreme security measures constantly ensure that the average American will make a personal connection between life in the United States and the military invasions in the Middle East. In addition, offering a rationale of expanding "homeland security," numerous governmental officials and private groups have inaugurated a renewed "war" against undocumented immigrants from Latin American countries, such as in the effort to build tall security fences on the Mexican border. In spite of this xenophobic effort to wall out needed workers—who are in fact economic refugees from countries wherein US corporations play a key role in creating economic crises—few US citizens see the irony in continuing to brag about the US role in the 1990s destruction of the Berlin wall in Germany and the end of a Soviet political system that routinely blocked and persecuted immigrants.

In the first and second editions, we predicted an increase in the aggressive international posture of a still imperialistic United States. At that time, very few US sociologists had ever systematically examined this US imperialism or colonialism in mainstream sociology publications. This is still the case. We still see few articles in the *American Sociological Review* and only a few books in the book list in *Footnotes*, the newsletter of the American Sociological Association, that indicate major research by US sociologists on this country's continuing overseas invasions and international imperialism. In our view, such social science research is still much needed if this country is ever to achieve its celebrated ideals of "liberty and justice for all."

Today, sociology ignites the imagination of countless students who choose to take sociology courses or elect sociology as a major in colleges and universities around the world. Indeed, we, the coauthors, share the experience of having our imaginations ignited when each of us, in separate countries, first encountered sociology in university courses. Joe Feagin decided to become a sociologist after attending his first lectures in sociology at Harvard University. Hernán Vera, at about the same time in Chile, became enamored with sociology when he first read C. Wright Mills's vision of sociology in *The Sociological Imagination*. Decades later in Canada, Kimberley Ducey decided to become a sociologist after reading the sociological work of Joe Feagin and Hernán Vera.

Students today continue to be attracted to sociology because of its promise to contribute to their political, social, and moral understanding of themselves and their social worlds—and often because they hope it will help them participate in building a better society. For generations now, not just college students but all who learn to read the world through sociological ideas have shared in the excitement and insight of being empowered by their newly acquired mindfulness. Community activists, union leaders, teachers, social workers, journalists, lawyers, politicians, theologians, and many others the world over have found sociology to be enlightening and useful in their careers and lives.

However, all too often sociologists choose to forget the activist, progressive, and radical traditions of the discipline they actively practice. Sociological theories are frequently taught as disembodied ideas on the margins of one's education. The passion and social change commitments of the great thinkers and activists in social science are frequently forgotten. The ideas and works of pathbreaking sociologists such as Jane Addams and W. E. B. Du Bois—to mention but two of the giants whose research and commitment to a better world have shaped our society and discipline—are only occasionally taught well. In this state of collective amnesia, it is easy to go with the flow and accept conventional approaches and ideas that circulate because of their immediate utility. New ideas and approaches are frequently seen as distractions from "career" work. We once asked a colleague what he thought of the work of Michel Foucault, the great European analyst of society whose work was then beginning to have a significant impact in US sociology. Naïvely, he said, "I have not read that work because I have had no need to quote it."

Yet new ideas are extraordinarily important to human progress. In 1905 a modest European graduate student wrote his doctoral dissertation and three research papers that, with one more research paper written in 1915, articulated the revolutionary ideas that constitute what is today referred to as "Einstein's universe." Photoelectric cells and lasers, fiber optics, space travel, semiconductors, our view of the birth and expansion of the cosmos, and nuclear power are just a few parts of the huge new universe that Albert Einstein's and other physicists' innovative ideas created. Einstein was, to use a term we employ in this book, a countersystem thinker. He did not work alone; he was gregarious and passionate about his scientific ideas. In his early days, he worked with Milena Marić, a scientist whom he married. Throughout his life, he developed scientific ideas in discussions with friends and colleagues. Over his lifetime, Einstein published hundreds of articles, many in scientific journals, but many others in liberal outlets on such progressive causes as pacifism and international human rights.[1]

In sociology today, a countersystem thinker is likely to research and document empirically such social phenomena as the increasing inequality among class, gender, and racial groups in this and other contemporary societies. Such a countersystem sociologist may, on the basis of that research, challenge the established and inegalitarian societal order on which many private and government policies are built. There is no question that those countersystem sociologists who believe that a better world is possible, and who have oriented their teaching and research to that viewpoint, sometimes have a harder time going through hiring and promotion rituals in the private marketplace, government agencies, and academia. Today, the idea that social justice and democracy are the better future for our society and world is far from being a matter of general policy consensus. If this difficult political reality should deter readers of this book from orientating their careers and lives toward participation in research on and construction of a much more egalitarian and democratic society, then they will miss out on one of the most exciting aspects of the discipline of contemporary sociology.

The amnesia surrounding the roots of sociology and an uncritical acceptance of conventional theories and methods too often influence the ways in which sociology is taught in the undergraduate curriculum and in courses for new sociologists in graduate schools. Conventional theoretical ideas and instrumental-positivistic methods (see Chapter 1 for a definition) are frequently taught as if they constitute the essential core of the discipline and the only way of doing a legitimate sociology. There is too much emphasis in graduate education on learning how to conceal from others, and from oneself, one's own cultural, class, racial, political, and gender biases. In many sectors, the most respectable sociology is that which takes a position of apparent social neutrality, yet one often uncritical of or unaware of its moral and political impact on other human beings.

Nonetheless, sociology remains a valuable social science, for it has great potential to assist in progressive and necessary social change. It has both the craft and the intellectual perspective to contribute to a deeper understanding of how any society works. Sociologists have the potential to probe the social complexity of life in ways that their colleagues in numerous other disciplines cannot. Indeed, in terms of significant ideas and research, sociology already has had an important impact on US society and the world. Politics, business, social work, and government would be difficult to conduct without the vocabulary and concepts borrowed from sociology. Ideas and terms such as *role, institution, ritual, variable, model, correlation, social class, social environment, social consensus, status, prestige, privilege, conflict, integration, social function,* and so on have often migrated from sociology into everyday life and popular discourse.

Like other social sciences, sociology has the potential to yield an image of a better world for all but also a potential for assisting in continuing oppression. It is the potential for social improvement that we want to support and reawaken with this book. This text is not a treatise on all one needs to know about the societal-liberation potential of sociology. Instead, it includes many sociological ideas and much data organized in such a way as to render its readers mindful of the moral and political dimensions of the craft and vocation of sociology. An awareness of these dimensions is the indispensable precondition for a critical understanding of social science and for contributing by means of that social science to the betterment of society.

We wrote this book with sociology and other social science teachers and students in mind. Indeed, we provide throughout the book, and especially in the epilogue, specific advice and suggestions for teachers and students. In addition, we believe this book to be useful for all those who want to learn how to understand the social dilemmas and future potential of the planet we live on—and for all those who would like to play a part in improving and saving the human and other species. Science and technology have moved at a blinding speed in the past century, but scientific knowledge and techniques will be only as liberating as our ability to put them to use for the common good. Otherwise, they will be used to construct more sophisticated systems of oppression that will likely benefit a few, while degrading the overall human condition.

We also wrote this book to assure young social scientists that a social science that openly acknowledges its moral concerns, its own biases and limitations, and its hopes and fears for the future is not only possible but also essential for the country's and the planet's survival. The pressures placed on graduate students and new faculty members to do conventional teaching, to conduct mainstream instrumental-positivistic research, or to obtain extramural funding for its own sake can make it appear that sociology can no longer be practiced without giving up humanistic goals and intellectual independence.

Indeed, graduate students at major universities have periodically reported that some of their professors no longer see room for idealism and activism in contemporary sociology. The examples in the pages that follow will clearly dispel the impression that such idealism and activism no longer have a place in contemporary sociology. Just to mention one expression of such new activism, we can note Sociologists Without Borders (Sociólogos Sin Fronteras; SSF), which was organized in Spain in 2001 and in the next year in the United States. This is a transnational organization of sociologists, faculty, and students with these stated goals from its website (www.sociologistswithoutborders.org): "That all people have equal rights to political freedoms and legal protections, to socioeconomic security, to self-determination, and to their personality. That is, old or young, regardless of where they live, their faith, and whether they are male or female, gay or straight, and regardless of their skin color they have the same universal rights, including their rights to their own particular cultures.... SSF is thus perfectly in synch with public sociology that advocates that sociologists be engaged and committed, and also reflective and critical. Besides SSF-US, there are chapters in Brazil, Chile, Iran, Canada, and Spain." This statement was prepared by the distinguished sociologist Judith Blau. The organization has a journal, *Societies Without Borders*, and made a significant impact in 2003 by putting a resolution against the Iraq invasion on the annual American Sociological Association ballot. With members in many countries, the organization has partnered with international human rights groups at the World Social Forum and the US Social Forum.

Currently, grassroots organizations across the globe are regularly undertaking field research projects designed for community betterment, projects for which social science knowledge and research are indispensable. In numerous countries, nongovernmental organizations are mushrooming to assist community groups in creating better lives for their people, and these organizations frequently use the talents of sociologists. Many sociologists wishing to pursue human rights ideals and activism will need to educate themselves in the innovative methods, ideas, and practices that will enable them to contribute to the goals of these community and other grassroots organizations. Although the ability to cross-tabulate data from survey data sets may occasionally be useful to people seeking more just communities and societies, there are many other sociological research strategies that can be quite useful. The latter can aid in the understanding of the social worlds that local people need in their struggle to transform and improve their lives. It is for those seeking a career in a change-oriented sociology, for those seeking a fulfilling life working as social scientists on behalf of human betterment, that we have written this book.

As numerous physical and social scientists are currently demonstrating (see Chapters 6 and 8), the human species may be running out of time. The evidence suggests that within the next century, major environmental crises, such as global climate change and ozone depletion, and the trend of increasing global income and wealth inequality along racial and class lines, will likely contribute to a significant decline in or destruction of numerous human societies across the planet.

We need a new generation of visionary social researchers and activists who think clearly and deeply about building a better human society now and in the future. Frederick Polak, a pioneer in social-future studies, strongly urged social scientists, political leaders, and ordinary citizens to ask what our vision of the human future is. Although sociological research and ideas can help us understand our societal dreams and decide which to accept or reject, such analysis is beneficial only if it allows us to choose a better social future. Let us conclude by closely paraphrasing Polak's final words: *We human beings have the ability to dream better futures than we have yet succeeded in dreaming. We have the ability to create a much better society than we have yet succeeded in creating.*[2]

Overview of New and Expanded Features

These are some of the new and expanded features of this thoroughly revised third edition of *Liberation Sociology*:

- Provides dozens of examples of the latest liberation-oriented social science research, with an emphasis on the new generation of liberation-oriented sociologists and other liberation-oriented social scientists
- Covers more types of liberation social science research and activism, including environmental, criminological, immigration, and animal rights research
- Probes more deeply into the sociological theoretical and empirical traditions and their links to related social science fields, such as history

- Provides more international examples of liberation-oriented social science, including in Canada, Africa, Latin America, and the Middle East
- Expands the coverage and analysis of important participatory action research
- Emphasizes with key examples how students can and do actively contribute to creating better societies
- Provides many case studies as tools to increase human abilities to understand deep societal problems, engage in better dialogues, and encourage more democratic participation

ACKNOWLEDGMENTS

In the preparation of the three editions of this book, we have been indebted to many supportive and helpful social science colleagues. Although we cannot name them all, we would particularly like to thank the following for their help, comments, and suggestions on various drafts of this book: Diana Kendall, Anne Rawls, Sidney Willhelm, Jennifer Mueller, Claire Renzetti, Ken Bolton, Nestor Rodriguez, Stan Bailey, T. R. Young, Gideon Sjoberg, Nijole Benokraitis, Noel Cazenave, Carl Jensen, Phil Nyden, Walda Katz-Fishman, Jerome W. Scott, Mary Jo Deegan, Barbara Finlay, Michael Hill, Kendal Broad, Paul Johnston, Maxine Baca Zinn, Bob Newby, Tony Orum, Leslie Houts Picca, David McBride, Rachel Feinstein, Bernice M. Barnett, Colin Goff, Peyman Vahabzadeh, Andrew Woolford, Elaine Weiner, Lucia Benaquisto, William K. Carroll, Elaine Coburn, Christopher Chase-Dunn, Vishwas Satgar, Yahilo Unno, Michael Dusseault, So'Lanna Dallaire, Donatella della Porta, Monte Bute, Tim Woods, The Manitoba Research Alliance, Elizabeth Comack, John Loxley, Jim Silver, Prairie Women's Health Centre of Excellence, David Naguib Pellow, Daniel Faber, Shirin Ahmadnia, Onwubiko Agozino, Joey Lywak, Jelena Tubin, David Nibert, John Sorenson, Tamari Kitossa, Scott Myers-Lipton, The Transformative Studies Institute, John Asimakopoulos, Ali Shehzad Zaidi, Leah Schmalzbauer, Al Gedicks, Alfonso Arrau, Raúl Urzúa, Daniel Chernilo, Juan Enrique Opazo, and Frank Lindenfeld. We are indebted to our Paradigm editor, Dean Birkenkamp, for his constant enthusiastic support for this project and its underlying goals.

*To Derek, Nicolás Bastián, Natasha María,
Marcos Antonio, So'Lanna, and all the world's
other children and grandchildren. May the world
you inherit be much more just than ours.*

CHAPTER I

What Is Liberation Sociology?

In the spring of 1845 one of the founders of the liberation social science tradition, the young Karl Marx, wrote that "the philosophers have only interpreted the world, in various ways; the point, however, is to change it."[1] Sociologists centrally concerned about human emancipation and liberation take this insight seriously. The point of liberation sociology is not just to research the social world but also to assist in changing it in the direction of expanded human rights, participatory democracy, and social justice.

Liberation sociology is concerned with alleviating or eliminating various social oppressions and with creating societies that are more just and egalitarian. An emancipatory sociology not only seeks sound scientific knowledge but also often takes sides with, and takes the outlook of, the oppressed and envisions an end to that oppression. It adopts what Gideon Sjoberg has called a *countersystem approach*. A countersystem analyst consciously tries to step outside her or his own society to better view and critically assess it. A countersystem perspective often envisions a society where people have empathetic compassion for human suffering and a real commitment to reducing that suffering. It envisions research and analysis relevant to everyday human problems, particularly those of the socially oppressed. The countersystem standard is broader than that of a particular society or nation-state. Using a strong human rights standard, such as the UN Universal Declaration of Human Rights, the liberation social scientist accents broader societal and international

1

contexts and assesses existing social institutions against a vision of more humane social arrangements.[2]

The consequences of taking this standpoint are explored throughout this book. We are eclectic in our approach and influenced by Enlightenment, modernist, and postmodernist theorists. Neo-Marxist, feminist, and antiracist conceptions have had their impact on our thinking. Moreover, the liberation theology of Latin America and Africa and important developments in the way we think about the mind and the body—no longer a viable dichotomy—have also been influential (see Chapter 2).

We do not propose here another abstract or doctrinaire approach but rather an emancipatory way to practice good sociology. Taking sides with, and understanding the outlook of, the socially oppressed can have profound consequences for the stages of social research: on how we know what we know, on what we choose to research, on the nature of our scientific endeavor, on the methods we choose, and on the conclusions we can draw from research.

A sociologist's, or a social research team's, choice of what to study is consciously goal-oriented. This always subjective choice is not made in social isolation but according to personal and collective tastes and convictions and is often in response to enticements such as grant monies, career prestige, or job security. Thus, many sociologists choose to deeply research US society with an eye to changing it for the better, whereas others choose to narrowly research topics whose description or analysis is mainly sought by leading agents of the status quo. Some social scientists go into the field and critically examine the impact that powerful nation-states or large corporations have on people's everyday lives and provide that information to proponents of change, whereas others limit their research to less critical descriptions of the views or attitudes of the general population for an establishment funding agency. Some choose to dig deeply into a society's foundations, including its systems of social control and information distribution, whereas others choose to do only surface-level research that helps those who head dominant institutions perform their roles more successfully.

Some social science research emphasizes its policy relevance for those at the helm of the nation-state or corporations. In contrast, the research of liberation sociology is generally defined by its usefulness to those who are oppressed and struggling for their liberation. A contemporary example of a sociologist who exemplifies the liberation sociology message is Peyman Vahabzadeh from the University of Victoria in Canada. As a student in Iran, he supported the overthrow of the reviled Shah of Iran, who with US help deposed a *democratically* elected government. As a refugee, he found a new homeland in Canada. Through it all, Vahabzadeh remained haunted by the fate of his fellow Iranians, including his brother, who survived one tyranny (the Shah) only to face another (the Ayatollahs). His brother was one among many murdered by Iran's leaders in the Islamic Republic.[3]

Presently, Vahabzadeh's research emphasizes the constitutive role of social movements in Iran. From the women's movement, to the student movement, to the workers' movements and trade unionism, to ethnic and environmental movements, he studies emerging secular politics. His path to liberation sociology makes clear an agonizing fact of society: the prevalence of violence in countless forms that coexists with innumerable injustices. He has dedicated his research, teaching, and activism to nonviolent alternatives for social change, while exposing systemic and frequently hidden forms of violence. But "most rewarding," for Vahabzadeh, "is training a new generation of activists."[4]

Radical phenomenology has become a guiding theory and method that informs Vahabzadeh's work on human collective action and social movements. A contemporary addition to the tradition of phenomenological sociology, radical phenomenology situates thinking and acting in epochal frames, presenting truth as temporal and conditioned by diverse periods and offering dissimilar and shifting possibilities for thinking and acting. Vahabzadeh reassesses democratic discourse, the notion of rights, liberal democratic regimes, time and epochs, oppression, and the practice of sociology itself.[5] As he told us,

> Radical phenomenology offers a glance into the epochal frames in which Truths become dominant and matters-of-fact. By showing that Truth has a temporal character and thus rises and falls, radical phenomenology cultivates an approach that is always in search of, and attuned to, the new. The new always reveals itself through action and as such the sobriety of the actors will decide the common future of humans and nonhumans in terms not imposed by regimes of truth.[6]

Another influential Iranian sociologist is Sarah Shari'ati Mazinani at the University of Tehran. She is a public intellectual and regular commentator on women's status and social justice. She is the daughter of Iranian liberation sociologist and theorist Ali Shari'ati—one of the most important Iranian intellectuals of the twentieth century. Shari'ati offered a liberationist reading of Shi'i Islam and is said to have influenced the younger generation that participated in the 1979 revolution. He supported the Algerian Front de Libération Nationale and had correspondences with Frantz Fanon and Jean-Paul Sartre.[7]

Like her father, Shari'ati Mazinani is a defender of social justice and insists that sociologists be interested in practical questions. Mohammad Amin Ghaneirad, a sociologist for the National Research Institute for Science Policy, an Iranian think tank, has explained Shari'ati Mazinani's position well. According to Ghaneirad, she endorses what some Iranian sociologists call "clinical sociology." Clinical sociology suggests that theory have an applied purpose, namely, to determine the most effective means for healing society. As Ghaneirad puts it, "The clinical sociologist enters the society and experiences various social phenomena and analyzes them with theoretical tools available to her/him rather than making judgments based on his/her theories from a distance."[8]

Commitments to alleviating human suffering or to peace, human rights, social justice, and real democracy, as evidenced in the research, teaching, and activism of Vahabzadeh and Shari'ati Mazinani, politicize the practice of sociology no more than the social science commitments that assert indifference and supposedly value-free methods or neutral knowledge.

One of the exciting developments over recent decades has been the emergence of an array of critical social theories in the humanities and social sciences. These include, among others, feminist theory, postmodern theory, queer theory, antiracist theory, and a variety of Marxist theories. Numerous sociologists have joined progressive social science organizations. Since the 1960s, critical social theory and research have frequently been published in books and certain social science journals.[9] As sociologist Berch Berberoglu has noted, "This new generation of critical scholars—envisioning a society without exploitation, oppression, and domination of one class, race, sex, or state by another—helped provide the tools for analysis for the critical study of social issues and social problems that confront contemporary capitalist society."[10]

In their research and analysis, most critical social analysts press for the liberation of human beings from oppressive social conditions. Most research the larger institutional contexts and macrostructures of oppression, domination, and exploitation and yet also view such structures as crashing into the everyday lives of human beings. The daily experiences of oppressed and subjugated peoples are a central focus and concern. Moreover, as a rule, critical social theorists do not focus only on the negative realities and consequences of oppression but often target issues and strategies of human liberation from that oppression (see Chapter 7). These theoretical frameworks generally see resistance to oppression and domination as beginning "at home, in people's everyday lives—sexuality, family roles, workplace."[11] These critical social thinkers support the agency and action of human beings in their own liberation.

EMPOWERING PEOPLE

One Effort at Liberation Sociology: Project Censored

Let us briefly examine an example of another sociological effort toward societal liberation—a research project called Project Censored that has had a significant impact in the United States. Carl Jensen, a Sonoma State University sociologist, launched this national research effort in the 1970s to explore whether there was systematic omission of important and newsworthy events and issues in the mainstream US media.

In discussions with us, Jensen has noted that his quest was stimulated in part by bewilderment over the reelection of Richard Nixon by a landslide only months after the news of the Watergate break-in, one of the more sensational political crimes in US history—in which Nixon's campaign organization was then known to be involved.[12] Jensen's knowledge of the mainstream press was useful in explanation: "While there was substantial information available tying the administration in with the Watergate burglary, the media did not put the issue on the national agenda until after the presidential election in November 1972."[13] Therefore, the American people who went to the polls in that fateful November were generally "uninformed about the true significance of Watergate." In effect, the mass media fostered the reelection of a criminal politician, Richard Nixon.

Jensen's bewilderment is an attitude toward events that has propelled the research of many generations of scientists. Galileo, Albert Einstein, Karl Marx, W. E. B. Du Bois, Ida B. Wells-Barnett, Charlotte Perkins Gilman, and many others also refused to accept what was happening before their eyes as unproblematic, routine, or natural. They asked, "Why?" "How?" and "Under what conditions?" As in other countersystem sociology projects, this attitude was coupled with a desire to change a problematical society, to make a difference. Jensen imagined a world with more democracy and one with a freer flow of honest and accurate information.

An attitude of concern about what happens in the social world is not easy to translate into research. Many other people may be looking at the same happenings and seeing something ordinary and not worth significant research. Jensen had come to understand an important issue but learned as well that "no one else seemed to share that knowledge."[14] He queried sociology departments at universities, seeking advice, yet received no response. Alfred McClung Lee, a past president of the American Sociological Association, whose work we examine later, was one of the few who encouraged this innovative media project.

Interestingly, Jensen's main support came from the lower-middle-class and working-class students who took his annual seminar on media censorship issues. In 1976 this seminar began to conduct the research he had in mind, and Project Censored was born. This project became "a personal crusade" that led him to cut back his teaching activities in the mid-1980s. Sociology departments seldom have resources or the inclination to finance internal research projects, particularly those with such a progressive intent. It was not until 1989 that Jensen got a grant from the CS Fund, one of the few foundations that support innovative boat-rocking research projects. This breakthrough allowed him to better produce and disseminate the media research results. In the twenty-first century, Project Censored continues to have an impact on domestic and global public access to mass media information. After Jensen retired from the project, sociologist Peter Phillips was brought in to shepherd the operations of Project Censored. In 2010 Mickey Huff, a historian, became the director and has labored with others to expand their affiliates program to include hundreds of faculty and students at many colleges and universities to help uncover important news stories.

According to Project Censored's mission statement on its website (www.projectcensored.org), "Project Censored educates students and the public about the importance of a truly free press for democratic self-government. We expose and oppose news censorship and we promote independent investigative journalism, media literacy, and critical thinking." To identify the news stories, Project Censored relies on numerous researchers, especially college students participating in the annual Project Censored seminar at Sonoma State University. These students analyze the news story nominations received from journalists, educators, librarians, researchers, and the general public. They examine the nominations and after a critical discussion decide which can be considered censored in the mainstream media. The research offers students an opportunity to learn by participating in field research.

Every year, Project Censored then publishes a list of the twenty-five most censored or ignored news stories. By ranking the serious news stories and disseminating the details about them, Project Censored better informs the public. For example, in 1995 the media ignored a story about sixty-eight elderly men and women who were dumped in a mass grave in Chicago. Most were poor people who died alone and unknown during that year's heat wave. For Jensen, "the traditional hallmark of a responsible press is that it should afflict the comfortable and comfort the afflicted; it would seem that today's press has turned that measure on its head."[15]

Over the years, Project Censored's Top 25 list has called the public's attention to the suppression of very important stories. In 2013, for instance, the most censored story was the dramatic growth of the US government as a type of police state. Beginning with the 2001 "Patriot

Act," the federal government has greatly expanded its ability to monitor many aspects of Americans' lives and, under the National Defense Authorization Act, to get the US military to jail citizens without a trial who are just *thought* to be involved in terrorism against the country. Ordinary protests protected by the US Constitution are under regular surveillance by police authorities. As the Project Censored pioneering report puts it, "the Department of Homeland Security's 'If You See Something, Say Something' campaign has encouraged the public to report all suspicious activity to local authorities, even though actions that the DHS identifies as 'suspicious' include the constitutionally protected right to criticize the government or engage in nonviolent protest."[16]

A range of poorly covered news stories across the globe emerges each year from the research of those affiliated with Project Censored. For example, there is the huge story that the negative impact of Japan's Fukushima Daiichi nuclear disaster (2011) is many times more serious than the mainstream media in the United States, Japan, and other countries have reported. The Project Censored report provides chilling data indicating that the fallout on the United States alone from this disaster will result in at least 14,000 excess deaths. The report also found that the US Environmental Protection Agency's radiation detection network was in poor condition to provide first-rate data on the dangers of this radiation.[17]

Walter Cronkite, the famous journalist who wrote the introduction for a 1996 Project Censored yearbook, noted that ideological diversity "is the strength of the free press, and since the nation's founding it has been so perceived by those who love democracy."[18] Project Censored counters to an extent what Cronkite calls "the awesome power" of elite mainstream media executives, deciding what news is worth exposing. The news stories that reached television journalists like him "have been culled and re-culled by persons far outside our control." People at local newspapers or at the wire services often decide which news items are passed to television network news centers in big cities, where producers and anchor people then decide what goes on the air. Colorful stories tend to get the most attention. As some journalists say, "if it bleeds, it leads." A small elite of professional journalists make the "significant judgments on the news of the day ... a lot of power for a few [elite] men."[19]

The social scientists and others guiding Project Censored have made it clear that they are not just concerned with zealous governmental officials who censor news, as when US military officials have limited press access to the theaters of war. There are other forms, including business-oriented actions that are in effect self-censoring. Peter Phillips, the former director of Project Censored, has explained that "media owners and managers are motivated to please advertisers and upper-middle-class readers. Journalists and editors are not immune from management influence. Journalists want to see their stories approved for print or broadcast, and editors come to know the limits of their freedom to diverge from the bottom-line view of owners and managers."[20]

In addition to identifying bypassed news stories, Project Censored keeps an eye on trends. One trend is the increased concentration of media ownership. A democracy cannot survive without a free flow of information. The managing editor of the *New York Times* once confided as much: "Year after year, newspapers have become concentrated into fewer and fewer organizations. Those organizations have become more and more centralized, less and less concerned about the flow of information to the public and more occupied with the flow of profits to the central corporation."[21] In the twenty-first century a few hundred top executives and directors on boards of the largest and most-influential media corporations have become the media elite of the world, yet they would fit in a medium-sized college classroom. Although these executives and directors may not agree on all issues, "they do represent the collective vested interests of a significant proportion of corporate America and share a common commitment to free market capitalism, economic growth, internationally protected copyrights, and a government dedicated to protecting their interests."[22] With still increasing concentration, only a narrow corporate-sanctioned version of the news will likely be presented. Moreover, as this concentration and censorship are placed in the hands of executives and directors at ever fewer multinational corporations, we will see ever more global media control and a narrowing of the news available to the majority of people on the planet.

The social scientists and others working on Project Censored show us how the sociological imagination can be applied for the common good. Without a strong commitment to participatory democracy and a vision of the importance of an educated citizenry, the research conducted in this project would not have been possible. Carl Jensen and his social science colleagues have been engaged in an important type of liberation sociology, one with a clear critical and countersystem approach to research and analysis.

ANOTHER EFFORT AT LIBERATION SOCIOLOGY: USING SOCIOLOGY TO FIGHT CONTEMPORARY SLAVERY

Social scientist Kevin Bales is another compelling example of a countersystem analyst committed to reducing human suffering. Locating few articles on modern-day slavery after completing an exhaustive review of thousands of articles, he established that no social scientist had conducted rigorous research on the topic. He decided to do something about it. "As a social scientist and a sociologist, I was thinking 'wow! There are millions of people in slavery'; [t]his is a very important thing to understand. This is an ancient form of social interaction and social control, which many believe had been eradicated.... So it was my curiosity and my sociological approach that drove me into the issue." Bales undertook a qualitative research project and traveled to meet slaves and slaveholders. "It had to be ... qualitative," he explains, "as the crime was so hidden. I looked at the economics of slave-based businesses in different parts of the world. I tried to tease out the different dimensions of what was going on."[23]

His book *Disposable People: New Slavery in the Global Economy* is the result of his research. There he tells the disturbing story of a "new slavery," one linked to the global economy.[24] In 1999, the same year *Disposable People* first appeared in print, Bales teamed with Simon Pell, head of Arts for Labour in the United Kingdom, to establish a fund-raising and research consultancy. The progressive company raises money for environmental campaigns, human rights groups, medical charities, overseas development, and other charities and voluntary sector groups.[25] In 2000, together with others, Bales founded Free the Slaves, a nonprofit organization that works to "liberate slaves around the world, helps them rebuild their lives and researches real world solutions to eradicate slavery forever." Free the Slaves works both on the ground to liberate individuals from slavery and on policy initiatives to eliminate slavery worldwide.[26] During a recent talk, Bales explained, "Liberation, and more importantly all the work that comes after liberation, it's not an event, it's a process. It is about helping people to build lives of dignity, stability, economic autonomy, citizenship."[27]

As in other countersystem sociology projects, Bales's approach is coupled with a desire to change the world, to make a difference. Like the social scientists at Project Censored, Bales has engaged in an important type of liberation sociology, with a critical approach to research and analysis. Recently, Bales has further explained his motivations:

> We have to ask ourselves, are we willing to live in a world with slavery? If we don't take action we just leave ourselves open to having someone else jerk the strings that tie us to slavery in the products we buy and in our government policies. And yet, if there is one thing that every human being can agree on, I think it's that slavery should end.[28]

Sociology and Societal Betterment

The sociology of liberation is part of a long tradition that aims at both studying and rebuilding society. Auguste Comte, the French social philosopher who coined the word *sociology* in the nineteenth century, viewed the new science as laying bare the reality of society and thereby helping to transform it (see Chapter 2). Comte gave lectures in France on his "positive philosophy" (later called *positivism*). However, Comte was not a progressive philosopher. The new directions for societal change that he envisioned were rather protective of a certain societal status quo. In a draft of his book on the civil war in France, Karl Marx noted that Comte "was known to the Paris workers as the prophet of personal dictatorship in politics, capitalist rule in political economy, hierarchy in all spheres of human activity, even in science, the creator of a new catechism, a new Pope, and new saints to replace old ones."[29]

In the 1930s, in one of the first probing analyses of the social meaning of what sociologists were doing, Robert Lynd proposed that the knowledge produced by a critical sociology is required so that democracy can "continue to be the active guiding principle of our culture."[30] In his major book *Knowledge for What?* Lynd argued that sociology should focus on practical problems in need of societal reform. Operating with an interdisciplinary focus that questioned the building of self-perpetuating academic traditions, Lynd called for research oriented toward truly democratic principles.

In this book we, too, call for the practice of more emancipatory and liberation sociology, but we do not seek an end to all conventional sociological research linked to funding by the nation-state or by mainstream foundations. These latter research efforts often do generate valuable knowledge about the structure and reality of US society, such as in sociological research projects dealing with the corporate abandonment of central cities.[31] Nevertheless, many traditional social science projects directly or indirectly reinforce the oppressive structures of society, if only by not challenging those social structures with strong alternatives going beyond the limits of present-day elite-controlled US politics. We also call here for greater democratic access to social science knowledge, which some regard as a commodity that confers the power to control nature, to shape other human beings, and to improve ourselves. Knowledge is power, and some, like Michel Foucault, use the combined word phrase *power/knowledge* to describe the two aspects of the same phenomenon.[32]

Thus, we call for the reassertion of a sociological practice designed to empower ordinary people through social science research and knowledge. By having better access to critical sociological knowledge, people will be in a better position to understand their personal and familial troubles, make better sense of the world we live in, plan their individual and collective lives, and relate in egalitarian and democratic fashions to others within and outside their own nation-state. This includes being in a better position to struggle for individual and collective human rights. A broad-based democracy can be fully developed in our era only if key types of knowledge are made available to all, not just to those at the top of the socioeconomic pyramid and their professional servants.

We envision here much more egalitarian access to relevant scientific knowledge. We believe that a renewed social science commitment to human liberation and social justice—a shift to the "for whom" and "for what" relevance of social science research and writings—can significantly reshape the scientific practice and product that sociology and other social scientific disciplines regularly generate. As we have seen in the examples of Project Censored and of Bales's slavery project, a major aim of a countersystem research project is to raise both the researchers' and the people's consciousness of society's oppressive structures. A related goal is to stop, or significantly reduce, human oppression and suffering. As we will make clear in subsequent chapters, liberation sociology follows in the paths of early sociologists like Jane Addams and W. E. B. Du Bois, who connected sociological ideas to social activism, and of later sociologists like C. Wright Mills, who proposed that a sociological imagination allows people "to grasp what is going on in the world and to understand what is happening in themselves as minute points of the intersections of biography and history within society."[33]

OPPRESSION: A CENTRAL SOCIOLOGICAL PROBLEM

Questioning Social Hierarchy

Liberation sociology is concerned with the oppression of various groups in society, including those who are poor or are discriminated against because of their physical appearance, alternative lifestyles, or orientations. Everyday life involves interaction, with most people coming into contact with others daily. Our relationships are shaped by societal structures and forces, including racism, patriarchy/sexism, heterosexism, class exploitation, and other processes of domination. Such societal forces are expressed in informal networks and formal bureaucratic organizations. Social scientists have long observed what the effects of these and other social forces are on people enmeshed in them—much in the way physicists infer the existence of the forces of gravity or electromagnetism.

Since early in the history of the discipline, progressive sociologists have questioned the major inequalities in the distribution of socioeconomic resources in societies where they have lived, as well as across the world. However, at least since the 1920s, mainstream sociology and other social sciences have too often tiptoed around major issues of elite power and coercion, especially in regard to class, racial, and gender oppression. In recent decades, when mainstream social scientists have examined power issues, they have often preferred to research legitimate power (sometimes called *authority*) rather than illegitimate power. In addition, they have substantially ignored the (mostly white male) ruling class at the helm of society. For example, most social scientists who have researched social class and social mobility in US society have limited themselves to social classes below the level of the very top elite.[34] Clearly, the social sciences sometimes play a traditional role in society. A glaring example is the once widely discussed book *The Bell Curve*, written by social scientists Richard Herrnstein and Charles Murray. This book, which has sold millions of copies, explicitly argues against the ideal of societal equality. By defending the meaningfulness of so-called intelligence test differentials (actually, learned-skills test differentials) between white and black and Latino students for US government educational policy, this social science book further attempts to legitimize racial inequality and discrimination.[35] As sociologist Alvin Gouldner once noted, social science has a "dialectical character and contains both repressive and liberative dimensions."[36]

In the United States, deeply critical analyses of power and hierarchy are resisted by most captains of industry, politicians, and mainstream intellectuals and by much of the general public. This country's traditionally white, male leadership resists such probing analyses because these will likely make more obvious the unfairness of the existing distribution of social positions and material and symbolic rewards. Since most leaders and much of the public do not ask for critical analyses of major power holders, it is easy for many social scientists to take the position that it is not their responsibility to research or correct the large-scale power and resource inequalities. In contrast, the sociology of liberation embraces concerns about this toxic social inequality and about the illegitimacy of the powers that be. It takes the additional step of choosing the societal processes and institutional arrangements that produce this deepening inequality as its central problem to study closely.

In this book we underscore the act of choosing what should be studied because this is a crucial decision in much social science practice. Injustice should be examined not just in its maldistribution of goods and services but also in the deep-lying social relations responsible for making that distribution possible. These social relations, among which oppressive power relations are a key part, are responsible for the way in which important societal goods are distributed. They determine whether individuals, families, and other groups are integrated into or excluded from society's decision-making processes. And they can shape the development of human identities and the sense of belonging and dignity. In the end, social justice is more than a question of redistribution of power, more than a matter of resolving within existing relations how goods are distributed. It is a matter of totally restructuring the larger framework of inegalitarian social relations for the greater human good.

As we have noted, important among the major social oppressions are racism, patriarchy/sexism, heterosexism, and class exploitation. Dorothy Smith has argued that mainstream sociology is linked to the dominant ideological apparatus of US society, which accounts for its historical emphasis mostly on research issues primarily of concern to white men. For the most part, mainstream sociology's themes are "organized by and articulate the perspectives of men—not as individuals ... but as persons playing determinate parts in the social relations of this form of society."[37] For many decades, feminist sociologists and others representing subjugated groups have pressured social scientists to research the social world from the perspectives of the oppressed and to take their experiences seriously as a source of societal understanding and knowledge (see Chapter 7).

The common social science term *social system* is often laden with the assumption that societal arrangements are more or less harmonious and that change in one element brings about change in other elements and in the general organization of the system (see Chapter 3). Although some societal relations exhibit an equilibrating or harmonious character, many do not show any such character. Expropriation, exploitation, domination, and oppression are processes that produce and reproduce the way Western societies like the United States are hierarchically arranged. To characterize a social arrangement as a more or less static social system without explaining how it was initially created and how it is being reproduced takes for granted as immutable what we need to actively observe and change.

Many influential social scientists—particularly those who have the best-paying, most-stable jobs—have been white men, and if they wish, they can isolate themselves from the many severe consequences of social oppression. C. Wright Mills once noted that "most social scientists have had little or no sustained contacts with such sections of the community as have been insurgent; there is no left-wing press with which the average academic practitioner in the course of his career could come into mutually educative relations." Such isolation has had significant and negative impacts on both the social sciences and on society.[38]

What Is Social Oppression?

In a probing analysis, political scientist Iris Young suggested that oppression and domination are disabling constraints that affect the "institutional conditions necessary for the development and exercise of individual capacities and collective communication and cooperation." Domination involves "institutional conditions which inhibit or prevent people from participating in determining their actions or the conditions of their actions."[39] These constraints operate at various societal levels. For example, loving parents who routinely make important decisions without consulting their children when they are old enough to make their own choices disable them through their domination. In like fashion, benevolent dictators have disempowered the people whose good they have claimed to seek.

Oppression consists of "systematic institutional processes which prevent some people from learning and using satisfying and expansive skills in socially recognized settings or institutionalized social processes which inhibit people's ability to communicate with others or to express their feelings and perspective on social life in contexts where others can listen."[40] The persecution and killing of Jews and Roma ("Gypsies") in Nazi-dominated Europe, the exploitation of farm laborers in the United States, the pillage of indigenous people's lands in the name of progress, the enslavement of Africans in the Americas, and the sweatshops still found in US and other Western cities are major examples of societal oppression. Those who must work for much less pay on account of their class, race, ethnicity, sexual orientation, or gender status are thereby socially oppressed. Oppression also eliminates or reduces human dignity and the capacity to express oneself and participate in society as effectively as those who are more privileged.

The oppression of women has been a central issue of the current era. In her famous 1960s book *The Feminine Mystique*, Betty Friedan wrote of the troubled North American housewife, especially the white suburban housewife, as being in a state of recurring personal distress. Though most such women lived in enviable circumstances by international standards, they often felt cheated and suffered from numerous gendered afflictions that came to be known as "housewives' fatigue." Friedan did not write her book merely to engage the reader's sympathy but to show that these women were being prevented from self-realization through gendered oppression and cultural conspiracy; this "feminine mystique" framing led women to believe that their happiness lay only in the kitchen and nursery.[41] Friedan's analyses were part of the feminist resurgence of the 1960s. In the years that followed, her analysis was criticized for seriously neglecting the central concerns of working-class women and women of color, especially those who had long worked outside the home. Eventually, the concerns of many women became part of a complex women's liberation movement.[42]

Here we underscore the institutional and embedded character of contemporary societal oppression. In one sense, the term *oppression* does cover the tyranny that a despot or ruling group exercises over others.[43] For example, in twentieth-century Europe, numerous fascist and Communist regimes oppressed their peoples in political terms. Yet there are other forms of contemporary oppression that do not involve this overt tyranny but rather are embedded in social norms and beliefs extending over long periods of time. Another term for this is *hegemony*, or domination with "a velvet glove."[44] In today's forms of societal oppression, many individuals who contribute to maintaining and reproducing the various oppressions see themselves as merely doing their jobs and living out normal lives. If asked, they would reject the view that they could be agents of oppression. Our emphasis on broad social processes and long-term institutions allows us to understand the apparent paradoxes of a society's oppressed peoples sometimes contributing to their own victimization—and even turning into oppressors of yet others.

In the United States and other countries around the world, there are privileged groups and oppressed groups that differ in the goods, resources, and opportunities that these countries make available to their members and in the degree to which they participate in societal decision-making that affects lives. These differences are hard to deny, even though some might choose not to see their continuing reality. As sociologist W. E. B. Du Bois once noted, some groups are privileged *because* others are oppressed. For example, for long decades in the nineteenth and twentieth centuries, the extreme poverty and degradation in the African colonies of European nations was "a main cause of wealth and luxury in Europe. The results of this poverty were disease, ignorance, and crime. Yet these had to be represented as natural characteristics of backward peoples."[45] Centuries of colonial exploitation of African labor and land have long been omitted from numerous historical reviews of the realities of European prosperity and development. A similar situation exists for generations of white Americans, whose prosperity is deeply rooted in centuries of exploitation of the labor and land of African Americans, Native Americans, and other people of color in North American history. A similar argument can be made for the privileges of men in regard to the conditions of women. This historical background of the United States is too often ignored or downplayed in contemporary accounts of racial discrimination and other oppressions, especially in the mainstream media.

The heterogeneous society that is the now United States is clearly differentiated in terms of oppressed and privileged peoples. Thus, we wish to gain some distance from arguments built upon the assumption of a homogeneous "American public," as found in much Western sociology of culture. Too often the term *Americans* in the media and in scholarly writings actually means "white Americans," and little thought is given by the commentators to the fact that a large proportion of the population may not share the view or behavior attributed to those "Americans."[46] Political and academic viewpoints that attempt to pass themselves off as neutral, or that claim a national consensus, are often the viewpoints of the privileged.

The particular meanings attached to social differences—which make them seem natural, traditional, or necessary—are deeply embedded in our stock of tacit understandings and knowledge. A sociology of liberation often questions and uncovers the hidden aspects of these concrete, historically given social arrangements so that they can be better understood—and perhaps acted upon so that their oppression is undercut.

HUMANIZATION AND CRITICAL CONSCIOUSNESS

Increasing Humanization

One conceptual starting point for our endeavor is the human vocation, the calling to be fully human. Seldom stated in conventional social science, the initial assumptions of the researcher need to be made explicit, for they shape research much more than just in its methodological principles. The statement of underlying domain assumptions is an important means for preserving the integrity of research, a topic we examine in detail later.[47]

A contemporary example of a sociologist who makes initial assumptions explicit is Donatella della Porta, a professor at the European University Institute. Like many scholars of social movements before, she has both studied and participated in social movements. She explains:

> My entrance to university corresponded with a very tense moment in Italian politics, with political violence and state repression closing down spaces for movements. Although still sympathetic to the left-libertarian movements in general, I left active politics, but not politics as a focus of attention. In fact, I started to study social movements in 1981, while I was doing a Master's degree at the École des hautes études en sciences sociales (School for Advanced Studies in the Social Sciences) with Alain Touraine. Social movements remain a main focus in my work.[48]

In addition to social movements, presently della Porta's research concerns political violence, corruption, police behavior, and policies of public order. She has conducted investigations in Italy, France, Germany, and Spain. Currently she is director of the comparative research project Mobilizing for Democracy, which addresses the role of civic organizations in democratization processes, thereby bridging social science approaches to social movements and democracy. From a theoretical point of view, she addresses structural preconditions and actors' tactics, and the main focus is on recent democratization processes in European Union member and associated states. Reflecting on how her research has been shaped by more than methodological principles, della Porta explains:

I think what helped me was that my parents—even if moderate in politics—were quite open-minded for Sicily, especially at that time. I could therefore develop autonomously. Cousins of my mother and her husband ... were active members of Medicina Democratica, a social movement organization that worked on health issues, such as the effects of pollution. In my youth, they were for me a source of political and social inspiration.[49]

Brazilian educator Paulo Freire wrote that while human beings have the potential for humanization and dehumanization, their true vocation is only humanization. Injustice, exploitation, the violence of oppressors—and their denial and dissimulation in euphemisms and ideologies—generate and undergird dehumanization. Our humanity is affirmed in struggles to achieve freedom and social justice. Dehumanization marks and defines the oppressor as much as it torments the oppressed. Activist sociologist Onwubiko Agozino, whose work we examine in later chapters, echoes Freire's sentiments:

> I have always argued that oppression does not harm only the targeted group ... slavery also harmed white men morally because they raped black women and then sold their own blood children into slavery as property; sexism harms men too because many men do not approximate the ideals of dominant hegemonic masculinity and because the women directly harmed are our sisters, daughters, friends, wives and mothers; and poverty is a problem for all because the rich cannot sleep safely knowing that the hungry man is an angry man.[50]

For Freire, the struggle to recover humanity is a struggle of the oppressed "to liberate themselves and their oppressors as well."[51] Oppressors who exploit and exclude by virtue of their power ordinarily cannot find the strength to liberate anyone. At best, they may soften their grip and may become gentler in exercise of power. In contrast, liberation sociology struggles to understand society well and then to disrupt the realities of oppression, the taken-for-granted, "natural" order that supports it and makes it possible.

Facing Challenges in Communities

In the United States, sociology originated as a field whose early practitioners were substantially committed to research for major social change. Among these were Jane Addams and W. E. B. Du Bois, whose work we examine in Chapters 3 and 4. Addams and Du Bois are examples of what Antonio Gramsci has called "organic intellectuals."[52] They are from or represent the oppressed sectors of society whose lived experience gives them an understanding superior to those intellectuals who come from highly advantaged sectors of society. Organic intellectuals work for liberation of their oppressed groups, often in local communities. For the first time, Addams and Du Bois brought into US social science the actual experiences, history, and culture of formerly excluded peoples. Not surprisingly, their research was aimed at improving the lives of the poor, the working class, immigrants, women, and Americans of color. Their progressive sociology sought mostly to better the lives of less powerful Americans, not to advance their careers or create a people-distancing social science discipline.

In later chapters we will observe that there is much interesting research linking community activists and social scientists in common efforts to understand various types of oppression and bring about social change. Some of this research is mainly evaluative; it attempts to assess the effectiveness of existing remedial programs. Another approach is broader and tries to collectively spell out community needs and how they might be addressed in new and innovative ways, and then works with people to help them deal with serious social problems. Such research is usually linked to community-defined goals.

Take the example of an organization called Project South: Institute for the Elimination of Poverty and Genocide, based in Atlanta, Georgia. This organization incorporates sociological research into education and organizing projects. An activist organization shaped in part by sociologists, it engages in workshops, action-research projects, and popular education projects across the country. Workshops are organized by and for community activists and activist scholars and are designed to help them better comprehend problems such as health care and the criminal "injustice" system. Project South's action-research efforts pull together teams of grassroots activists and social scientists to develop materials for popular education and community organizing. One project has gathered oral histories and statistical data to describe socioeconomic conditions in Georgia's communities and to discover what impact political campaign funds have had on these areas. Low-income neighborhoods in several cities have been part of the project, and in each case the findings have been put into videos and pamphlets for use in workshops and for community organizing. Project South researchers begin the process of community discussion by conducting at least one local workshop to examine the research findings and often work with community leaders. Project South has also developed other projects, such as the Grassroots Popular Education Project, which is a resource-building program for grassroots organizations, and the Leadership Development Initiative, a development program for low-income grassroots leaders in Georgia.[53]

In 2007 the first ever US "Social Forum" took place in Atlanta under Project South auspices. Project South organized this forum over two years of intense efforts. Some 15,000 people, young and old, men and women, participated in many workshops spread over the city. After the 2007 Social Forum, and after working with other activist groups, Project South set up the Southern Movement Assembly. The purpose of this organization is to groom grassroots leaders, especially youth leaders, and to support progressive grassroots organizations in the Southern states. The goal is to regenerate a twenty-first-century freedom movement for the South's many underserved communities. Included in this effort is a strong accent on a National Student Bill of Rights. The forum's major themes have included Gulf Coast reconstruction in the post-Katrina era; persisting US imperialism, invasions, militarism, and oppressive prison systems; indigenous people's issues; immigrant rights; liberating people from gender and sexuality discrimination; and workers' rights in a global economy.[54]

Significantly, several sociologists have been active in this organization, two of whom we can mention briefly. One is Jerome W. Scott, who once served as the director of Project South. Growing up in working-class Detroit, Scott "lived the reality of its poverty-stricken neighborhoods."[55] He is an organic intellectual whose sociological ideas have been honed by experience. After serving in Vietnam, Scott took courses at Lawrence Technical College but left for a job in an auto plant. There he participated in the League of Revolutionary Black Workers, a workers' group that pressed unions and management for more racial integration in auto plants. He became part of groups of workers and scholars studying sociopolitical theory, including that of Marx, Du Bois, and Malcolm X, in the context of building movements for change. This provided an important part of his broad sociological and political education. As he has noted to us, "From both my lived experience and theory I developed an understanding of society rooted in class analysis and social struggle, as the larger historical and institutional context of white supremacy, male privilege, and US global domination."[56] Moving to Atlanta in the 1970s, he began work on social justice issues. Soon he was working with community activists and activist sociologists and helped to found Project South. He also became involved in the American Sociological Association and the Association of Black Sociologists.[57]

An activist sociologist, Scott has coauthored articles and book chapters on US history, globalization and the electronic revolution, race and class issues, and people's movements for social change. He has noted current challenges facing sociologists: "Today, as globalization in the electronic age sweeps the world, liberation sociology is being transformed; and those of us who are engaged are building bridges to the emerging bottom-up movement for global justice and equality. For me, liberation sociology is an essential part of the larger project of human liberation."[58]

Another sociologist active for a time in Project South is Walda Katz-Fishman, who once served as chair of the board of Project South. In a communication to us, she noted that her activism is rooted in her background. Growing up in the South, she saw her parents active in the civil rights movement, civic and Jewish organizations, and the Democratic Party. At an early age, she became aware of racial, class, and gender inequalities, "but did not have a framework for truly understanding the world, a clear vision, or a strategy for how to change it."[59] After graduating from college, she attended graduate school at Wayne State University, where she became educated in a working-class perspective and Marxist interpretations of society. "From that point on," she reported, "I was always developing my historical materialist world-view and participating in many activist arenas—from scholar activism among professional groups to anticapitalist movements building in multiracial and multiclass organizations, often with women in the leadership."[60]

Moving to Washington, DC, in 1970, Katz-Fishman took a teaching position at Howard University. She continued developing her liberation sociology ideas and has taught many students about ideas and strategies of societal transformation. Like Scott, she has worked as an educator who uses her research on class, racial, and gender inequality to help grassroots organizations working for social justice. Katz-Fishman views her sociological education and research work as a crucial background and constant resource for her community activism: "To me sociology is a key to understanding social history and society—its past, its present, and its future, that is, what it is becoming. It offers me the tools for theoretically understanding the world and for practically transforming the world. But I have done and continue to do this within the collective process of study and movement building."[61]

More recently, Katz-Fishman and Scott have moved on from Project South to other group organizing projects, including some that focus on global social issues and movements. They have participated in the US Social Forum National Planning Committee as representatives of the League of Revolutionaries for a New America. They also continue to focus on educational curricula and programs to build progressive people's movements. As Katz-Fishman has recently stated, we "conduct movement schools for liberatory transformation with Move to Amend, a national organization working to end corporate personhood; the Green Party, an independent political party committed to economic justice, peoples' democracy, and ecological sustainability; and the Wayside Center for Popular Education in the DC and Virginia area."[62]

Listening to the People

At its best, social action research involves a willingness of both community participants and social science researchers to listen carefully and democratically to each other. Historically, some community-based research has involved social scientists who were not seriously interested in listening to community residents. For example, one group of experienced action researchers, sociologists at Loyola University in Chicago, has noted that too often social science researchers have come in, gathered community data, and left without giving anything back to the community.[63] In such settings, one problem is getting researchers and local community activists to listen well to one other and communicate without jargon.

Although some mainstream social scientists may see it as "too subjective," good collaborative research with community residents can be as carefully done and meaningful as other social research (see Chapter 4). From the community point of view, good social science research provides people with solid ideas about the depth of their problems and about how change strategies can be more effective. All social science research is pervaded by the perspectives of the researchers and of those funding or supporting the research. No research is conducted without underlying assumptions or without linkages to the structures of power and inequality in society. Francis Moore Lappé has noted that "each of us carries within us a worldview, a set of assumptions about how the world works—what some call a paradigm—that forms the very questions we allow ourselves to ask and determines our views of future possibilities."[64]

TEACHING LIBERATION SOCIOLOGY

In the United States and other parts of the world, sociology is an academic discipline, with its teachings being part of the mainstream curriculum in institutions of higher education and sometimes in high schools. Much of what is published and read within the disciplinary boundaries of these institutions is written by academicians. We should pay particular attention to the teaching of sociology because the sociology taught in high schools, colleges, and universities is, or can be, practiced in everyday life—as a way for individuals and small groups to examine the societal conditions in which they live and the consequences of individual and collective actions.

Teaching the sociology of liberation typically involves a process of creation of awareness, what Paulo Freire has called "conscientization"— a pedagogy of how oppressed people struggling for liberation can free themselves. It refers to "learning to perceive social, political, and economic contradictions, and to take action against the oppressive elements of reality."[65] The sociology of liberation is not just a sociology that discusses liberation; it is a sociology that can show or facilitate the way to it. A famous educator, Freire discovered that his pupils learned how to read and write better when language details were associated with acquisition of a critical consciousness. Learning how to read and the process of education in general were thus projects of human liberation.

Freire contrasts radicalization, the aim of his pedagogical method, with the more typical political sectarianism. Whereas radicalization nourished by a critical spirit is creative, "sectarianism, fed by fanaticism, is always castrating."[66] Radicalization literally means going to the *root* of things, a process that in Freire's experience involves "ever greater engagement in the effort to transform concrete, objective reality." Political sectarianism of the right or the left, because it is usually "mythicizing and irrational," can create a wrongheaded image of social reality and a sense of futility in changing that reality.[67] This distinction between radicalization and sectarianism is vital to a viable sociology of liberation. As we see it, the goal of liberation sociology is not to replace one dominant mythology with another but to contribute substantially to the freedom of human beings to think critically about society and to liberate themselves from dominant reality-distorting mythologies.

Consider this contemporary example. Alia Tyner-Mullings, professor of sociology and founding member at the New Community College at the City University of New York, connects the theoretical perspective of Freire with the teaching and learning styles of teachers and students at Central Park East Secondary School, a public alternative high school in Harlem (New York) that successfully serves predominantly low-income students. She has examined some of the ways the Freirean model has worked within the public school system and considers the challenges in implementing it. An article published in *Schools: Studies in Education*, based on research conducted on former students of the high school, concludes that while much of the Freirean model has been used successfully there—especially those aspects that focus on relationships inside the school—critical questions remain about the implementation of Freire's curricular recommendations.[68] Tyner-Mullings was once a student there and invites all who read her work to contemplate the potential of alternative educational models to deliver quality education to low-income students otherwise underserved by public schools.

Consider another contemporary example. Tim Woods, who teaches at Manchester Community College in New Hampshire, expects his students to bring their communities into the classroom. Service-learning is a requirement in most of his courses.

One of the great opportunities about teaching sociology in a community college is that nearly all of the students are genuinely enmeshed in the community while simultaneously attending classes.... Bringing the community into the classroom feels natural under these circumstances. In fact, expecting students to leave their social backgrounds, personal troubles, family issues, and job worries at the door is nearly impossible. Rather, the goal of teaching becomes connecting the classroom to the community to strengthen both.[69]

While Woods and his students are involved in a range of community issues, his students' commitment and engagement toward ending homelessness stands out. For instance, one student stayed after class to visit with him about the troubles he was having studying. The student was a veteran and, while motivated toward educational success, could not find time to study. After several days of the student staying after class, he finally admitted that he was living in a homeless shelter. He wanted to study but could not find any free time or quiet space in the shelter to do so.[70]

Trying to assist this one student and walking with him (sometimes literally) to learn the story of homeless vets, Woods and his students started on the path toward homeless advocacy. With the college's help and collaboration with community members, the Manchester Initiative for Supportive Housing was created. They utilized the strength of each community member, including students, to advocate in their town for more supportive housing. Meanwhile, students were reading social science books like Elliot Liebow's *Tell Them Who I Am* and John McKnight and Peter Block's *The Abundant Community*. Most importantly, they were connecting class readings to their community, both in writing and in actions they were involved in during the course. For example, students successfully invited community leaders to class discussions on homelessness and housing. Community members and students decided to host a public forum at the college to advocate for the building of supportive community housing in the community. Some students took on the task of media coordination, while others invited local residents. Students who had their own band wrote a song about homelessness and started the conference by debuting the song.[71]

All of this community collaboration eventually resulted in the construction of new housing apartments in the community. Students reportedly view the housing with pride, knowing that they played an important role. Additionally, they have discovered strong connections within their community and realized the power of those connections to help others and themselves.[72]

The activist social scientist Karl Marx once wrote that he did not seek to anticipate the world for all time to come but to engage in relentless criticism of existing reality. This does not mean hurling distorted or undocumented critiques at the way other people act or think. In our view, liberation sociologists should stay deeply connected to empirical reality, with what they can discover about the daily experience of the members of a society, including global society. A full empirical understanding of a society like the United States leads to the knowledge that it, and especially its social hierarchies, is systematically structured in the wrong way for full human self-realization. In the nineteenth century, Marx carefully studied the concrete realities of Western capitalism and came to the savvy conclusion that the logic of modern capitalistic societies "made injustice, alienation, and exploitation inevitabilities rather than contingencies."[73]

Without this empirical connection to everyday life and its constraints, there is no viable sociology. For liberation sociology, this connection between the empirical reality that sociologists study and sociologists' subjectivity—personal commitments, social biases, and existential coefficients of all sorts—is part of an ongoing dialectical and reflective process. Indeed, subjectivity usually provides the impetus to explore the social world.

Liberation sociology thus does not seek to establish certainty for all time, as some sociologists have tried to do. Practitioners of liberation sociology study current societal realities so they and others can better transform them. Thus, much new knowledge is tied to the transformations that such social science study and research bring about, to the remedial practices that are paired to what field researchers find in their work. They are not afraid of ordinary people or participating with others in the search for knowledge. The liberation sociologist is not afraid of becoming an activist-researcher committed to an oppressed people's history or to fight on their side of human history. The critical consciousness at the heart of liberation sociology is self-reflective and part of an interactive learning process. Reflective decisions about studying a societal problem and about methods for its analysis are acts of judgment and are made possible only by previous experience listening to and communicating well with other human beings.[74]

WHAT TYPE OF SOCIETY WILL WE HAVE?

Taking Sides with the Oppressed

If sociology is to become a stronger intellectual framework for people struggling for liberation from the structures and mystiques of domination, then sociologists need to decide on the type of sociology they will practice and whose interests they will serve. All sociologists, like all other social scientists, make personal choices as to the problems they are going to devote their energies to, the terms in which they will cast research questions, and the research methods they will utilize. They do not make such choices in a social vacuum but typically as they struggle to provide for themselves and their families.

The noncommittal attitude of much sociology and other social science today—usually formulated as scientific detachment, objectivity, or value freedom—is too often a cover-up for the accommodation the research has made with dominant group interests. Mainstream sociology, like other intellectual endeavors, is part of the political, social, and psychological status quo. To ignore or deny the political, social, and psychological standpoints of our own sociological thinking and discipline is to make sure that the latter will stay rooted in a deeply troubled status quo. W. E. B. Du Bois provided an eloquent examination of the social forces at play in the decision to take sides with the oppressed: "The educated and cultured of the world, the well born and well bred, and even the deeply pious and philanthropic" cannot escape the contradiction that they "receive their training and comfort and luxury, the ministrations of delicate beauty and sensibility, on condition that they neither inquire [too closely] into the real source of their income and the methods of distribution nor interfere with the legal props which rest on a pitiful human foundation of writhing white and yellow and brown and black bodies."[75]

In our view, social science researchers should make every effort to do honest and open research work and to minimize as best they can the intrusion of unstated assumptions that can distort that research. We support "objectivity" in this sense, although we recognize that this task is not an easy one since the mainstream accent on "objectivity" is often part of an argument to coerce research into a certain conventional mode. Indeed, it is frequently the countersystem sociologists who have the greatest ability to be objective and socially truthful because they critically analyze and demystify established interpretations of oppressive social arrangements. According to Sandra Harding, the truly democratic values that legitimate critical analysis of established structures from the viewpoint of the dispossessed "tend to increase the objectivity of the results of research."[76] As the social sciences become more diverse in terms of who does social science, these fields embrace a broader array of human perspectives and knowledge, and more critical questions are raised about traditional perspectives and hidden societal realities. In addition, by regularly bringing in the social and historical contexts of social science, one can increase its objectivity by reducing its parochialism. Democracy-enhancing practices can only improve science, whereas democracy-reducing practices—the traditional practices of much natural and social science—can only limit science.

One of sociology's great contributions to modern thought is that at its best it encourages us to think critically about the socially patterned nature of the world around us. Early European sociologists like Max Weber and Emile Durkheim researched, and wrote insightfully about, broad societal forces such as industrialization, bureaucratization, and urbanization. Yet these are not the only processes that characterize the modern period in Western societies. The differentiating processes of exploitation, social discrimination, and oppression also distinguish the modern period.

These latter realities were perhaps best understood by other early sociologists such as Jane Addams, Charlotte Perkins Gilman, W. E. B. Du Bois, and Ida B. Wells-Barnett. All of them analyzed issues of discrimination and exploitation in their efforts to understand US society.[77] Experiencing social oppression firsthand, these white women and black men and women sociologists saw what most white men at the time could not—that major "social difference is the first consequence of modern society and, thus, the more reasonable first principle of sociology."[78] A relevant sociology must be grounded in the studied realization of the extent to which US society, as well as other societies, are founded in social differentiation, inequality, and oppression.

Taking an Overt Moral Stance

The flight from serious discussion of issues of morality and ethics in social science must be ended. Beyond a desire for a deeper understanding of exploitation and oppression, liberation sociology takes an overt moral stance, which includes identification and empathy with the victims of oppression and a calling for and working toward their liberation from misery and inequality.

Sociology can liberate when it applies its humanistic concern and empathetic reasoning to solving the everyday problems afflicting human beings. In this book we advocate a broad human rights standard for social research, affirm the value of humanization, and call for maximizing human self-realization and achievement. One starting place for a broad human rights standard, which has international resonance, is the United Nations' Universal Declaration of Human Rights. This international agreement stipulates in Article 1 that "all human beings are born free and equal in dignity and rights" and in Article 7 that "all are equal before the law and are entitled without any discrimination to equal protection of the law." Article 8 further asserts: "Everyone has the right to an effective remedy . . . for acts violating the fundamental rights," and

Article 25 states that these rights extend to everyday life: "Everyone has the right to a standard of living adequate for the health and well-being of himself and his family, including food, clothing, housing."[79] From this influential international human rights perspective, no one can be expected to take care of their family and civic responsibilities without adequate daily sustenance and freedom from intrusive oppressions (see Chapter 9). We believe that this commitment to broad human rights and freedoms should be the starting point for much sociological research and analysis. Interestingly, the American Sociological Association now has a research section explicitly on human rights, one in which both social science specialists and interested practitioners can exchange ideas about research and practice.

An important example of sociological analysis interweaving with moral concerns is liberation theology, a powerful tradition among Catholic activists in numerous postcolonial countries, especially in South and Central America. For some time now, liberation theology has drawn in part on sociological writings, and, in turn, liberation theology has influenced the thinking of progressive sociologists, including ourselves. Stan Bailey, a former priest and sociologist, made this cogent comment on an early draft of this book:

> I am an ex-priest trained in liberation theology in Córdoba, Argentina, where I spent nearly a decade working with oppressed communities. As a priest, what kept me going was the perspective of solidarity with the poor, and doing theology from the bottom up—being a voice for those denied a voice. Now, to hear the same terms being used to indicate a certain type of sociological praxis is gratifying.... We reduce the world to our disciplines with their internal rules and regulations, and their authorities who determine the true path. Don't we realize the futility of our intellectual conclusions for most of the world's population living in subhuman conditions? Our "ivory towers" distort our visions and move us along in the justification of the powerful.[80]

Liberation theology emerged in Latin America in response to the inadequacy of doctrinaire European theology for Catholic priests doing pastoral work among the poor and politically disenfranchised. In 1968 liberation theology came to the world's attention as a result of the second meeting of the Latin American Bishops' Council in Colombia. At that meeting Father Gustavo Gutierrez, "the father of liberation theology,"[81] and others called for new church initiatives to meet the economic and social justice needs of the poor in Latin America. As a result, these Catholic bishops declared that the Catholic Church should have a "preferential option for the poor," the liberation theology phrase for taking sides with the oppressed. This movement was criticized by Catholic Popes John Paul and Benedict, but more recently, Pope Francis has accented the importance of serving the poor and has met informally with Father Gutierrez. As we discuss in Chapter 8, while Francis has distanced himself from the liberation theology movement, he has included some elements of its philosophies in his speeches.[82]

Looking beneath the Surface

In ancient Roman myth, the giant Cacus lived in a cave and once stole some oxen from Hercules, then dragged them backward into his cave. When Hercules came seeking his cattle, he saw tracks that appeared to indicate that the cattle had gone out of the cave, and he was initially deceived. All too often, modern social science analysts are like the puzzled Hercules. They note the shape of the cave and count the number and direction of the footprints but do not dig deeper into the social realities that their observations often represent.[83] Indeed, several social science commentators have noted that if social life were only what it seemed to be on its surface, there would be no need for social science.

Too much mainstream analysis of US society, economy, and politics reflects a status-quo ideology that denies or hides many of this society's most serious "distorting contradictions."[84] One of the tragedies of any society is the failure of its people and leaders to understand the real social problems confronting them. For example, today modern capitalism seems to be riding high, with many mainstream analysts, business leaders, and academics singing its praises. Indeed, there is a general denial that the mechanisms and machinations of modern capitalism are creating very serious social and economic troubles for the billions of residents of planet Earth.

The United States appears to be on a path of continuing social conflicts, of accentuated economic and other inequalities, and of environmental degradation shaped by such trends as global warming and the deterioration of air and water. The social contradictions of contemporary capitalism are becoming ever more evident to those who attend to the empirical data. Clearly, there is no historical reason to expect the system of capitalism to last forever. The failures of other societal systems, such as the demise of state communism in Eastern Europe, have received far more academic and media attention than the continuing crises of US and global capitalism. Politicians' debates over cutting social programs, over job losses, and over trends in Social Security and Medicare have often been conducted with little sustained reference to the growing income and wealth inequalities underlying capitalistic societies like the United States. Today, most large US corporations are part of a global market system and have periodically directed many of their profit-making activities to low-wage areas overseas as they close US plants and eliminate many decent-paying jobs. Although many US corporations have made very good profits, their economic "advances" have frequently come at great cost to US workers and their families. In the United States the real wages of a majority of ordinary workers are lower today than they were a few decades ago, a situation that has forced many to take on extra jobs or put more family members to work.[85] The so-called free market is celebrated by mainstream analysts as the solution for social and economic problems overseas at the same time that it is creating recurring serious economic problems and severe environmental problems for workers and their families across the globe.

The increasing inequalities of income and wealth have often been rationalized by an array of US politicians, media commentators, and intellectuals. Most societies are controlled substantially by elites who take overt and covert actions to shape society in terms of their group interests. The oppressing classes and the bureaucratic organizations they control hide many of their exploitative operations from the public and do not wish for social scientists to do research on systems of oppression they create or uphold. In analyzing society, liberation sociologists typically try to dig beneath these overt rationalizations and everyday fictions. Major tasks for critical social scientists are to ascertain the larger social framework around such elite actions, and how the actions arose or developed. At its best, sociology provides a useful collection of interpretive concepts and methods, and it relies on actual field observations, interviews, experimentation, and comparison to reach critical conclusions about conditions in society.

Empirical Social Science

Our defense of empirical social science appears to fly in the face of postmodernist questioning of science. Early in the history of social science, the application of observation and analysis through the scientific method was thought to bring societal progress. Scientific reasoning would make us free once we rid ourselves of conventional prejudices, but this promise was never delivered. Thus, a critical questioning of the physical and social sciences is justified. Although reasoning in science can be used to liberate, it has been used to exploit, oppress, and exterminate.

However, as we show later, some sociological methods used to buttress systems of oppression can also be used to liberate human beings. For instance, sociological methods in the hands of many corporate advertisers hide the business interest in manipulating human needs and generating unnecessary consumption. An example is the use of focus groups, an old sociological method, to find out how to manipulate people into buying products they do not need. Social science research can have a repressive potential, as in the marketing research designed to get people to behave against their interests. The tobacco industry availed itself of social science research techniques to produce advertisement campaigns, such as those targeting younger people and those in low-income neighborhoods. Nonetheless, the same methods can be used to help human beings be more conscious of, and better equipped to fight, advertisers and related corporate interests that try to ensnare them.

Many social scientists who go into the field are often dramatically enlightened if not radicalized. Field research has radicalizing potential because it frequently reveals what researchers do not expect, or do not wish, to see. Thus, field sociologists have been among the first to bring to public attention the issues of youth culture, bureaucratic structure, racial discrimination, changing roles for women in society, the problems of individualism, divorce's impact on society, and the regulation of the poor by government agencies in the interests of capitalism. An example of the latter is a book by sociologists Richard Cloward and Frances Fox Piven (Piven is a former president of the American Sociological Association). In their influential book, *Regulating the Poor* (1971), they showed how government programs for the poor have regularly expanded or contracted in direct relationship to the needs of employers for low-wage labor.[86]

Recently, another of their works received hostile responses. Glenn Beck, a conservative television host for Fox News, coined the phrase *Cloward/Piven Strategy* to explain his view of US crises. His target was Cloward and Piven's 1966 article, "The Weight of the Poor: A Strategy to End Poverty," in which they suggest that economic and political pressure on the US system could drive much needed reform. The article was the impetus for Beck's condemnation of Piven, who he claimed deliberately set out to ruin the US economic system. Visitors to Beck's website even called for Piven's death. These events led the Center for Constitutional Rights to contact Fox News to ask that Beck's "false accusations" be discontinued. "Mr. Beck is putting Professor Piven in actual physical danger of a violent response," the group argued. Fox News refused to comply. Exemplifying how dramatically enlightened sociologists who go into the field can become, Piven explained Beck's attack as "a kind of rhetorical trick that is always used to denounce movements of ordinary people, and that is to imply that the massing of people itself is violent."[87]

Piven's book *Who's Afraid of Frances Fox Piven?: The Essential Writings of the Professor Glenn Beck Loves to Hate*—which includes her work on welfare rights and poor people's movements, US voting habits, and the possibilities for new progressive movements—serves as a guide to her thoughts that alarmed the sociologically misinformed Beck.[88]

Sociologists have been at the forefront of those documenting the oppressive conditions faced by African Americans, Native Americans,

Latinos, and Asian Americans. Examples of this include the classical field study of African Americans under Jim Crow segregation by Gunnar Myrdal and his sociological associates, *An America Dilemma* (1944), and the field study of Mexican American conditions by sociologists Leo Grebler, Joan Moore, and Ralph Guzman, *The Mexican-American People* (1970).[89] Field sociologists have often given the best pictures of poverty, juvenile delinquency, drug cultures, the homeless, and working-class lives. Take, for example, sociologist Cheri Jo Pascoe's recent book, *Dude, You're a Fag: Masculinity and Sexuality in High School,* which is based on months of fieldwork in a racially diverse, working-class US high school. She analyzes emerging masculinity as a highly gendered and sexual process, exploring the "specter of the fag" as a disciplinary device for regulating straight and gay boys. In the process, she charts some of the complexities involved in the relationships between sexuality, gender, race, and class in contemporary North America.[90]

Probing the Underlying Assumptions

Whether it is acknowledged or not, all social research has an underlying perspective and moral stance. Critically examining the problems of powerful nation-states and corporations requires a bold moral position that asserts the rights of all human beings as world citizens. As noted previously, researchers who work for or who are significantly supported by a nation-state are less likely to collect data or develop analyses subversive to that state, including such phenomena as overseas colonialism and imperialism.

Alvin Gouldner noted the ways in which the social sciences have been shaped by their sociocultural environments. Thus, major social theories, such as the structural-functionalist theory of Talcott Parsons, provide an "anxiety-reducing reorientation" to the world for those who more or less prefer the status quo.[91] Historian Dorothy Ross has suggested that in the United States the social sciences have often been shaped by a shallow historical perspective, a practical outlook, and a naïve confidence in technical methods. US social scientists have often shared the optimistic views of ordinary citizens that the United States is different from European nations and can more easily solve the problems of class conflict and poverty.[92] By arguing for an American exceptionalism, US social scientists have too often embraced "a scientism that proceeds in dangerous ignorance of historical differences and societal complexity."[93]

In social science research, various types of bias appear in many places, including in the choice of research topics and agendas. Too often those who do conventional social science research become hired hands, selling their research skills to those who have the power to command them. In such cases, "objectivity" has frequently meant the use of statistical methods operationalized so narrowly that the choice of topic is not considered to be an area of possible bias. Sandra Harding has noted that "many critics of the natural sciences argue that racist and Eurocentric political concerns shaped the questions the sciences have asked and this is why the results of such research have been racist and Eurocentric."[94] Similarly, the choice of research topics in the social sciences is not independent of the values of the researchers.

When *New York Times* reporter Jennifer Schuessler wrote about social scientific research conducted on the Occupy Wall Street movements of 2011 and 2012, she inadvertently exposed how some who engage in orthodox social science research offer their research skills to the powerful. She describes the research of a criminologist who studied attitudes of protesters toward law enforcement in six cities: "Some researchers … say that the sympathy many academics feel for the movement risks undermining objective research." Schuessler describes a research assistant who, at a demonstration in Washington, "handed in her ID, turned in her clipboard and within minutes got arrested." The reporter quotes the criminologist researcher as saying, "Part of where our research is heading is making recommendations to police departments. When they look at our research, I want them to trust it. Having people involved in the movement wouldn't work for us."[95]

These comments contrast with those of Alex Vitale, a sociologist at Brooklyn College who has also studied the policing of such demonstrations: "Occupy Wall Street, with its defiant style of non-violent protest, has consistently clashed with the NYPD's obsession with order maintenance, resulting in hundreds of mostly unnecessary arrests and a significant infringement on the basic rights of free speech and assembly."[96] Vitale's views might be understood in terms of Howard Becker's classic 1967 argument. A field researcher himself, Becker sarcastically stated this view of those in power, such as the police:

> We are, if we are proper members of the group, morally bound to accept the definition imposed on reality by a superordinate group in preference to the definitions espoused by subordinates.... [T]he sociologist who favours officialdom will be spared the accusation of bias. "Everyone knows" … that police are more respectable and their words ought to be taken more seriously than … deviants and criminals.[97]

In his research writings on "deviant" behavior, Becker famously defined *deviance* as just something that people, especially those with power, *label* as such—and thereby *create*.

Questioning an Instrumental-Positivistic Social Science

As we show in the next chapters, an instrumental-positivistic perspective has come to dominate numerous areas of social science research in the United States and other countries. Clearly, the phrase *positivistic science* has had several different meanings since Auguste Comte accented the idea in the nineteenth century (see Chapter 2). For example, some analysts have used the phrase for any social science approach that seeks to develop empirical data and laws of human social behavior.

However, in this book we define contemporary positivistic social science as having at least these elements: (1) attempting to delineate enduring laws of social life with little consideration of historical contexts; (2) accenting a conventional quantitative (statistical) processing of data on social life as the main or only legitimate way to gain knowledge; (3) not researching those aspects of human life that cannot be measured by conventional quantitative methods, such as human imagination and the holistic complexity of phenomena; (4) conceiving of knowledge as something generated by certain instrumental methodologies—and downplaying other types of human knowledge; and (5) emphasizing "value-free" research and downplaying the underlying assumptions of those doing that research, including assumptions that the current political-economic status quo is generally legitimate.[98]

This contemporary positivistic social science is distinctively North American. Some have termed it an *abstracted empiricism*, or perhaps more accurately, an *instrumental positivism*. It is "instrumental" in that it limits serious social research to only those questions that certain research instruments and quantitative techniques will allow, and it is "positivism" in that it commits social scientists to research approaches attempting to mimic those of the natural sciences.[99] One of the founders of US sociology, Franklin H. Giddings, put the matter succinctly, and in gendered language, in a definitive and influential 1909 *American Journal of Sociology* commentary: "We need men not afraid to work; who will get busy with the adding machine and the logarithms, and give us exact studies, such as we get in the psychological laboratories, not to speak of the biological and physical laboratories. Sociology can be made an exact, quantitative science, if we can get industrious men interested in it."[100]

In this book we use the terms *quantitative positivism* or *instrumental positivism* for the social science research that more or less encompasses these several assumptions and inclinations. However, we should emphasize a broader point here: The practice of social science in the United States is generally permeated by what might be termed a *positivistic culture*. This larger positivistic culture is so powerful that some who practice a social science that is often considered antipositivistic—such as phenomenologists, ethnomethodologists, and discourse analysts—can adopt in their qualitative research procedures some of the traits and trappings of positivism. Thus, sociologist Abigail Fuller notes that in our positivistic culture, much "knowledge is fragmented, specialized, and divorced from its historical and social context, and as such, is robbed of its critical functions."[101]

Since World War II, many leading sociologists have emphasized the need for sociology to standardize and develop methodological "rigor" by using certain statistical techniques, survey methods, and the hypothetico-deductive framing of social analyses. As conventionally stated, this instrumental positivism should involve developing formal hypotheses, using specified falsification procedures, basing theories only on statistical measurements, and being "value-free," whatever that may mean.[102] The value-free position asserts that sociological research should be done in a technical and neutral way that allows it to be used by anyone who wishes to do so. However, the "idea of sociology for sale to all-comers also loses sight of the economics of truth." Too often "empirical social research is expensive and therefore only available to those who can afford it."[103]

The repeated emphasis on traditional quantitative or survey research methods as the only way to do serious science, and the teaching of narrowly defined social research techniques to undergraduate and graduate students, has far-reaching societal consequences. Sheldon Wolin has noted that a heavy accent on traditional positivistic research techniques "affects the way in which the initiates will look upon the world and especially the political portion of it. 'Methodism' is ultimately a proposal for shaping the mind. [Its] assumptions are such as to reinforce an uncritical view of existing political structures and all they imply."[104] Furthermore, Thomas Kuhn, in *The Structure of Scientific Revolutions*, is critical of much scientific education for being as narrow as orthodox theology. For that reason, this type of education produces relatively few researchers who ask new boundary-breaking questions and discover new paradigms and pathbreaking approaches.[105]

Countersystem sociologists are often interested in looking critically at their own field—engaging in a self-reflective sociology that looks closely at their academic settings. Gouldner commented on the dilemma of academic sociologists: "For tenured faculty, the university is a realm of congenial and leisured servitude. It is a realm in which the academician is esteemed for his learning but castrated as a political figure." That is, the professor can be a "tiger in the classroom" while being a "pussycat in the dean's office" and, too often, in society.[106] All social scientists have to accept the existing system some of the time, but many rarely or never make attempts to question or change the often oppressive systems around them. In contrast, the liberation impulse in sociology teaches us that we must resist the social oppressions in our own circumstances and elsewhere in society.

"PUBLIC SOCIOLOGY": A LIBERATION SOCIOLOGY PERSPECTIVE?

Since the first edition of this book, an extensive discussion of what is termed *public sociology* has emerged within the field of sociology. The first to dramatically emphasize this approach was Ben Agger, whose book *Public Sociology* (2000) preceded the publication of our book by some months.[107] Soon after Agger's book was published, sociologist Herbert Gans articulated the need for a public sociology in the 2002 newsletter of the American Sociological Association (ASA). And in 2004 then ASA president, Michael Burawoy, made the plural of this phrase—*public sociologies*—the theme for that national sociology meeting. In his presidential address, Burawoy spoke of the complexity of contemporary sociology and distinguished four legitimate types of sociology, all part of a "sociological division of labor": professional sociology, policy sociology, public sociology, and critical sociology. Although Burawoy's own research has often articulated a critical neo-Marxist perspective, in his address he portrayed a vision of contemporary sociology as a broad tent that includes these four forms of sociology. By *policy sociology* he means sociological research done for a specific client such as the US Department of State (e.g., on issues of terrorism). By *public sociology*, he means research whose sociological practitioners engage directly in interactive dialogue about that research with some public, though they do not necessarily accept that public's views. By *professional sociology*, Burawoy means the "true and tested methods, accumulated bodies of knowledge, orienting questions, and conceptual frameworks" of contemporary sociology, which he sees as undergirding both policy and public sociology. By *critical sociology*, he means sociology that is critical of the established research programs of professional sociology.[108]

Significantly, the corrosive character of major instrumental-positivistic "true and tested methods" in much professional sociology is nowhere critically assessed in Burawoy's address. As suggested above, a central problem in contemporary sociology is this instrumental positivism and often associated methodological dogmatism that sees the only way to gain legitimate social science knowledge of the world as being through certain quantitative methods and that uncritically accepts the assumptions or interests of the surrounding status quo. By accepting instrumental positivism as one of the important types of sociology under his big tent, Burawoy provides support for the undeserved power of those positivistic sociologists who are dominant in the major journals and numerous graduate departments of sociology, those who generally do not seek to challenge the oppressive status quo. Unfortunately, at no point in his address does he offer a critical analysis of how much of government- and foundation-funded sociology is linked to the often oppressive needs of the US nation-state. Although he cites earlier sociologists who raised important questions of sociology "for whom" and "for what," his discussion of these matters never covers the issues of sociology for "the oppressed" or sociology "to reduce that oppression" in society. In his view both traditional positivistic sociology and a critical nonpositivistic sociology can make for a viable public sociology. Even so, he does briefly note that public sociology and critical sociology, as he has named them, are in some danger because the professional and policy sociologies have much greater control over important career positions in sociology and over most government funding.[109]

Nowhere in his presidential address does Burawoy acknowledge the earlier work of Ben Agger. This may be because Agger's public sociology is centrally a *critical* liberation sociology like that accented in this book. We agree with Agger's view that in this process Burawoy watered down the concept of a public sociology committed to progressive societal change, the public sociology articulated by many progressive sociologists since the daring Jane Addams and W. E. B. Du Bois (see Chapter 3). Interestingly, since Burawoy's presidential address, the American Sociological Association has set up a committee on public sociology and periodically highlighted the concept on its website. Yet there is little evidence of a significant shift away from instrumental positivism in mainstream sociology journals or in numerous major sociology graduate programs' educational curricula. Thus, in Agger's periodic reviews of those journals, he has found that instrumental positivism and its focus on a selected range of conventional quantitative methods still predominate. Agger's research on the discipline of sociology also concludes that it is still "training" younger sociologists "to be careerist civil servants and not as public and activist intellectuals."[110]

Still, Burawoy brought important public sociology questions to the forefront of contemporary sociology and helped to inaugurate important debates. In his presidential address, he distinguished the discipline of sociology as different from economics and political science, which focus on issues of the market and nation-state. He views the special standpoint of sociology as defending the interests of "civil society," by which he means civic organizations, such as trade unions and community groups, lying beyond market corporations and the nation-state. He briefly indicates that numerous sociologists are critically aware of the "segregations, dominations, and exploitations" of society, and that sociology has some-times been invaded by government and market concerns.[111]

Significantly, Burawoy explicitly notes that in most other countries, sociology is not focused on professional sociology as he has defined it. In numerous countries the practice of sociology is often more critical and liberation oriented. In South Africa, for example, there has been a strong connection between sociological research and teaching and the antiapartheid struggles. A similar connection between progressive social struggles can be seen in numerous European and Latin American coun-tries, a point we cover later. In his conclusion Burawoy expresses the hope that a progressive public sociology will eventually come to the United States, probably generated by civil-society organizations and move-ments: "It will come when public sociology captures the imagination of sociologists, when sociologists recognize public sociology as important in its own right with its own rewards, and when sociologists then carry it forward as a social movement beyond the academy."[112]

CONCLUSION

Throughout this book, we have asked the hard questions, "Social science for what purpose?" and "Social science for whom?" In proposing a libera-tion sociology, we give a strong humanistic, democratic, and progressive-activist answer to these questions. Liberation sociology can be a tool to increase the human ability to understand deep societal realities, to engage in dialogue with others, and to increase democratic participation in the production and use of knowledge. Making oppression more visible and forcing public discussions of it are essential. C. Wright Mills put it thus: "It is the political task of the social scientist ... continually to translate personal troubles into public issues, and public issues into the terms of their human meaning for a variety of individuals."[113] A critical, commit-ted sociology can help those who are powerless to become more powerful. It can give voice to those who are oppressed and voiceless. For example, it can help women and people of color to understand better where and how sexism and racism operate and suggest useful countermeasures. Or it can help white male workers who join right-wing supremacist groups to understand why they feel alienated and why reactionary ideologies play into the hands of their own class oppressors.

Well-established research methodologies, including face-to-face interviews and social surveys, can be coupled with newer approaches such as Dorothy Smith's institutional ethnographies of US schools.[114] For Smith, field ethnography means more than observation and inter-viewing; it means a commitment to finding out how a social entity really works in its practices and everyday relationships. Discovering social facts can thus involve a diversity of social science methods. For example, some researchers have made good use of the diaries and other materials left by the victims of the German Nazi Holocaust to get a sense of everyday realities of extreme oppression and genocide. In South Africa, new methods were pioneered by that country's Truth and Reconciliation Commission, which has looked into the atrocities of the old apartheid system. They sought out the voices of the survivors of this violent oppression in order to air the truth about its horrors and allow the country to better face its future with its eyes wide open. Similarly in Chile, after Augusto Pinochet's dictatorship (1974–1990), a special national committee investigated and assembled data on the civil rights abuses of that brutal regime with the hope of bringing about societal openness and eventual reconciliation.

The ultimate measure of the value of social science knowledge is not some type of academic propositional theory building but whether that knowledge sharpens our understanding of society and helps to build a more just and democratic society. Liberation sociology seeks to stimulate debate in the field of sociology and in the larger society over what humane societal arrangements would look like and how they could be implemented. To bring change, powerless human beings must be empowered. Liberation sociology can provide probing research that supports the struggles of the oppressed against classist, racist, sexist, heterosexist, and other authoritarian types of oppression. Liberation sociology is oriented toward people acting to change oppressive conditions. Karl Marx once wrote that people "make their own history, but they do not make it just as they please; they do not make it under circumstances chosen by themselves, but under circumstances directly encountered, given and transmitted from the past."[115] C. Wright Mills noted a qualification to this: "Men are free to make history, but some men are much freer than others. Such freedom requires access to the means of decisions and of power by which history may now be made."[116]

Both Marx and Mills recognize that people are acting agents and actually can and do make or remake their history. A former secretary general of the United Nations, Dag Hammarskjöld, put it this way: "We are not permitted to choose the frame of our destiny. But what we put in it is ours."[117] Each member of this society is a part of the systems of oppression, for no one can escape and all are part of the struggle to maintain or remove these systems. But we can choose which side to be on.

CHAPTER 2

Improving Human Societies

Reassessing the Classical Theorists

Let us now turn to the theoretical background of modern sociology and examine several sociologists of different epochs and political persuasions, all of whom have emphasized a sociological concern with life improvement and societal betterment. We include views that shed light on sociologists' early commitment to social justice or to building a better world. We argue that the pure-science, objectivist ideal of social science is a relatively new invention, mostly emerging in the 1930s and 1940s. As we will see, numerous early sociologists in Europe and the United States viewed sociology as generating new knowledge and as being directly applicable to building a better society. One central argument is that the scientific discipline of sociology, in its inception, was mostly conceived *as a way to improve the human condition.*

Many contemporary sociologists have reinterpreted the perspectives of key "classical" sociologists, such as Émile Durkheim and Max Weber, to support instrumental-positivist trends and certain other mainstream analytical commitments. Recent advocates of professionalism in sociology and other social sciences have often tried to denigrate or downplay the activist and change-oriented aspects of the sociological tradition and emphasize instead a careerist and instrumental positivism. They commonly appeal to a tradition of "pure science" and "value-free" social science. To do this they must ignore, if not greatly distort, the history of sociological theory and research. In order to fully understand the perspectives of sociological theorists, we need to understand the social and intellectual climates in which they lived. Most important perhaps, we need to understand the theorists' social positions and their commitments to particular values and to societal change.

EARLY ROOTS OF SOCIOLOGY

A good case can be made that both Auguste Comte (1798–1857) and Harriet Martineau (1802–1876) were the early founders of sociology. In the early 1800s, Comte, a French philosopher, gave "sociology" its composite name, one constructed from Greek and Latin linguistic roots. However, the idea that human relations should be studied empirically predates Comte's idea of sociology by about a century. When the possibility of a realistic study of society was first proposed in the 1700s, it was a revolutionary idea. "In the eighteenth century," writes historian Peter Gay, "for the first time in history, confidence was the companion of realism rather than a symptom of the Utopian imagination."[1] During the Enlightenment, which took place mostly in the eighteenth century, many intellectuals reacted against the dominant ideas and methods of established Christian theology. In countries across Europe, these intellectuals included "religious skeptics, political reformers, cultural critics, historians, and social theorists."[2] The empirical study of human relations was viewed as replacing the dominance of knowledge by religious authorities.

Scottish philosopher David Hume (1711–1776), an influential Enlightenment thinker, repeatedly reminded his readers that ignorance is the mother of religious devotion. At the same time that Enlightenment analysts like Hume rejected the irrational in religion, they also rejected what they saw as the excessive rationalism of earlier philosophers such as René Descartes (1596–1650). Thus, Hume understood that reason was limited by the power of emotions: "Reason is, and ought only to be the slave of the passions, and can never pretend to any other office than to serve and obey them."[3] Hume understood that ideas like "causality" were only conventional and constructed. Immanuel Kant (1724–1804), a German professor and perhaps the leading philosopher in the Western tradition, broke new ground that paved the way for the rise of the social sciences. In contrast to England's influential social philosopher, John Locke (1632–1704), who viewed the human mind as passive and mirror-like, Kant viewed the human mind as creative and active in interpreting empirical experience. For Kant, scientific and nonscientific knowledge are derived from experience, and both are valid ways of understanding nature and society.[4] Hume and Kant influenced key sociological thinkers like Karl Marx, Max and Marianne Weber, and Émile Durkheim.

The American and French Revolutions took place near the end of the Enlightenment period, in the late 1700s. They inspired other liberation movements. For example, soon thereafter, enslaved people of African descent in Haiti rebelled against the French colonial system. In 1791 those enslaved rose up against their masters in a successful revolution. Haiti became an independent republic on January 1, 1804, thereby becoming the second independent country in the Americas. After 1808, Latin American countries declared their independence from the European colonial powers. To one extent or another, these movements were inspired by the writings of Enlightenment intellectuals in Europe and the Americas. Numerous Enlightenment intellectuals had pressed for the liberation of human beings from fear and oppression and for establishing sovereignty over their own lives.[5] Many European and American intellectuals viewed the American Revolution as a confirmation that their ideas could be applied—that human beings had a "capacity for self-improvement and self-government, that ... reason and humanity might become governing rather than merely critical principles."[6]

Auguste Comte

Reflecting the Enlightenment idea of human capacity for societal improvement, Auguste Comte initially sketched his ideas in the 1820s, in articles that caught the eye of England's major theorist of liberty, John Stuart Mill (1806–1873). Mill agreed with Comte in his attack on the societal subjugation of women.[7] Mill enthusiastically recommended to colleagues the series of lectures Comte offered in Paris on "positive philosophy." The word *positive* was chosen to indicate that the philosophy being proposed was a reaction against the highly critical (considered "negative") philosophy of the German Hegelian system.[8] Georg Hegel started from the errors made by philosophers before him. Comte believed one should start not with the errors of the past but with a positive statement of what is discovered through actual observation and comparison. Comte believed that he had discovered a fundamental law of the stages "through which the human mind has to pass, in every kind of speculation."[9] The laws of human behavior could be discovered in the same way that Isaac Newton had discovered laws in physics.

Comte sought to set in place a natural science that would lay bare the reality of a society and help to transform it. The sciences had developed from an understanding of simple abstract principles to an understanding of complex concrete phenomena. In this schema, mathematics was the initial science and the more complicated sciences were, in order, astronomy, physics, chemistry, and biology. Sociology was the queen of sciences at the top, the last science and the one that would discover laws governing social facts and synthesize the whole of human knowledge. Sociology would thus be equipped to assist in the reconstruction of society. In spite of his rejection of numerous progressive Enlightenment ideas, Comte was a child of the Enlightenment, who believed in the power of reason to make sense of the way the world works.

Thus, sociology has resulted from a blending of many perspectives and theories, including "natural law, science, materialism, determinism and inevitability, the romantic emphasis on organic wholes and on conflict, ideas of progress and evolution."[10] The concept of social order, so important in the history of sociological theory and analysis, is a legacy of sociology's historical roots in nineteenth-century conservatism in Europe.[11] Comte wrote in the period following the French Revolution, a social explosion that had destroyed the fabric of society in France. Although Comte was a political conservative opposed to democracy and was supportive of much social hierarchy, he was not for a return to the old French monarchy destroyed by the Revolution.[12] Comte saw European society as advancing through stages, from a theological stage to a modern, positive stage where business and political leaders would rule with the help of sociologists. In this last phase, there would be reliable knowledge, rational government, and a human-oriented religion.[13]

Thus, sociology began as a grand science of reform and social harmony. Comte suggested that if people learned about the real laws of society—determined by sociologists through empirical investigation—and how to adapt to them, then social harmony would follow. However, he turned his back on the Enlightenment's idea that society should be changed to allow for the continuous perfection of all individuals. Instead, he stressed human adjustment to natural social laws. He saw individualism as a disease of Western civilization. Social order rested on moral consensus.

Interestingly, Comte viewed positivism as the "secular religion of humanity devoted to the worship of society."[14] Over time, a positivistic movement became popular in many countries, in which social circles and foundations were created to promote positivistic ideas. For others, however, a positive religion of humanity was an aberration that seemed to violate some ideas that Comte himself had proposed. John Stuart Mill, the British philosopher originally impressed with Comte's ideas on the scientific study of society, eventually became a staunch critic.

Harriet Martineau

Without the efforts of the English sociologist and social activist Harriet Martineau, the ideas of Auguste Comte would not have become widely known outside of France. Martineau translated and condensed Comte's work into a popular one-volume English edition, which Comte had translated back into French.[15]

More importantly, although she remains little known today, Martineau was the first social scientist to see herself as a sociologist and to do systematic empirical research in the field. Over her lifetime, Martineau traveled extensively in Ireland, the United States, and the Middle East and kept detailed sociological accounts of what she observed. Her first major sociological analysis was of her careful observations during her visit to the United States, which were published in an important three-volume set called *Society in America* (1837).[16]

In her pioneering assessment of US society, this British sociologist developed sociological insights at least as original as those of her more celebrated male counterpart, Alexis de Tocqueville. The young Martineau, at this early point in the history of sociology, helped to create a new research approach using empirical data to assess theory and public policy. Indeed, she wrote the first book on sociological methods, in which she argued—preceding Émile Durkheim by a half century—that research on social life is centrally about studying social "things" accurately and should involve research on "institutions and records, in which the action of a nation is embodied and perpetuated."[17] In addition, Martineau used her sociological insights in her social activism, which in turn helped to hone numerous sociological insights. She was an antislavery activist and a feminist and wrote extensively for the popular press about important issues of her day. It is time to recover Harriet Martineau as one of the early founders of Western sociology and as the first publicly influential sociological analyst in Western history.

THE DISTORTION OF MAX WEBER'S THOUGHT

Western sociology has long had competing social perspectives. Many sociologists and other social scientists have offered theory or engaged in research that supports the established order. Typically, in these social science analyses, they have emphasized the harmonious working of established institutions, and when they consider change, they have preferred slow rates of evolutionary change. In contrast, another sizeable group of sociologists has viewed the discipline of sociology as an enterprise that can help liberate human beings from their misery and social troubles through accurate sociological research on oppressive institutions and the introduction of societal reforms or more revolutionary changes based on that research.

The ideas of a value-free sociology and of the ideal type method are considered by many to be cornerstones of the work of the prominent German sociologist Max Weber (1864–1920). His cautions about values in social science are generally interpreted as proposing a sociological understanding not shaped by the researcher's social position, one free of the sociological researcher's values. The US theorist Talcott Parsons introduced much of the work of Max Weber to North American social scientists, and this was generally his interpretation of Weber. Such an interpretation portrays Weber as a father of mainstream instrumental positivism, which often presents itself as value-free and detached.[18] This view is too simplistic, for Weber was a sophisticated sociologist who struggled throughout his career with sociology's need to be socially useful but politically neutral. An in-depth discussion of Weber's ideas is necessary to gain an understanding of the complexities involved in claiming neutrality or objectivity in the practice of social science—as well as to understand the ways in which the evolving discipline of sociology has often constructed itself.

An early controversy over value-free social science flared up at a 1909 Vienna conference. At a session there, Weber was upset by a colleague's narrow use of the concept of productivity to judge agriculture in Germany. Weber suggested that three different problems had to be recognized: (1) productivity in the sense of maximum grain production for a given area, (2) the interest or the welfare of the people in an area, and (3) the sociopolitical interest of an even distribution of property among the people of the area. As Weber saw it, these different concerns and interests compete with each other. Equating productivity with a certain profitability, as his colleague did, was *objectionable* because several economic interests were at stake in the situation studied. Weber objected to the use of concepts that represented a premature "value judgment." He analyzed explicitly the role of value judgments and the interests then in conflict.[19]

More generally, Weber's advocacy of value freedom was not a call for a social science devoid of values but rather a call for a social science that was protected from intrusion by established political authorities and their values and that took social values seriously and was careful not to transform questions of values into purely technical questions. Weber abhorred the unquestioned acceptance of conventional definitions of social phenomena. At the aforementioned Vienna conference, Weber was eloquent on the need for ideals in social science: "I cannot bear it when problems of global proportions, with consequences that concern great ideals, in a certain sense the utmost problems that move the heart, are here turned into technoeconomical questions of 'productivity,' and are made a matter of discussion of a specialized discipline, as is the national economy."[20]

Probably influenced by his sociologist and activist wife Marianne Weber, Max Weber was clear about the impossibility of social sciences unshaped by values. In an essay for the social science journal *Archiv*, Weber was unequivocal: "There is no absolutely 'objective' scientific analysis of culture ... of 'social phenomena' independent of special and 'one-sided' viewpoints according to which—expressly or tacitly, consciously or unconsciously—they are selected, analyzed and organized for expository purposes."[21] Moreover, while Weber remained doubtful that societal inequality could be eradicated, he clearly saw the need for progressive values and ideals in social science. During World War I, he drew on social science to publicly voice concerns against the annexationist policies of the German government. He criticized such policies, writing news articles, memos to public officials, and various research papers. He advocated for a democratically elected parliament and against the extreme ideologies of the German left and right.[22]

Nonetheless, since Weber's time, many instrumental positivists have argued for a "value-free" social science. This is supposed to be achieved through the application of technical methods said to be independent of the researcher, of the problem at hand, and of the object studied (see Chapter 3). These instrumental methods are said to be generic and to exist before a societal problem is tackled. Weber rejected this notion. He saw linkages between observers, the observed, and the methods used."[23]

A look at Weber's conception of "ideal types" makes it clear how far his sociology is from the instrumental positivism of contemporary social science. These ideal types are stylized images designed as "standards of value by reference to which empirical existence can be evaluated."[24] Weber's ideal types are culturally specific ways of classification. A researcher's interests determine the significance attributed to events in the past. The simplification involved in the strategy of ideal types reflects those elements the experienced researcher sees as significant—to the exclusion of other elements because of the researcher's particular interests. Weber does not claim that the facts that sociologists include in an ideal type are more essential than those excluded; rather, they are regarded as being more significant by the researcher. In this way, the ideal type that a social scientist constructs to organize data is not an arbitrary simplification but one that reflects the understandings and values of the researcher. Ahmad Sadri notes that Weber "recognized that 'our' history inevitably bears the imprint of our particular interest in it. Thus, he liberated sociologists as well as other social scientists and particularly historians from the burdensome pretension of German idealism, which required them to be selfless oracles of reason (or revolution)."[25]

Ideal types are thus bound to the values of the researcher at a particular point in history. They have a liberating effect because the social scientists who use them are forced to make explicit their mental models and to examine those models for adequacy, keeping in mind that this conceptual tool is affected by their values and existential circumstances. The use of ideal types makes it possible to accept, rather than deny, the fact that "we confront our society and history as finite human beings whose interests define the past as much as they are defined by it."[26] In Weber's terminology, the measure of meaningfulness of an ideal type is its "subjective adequacy"—that is, its agreement with "our habitual modes of thoughts and feelings."[27] It should be in agreement with our common sense, not in conformity with some abstract principles of logic. Social researchers determine the empirical validity of the ideal types by estimating their "causal adequacy," the odds of their actual occurrence.

For Weber, social researchers can look at history and societies *only* from the point of view of their values and interests. Age, gender, class, racial group, religion, education, urban-rural location, occupation, and nationality are among the social factors that shape one's vision. However, these limitations can be turned into leverage for understanding. It is not necessary to claim that one has reproduced the worldview of the other or that one has transcended one's own culture. When social scientists erect the logically consistent structures called ideal types to accent certain aspects of the societal problems studied, they submit their values and interests to examination. A self-righteous affirmation of cultural or methodological superiority only highlights the blissful unawareness of one's standpoint.[28]

Clearly, Weber did not call for a sociology devoid of human interests. In his strongest statements on values and social research, he was reacting against political intrusions into the German academy and against the transformation of social life into supposedly value-free technical questions. In fact, the ideal type method furnishes sociologists with a practical way to examine the values and interests they incorporate into their research.

In the next two chapters, we examine in detail how many mainstream sociologists came to accent the view of sociology as devoid of human values, as detached and as distancing of the subjects studied. This view did not develop without opposition. In an appendix to his 1944 pathbreaking book on US racism, called *An American Dilemma*, Gunnar Myrdal took a Weberian position on values. Myrdal specifically criticized the detached positivism of then prominent US sociologists: "The specific logical error is that of inferring from the facts that men can and should make no effort to change the 'natural' outcome of the specific forces observed. This is the old do-nothing (laissez-faire) bias of 'realistic' social science."[29] He added as well: "Scientific facts do not exist per se, waiting for scientists to discover them. A scientific fact is a construction abstracted out of a complex and interwoven reality by means of arbitrary definitions and classifications. The processes of selecting a problem and a basic hypothesis, of limiting the scope of study, and of defining and classifying data relevant to such a setting of the problem, involve a choice on the part of the investigator."[30] Value neutrality in social science is impossible, for in choices about how to assess society there is always something of value at stake.

In the 1960s, Myrdal expanded his view of how social scientists can provide a maximum of objectivity only by being candid about their values and biases. In a book titled *Objectivity in Social Research*, he argued the following:

> The logical means available for protecting ourselves from biases are broadly these: to raise the valuations actually determining our theoretical as well as our practical research to full awareness, to scrutinize them from the point of view of relevance, significance, and feasibility in the society under study, to transform them into specific value premises for research, and to determine approach and define concepts in terms of a set of value premises which have been explicitly stated.[31]

One lesson here for contemporary social scientists is that we should not abandon the idea of objectivity to the instrumental positivists. Instead, as social scientists, we should watch carefully how concealed biases and assumptions, both our own and those of other researchers, affect the sociological craft, and we should try to minimize the possible distortions from these influences.

THE COMMITMENTS OF ÉMILE DURKHEIM

We need to demystify others among the classical theorists as well. Émile Durkheim (1858–1917), the pioneering French sociologist, has often been portrayed in relatively conservative terms as principally concerned with social order. However, the transformation of Durkheim into a sociologist of value-free positivism by some contemporary sociologists ignores his deep concern with morality, social justice, and societal change. He often saw his sociological analysis as a type of moral philosophy. The center of his thought system was the concept of the *conscience collectif*. However, the common translation of this French word *conscience* with the English word *consciousness* obscures the fact that *conscience* in French also means "conscience" in the English sense of an ability to make moral judgments. If one reads Durkheim in the original French, it is clear that he was centrally concerned with the moral dimensions of society.[32]

In his important book *The Elementary Forms of the Religious Life*, Durkheim offered seminal ideas about religion and fundamental human concepts that were much more than an abstract discussion when he first proposed them. His central ideas were that religion involves a view dividing the world into the sacred and the profane and that the sacred is the social par excellence. Moreover, as Durkheim saw it, his perspective had concrete political implications. At the time, the French government was expropriating the property of the Catholic Church. Catholic parishioners and their clergy, who were for the most part monarchists opposed to the French republic, vigorously opposed this on the grounds that the church's riches were "sacred" and that the "profane" authority of the government had no right to intervene.[33]

Rather than dismissing this division of the world into sacred and secular as a sign of backward thinking, as many scholars did in his time, Durkheim viewed it as a characteristic of the religious way of thinking. Durkheim wrote of "religious facts," and not just of "religion," in order to emphasize that religious expression in a given society did not have to be part of organized religious systems.[34] Durkheim showed that organized religions like Catholicism did not have a monopoly over religious rituals and sentiments. He argued that the sense of God and of moral control that all believers feel, whatever their religion, stems ultimately from society: "The forces before which the believer bows are not simple physical energies, as they are given to the senses and imagination; these are social forces."[35] Religious and moral forces are actually social forces.

Rather than segregating sacred things as beyond the reach of society, Durkheim declared them to be at least as social as other important phenomena:

> Sacred things are those in which society itself has elaborated the representation; in it enter all sorts of collective states, of traditions and common emotions, of sentiments that relate to objects of general interest, etc., and all these elements are combined following laws of social mentality. Profane things, on the contrary, are those that each of us constructs with the given of our senses and our experience; these notions concern all new individual impressions, and this is why they do not have, in our eyes, the same prestige than the precedent.[36]

The sacred takes precedence because it symbolizes collective images and reflects collective forces and pressures. Durkheim did not come to this fertile sociological idea from neutral and detached reflection on a random topic. On the contrary, it was from applying Durkheim's sociological reason to the historical turmoil burgeoning around the wealth of the Catholic Church in this era of France's history.

Although Durkheim did not extensively analyze the role of major oppressive structures such as imperialism, systemic racism, and patriarchy in his day, he did underscore in some writings the critical importance of social justice and the move to equality. Indeed, he wrote eloquently about the need for justice. For Durkheim, a forced division of labor like that found in a capitalistic society was pathological: "The lower classes not being ... satisfied with the role which has devolved upon them from custom or by law aspire to functions which are closed to them and seek to dispossess those who are exercising these functions."[37] He was critical of any societal inequalities generated by such mechanisms as inheritance over family generations.[38]

Durkheim used the term *organic solidarity* for a healthy society. In his view, "justice" required the elimination of social inequalities that are not generated by variations in personal merit and abilities: "If one class of society is obliged, in order to live, to take any price for its services, while another can abstain from such action thanks to the resources at its disposal which, however, are not necessarily due to any social superiority, the second has an unjust advantage over the first at law."[39] Moreover, he makes it clear that "the task of the most advanced societies is, then, a work of justice.... [O]ur ideal is to make social relations always more equitable, so as to assure the free development of all our socially useful forces." The trend toward ever more complex and organic societies requires ever more social justice and equality. "Just as ancient peoples needed, above all, a common faith to live by, so we need justice, and we can be sure that this need will become ever more exacting if ... the conditions dominating social evolution remain the same."[40]

An additional illustration of Durkheim's concern with social justice is his work entitled "Anti-Semitism and Social Crisis," written in 1899 during the Dreyfus Affair in France. The Dreyfus Affair was precipitated by the wrongful conviction of Captain Alfred Dreyfus, a French army officer of Jewish background, for allegedly selling military secrets to the Germans. Through his role as an active member of the Dreyfusard Ligue pour la Defense des Droits de l'Homme, Durkheim vigorously defended Dreyfus.[41] The social and political context in France in which Durkheim, the agnostic son of devout Jews, penned "Anti-Semitism and Social Crisis" and defended Dreyfus can best be summarized as "hostility to the country's Jewish population ... in both word and deed."[42]

Drawing on this work, sociologist Chad Alan Goldberg has emphasized Durkheim's concern with morality, social justice, and societal change, while underlining the contemporary relevance of Durkheim's ideas for the sociology of racism and anti-Semitism. According to Goldberg, in keeping with Durkheim's assertion elsewhere that sociology should be interested in practical problems, the conclusion to "Anti-Semitism and Social Crisis" includes a discussion of the most adept means for challenging anti-Semitism. For Durkheim, however, sociology could usefully tackle such practical questions only by retaining methodical independence and consequently offering scientific and objective recommendations.[43] Goldberg describes Durkheim's "long-term" corrective to anti-Semitism as such:

> If anti-Semitism is primarily a reaction to and a means of coping with anomie, then anomie is its root cause.... [Durkheim's] chief remedy was the reorganization of economic relations through the revival of occupational groups, linked to but independent of the state.... By realizing a healthy, organic form of social solidarity appropriate to a complex society with a highly developed division of labor, these measures would obviate the need for dysfunctional substitutes that ultimately divided rather than integrated French society.[44]

Clearly, the sections of the classical founders that emphasize concerns of social justice have been neglected in contemporary social science, probably because they do not fit well with numerous mainstream perspectives. For example, in putting his influential structural-functionalist theory in place, sociologist Talcott Parsons drew on a sanitized Max Weber and relied heavily on the work of Durkheim, whom he positioned as a premier theorist dealing with problems of social order and stability.[45] He does not even mention Durkheim's concern with and recognition of issues of equality and social justice. Parsons was but one of a number of major Western social scientists who have developed and perpetuated one-sided misinterpretations of Weber and Durkheim in contemporary sociology.

CHALLENGES OUTSIDE ACADEMIA: KARL MARX

Unlike Durkheim and Weber, Karl Marx (1818–1883) was not an academic and he wrote frequently for a nonacademic audience. He attempted to write for workers and about the political-economic sources of their suffering. His aim was not just to understand the world but also to change it. In fact, his influential ideas have changed—and continue to change—the modern world in major ways.

In US sociology, Marx has often been ignored or treated as "insignificant." For example, in one 1960s theory textbook that taught social theory to a generation of sociologists, the author deals with Marx in just two and a half pages in a catchall chapter devoted to "other pioneers."[46] Marx is erroneously labeled as an economic determinist. Another popular theory textbook of the 1960s devoted seven pages to the seldom-read idealist philosopher Georg Hegel but gave only six to the still-influential materialist thinker Karl Marx.[47]

In many textbooks and other social science discussions, Marx's dialectical approach is misunderstood or dismissed. Much mainstream discussion inside and outside academic circles views this "dialectics" as describing a rigid social cycle: a thesis, opposed by an antithesis, which is resolved in a synthesis. This is alleged to be the central Marxist approach to analyzing history and society. Yet, Marx's dialectics entails an approach quite different from this simplistic portrait. For Marx, a dialectical approach involves *asking whether things really are what they seem to be*. Through dialectics, Marx dug beneath the surface realities and tensions of socioeconomic life under capitalism and found that the apparently fair exchanges of labor and commodities hid an economic structure that dominated not only workers but also the development of various institutional structures of a capitalist society. A dialectical approach recognizes that in the social world there is an ongoing tension and reciprocity among different social phenomena; one set of social arrangements can be in contention with another set of social arrangements, even to the point of replacing the latter. Capitalism is not just a social system but an unjust way of living in a society, and it is a political-economic system that is periodically challenged and ever changing.

Marx contrasted his research method, later called *dialectical materialism* or *historical materialism*, with Hegel's idealism and argued that dialectical movements are part of the material world. Marx's idea is that human experience can be understood only as a complex and living whole, a dialectical whole with contending social realities—one always moving and in process. Marx does *not* reduce social phenomena to economic phenomena, as has often been claimed. Instead, Marx placed economic life in the context of society, of the whole that is human experience. An important contribution of Marx was to show how capitalism, apparently a purely economic system, actually shapes, interacts with, and often dominates the larger cultures and societies of which it is an integral part.

In recent decades, one of the better-known sociological proponents of the dialectical method has been French sociologist Georges Gurvitch. In his view, Marx's dialectics focuses on the dynamic character of everyday life. The nature of human social reality is fundamentally dialectical. Dialectics is a way to affirm "the complexities, sinuosities, flexibilities, and constantly renewing tensions, along with the unexpected turns of events of social reality."[48]

As we see it, liberation sociology should be contextual, historical, and dialectical in assessing the movement to a more just society. It should carefully assess the context around and processes behind current social observations. Particular social phenomena have histories and weblike relations to other, often less obvious, social phenomena. This approach examines contradictions and complexities within the whole and across space and time. In sociology, this approach can be liberating and revolutionary "because it helps us to see the present as a moment through which our society is passing, because it forces us to examine where it has come from and where it is heading ... and because ... we have the power to affect it."[49]

Using this dialectical perspective, liberation sociologists view social reality as filled with tension, movement, backtracking, and renewal. No oppressive system lasts forever, and during its life it is periodically, if not constantly, challenged. Thus, social life is dynamic, not static—with much counterpoint. Human societies like that of the United States are riddled with social contradictions and are shaped by people who make errors in arrangements, beliefs, and choices. Often these errors are covered over with rationalizations and myths. In analyzing society, sociologists working in a critical dialectical tradition dig behind these rationalizations and fictions. Recall the Roman myth of the giant Cacus, who stole Hercules's cattle and then made them walk backward into his cave to deceive Hercules into thinking they had walked out of the cave and vanished. Too often, social scientists count the number of footprints but do not see where they come from or where they are going. A liberation sociology approach attends to the larger social framework around observations, to how observed phenomena arise and develop, and to how they fit into the larger environment.

Much contemporary social theory, such as exchange theory and rational choice theory, leaves out the flow of history and the deeper layers of social reality. In Marx's view, when we apply the standard logic of modern capitalistic societies, injustice and exploitation falsely appear to be inevitable. Yet, a particular injustice is not a static thing found at one point in time or place but ordinarily has a long history of social reproduction. Oppression at one place is part of a process that contains both the history of that oppression and its possible futures, including futures of resistance. A dialectical approach emphasizes that the aspects of oppression are but segments of a larger whole, which includes not only the present, past, and future of oppression but also the agents and individuals involved, including the researchers. The perspectival element, accenting the standpoint from which one views reality, is a critical element of the dialectical approach.[50]

Dialectical methods reject static truths. Everything in the social world, including our ideas of it, is in tension or contradiction with something else. There is nothing permanent; the apparent stability that human beings give to their affairs, such as through the creation of societal institutions, is temporary at best and the result of continuing negotiation and struggle.

A sociological method that produces statements about social realities as if they were crystallized and immobile contradicts the fact that human beings and their groups are alive. To affirm the dynamic nature of social life, we need instead a method that concentrates our attention on that dynamism. At its best, a dialectical approach also has the advantage of making the changing humanity of the researchers part of its investigation. The practice of research is a human experience. The claim to be "value-free," seen from this dialectical approach, is just a social construction of certain mainstream social scientists. C. Wright Mills criticized the "abstracted empiricism" of mainstream sociology in the 1950s and 1960s. Practitioners of abstracted empiricism, then and now, often claim objectivity and detachment, a freedom from conceptual presuppositions, when in fact what they do is "embrace one philosophy of science which they now suppose to be the scientific method."[51]

For many social scientists, physics has been the model for those who want to discover scientific laws that determine human behavior. From this viewpoint, one proposes coherent hypotheses that, when tested correctly through certain limited types of empirical observation and experimentation in regard to research objects, become scientific laws. However, we should place in quotation marks conventional social science terms like "subject," "object," "discover," and "determine" to call attention to how problematic these terms are. In reality, many of the "objects" studied by social scientists are as much "subjects" as the researchers who are supposed to discover relations among the "objects." Use of this type of distancing language makes it seem that the social research endeavor is not itself a type of human social relationship. It is as if the human beings studied by researchers were no different from rocks, bugs, or any other thing studied by the natural sciences. Yet, they are quite different, for they are sentient beings that can "bite back," and they are ever changing.

THE PROGRESSIVISM OF GEORGE HERBERT MEAD AND LESTER FRANK WARD

Durkheim and Weber are not the only major theorists whose ideas and proclivities have been distorted to fit contemporary interests and concerns. Note the important work of the great US social theorist and founder of the symbolic interactionist tradition, George Herbert Mead. Mead is usually considered a major member of the Chicago School of sociology, though in fact he taught in the areas of philosophy and social psychology. However, Mead had many sociology graduate students and interacted regularly with members of the University of Chicago sociology department and the sociologists at Chicago's Hull House (see Chapter 3). His ideas about symbolic interaction have influenced subsequent generations of sociologists and social psychologists. Mead is best known for a book later constructed from his classroom notes, called *Mind, Self, and Society*. The cover of the paperback edition claims that Mead published little in his lifetime. Yet, Mead published more than eighty articles, most of which have been forgotten. One likely reason for this amnesia about Mead's work is that over half of these articles are concerned with *progressive reform* issues, such as the conditions of workers and immigrants, war and peace, democracy, and public education.[52] Indeed, Mead was an activist intellectual who participated in numerous local and national reform movements.

Contributing to the distinctive US philosophical tradition of pragmatism, Mead took a dialectical approach to the human self. He rejected the dualistic division of "mind" and "body" common in Western thought, as well as the division of person and environment. As he saw it, the individual "constitutes society as genuinely as society constitutes the individual."[53] Human beings interact with each other substantially in terms of symbols such as language, and human thinking is an internal conversation involving social symbols, much like the conversations carried on with other people. Linguistic and other symbols have meaning because they are developed in the social interaction of human beings.[54] Social conflict arises when there is a breakdown in this symbolic communication and people are not able to understand the positions or roles of important others.

Moreover, while past experience certainly shapes symbolic meanings and communication, the acts of human beings are not strictly determined but have major aspects of creativity and spontaneity. All human beings are thinking creatures working to shape their surrounding environments. Thinking involves problem solving in order to take practical action in social and physical environments.[55] Central to Mead's perspective is the idea that human beings think critically about environments, as well as about the thinking process itself. They are reflexive (reflective) and can act in a proactive manner. The reflective mind is social and is shaped by the societal milieu in which people find themselves. As Gideon Sjoberg and Ted Vaughan note, human beings spend much effort in "justifying their moral beliefs and their normative order" and have the ability to "take the roles of others and to recognize another's humanity and commonality with oneself."[56] This ability, though in many settings seldom used, can be a critical step toward developing respect for the rights of others.

Democratic rights and freedoms, especially the freedom of communication, were critical for Mead. He accented the advance toward equality as essential for the development of healthy societies. His approach to sociological research and social reform was humanistic; people and their ideas had to be respected. This was in contrast to the social scientific analysts of his day who just studied human subjects as "objects." Human beings had critical minds and intelligence and could change themselves and their surroundings, and thus were different from the usual objects of the physical sciences. Not surprisingly, Mead gave great weight to progressive and critical education, which he saw as encouraging scientific inquiry that was self-reflective and that integrated the social milieu into self-understanding.[57] Such education was essential to progress in equality and democracy, especially education for the poor, immigrants, and others who had been marginalized.

Although Mead has often been portrayed as an ivory tower scholar interested in abstract ideas about self and mind, he was in fact a community activist and progressive reformer who worked with Jane Addams and other sociologist-activists in Chicago (see Chapter 3). Mead worked in city settlement houses and played a role in the educational committee of the Chicago City Club. He was an editor of a publication of the Chicago Laboratory School, which was set up to experiment with progressive ideas in education. He worked on behalf of workers in an era when this stance was considered radical, and he was a vice president of an organization committed to immigrants' rights. He spoke at meetings on behalf of women's right to vote and generally supported the movement for women's suffrage.[58]

Another important progressive scholar among early sociologists was Lester Frank Ward, the first president of the new American Sociological Society. In contrast to most male sociologists, who viewed women as naturally subordinate, Ward was egalitarian and feminist in his research and writing. In the first decades of his career, he published in the areas of geology and anthropology but later did sociological research, becoming a professor at Brown University in 1906. In his book, *Pure Sociology*, Ward lays out a view of sociology as contributing significantly in its research and analysis to human achievement and societal reform. Perhaps most pathbreaking in Ward's research work is his conceptual analysis of gender and the subordination of women, work so important that women sociologists of his time, such as Charlotte Perkins Gilman, cited his research as influencing them. Ward coined the term *androcentric* to describe the contemporary popular and social science theories that put men as primary in the biological order and the center of all important aspects of society and that played down the role of women as key societal actors outside of procreation. Ward countered the prevailing view with a "gynaecocentric" theory that viewed women as primary in the biological order and argued that the natural superiority of women had long ago been reversed by men who used their size and force to create androcentric patriarchal societies.[59] Gender subordination of women was rationalized extensively with "epithets, slurs, flings, and open condemnation of women as being in some manner vile and hateful, often malicious and evil disposed."[60]

Ward argued assertively for an egalitarian society in which men and women would have equal access to virtually all political and economic positions. He advocated openly for such a society and for women's rights in an era when this was considered "radical." In this regard Ward's views and activism were very much in line with the views and work of the early women sociologists whom we previously discussed.[61] Clearly, both Mead and Ward were early contributors to the liberation sociology tradition.

INSIGHTS FROM THE PHYSICAL SCIENCES

In his influential work on paradigm shifts in science, Thomas Kuhn rejects the idea that physical science has developed only in a gradual and accumulating fashion.[62] Instead, he accents the revolutionary breaks that define much of the history of science. What he calls "normal science" is a period during which a dominant paradigm is gradually reinforced by accumulating knowledge. As scientific findings develop that cannot be explained by the dominant paradigm, pressures build and often lead to a scientific revolution and a new paradigm. George Ritzer has clarified what Kuhn means by *paradigm*: "It serves to define what should be studied, what questions should be asked, how they should be asked, and what rules should be followed in interpreting the answers obtained. The paradigm is the broadest unit of consensus."[63] Kuhn also criticized education in the physical sciences for being too "narrow and rigid" and for not producing students "who will easily discover a fresh approach."[64]

Niels Bohr, a Nobel Prize–winning physicist, explained the old Newtonian way of thinking in a 1958 essay: "In Newtonian mechanics, where the state of a system of material bodies is defined by their instantaneous positions and velocities, it proved possible, by the well-known simple principles, to derive solely from the knowledge of the state of the system at a given time and of the forces acting upon the bodies, the state of the system at any other time."[65] However, at the end of the nineteenth and beginning of the twentieth century, a series of new ideas revolutionized the paradigm central to physical science. The new idea of relativity—that the "description of physical phenomena depends on the reference frame chosen by the observer"—was revolutionary for the physical sciences.[66]

A new era for atomic physics began with the discovery of subatomic particles and the complexity of matter and radiation—what came to be called "quantum" physics. What were once seen as only particles could also be viewed as waves, and vice versa. The new physics showed that there was a holism to atomic phenomena. There was also a major challenge to the distinction between the measuring apparatus, the person doing the measuring, and the objects being studied. According to the "uncertainty principle," the interaction between the instruments of observation and the observed particles is critical in the research process. Viewed broadly, one cannot be said to be measuring something exactly if one cannot tell whether the changes recorded on instruments are the result of what is being observed, of something going on inside the instrument, or both.

Similarly, in the social sciences, the instruments of observation and the observers are inseparable parts of a whole reality with the researched subjects. Indeed, Bohr even noted that the methodological situation in twentieth-century social science and biology reminded him of what quantum physics had gone through.[67] A rigid and neat distinction between the researcher, the method, and the object studied is no longer tenable in either the physical sciences or the social sciences.

CONCLUSION

Sociological dialectics is a method that allows social scientists—to use the same terminology that Bohr uses for physics—to "include a description of all the relevant features of the experimental arrangement."[68] Science is defined by the application of a method to the production of knowledge. Yet the method is to a large extent determined by what is to be observed. The use of a microscope allows scientists to observe realms hidden from the naked eye. But no matter how wonderful the method of using a microscope is, it is not appropriate for observing the stars. A different method needs to be used. It is always the human researcher who decides which method to use and why it is appropriate to use it.

In the social sciences, the researchers observing human beings are, of course, as human as those under observation, and a social research project would seem to have the greatest potential only if the researchers establish a human relationship with the people being studied. However, in recent years, government survey and demographic data sets have been made available to social science researchers who did not participate in their collection. There are at least two types of potential problems here. First, it is often the case that these governmental statistics are produced by human beings whose careers depend on their turning out numbers acceptable to their bureaucratic superiors, whether they be in the executive or legislative branches.

Second, social scientists using the data collected by government agencies or other researchers may work under the illusion that their job as social scientists is only one of reporting statistical distributions or coefficients rather than understanding well the human relations those data usually represent. Typically, these researchers do not meet or talk with the people they study, or often even with the people who participated in the original generation of the data. And they frequently do not inquire into the biases of the data collectors.

Those studying human relations in this fashion—and they include numerous social scientists in key research areas—are producing unduly limited, if not distorted, images of those human relations. The study of disembodied numbers from survey data can manufacture human beings who, like billiard balls touching each other in a game of pool, have only isolated or individualistic existences and random encounters. Yet this is not the social world in reality. Whether or not they realize it, social scientists study behavior that is more or less actively willed by their fellow human beings, who are interacting in situations meaningful to them and that they often define or redefine.

As we have seen, all the "classical" sociological theorists examined in this chapter were concerned with the moral and ethical issues of their immediate social contexts. They were in no sense detached scientists trying to be value-free, instrumental-positivistic researchers. All were actively involved in studying societal trends and structures sociologically and all tried to effect positive change in their own societies.

CHAPTER 3

US Sociology from the 1890s to the 1970s

Instrumental Positivism and Its Challengers

Like other academic disciplines, sociology has long been molded by its national and international contexts, central to which is the economic system of modern capitalism. For more than a century, capitalism and its elites have shaped the dominant assumptions underlying sociology and the other social sciences—in Europe and the United States.

In the late nineteenth and early twentieth centuries, the new discipline of sociology had several prominent advocates. Some of the early sociologists, such as Herbert Spencer in England and William Graham Sumner in the United States, strongly supported free-market capitalism and were opposed to government intervention in the capitalistic economy. Spencer generated the concept of "social Darwinism," with its idea of the survival of the fittest in society. Sumner picked up on Spencer's ideas, arguing, for example, that the rich were rich because natural selection sees to it that the "best" people rise to the top of society.

However, with the rise of progressive movements in the decades just before and after 1900, many of the new sociologists and other social scientists came to see this as an untenable position. This was a period of growing labor conflict and progressive ferment in the United States, and many leading academics, including some sociologists, supported moderate reform and some government intervention in the operation of capitalism, a "corporate liberal" approach. Indeed, the US university has long been a center of this moderate-reform approach. Such corporate-liberal social scientists have argued that without some "political regulation of economic life, capitalism would be destroyed by class conflicts involving militant labor unions and socialist movements on the one hand, and gigantic monopolies or monopoly trusts on the other."[1] Viewing capitalists and corporations as necessary and productive, corporate liberals have traditionally backed some government intervention in the economy. Moreover, they have supported substantial government aid to corporations when the market fails and some modest government aid to working people, especially if they protest. For decades, many mainstream sociologists have adopted some version of the corporate-liberal, moderate-reform perspective.

CAPITALISM AND THE FOUNDERS OF SOCIOLOGY

The "founding fathers" of US sociology are sometimes said to be Lester Frank Ward (1841–1913), William Graham Sumner (1840–1910), Franklin H. Giddings (1855–1931), and Albion Small (1854–1926). Not surprisingly, given the lack of early academic programs in sociology, not one was actually educated as a sociologist. Ward worked for the federal government as a clerk and paleobotanist, Giddings was a journalist, and Small and Sumner were educated in theology.[2] Note that these commonly listed sociologists were all white and male. All were aware of the major social and political issues of their period, and Ward, Giddings, and Small were committed to using sociology to bring some reform and thereby make a better society. Thus, in 1900 Albion Small presented a paper at the first meeting of the American Sociological Society in which he argued vigorously that sociological study and research were not ends in themselves but should serve to improve society.[3]

Some early male sociologists had been ministers, including Small, while Giddings and Ward had fathers or grandfathers who were ministers. Their backgrounds tended to be urban or rural and Protestant. Not surprisingly, they were often concerned with the negative effects of urbanization and industrialization. The "social pathology" and "social disorganization" of cities became early topics in their social research.[4]

A few prominent male sociologists were moderately critical of capitalistic enterprises. For example, Small and Edward Alsworth Ross (1866–1951) occasionally went beyond the conventional wisdom espoused by the dominant intellectual and business elites to argue that workers should have greater power in enterprises and the right to organize. Indeed, at the turn of the twentieth century, Ross was fired from Stanford University for his critical views on the exploitation of Chinese laborers by white capitalists. Nevertheless, even sociologists like Ross were unabashedly racist in their views of people of color, and they were by no means sympathetic to the views of more radical social reformers who sought to substantially remake capitalist society or replace it with a more just political-economic system.[5]

Among these early white male sociologists, there was some criticism of the existing society, but mostly from the corporate-liberal perspective. Very few took issue with the use of government force and related actions to expand the interests of the capitalist elite, and they rarely took the perspectives of working people, immigrants, women, or African Americans in their research or public actions. A more assertive liberalism among sociology's founders can be seen in some statements of Lester F. Ward—as noted previously, the first president of the American Sociological Society (now the American Sociological Association). Ward believed that there should be a practical use for sociology. He argued that "the true guide, the Moses that is to lead man out of the wilderness, is science" and that "the real object of science is to benefit man."[6]

Ward, writing in the early 1900s, viewed sociology as divided into "pure" and "applied" areas. Pure sociology ignores what ought to be and aims at "truth for its own sake." Applied sociologists should apply sociological intelligence to everyday life and should deal only in broad generalizations to guide action. An applied sociologist should not "abandon his science."[7] As we saw in Chapter 2, Ward made intensive scientific efforts to examine gender issues and concluded that a highly patriarchal society was not a healthy society.

A SOCIOLOGY FOR THE PEOPLE: EARLY WHITE FEMALE AND BLACK SOCIOLOGISTS

The Early Women Sociologists

From the beginning, US sociology has had a strong countersystem tradition, one that often aggressively sides with the oppressed against social injustice and calls for a publicly involved sociology. Scholar-activists like Jane Addams and W. E. B. Du Bois were "organic intellectuals" who emerged out of the aggrieved sectors of society to articulate the experiences of the oppressed. Addams and Du Bois sought the liberation of women and African Americans from the deeply oppressive structures of US society. To a significant degree, their sociological sensitivity and sophistication stemmed from their experiences in dealing with oppression in their lives and those of friends and relatives. They were sociologists whose interpretive, epistemological, and theoretical insights grew, in part, out of concrete everyday encounters with societal oppression.

In the late nineteenth and early twentieth centuries, numerous women sociologists took strong positions on behalf of women, children, the poor, and immigrants. Among these were Jane Addams, Emily G. Balch, Florence Kelley, Julia Lathrop, Lucy Salmon, Ann G. Spencer, Mary Eliza McDowell, Charlotte Perkins Gilman, and Marion Talbot. These women were practicing sociologists and early members of the American Sociological Society, founded in 1905. Some gave presentations at Society meetings. Early on, numerous female sociologists were committed to bringing real societal changes that would stem from alliances between sociologists and communities of the poor, immigrants, and African Americans.[8]

Between the 1890s and the 1910s, many of these female sociologists were linked to Hull House in Chicago, a major settlement house and intellectual center of the day. The settlement house movement was part of a large progressive movement to better conditions and opportunities of the poor and immigrants in US cities. Out of the group of female sociologists, and a few associated male sociologists, came a major humanistic perspective termed *feminist pragmatism*. Pragmatism was a US intellectual movement of the late nineteenth and early twentieth centuries; its central idea was that the real test of a concept lay in its observability and practical significance in the real world of everyday experiences. A developed variant of the prevailing pragmatist perspective, feminist pragmatism emphasized a strongly cooperative and nurturing humanist ethic. It emphasized the values of liberal education and democracy as essential to progressive development in the everyday world.[9]

As a pioneering scholar of US sociology's history, Mary Jo Deegan has shown that Jane Addams and certain colleagues inside and outside sociology were part of a decades-long successful attempt to bring a "feminist pragmatist welfare state" to Chicago, to the United States, and ultimately to the world. These activist-intellectuals were perhaps the "most powerful network of women" in US history, a network that aggressively articulated an activist framing of society that was much more democratic, feminist, and antiracist than the dominant interpretive frame, which was strongly patriarchal, corporate-capitalistic, and white-racist. The women and a few male colleagues developed an important counter-frame to the dominant frame of the white male elites, and then they pressed hard to bring major changes in societal support programs. Although the major credit is often given to male politicians in the 1930s and 1940s in Europe and the United States, to a very substantial degree the ideas lying behind the modern social-welfare state come from these feminist pragmatists and their aggressive efforts to provide major socio-economic support programs for people in US society.[10]

Significantly, the first graduate department of sociology was created in the 1890s at the University of Chicago, not far from Hull House. There, in the early days of US sociology, white men dominated the development of academic sociology. However, even *before* this famous department was founded, and as it was growing, women sociologists at Chicago's Hull House (a community facility) were pioneers in empiri-cal field research. These women sociologists—including Jane Addams, Florence Kelley, and Julia Lathrop—worked and did empirical research from the feminist-pragmatist point of view at Hull House. They should be listed among the early founders of US sociology.

The Chicago sociology department was a male bastion, and numer-ous white men there saw themselves as intellectually superior; they often viewed women as data collectors who could implement the ideas of the male sociologists. These men viewed Hull House, and the city of Chicago, as a "sociological laboratory."[11] Albion Small, a founder of the department at the University of Chicago, first used the term *sociologi-cal laboratory* in the 1890s. Later, the men in the Chicago department who did undertake what became famous urban sociological research came to view the city as such a sociological laboratory.[12] However, this conception of Hull House and of the people of Chicago was rejected by Addams and other women sociologists at Hull House. Instead, they viewed the needs of the working people in the area as more important than the needs of sociological lab researchers. The people in cities were not primarily "specimens" to be studied and objectified.

These women sociologists were—and perceived themselves to be—scholars, researchers, and intellectuals, and some were faculty members or students at the University of Chicago. Indeed, at this university a group of female sociologists, including Marion Talbot, Ella Flagg Young, and Sophonisba Breckinridge (initially in a subordinate division of the sociology department), worked with the more progressive men there such as George H. Mead and William I. Thomas to educate Chicago students, often in the ideas of the feminist pragmatism.[13]

By the 1920s, most leading male sociologists saw sociology as hav-ing moved from the early rudimentary stage in which female sociologists at community settlement houses facilitated sociology's development, to a more "mature" stage of academic research, which was increasingly done with support from corporate foundations. Sociology students from the department at the University of Chicago came to Hull House, yet the men who controlled the department had increasingly negative views of Addams's "uplift" sociology.[14] Indeed, by 1920 all the women sociologists affiliated with the department of sociology at the University of Chicago had moved out of the sociology department, usually into the school of social work. Whereas in the first two decades of US sociology, when leading white male sociologists spoke of both disinterested knowledge gained for its own sake and the need for justifying knowledge on the basis of its societal utility, by the 1920s and 1930s, the leading white male sociologists were mostly dropping this accent on the social and policy utility of social science knowledge.[15]

WOMEN AND THE ORGANIZED PROFESSION

In the early 1900s, the American Sociological Society (ASS) was established by several sociologists who were members of the American Economics Association. Significantly, during the earliest (1905–1931) period of its existence, not one woman was elected to its highest offices, and only a few were included at professional meetings. Even most moderately progressive male sociologists saw the spheres of women and men as different and separate and openly stereotyped women. As the chair of the first graduate-level department and an early ASS president, Albion Small hired women sociologists only for such specialized areas as household administration, social settlements, and sanitary science. Indeed, the ASS began in the sociological old-boy networks and was viewed by most as an association for white men. A few women were allowed as presenters or discussants at association meetings, if they engaged in a type of women's sociology viewed as acceptable by the white male sociologists.[16]

The Influential Jane Addams and Her Colleagues

Despite their marginalization or exclusion, some early white female and black male and female sociologists were influential, if more outside the academy than inside. Between 1892 and 1930, Jane Addams was one of the country's leading sociologists and policy intellectuals. She was cofounder and head resident at Hull House and a leader of the community settlement movement across the United States. She had a major impact on the political and intellectual life of her era. At first taking a Christian humanist approach, she soon came to express strong ideas about expanded democracy, arguing that all people should have a voice in decisions affecting their lives. She advocated participatory democracy and social equality and pressed for reforms to improve the lives of African Americans, the poor, immigrants, and young people. In facilitating people working together, she felt that gathering scientific facts was important to convince people of the correct type of action needed. Addams wrote effectively on important sociological issues of the day—including immigration, poverty, women's issues, delinquency, and aging.[17] An early social science analyst of the problems of cities, she was advanced in her sense of justice. Her perspective on democracy saw it as more than fairness and legal equality: "We are brought to a conception of Democracy not merely as a sentiment which desires the well-being of all men, nor yet as a creed which believes in the essential dignity and equality of all men, but as that which affords a rule of living as well as a test of faith."[18] As she viewed US society, for there to be participatory democracy, working-class Americans had to actively take part in major decisions affecting their lives.

Clearly, Addams saw herself as a sociologist, and she was at the center of a network of important sociologists and activists. Yet, over subsequent decades, numerous mainstream scholars have tended to view her as "only" a reformer or social worker and as a person with a moralistic and status-quo view of the world. Even C. Wright Mills, one of the few later sociologists to recognize her importance in sociology, viewed her in this light. This perception is highly inaccurate, for Addams, who was often attacked as a "radical" in her day, had a critical emancipatory view of society in contrast to many of the men of the Chicago School, most of whom had a moderate corporate-liberal and technocratic view.[19]

This was especially true of the later men in the powerful Chicago department, who viewed sociologically informed action as not involving "real science" and distanced themselves from it. The science of sociology, which had begun as a commitment to the betterment of society, increasingly became a science that was more distant, abstract, and based on a natural science model.[20] Most of the Chicago men were allied with the corporate-liberal wing of the controlling elite and rejected a more critical and emancipatory perspective. In contrast, Addams and a number of other white women—as well as some black male and female sociologists—stayed involved in aggressive social change organizations, such as the antiwar movement, the women's movement, and labor unions.[21]

The women of Hull House were among the first scholar-activists to recognize that "not all people are polluted equally." As early empirical sociologists, they established that disease rates were increasing in the poor immigrant communities with whom they worked. They believed that inadequate public services like poor trash collection were very serious issues in many low-income urban neighborhoods. Rose Marie Berger explains:

> The Hull House Woman's Club launched a major investigation into the city's garbage collection system, then Addams submitted to the city government her own bid to collect garbage. The resulting public uproar forced the mayor to appoint Addams as garbage inspector for

her ward. The Hull House women formed a garbage patrol, getting up at 6 a.m. to follow the garbage trucks, mapping routes and dump sites, and making citizens' arrests of landlords whose properties were a health hazard. Their vigilance moved garbage reform to the top of Chicago's civic agenda, forcing industry to take responsibility for its trash.[3]

The First Empirical Sociology

Conventionally, the department of sociology at the University of Chicago has been given credit for inventing empirical field sociology, particularly the social-demographic mapping of urban areas. Yet it was the *women* sociologists at Hull House who first developed this major sociological research technique. In their book *Hull House Maps and Papers* (1895), they collected extensive data on Chicago's urban areas and analyzed it using detailed maps *two decades before* it became important in the work of white male sociologists at the University of Chicago. Engaging in the first collaborative research in the field done by US sociologists, they used this technique for some years as a way of gathering and interpreting information on income, occupation, nationality, family size, and housing conditions. These data were used to help local residents understand community patterns in order to make better decisions, not to provide abstract data just for published sociological analysis. Addams worked to get women of various class levels, rich and working class, involved in meetings and community organizing. She sought their advice and brought them onto the stage at gatherings, breaking down class and gender lines.[24]

The quality and importance of the research done by Hull House researchers is evident in the more than *fifty* articles published between 1895 and 1935 in what was then the leading journal of sociology, the *American Journal of Sociology*. Some twenty-seven books by the Hull House researchers were reviewed in the journal.[25]

The fact that the women sociologists were pioneers in empirical sociology was occasionally noted in the 1910s and early 1920s by the men in the University of Chicago department of sociology, but later these men criticized the early work as little more than social work or they ignored it. Subsequently, numerous methods textbooks rewrote the history of sociology and misrepresented the technique of demographic mapping as being the invention of male sociologists at the University of Chicago![26]

During World War I, a strong new wave of political repression was aimed at US political radicals and liberal reformers. This government and private-sector repression forced a reduction in the involvement of social scientists and social workers in reform activities. Some of this attack continued into the 1920s and 1930s. Addams, who won a Nobel Prize in 1931 for her antiwar activities (the first ever won by a sociologist), noted that "any proposed change was suspect" and that social researchers and social workers "exhibited many symptoms of this panic and with a protective instinct carefully avoided any phraseology of social reform."[27] This political attack by repressive governmental and private authorities on progressive dissent played an important role in generating the move to a more detached, academic, and distancing social science. Even urban settlement houses were seen as "radical" by the white male elites obsessed with any challenges to the corporate-capitalist system. Moreover, from this period to the present day, "any attempt of [sociologically oriented] community organizers to become involved in the development of militant grass-roots movements has been seen as a blatant disregard of professionally defined functions."[28]

Another Critical Sociologist: The Pioneering W. E. B. Du Bois

One of the most important of the early sociologists, W. E. B. Du Bois taught sociology in US colleges and universities from 1894 to 1910. He had close ties to the settlement house movement, which had spread to Philadelphia by the 1890s with its emphasis on community-based research. In 1896 Du Bois became an "assistant in sociology" at the University of Pennsylvania and conducted a major study of African American conditions in that city using the "best available methods of sociological research." The book resulting from this research, *The Philadelphia Negro*, was the first systematic sociological field study of life in an urban black community.[29] Du Bois drew on the earlier studies and demographic mapping of immigrants by the settlement house researchers (see Chapter 4). Du Bois's book and the *Hull House Maps and Papers* were the first major community studies in US sociology. These origins of urban sociology have often been ignored by later social scientists. For example, Stephen P. Turner and Jonathan H. Turner locate the origins of empirical research in sociology in the labor statistics movement after the Civil War. Showing an unawareness of the actual history of US sociology, they ignore the Hull House studies in urban sociology and the pioneering sociological work of Du Bois.[30]

In his urban monograph, Du Bois gave recognition to a community of black city dwellers, analyzing their conditions and exploring the impact of racial discrimination by whites. His book received good reviews by historians but little support from white male sociologists. In spite of Du Bois's stellar qualifications—major field research, a PhD from Harvard, and study abroad with major social scientists like Max Weber—no historically white sociology department made Du Bois an offer to be a regular colleague. In contrast, white female sociologists in the settlement house movement strongly supported him.[31] Du Bois, like early women sociologists, should be given credit as one of the significant founders of the new US discipline of sociology.

In the mid-1890s, Du Bois was invited to teach sociology and develop a research program on black Americans at Atlanta University, a historically black institution. He helped to build a "center of sociological research" and developed plans to study aspects of black life, from mortality and urbanization to religion and crime.[32] Du Bois sought substantial scientific data on the conditions of African Americans in the North and South. However, as with some other early social scientists like Addams, Du Bois did not see social science as an end in itself or isolated from the world of policy and action for change, but rather he saw it as working to better society, particularly for African Americans.[33]

In his research work at Atlanta University, Du Bois envisioned close ties to the sociology departments at Harvard, Columbia, Johns Hopkins, and the University of Pennsylvania.[34] However, Du Bois's opposition to the educational views of the leading black educator of this time, Booker T. Washington, created difficulties. Washington had the backing of powerful corporate capitalists who liked his approach to change in US racial relations. (Washington proposed gradualism and an orientation to vocational education for African Americans.)

Not surprisingly, Du Bois had trouble getting research funds from corporate foundations for important projects. Nonetheless, at Atlanta University, he did engage in a successful research program studying African American issues, which resulted in major conferences and many publications. However, by 1910 opposition to him from corporate officials associated with Washington led him to leave Atlanta University to begin new activist work, principally as director of publications and research of the National Association for the Advancement of Colored People (NAACP).[35]

But Du Bois did not abandon his ties with the women sociologists. Significantly, between the late 1890s and the 1930s, he had nearly twenty professional exchanges. For example, in 1907, Addams invited him to speak at Hull House. Moreover, several sociologists linked to Hull House, including Addams, Du Bois, Florence Kelley, Ida B. Wells-Barnett, Mary McDowell, Anna Garlan Spencer, William I. Thomas, and Charles Zeublin, signed the initial call for the NAACP, which was established in 1909.

The Sociological Ideas of Du Bois

In his books and as editor of the influential NAACP journal, the *Crisis*, Du Bois was an early articulator of the intellectual foundations of the movement for social justice for African Americans. In his work on the Philadelphia black community, Du Bois had gone beyond a documentation of realities of poverty and discrimination to make clear his moral position and the role of whites: "Such discrimination is morally wrong, politically dangerous, industrially wasteful, and socially silly. It is the duty of whites to stop it, and to do so primarily for their own sakes."[36]

Later on in the 1930s, drawing on Marxist class analysis, Du Bois was perhaps the first major sociological theorist to emphasize the link between racial and class exploitation. For him the interplay of institutional racism and modern capitalism explained why there had never been real democracy in the United States. Both white capitalists and white laborers maintained the system of racism: "The resulting color caste founded and retained by capitalism was adopted, forwarded and approved by white labor, and resulted in subordination of colored labor to white profits the world over. Thus, the majority of the world's laborers, by the insistence of white labor, became the basis of a system of industry which ruined democracy and showed perfect fruit in World War and Depression."[37]

White capitalists and workers were more or less united in their whiteness—with its array of material and psychological privileges. Du Bois asserted that white workers accepted lower than necessary money wages in return for a "public and psychological wage" of whiteness. White elites allowed white workers to participate in the dominant racial hierarchy; for example, they were admitted to certain public areas (e.g., segregated parks) and functions off-limits to people of darker color. Yet by not organizing with workers of color, these racially privileged white workers paid a heavy economic price (e.g., lower wages) for their bequeathed sense of "superior white selves."

In a chapter in his book *Darkwater* (1920), the first extended analysis of whiteness in the social science literature, Du Bois noted that "the discovery of personal whiteness among the world's people is a very modern thing.... The ancient world would have laughed at such a distinction.... We have changed all that, and the [white] world in a sudden, emotional conversion has discovered that it is white and by that token, wonderful!"[38] Indeed, Du Bois was the first sociologist to deal with the sociology of racial emotions. As he noted, color barriers are created not only by maliciousness but also by "unconscious acts and irrational reactions unpierced by reason."[39]

Du Bois offered some of the first sociological analyses of a globalizing capitalism and imperialism. Writing of the years around 1900, he argued, "White supremacy was all but world-wide. Africa was dead, India conquered, Japan isolated, and China prostrate.... The using of men for the benefit of masters is no new invention of modern Europe...

But Europe proposed to apply it on a scale and with an elaborateness of detail of which no former world ever dreamed."[40] Analyzing Europe's colonization of Africa, Du Bois demonstrated that extreme poverty and degradation in the African colonies were "a main cause of wealth and luxury in Europe. The results of this poverty were disease, ignorance, and crime. Yet these had to be represented as natural characteristics of backward peoples."[41]

He summed up European imperialism and the damage it did to peoples of color around the globe: "There was no Nazi atrocity—concentration camps, wholesale maiming and murder, defilement of women and ghastly blasphemy of childhood—which the Christian civilization of Europe had not long been practicing against colored folk in all parts of the world in the name of and for the defense of a Superior Race born to rule the world."[42] Few social science analyses of more recent racialized atrocities have examined the deep roots of racial oppression as well as Du Bois did a century ago.

Du Bois was the first US sociologist to analyze racial oppression in the Americas as thoroughgoing systems of white racism. In the Americas, the European-origin peoples applied slavery "on a scale and with an elaborateness of detail of which no former world ever dreamed. The imperial width of the thing—the heaven-defying audacity—makes its modern newness."[43] An essential feature of North American slavery was the denial of most human liberties.[44]

Du Bois was a pioneer in an activism that was sociologically informed and oriented to expanding human rights. He was a leading thinker and activist in regard to Pan-Africanism. Pan-African nationalism was a partial solution for the conditions in which people of African descent found themselves across the globe. Against major objections by officials at the US State Department, Du Bois put together the first Pan-African Congress in 1919, which was attended by delegates of color from fifteen countries. The Congress called for the abolition of slavery and curtailment of colonial exploitation.[45]

The impact of Du Bois is increasingly being recognized. In a contemporary book, several contemporaries have explored connections between Du Bois's influential book *The Souls of Black Folk*; his other academic works; and his larger venture relating to racism, racial identity, and the social objectives of scholarly engagement. They show how *The Souls of Black Folk* extends, enhances, or presents ideas developed in his other sociological books, including *The Philadelphia Negro*, and what *Souls* offers in regard to Du Bois's ideas about activism on behalf of African Americans. They establish just how important *The Souls of Black Folk* is for Du Bois's racial theorizing, his understanding of the potential for social justice, and his views on the social conditions influencing race.[6]

Early Black Women Sociologists

Among the early sociologists were a number of African American women, perhaps the most visible of whom were Ida B. Wells-Barnett and Anna Julia Cooper. Wells-Barnett, together with Fannie Barrier Williams and Mary Church Terrell, was active in the Hull House group of sociologists. The important sociological work of Wells-Barnett and Cooper is being rediscovered by contemporary sociologists.[47] Both were practicing sociologists and penetrating theorists of US society.

Ida B. Wells-Barnett was born to enslaved parents in Mississippi. Once freed, her parents put her into Rust College. However, when her parents died from yellow fever, she dropped out and became a teacher to keep the rest of her family together. She spent her life writing about, and fighting against, the often-violent discrimination faced by African Americans at the hands of whites. Around the turn of the twentieth century, she researched and wrote tirelessly about white lynchings of African Americans, using accounts from white newspapers to build a lynching database. She approached such data with a profound understanding of US racism: "The purpose of the pages which follow shall be to give the record which has been made, not by colored men, but that which is the result of the compilations made by white men, of reports sent over the civilized world by white men in the South. Out of their own mouths shall the murderers be condemned."[48]

She wrote in detail of the myth of "black male rapists," many of whom allegedly desired to rape white women, and she herself barely escaped being killed for suggesting that white men's desire for black women might be related to this obsessive rapist mythology. At this early point in the history of US sociology, Wells-Barnett developed deep empirical and theoretical understandings of the connections of racial and gender stratification.

Anna Julia Cooper was born a slave in 1858 in North Carolina. Her father was likely the white slaveholder. She learned to read at an early age, later attended Oberlin College, and became a teacher, school principal, and gifted social theorist. In a major 1892 book, *A Voice from the South,* Cooper developed a sociological analysis and articulated the idea that black women have a distinctive standpoint because of the double oppression they face. Like Wells-Barnett, she was critical of distorted representations of African American history and of their contemporary impoverished conditions in the often aggressively racist white media and academic scholarship.[49] Wells-Barnett and Cooper created a sociology from the viewpoint of the oppressed and one dedicated to full social justice. They were among the first social scientists to analyze data on the social situations of both black Americans and women in terms of such critical concepts as social "domination," "subordination," and "repression."[50]

ESTABLISHMENT SOCIOLOGY: THE CHICAGO SCHOOL

Numerous textbook writers and other social science writers regularly assert that the first well-developed sociological research program at a university, the first research-oriented "school of sociology," was set up at the University of Chicago in the 1910s or 1920s. This program is usually termed the *Chicago school of sociology*. However, several researchers have demonstrated that the first extensive sociological research program at a university was the one developed in the 1895 to 1917 era at Atlanta University (now Clark Atlanta University), a historically black institution established after the Civil War. The Atlanta Sociological Laboratory played a critical and early role in developing the "discipline of sociology, including the establishment of the first US school of sociology, institutionalization of method triangulation, institutionalization of the insider researcher, and institutionalization of the public acknowledgment of one's research."[51] In 1895 this laboratory was established by the Atlanta University president and trustees to do extensive research on the socioeconomic conditions faced by African Americans, especially as they moved from slavery to freedom in the decades after the Civil War.

As noted previously, after his graduation from Harvard and research in Philadelphia, W. E. B. Du Bois became the head of this research laboratory in 1896. There he developed an extensive and important research program, one that accented one research problem for each year over a substantial period of time. Du Bois instituted a series of important conferences on this research during the years between 1896 and the 1920s. Liberation-oriented researchers like sociologists Jane Addams and Monroe Work, anthropologist Franz Boas, and educator Booker T. Washington came to these conferences, at which the field research was presented, and the research reports were published annually.[52]

This was the first research-oriented "school of sociology," yet because it was headed up mostly by African Americans, it has been ignored in the mainstream history of sociology. Moreover, we should underscore the point that some similar sociological research had already been done at Chicago's Hull House. Jane Addams and other women sociologists had not only pioneered in sociological field research but also been the teachers and supporters of Du Bois in his involvement in a major sociological research program on African Americans, including the field research program at Atlanta University.

By 1920, there were at least 400 colleges and other institutions of higher education offering sociology courses. A 1909 *American Journal of Sociology* report on courses in sociology based its calculations on questionnaires from 173 colleges, universities, and theology schools. A few institutions reported having a sociology course by the 1880s (Yale reported the first, in 1873), but most did not offer such courses until the 1890s and early 1900s. In the academic year 1907 to 1908, only 35 of these higher-education institutions had at least one professor teaching sociology full-time; most institutions had only part-time teachers at this stage in sociology's history. Just 20 institutions had full-fledged departments of sociology under that name, and only six reported offering ten or more courses in sociology. Chicago was the leading department in 1907 through 1908, in terms of having the most developed program of sociology courses.[53]

A Key Figure at Chicago: Robert E. Park

During the 1920s and 1930s, sociology did blossom at the University of Chicago, and many students there focused on field research on urban problems. In field studies in the city of Chicago, Robert E. Park, his students, and his associates often highlighted the idea of urban "disorganization." Urban phenomena such as prostitution, "slum" communities, and the homeless were primary topics for this new sociological research. Although there was some demographic and ethnographic work on the communities of the black and immigrant residents of the city, the deeper dynamics of gender, racial, and class oppression were rarely examined.

Dozens of dissertations, theses, and books were written by students and faculty during Park's years at Chicago, and they collectively influenced the shape of US sociology in this period. They included books like that by Nels Anderson on hobos, by Paul Cressey on taxi-dancers, by Edwin Thrasher on gangs, and by Louis Wirth on the Jewish "ghetto."[54] Park had a major impact at the University of Chicago; he taught there for nearly two decades and became the national American Sociological Society president in 1925. Interestingly, he was not educated in the discipline of sociology. As an undergraduate, Park had specialized in philology and philosophy. Then, after a decade of work outside academia as a journalist, he went to Harvard, where he took a master's degree in philosophy. Then he migrated to Friedrich-Wilhelm University in Berlin; there he took mostly history, philosophy, and political economy courses—and his only sociology course ever, with Georg Simmel.[55] Park then followed one of his professors to the University of Heidelberg, where he did much work on his doctoral dissertation, titled "Crowd and Public." His first academic position was as an assistant in the department of philosophy (not sociology) at Harvard, where he finished his PhD dissertation.

In 1905, Park went to the Tuskegee Normal and Industrial Institute, where he became a publicist for this historically black college created by Booker T. Washington.[56] During the Tuskegee years, Park traveled and interviewed many black residents in the South. The impact of his seven years there was such that he once commented, "I became for all intents and purposes, a Negro myself."[57] He was a student learning about the "curious and intricate system" that defined the black Southerners' relations with white Southerners.[58] Significantly, he reported that in studying black people, he remained "sufficiently detached to see it in more general social and sociological significance," and he argued that the "Negro in his American environment is a social laboratory," using the subject-distancing language that the early women sociologists had rejected in their work.[59] In 1910 Park toured Europe with Booker T. Washington and began a coauthored book with him called *The Man Fartherest Down*.

Though relatively liberal for his time, Park openly reflected the white-racist thinking of the era, as did numerous other white sociologists. In his writings, Park suggested that racial characteristics, seen as "innate biological interests," determine characteristic features of groups, including their "racial temperaments": "The Negro is, by natural disposition, neither an intellectual nor an idealist, like the Jew; nor a brooding introspective, like the East Indian; nor a pioneer and frontiersman, like the Anglo Saxon.... His metier is expression rather than action." Park, like virtually all of his white colleagues, generally saw the social world from a distinctive white racial frame.[60]

In April 1912, an International Conference on the Negro was held at Tuskegee Institute. The conference—with its racist theme "The Education of Primitive Man"—was the brainchild of Park, who saw education in racialized terms as helping the "primitive younger races" (blacks) relate better to the "civilized older races" (whites). Park invited William I. Thomas, a professor at the University of Chicago, to give a talk. This led to Park's being offered a position in sociology at the University of Chicago, where he gave his first course in 1914 on "The Negro in America." This was one of the first such courses at a historically white university. There in Chicago, at a time when the NAACP and the Urban League were growing, Park chose to work with the less militant Urban League. Nevertheless, he was opposed to discrimination and saw black Americans as eventually becoming socially integrated into mainstream white institutions.[61]

One incident suggests that Park and his associate Ernest W. Burgess were reluctant to take overt action against discrimination. At the 1923 meeting of the American Sociological Society (ASS) in Washington, DC, E. Franklin Frazier—who would later be the first black president of the association in 1949—engaged in a protracted battle with hotel management and staff over hotel policies of racial discrimination. The hotel had a policy of not letting blacks use the regular elevator, insisting instead that they ride the freight elevator. One elevator operator insisted that Frazier could not ride the main elevator. Two white men on it pushed him out, commenting, "Why don't you go back to the jungles of Africa where you belong?" Holding his ground, Frazier replied, "No, thank you, I prefer to remain in the jungles of America with you white savages."[62] A police officer tried to put Frazier on the freight elevator. Frazier sought out the assistance of Burgess, then the official ASS secretary. Burgess went to the white manager and reported back to Frazier that he was adamant in refusing to let black sociologists use the regular elevator. Frazier was also harassed by hotel police officers when in the lobby of the hotel. At the time, Burgess took no further action to challenge the color line. Park had witnessed one of the discriminatory incidents and offered to ride the elevator with Frazier, but he did not intervene further. In this case, "liberal" Chicago School racial relations experts reacted meekly to the brutal exclusion of a black colleague. There is no record of any individual or ASS organizational protest against the racial harassment of Frazier, and the association met in the same hotel the following year.[63] Later, in the 1950s, Frazier would face discrimination at the University of Chicago, where he had earlier done his graduate work. The "liberal" university turned him down for a faculty position because "the wives of white professors would object."[64]

The Chicago Department Becomes Dominant

In 1916 the young Ernest W. Burgess was hired as an instructor at the University of Chicago, and Robert Park helped him organize readings for an introductory course. This course led to the development of an influential textbook, *Introduction to the Science of Sociology*, by Park and Burgess.[65] This is a large textbook, with 1,000 pages and nearly 200 readings with interspersed commentary. Georg Simmel, Charles Darwin, Herbert Spencer, Émile Durkheim, Gabriel Tarde, Gustave Le Bon, William Graham Sumner, Charles Cooley, William I. Thomas, and Park himself are the ten most excerpted scholars. There is *no* mention of Karl Marx and *no* serious discussion of the work of pioneering sociologists like Jane Addams or W. E. B. Du Bois. Park and Burgess considered the book to be a major and comprehensive treatise on world sociology.

In their view, the permanence and solidarity of social groups rested on common traditions and voluntary consensus. Their general theory of social conflict, competition, assimilation, and accommodation had social Darwinist assumptions and was taken to be universal and applicable to all social interaction. Yet their analysis was actually grounded in assumptions about a stable society centered in modern capitalism. This was a corporate-liberal view like that of other early white male sociologists, who also did not deal seriously with systems of class, racial, and gender oppression and coerced social order all around them.[66] The Park and Burgess textbook was widely used, and subsequent sociologists have considered the book one of the most influential sociology textbooks ever written. The book helped set the direction of sociology in the United States for decades thereafter.

When it came to issues of social class, Park, Burgess, and most of their sociological associates took a moderate corporate-liberal approach that viewed capitalism as basically a good system but requiring some technocratic reform and regulation. Indeed, from the 1920s to the 1940s, numerous sociology textbooks took an approach accepting, more or less uncritically, the central features of the capitalist framework yet sometimes calling for moderate reforms. For example, in one textbook, *Social Pathology* (1925), Stuart Queen and Delbert Mann argued that sociological interpretations of societal problems should include ideas of maladjustment, demoralization, and disorganization.[67] In most textbooks like this one, there is a preoccupation with the failure of individual Americans to fit in with established norms and roles, although sometimes attention is given to modest reforms that might be implemented by government. Some structural elements of urban problems may be considered, but little sustained attention is given to their deeper roots in the class-driven, racialized, and gendered capitalistic system.

Criticizing Activists in Sociology

In the sociology departments at the University of Chicago and elsewhere, many graduate students were interested in reform-centered careers and organizations, and there was much student demand for courses on social problems. Over time, the founder, Albion Small, had moved away from his strong commitment to social reform, but it was Park who played a major role at Chicago in shifting the emphasis from a sociology concerned with studying and eradicating serious social problems to an "objective science." Using grant money from the Rockefeller (corporate) foundations channeled through the University of Chicago, Park headed up the Local Community Research Committee, which had control over research projects. He shaped these projects and the graduate program away from the reform-oriented concerns of many incoming graduate students. From his perspective, the urban reform movements had too much concern for "unwholesome" activities such as dance halls and alcohol. Park moved sociological research in the direction of looking at urban issues without what he saw as the earlier "do-goodism," of which he often made fun.[68] Some graduate students came by way of the settlement houses, and Park pressed them hard to change their often aggressively reformist orientations.

In addition, and in contrast to more progressive male sociologists there like William I. Thomas and George H. Mead, Park did not develop close relationships with the women sociologists, such as Sophonisba Breckinridge and Jane Addams. The latter were at Hull House or were members of a subdepartment in the sociology department. Although he did admire a few research studies done by the women sociologists, he argued that the women reformers had done more damage to Chicago than the corrupt local politicians.[69]

Park was complex and contradictory. He had in his earlier life been involved in muckraking journalism supportive of reform movements, and into the 1920s he sometimes got involved in reform activities. He clearly wanted to see the lives of the urban poor become less trying and more democratic, yet at the same time he pressed his university colleagues and students to move away from the emancipatory sociology of sociologists like Addams and Du Bois. He and his urban sociology colleagues at Chicago were broad in their methodological understandings. One scholar who visited Park's sociology classes commented that the latter emphasized the importance of "life history cases, the value of contemporary newspaper accounts, the place of the participant observer, the need for defining fundamental concepts, and the proper role of statistics. He had an unearthly horror of the use of statistics for trivial or unproductive purposes."[70] In his letters, Park suggested that good social science requires not only accuracy but also wide experience, and he pressed for the naturalistic study of humans.[71] All social facts are situated in space and time, and the Chicago School studies of gangs, prostitutes, poverty, and delinquency were set constantly in their immediate settings and at specific times in a city's urban history. However, this approach to accenting the important spatial and temporal contexts of social life became less central as US sociology developed ever more in the instrumental-positivistic direction in the ensuing decades.

Oliver C. Cox: A Dissident in the Chicago Tradition

An early power-conflict analyst who drew on Du Bois and on a critical class analysis was Oliver C. Cox. Like Addams and Du Bois, Cox was an organic intellectual emerging from and concerned with the impact of social oppression on working-class Americans and on Americans of color. He clearly was motivated by the experiences of Americans of color and their history of exclusion and oppression, and he wanted to bring these issues to the forefront of sociological analysis in the 1940s and 1950s. An African American, he himself came from the ranks of the aggrieved. Although Cox's research and writings are not familiar to many sociologists today, he engaged in pathbreaking work on issues of racial and class stratification in US society, and his work has greatly influenced our own thinking on institutional racism.[72]

Although educated at the University of Chicago, Cox rejected the objectifying and "value-free" sociology often found there and at other major sociology departments of his era. Recall that instrumental positivism views "good" sociological research as being more or less limited to those research questions that certain research instruments and statistical techniques will allow. Cox's work shows that this turn to instrumental positivism did not take place without resistance. He argued that human beings can design a better social order, and he took sides with the socially oppressed. He practiced sociology from their standpoint. For black Americans, "the very process of living in America as citizens implicates them in an interminable struggle for social equality."[73] As a good sociologist of knowledge, Cox noted how a scholar's social position shaped the production of scientific data and ideas. He was an early pioneer in what has come to be called "standpoint" analysis.

Consider Cox's analysis of Robert Park's work: "Park's theory of race relations is weak, vacillating, and misleading; and to the extent that it lends a 'scientific' confirmation to the Southern rationalizations of racial exploitation, it is insidious."[74] This is a strong indictment of the use of sociology as a political weapon by the ruling elite. His quotation marks around the term *scientific* suggest he questioned the nature of Park's sociological perspective. Cox further wrote: "If social science has any claim at all to be science, it should at least refrain from distilling social data through a context of designedly developed, popular prejudices."[75] Cox impeaches Park's sociological perspective for not being a self-reflective science and for using a scientific cloak to support, if indirectly, racial prejudices and other racial notions. Cox was also one of the first social scientists to examine the role of the US ruling class in shaping US and world history.[76]

Committed to a sociology that would assist in bringing major change, Cox defined his own sociology as a reaction against a detached eclecticism or "tradition of tentative expression," the perspective that he attributes to mainstream sociologists. Much mainstream sociological work was often irrelevant. "To be sure, it is well to keep our heads while the world is in convulsions, yet we may become inane if we discuss them as if we were describing an Egyptian mummy."[77] Taking a sophisticated and nuanced position on the role of values in sociological practice, he proposed that one could not remain neutral: "Clearly the social scientist should be accurate and objective, but not neutral; he should be passionately partisan in favor of the welfare of the people and against the interest of the few when they seem to submerge that welfare. In a word, the reason for the existence of the social scientist is that his scientific findings contribute to the betterment of the people's well-being."[78] The contribution to the people's well-being is not just another trait of the sociological craft; it should be the reason even for the existence of sociological practitioners.

This was not a sociology just for those "immediately engaged in research," but for a broader audience.[79] Cox's work is replete with tactical advice for those struggling against oppression. For example, he insisted that ideas of racial superiority are rooted in the social system and not the other way around: "We cannot defeat race prejudice by proving that it is wrong. The reason for this is that race prejudice is only a symptom of a materialistic social fact.... The articulate white man's ideas about his racial superiority are rooted deeply in the social system, and it can be corrected only by changing the system itself."[80] Moreover, Western capitalism's subordination of non-Western societies and its transformation of cultures around the globe are crucial for the explanation of systemic racism, because in the process of capitalist transformation, the "other peoples became convinced that their way of life was relatively static and impotent."[81] Cox is not ignoring the physical violence responsible for the expansion of capitalism but is anticipating the idea of domination by seduction of the oppressed, well captured today by the concept of social "hegemony."

The international hegemony linked closely to racial oppression is that of the world capitalist system. Cox thus did pioneering work on what we now call *world systems theory*. The capitalist system's expansive nature is a form of societal organization that tends "to systematize the world in a hierarchy of interdependent, economically centered communities," which cannot easily remove themselves from this all-encompassing international system.[82]

Working alone as a black sociologist dissenting from the University of Chicago tradition, from which he had learned the craft of sociology, Cox and his work received little attention from the sociologists of his time. It is only recently that his brilliant and critical work has been partially rediscovered—work very much in the liberation sociology tradition.

THE GROWTH OF INSTRUMENTAL POSITIVISM

East Coast Departments: Social Surveys

During the 1930s and 1940s, several East Coast departments of sociology, particularly those at Columbia University and Harvard University, gradually became influential in US sociology. During the 1920s and 1930s, the roots of a more statistically oriented sociology were established at Columbia University. A key figure was Franklin H. Giddings, a major force in Columbia University's sociology program from 1894 to the late 1920s. Giddings was one of the first to insist that the use of statistics should become the central method of social science. Recall his comments from an earlier chapter: "Sociology can be made an exact, quantitative science, if we can get industrious men interested in it."[83] At Columbia University, the idea of a rational social science came to be linked to statistical surveys and quantitative methods.

By the 1940s and 1950s, opinion polling had become a common research technique used in the fields of market and consumer research, advertising, and political campaigns. One of the key figures at Columbia was Paul Lazarsfeld, who was very interested in survey research on consumer issues. Lazarsfeld became known for his view that the study of the buying of consumer goods could lead to the development of a paradigm for studying and theorizing human social actions more generally.[84]

Leaders in the survey research movement, which remains central in social science today, also included the prominent Harvard sociologist Samuel Stouffer (see below). Stouffer saw survey research as the only way to effectively build up the discipline of sociology. As Andrew Abbott has noted, decontextualization was central in this opinion-survey approach to sociology:

> The necessary decontextualization of particular social attributes was then accomplished through the rapidly advancing discipline of [statistical] sampling, which not only separated individuals from their social context of friends, acquaintances, and so on but also deliberately ignored an individual variable's context of other variables.... This would later enable a whole generation of sociologists to act as if interaction were a methodological nuisance rather than the way social reality happens.[85]

Relying on public opinion surveys has meant in practice that the social researcher emphasizes only a limited number of (often short and superficial) survey questions, seen in the subsequent analyses as variables, and analyzes them statistically in relation to a modest number of other survey questions (variables). Typically, this type of sociological analysis assesses these survey variables substantially in isolation from their usually rich social contexts. In an article in an influential 1955 book, *The Language of Social Research*, Lazarsfeld and Morris Rosenberg codified this focus on variables, noting that the term is borrowed from mathematics. They describe how one moves from vague concepts to a "battery of indicators," with explicit reference to examples from survey and census research.[86] They go so far as to say that the end result of this "indicators" stage of research is always the same:

> The investigator will have transferred a piece of social reality into a set of objects which are given a place in a variety of conceptual dimensions which the investigator considered pertinent to his purpose. The symbol and the complete formal equivalent of such a representation is the IBM [punch] card. To each dimension corresponds a column; the position along the dimension is given by the punched square.[87]

Lazarsfeld and Rosenberg refer here to the early computerization of social science research, in which punched computer cards were used to enter data on survey variables into the computer for statistical analysis. For these instrumental-positivist social scientists, "any subject matter under investigation has to be translated into IBM language."[88]

The richness of social life can thus be reduced to numerous columns on punch cards for computer processing; the new language of statistical analysis and computers becomes the "language of social research." Unquestionably, we have here a clear break not only with the work of activist sociologists like Addams and Du Bois, but even with the central methodological commitments of the earlier Chicago School. Most of the earlier sociologists believed one could understand particular phenomena only by situating them firmly and substantially in their social and ecological contexts.

Instrumental Positivism and New Sources of Funding

This new survey-variables approach got substantial financial support from major foundations, such as the Russell Sage Foundation and the Rockefeller Foundation, which sometimes channeled funds through such organizations as the Social Science Research Council (SSRC). As early as the 1920s, considerable money from the Rockefeller foundations flowed into the SSRC, where the goal was to create a social science relevant to public policy—but one that accented quantitative and business-oriented research. Under the leadership of sociologists like Giddings at Columbia University, an active effort was made to make survey research the central sociological method and to link sociologists' research to funding by elite foundations or the government. Giddings's students, particularly William F. Ogburn, spread the doctrine of quantitative and survey-based sociology as the best sociology. Ogburn served on the SSRC. From that position, he worked aggressively to promote the quantitative-positivistic approach and identified it as the way to unify the social sciences.[89]

During the decade before World War II, sociology gradually became a common element in the curricula of colleges and universities, and the focus on survey methods and quantitative techniques became more commonplace. President Herbert Hoover set up a Research Committee on Social Trends, and many of the thirty studies of that committee were conducted by sociological researchers trained by Giddings. This was one of the few times before the war that this type of quantitative (survey) methodology was used in studies for government policy. The final report of this committee called for an integration of social science efforts to provide new knowledge of social problems, knowledge on the basis of which the (white male) business and government elites could then make social and political policy.[90]

Ogburn soon brought his strong instrumental-positivist perspective to the University of Chicago when he was appointed a senior professor there in the late 1920s. Between the 1930s and the 1960s, the PhD dissertations and other research conducted in that department became increasingly quantitative in methodology.[91] In his presidential address to the American Sociological Society in 1929, Ogburn called for a rigorous sociology emphasizing quantitative methods and statistics. He underscored the point that sociologists as professionals should not be interested in improving society but should focus only on discovering new knowledge.[92]

In 1935 a group of statistically oriented sociologists established a journal, the *American Sociological Review*, to propagate the new instrumental positivism. In the 1940s, two advocates of this quantitative positivism, Read Bain and F. Stuart Chapin, served as editors. During World War II, a growing number of sociologists moved into positions in government agencies or were the beneficiaries of government funding. Harvard's Samuel Stouffer became director of research for an office of the War Department. With several dozen social scientists, this office conducted many (later influential) survey studies of the US Army and its soldiers. Sociologists also worked as researchers in numerous other capacities for the federal government.[93]

At Vermont's Bennington College, and after 1945 at the University of Washington, the prominent sociologist George Lundberg was one of the most visible promoters of instrumental positivism. Lundberg served as American Sociological Society president in 1943 and wrote books that carried his influence beyond academic settings. Lundberg emphasized a separation of fact and value in sociology. Writing in his 1947 book *Can Science Save Us?*, Lundberg argued that if social scientists had a body of knowledge as developed as that of physical scientists, then their "knowledge would be equally above the reach of political upheaval. The services of real social scientists would be as indispensable to Fascists, as to Communists and Democrats."[94]

In his presidential address of that year, Lundberg "seemed to some to verge on open anti-Semitism, while his other public statements appeared to repudiate democracy."[95] Recently, in his book *Holocaust, Religion and the Politics of Collective Memory: Beyond Sociology*, Ronald Berger has summed up Lundberg's highly problematical position:

> Lundberg . . . asserted that as "a value-neutral social scientist he could function as well in Hitler's Germany as in [Franklin] Roosevelt's America."... When accused by his colleague Read Bain of being a Nazi, Lundberg replied that he disliked the Nazis as much as the Hebrews.... After learning of the extermination of the Jews, Lundberg reasserted his opposition to the intrusion of values and morality into social science: "[W]e find ... large numbers of organized and articulate Jews in their unhappy predicament devoting themselves to legalistic and moralistic conjurings so that their attention is entirely diverted from a realistic approach.... [T]hey demand international action outlawing anti-Semitism instead of reckoning with the causes of the antagonism in a purely scientific way."[96]

Indeed, during the 1930s and 1940s, remarkably few of the country's leading sociologists researched, or spoke out publicly against, the numerous fascist movements and governments of the time, including major fascist organizations in the United States. One reason for this was perhaps the new focus on a detached social science of survey and statistical methods. Roger Bannister puts it this way:

> As sociology professionalized, a rising cult of scientific objectivity inhibited public statements on public issues while at the same time marginalizing those most inclined to speak out against developments in Europe. Intellectually, the treatment of fascism during the 1930s and 1940s revealed the continuing isolation of American sociology from European social theorists (Marx, Weber, and Freud, among others), an isolation that grew more marked as a second and third generation of American sociologists, unlike their founders, sought their training at home [in the United States].[97]

There were important exceptions to this trend. In his 1938 book, *Nazi Germany: Its Women and Family Life*, Clifford Kirkpatrick noted he had "no illusions about his capacity for purely objective description," arguing instead that the sociologist is necessarily "liberal in the sense that he values reason, toleration, and co-operation." Even Talcott Parsons, the American Sociological Society president in 1949 and an establishment intellectual, penned numerous articles that critically examined the effects of Nazism on German society. He rallied popular opinion against fascist Germany by helping launch the Harvard Defense Committee. However, after the war and in keeping with his structural-functional thinking that tended to downplay serious societal conflicts, Parsons helped recruit Russian collaborators of the Nazis to Harvard's Russian Institute. Some current commentators on Parsons's life and work have suggested these various actions are proof that he took issue with fascism's potential impact on democratic institutions and academic freedom during the Nazi years, but not as much with its virulent anti-Semitism then or later on.[98]

More Critics of Instrumental Positivism

By the late 1930s and 1940s, sociology and other social sciences had reached the point where the "tail" of the new technical methods was beginning to wag the social science "dog." As early as 1938, a prominent social scientist, Gardner Murphy, warned of this in a presidential address to the Society for the Psychological Study of Social Issues:

> Undoubtedly a large part of our trouble has been an over rapid development of research techniques which can be applied to the surface aspects of almost any social response and are reasonably sure to give a publishable numerical answer to almost any casual question.... Woe to that science whose methods are developed in advance of its problems, so that the experimenter can see only those phases of a problem for which a method is already at hand.[99]

As Robert Lynd put it in 1939, in a farsighted book dealing centrally with the problematical character of these trends in social science, the modern social scientist is "deeply committed, by training and by the need for security and advancement, to the official concepts, problems, and theoretical structure of his science. Quantification and refined measurement carry heavy prestige, in part related to the reliance upon them by the authoritative natural sciences."[100] Lynd noted the way in which social scientists often become "organization men." When social scientists were asked to "experiment in the manifestly safe enterprise of quantifying their familiar problems and to engage in the more hazardous venture of faring forth into unfamiliar problem-areas," they usually opted for the first choice.[101] Lynd saw a strong reluctance to get involved in innovation and intervention: "So one observes these grave young scientists hiding behind their precocious beards of 'dispassionate research' and 'scientific objectivity.' They observe, record, and analyze, but they shun prediction. And, above all else, they avoid having any commerce with 'values.'"[102]

Lynd argued that sociology and the other social sciences should instead target crucial problems that involve the pain and frustrations of large numbers of people. He called for an expansion of democracy in US government, industry, and other areas—an expansion informed by good sociological research.[103] From his perspective, another deep-seated crisis lay in the "disorganizing confusions" of modern capitalism: "Private capitalism does not now operate, and probably cannot be made to operate, to assure the amount of general welfare to which the present stage of our technological skill and intelligence entitle us; and other ways of managing our economy need therefore to be explored." From Lynd's viewpoint, social science should be a holistic enterprise, with each social scientist linking her or his problems to an "inclusive totality."[104] In effect, he called on social scientists to examine what kind of world would exist if we used our social science knowledge and resources to maximize the "quantity, quality, and useful variety of daily living" for all people.[105]

Lynd was joined in his criticism of value-free sociology by perhaps the most distinguished European social scientist (economist) of the day, Gunnar Myrdal. Recall from Chapter 2 that in the early 1940s, Myrdal specifically criticized the move by Park and Ogburn to a detached academic sociology: "The specific logical error is that of inferring from the facts that men can and should make no effort to change the 'natural' outcome of the specific forces observed. This is the old do-nothing (laissez-faire) bias of 'realistic' social science."[106] He rejected the faddish accent on a "value-free" social science: "Scientific facts do not exist per se.... The processes of selecting a problem and a basic hypothesis, of limiting the scope of study, and of defining and classifying data relevant to such a setting of the problem, involve a choice on the part of the investigator."[107]

THE GROWTH AND BUREAUCRATIZATION OF SOCIOLOGY

Anticommunism and Expanded Funding for Sociology

Before the 1930s, most sociologists had conducted relatively small-scale research projects, and most used qualitative or descriptive-statistics research methods. Indeed, there was a significant diversity of qualitative and descriptive-statistics research in the early period of US sociology. There were few large grants from any source. During and after World War II, however, the funding for sociology and other social science research increased dramatically. Even so, during the 1940s and early 1950s, there was tolerance for methodological diversity in numerous established sociology departments. "Case study" researchers often coexisted with quantitatively oriented researchers. However, in the mid-1950s, the prominent Chicago department reportedly purged some qualitative researchers in its move toward more quantitative research. There was also a dramatic expansion of funding for survey research by government and private foundations.[108]

From the 1940s to 1960s, the growth in the scale and influence of the US government, especially in the form of social welfare and military programs, provided new positions for sociologists. Numerous sociologists were employed during World War II on a variety of survey and other quantitative research projects. Moreover, the Soviet Union's achievement in launching the first satellite in 1957 created serious concern in the US government over a technological lag. Such events helped to spur increased spending for the Defense Department and natural science research, with the social sciences also benefiting.[109]

Since World War II, sociology has been reshaped into a discipline in which many of its most prestigious members are linked to government agencies, foundations, and other bureaucracies that supply much of the money for conventional social research. After 1950, there was a great expansion of federally funded research in the physical sciences, and some sociologists pushed for a share of the new federal money. Indeed, in the late 1950s, fifteen prominent social scientists, including Robert Merton and Samuel Stouffer, signed a statement called "National Support for Behavioral Science"; this pressed the government for more funds for social science, in part to help with fighting the Cold War against the Soviet Union. These scholars commented on trends in social science: "We assume the probability of a breakthrough in the control of the attitudes and beliefs of human beings.... This could be a weapon of great power in Communist hands, unless comparable advances in the West produce effective counter-measures."[110] The anticommunist orientation of the statement led Robert Friedrichs to describe it as an "essentially evangelical tract" put out by sociologists who had previously argued for "value neutrality" in social science.[111] There was no value neutrality here. This was a period of intense anticommunist fervor, with loyalty oaths to the United States being imposed on many college faculty members. Being critical of established US institutions was often all it took to be labeled a political subversive by leading politicians and media commentators.

In 1960 the National Science Foundation (NSF) established a Division of Social Sciences and appropriated $3.5 million to fund social science research projects. Also in 1960, the American Sociological Association (ASA) moved to Washington, DC, with a full-time congressional lobbyist. Funding from corporate foundations was growing.[112] Between 1956 and 1980, private research money flowing to the social sciences increased from $21 to $41 million, while federal grants increased from $30 million to $424 million. Outside the universities there was new demand as well for contract research projects from private agencies and all levels of government. Graduate enrollments and degrees increased dramatically.[113]

Large bureaucracies developed under the auspices of private foundations and at the federal government level to fund social science research, and these agencies helped develop large research institutes at selected universities. This governmental underwriting of research fed the growing emphasis on advanced survey and statistical methods and on social scientists as research entrepreneurs. To facilitate this funding, many sociologists put on the protective clothing of "hard scientists" who, like physical scientists, accented quantitative methods of research. Apparently, a majority of the sociologists who sought the new funding from government agencies or private foundations made a conscious attempt not to research controversial social issues. The instrumental-positivism tradition became dominant, with its emphasis on advanced statistical methods, on variables, on demographic and survey techniques, and on the *unimportance* of assessing domain assumptions or using critical social theories.[114]

By the 1960s, numerous sociology departments at large universities became influential as this type of sociological research was increasingly sought out by the private and public sectors. One underlying assumption of much of this research was an optimistic image of US society as relatively fair and open. At that time, numerous researchers contended that their data showed that the United States had an open mobility system.[115] Moreover, by the late 1960s, sociology departments were growing in colleges and universities across the country. Large-scale federal and corporate funding brought major PhD-granting departments into prominence. Today, these powerful research departments often disproportionately control major sociological publication sources such as the *American Sociological Review*, and thus can act as gatekeepers for much sociological research and debate.

On occasion, nonetheless, some sociologists have used their government or private research grants to develop very critical and probing approaches to significant structural problems in US society. Those who have made this attempt have often had difficulty getting additional state or private foundation funding. In addition, periodically, sociological grant projects do uncover data and provide critical analyses that the country's governing elites would prefer to keep hidden.

State Bureaucratic Expansion and Sociology

During and after the 1960s, the major increase in US welfare-state operations—such as new educational programs at all levels, new hospitals, and new public health programs—was very important for the development of the social sciences, including sociology. For example, when the 1960s' War on Poverty started involving sociologists, many who got the call from government for contracts were the social statisticians who utilized opinion surveys or government-generated statistics in their analyses. Since that time, sociologists and other social scientists have tended to study social problems in terms of opinion surveys or government-generated (official) statistics. As sociology has become ever more linked to the governmental apparatus, it has lost some of its progressive reform roots. As C. Wright Mills put it, "Liberalism has become less a reform movement than the administration of social services in a welfare state; sociology has lost its reforming push; its tendencies toward fragmentary problems and scattered causation have been conservatively turned to the use of corporations, army, and state."[116]

With the rise of the United States to global dominance, sociology and the other social sciences have been shaped into disciplines whose most prestigious members are often closely linked to research university social science departments and to government agencies that put significant dollars into social science research. "Being closely tied to American capital and the US state for both funds and jobs, American sociologists bought and sold a very [corporate-liberal] analysis. Stratification was good and necessary; mobility was based on merit.... The state played a beneficent role; social problems were tractable and sociology would help the state manage them."[117] Not surprisingly, these government and corporate links have meant that, at best, only a small minority of social scientists in the major research universities have done substantial critical research on the most privileged racial, gender, and class groups and their role in maintaining a hierarchical and oppressive society.

Sociology courses and programs benefited greatly from the expansion of the federal government after World War II. The number of graduate students and sociology professors grew dramatically. In the 1950s and 1960s, as a result of popular books by sociologists and because of growing social unrest, sociology came more to the attention of college students, the general public, and policymakers. Contemporary sociology, in the United States and Europe, was reinvigorated by social protest movements of the 1960s and 1970s, including on college campuses. By the

1960s, hundreds of thousands of college students were taking sociology courses, thousands of sociology books were being sold, and thousands of credentialed sociologists were teaching and doing research. Sociology degrees increased significantly in the 1960s and 1970s.[118] Sociology was not alone in this regard, for most social sciences experienced much growth during this period.

Significantly, this era brought a new concern with social problems, and many sociological studies were oriented toward greater government intervention to repair them. This period also saw a reinvigoration of more critical sociologies. Critical social theories, such as Marxist, feminist, and black nationalist theories, developed and expanded. Some sociologists were involved in research associated with important student or civil rights movements or in the movements themselves. During the 1960s, many activist students, including student leaders in protest movements in France, Germany, and the United States, were undergraduate students, graduate students, or younger faculty members in sociology departments.

For example, in the 1960s, Dick Flacks (later a member of the American Sociological Association's governing council) was an untenured faculty member in the sociology department at the University of Chicago. In spring 1968, he was involved in organizing the New University Conference (NUC), which sought to bring together radical faculty and students to support student protest movements of the period. NUC sociologists and students at Columbia University joined together to form the Sociology Liberation Movement (SLM), which collapsed in 1972.

Flacks supported student protests and at one point was brutally assaulted by a man opposed to his activism. Sometimes, senior faculty members at various major universities took the position that the nonviolent student demonstrations were "Communist led," thereby often radicalizing more students.[119] Across the country, mainstream sociologists attacked the counter-establishment ideas of the many activist students and faculty members and called for more ties between sociological research and the making of conventional government policy. In 1967 the council of the American Sociological Association defeated a resolution in opposition to US intervention in the Vietnam War. Contemporary commentators suggest that a majority of American Sociological Association members were opposed to the war at the time but favored the council's seemingly neutral position.[120] Clearly, sociology was then to some degree at war with itself.

Despite the official collapse of the SLM in 1972, Flacks's commitment to the movement never wavered. From his radio program, *Culture of Protest*, to his subsequent liberation sociology publications, the goals of SLM live on today. In 2010, Flacks reflected on the decade when the SLM was born:

I'm still puzzled fifty years later by what it was about the climate and the culture in 1960 that encouraged many young people to think they could make the world over. That was the year when little groups of black students brought down entrenched segregation by putting their bodies over lines they weren't supposed to cross.... The main point of claiming the need for a "New Left" was to envision a way of acting and speaking politically that connected with experience, that was experimental, that had effects on the world, that could be seen as good for people's lives.[121]

Significantly, many contemporary sociologists who participated in these various protests of the 1960s, as activists or activist-researchers, have maintained their critical or radical commitments to the present day.

The dominance of instrumental positivism in US sociology was not unique. In the first few decades after World War II, many other disciplines in the physical and social sciences experienced a similar trend.[122] Reinhard Bendix described how mainstream social scientists were trying to become priestly interpreters of truth for laypeople. He noted that contemporary social scientists

no longer believe that men can rid their minds of ... impediments to lucid thought: only scientists can.... They assert that there is only one escape from the consequences of irrationality: that is by application of the scientific method. And this method can be used effectively only by the expert few.... Instead of attempting to make people more rational, contemporary social scientists often content themselves with asking of them that they place their trust in social science and accept its findings.[123]

THEORIES OF SOCIAL ORDER AND CONSENSUS

From the mid-1940s to the late 1970s, the US economic system dominated the world economy. In addition, the United States was then one of the world's two great military powers. For the first time in its history, the United States substantially dominated the globe. Meanwhile, at home, economic prosperity enabled the country to provide many ordinary families with an ever-improving standard of living.

Writing sociological theory in this buoyant environment, Talcott Parsons, a leading sociological theorist, and his associates accented a renewed concern with issues of social order and consensus. From World War II to the mid-1960s, their structural-functional perspective was dominant in English-language social theory, and to some degree, portions of it can still be found today. One reason for its popularity was that structural functionalism claimed to be able to embrace all societal phenomena.

This structural functionalism was generally compatible with the mode of operation and the writings of most instrumental-positivist researchers in sociology, in that it provided a theoretical framework with little questioning of the status quo. Most social science positivists used data generated by government agencies or by research grants, and many wrote up their data with little theoretical analysis. Those who did make use of theory often did so in a perfunctory or uncritical way, providing citations to theorists like Parsons, Émile Durkheim, or Max Weber (but usually not Karl Marx), yet they usually viewed theory as subsidiary to their main purpose of presenting "hard data."[124]

Social science often draws on underlying models of social reality, and these models usually elaborate on iconic metaphors. In much social science there are several basic metaphors that are used as broad images of the societal world: society as organism, machine, market of exchange, drama, game, conversation, and war. One of the oldest overarching metaphors is that of society as biological organism. Drawing on the metaphor of a living organism, structural functionalists explain the parts of a given society in terms of how they function in the larger social system. Just as the human body has certain requirements, such as food digestion, society has common and interrelated parts, such as the economic system, which function to meet societal requirements.

However, research by cognitive scientists on such use of metaphors suggests that metaphors are not simply figures of speech that map one domain of life onto another but rather are critical to the structuring of the understandings themselves. As George Lakoff notes, metaphors give rise to a "rich system of metaphorical entailments."[125] That is, ideas from the source domain of a metaphor, such as the digestive system of the human body, suggest new ideas in the target domain, such as the economy being like a digestive system in certain adaptive ways. These entailments can stimulate thinking in the target domain in new ways. Yet, as Naomi Quinn has cautioned, particular metaphors do not underlie thinking as much as they are chosen by speakers and analysts "because they provide satisfying mappings onto already existing cultural understandings."[126]

Structural functionalists such as Talcott Parsons are, to be more accurate, "system functionalists." British sociologist Ian Craib has noted, "The idea of a system gives us the crucial analogy or metaphor in Parsons's theory: that of the biological organism or living system.... He does not stop at saying that social life is like a living system; he says that it is a living system of a particular type."[127] These system functionalists typically highlight the importance of social consensus and stability and view a major aim of theorizing as explaining social order. For example, in his 1959 presidential address to the American Sociological Association, Kingsley Davis argued that the structural-functional approach was so pervasive that it was no longer a distinctive school of sociology; whatever was valid in functional analysis was to be found in one form or another in most sociological analysis.[128] Thus, as of 1964, a large survey of sociologists found that 80 percent were favorably disposed toward structural-functional theories of society.[129]

Structural-functional analysis has played a more or less conservative role in US sociology because of its strong emphasis on the status quo and deviations therefrom. Working in the golden age of US global hegemony (1944–1970s), and with the federal government moving to bring modest welfare and civil rights reforms, structural-functionalist sociology reflected a relatively optimistic approach to societal change.[130]

Unfortunately, Parsons and other dominant theorists of this era rejected critical power-conflict theories, such as black-nationalist and neo-Marxist theories, that were skeptical about the long-term survival of capitalist societies and that forecast substantial resistance by society's oppressed groups. Significantly, in his influential theoretical book, *The Structure of Social Action*, Parsons makes no reference to earlier US sociological theorists and analysts of social conflict and oppression such as Jane Addams or W. E. B. Du Bois.[131] Thus, he also does not include a theoretical analysis of social oppression that would likely have come from a serious reading of the early white female and black male and female sociologists. As an establishment intellectual, Parsons was committed to moderate social reform and orderly change and was optimistic about agreement on values between groups often in conflict, such as privileged whites and oppressed blacks, and about a forthcoming inevitable decline in social injustice in capitalistic societies. Parsons and the many sociologists influenced by structural-functional thinking have tended to downplay the serious problems of social class and racial and gender discrimination and conflict within societies like the United States.[132]

Parsons and his followers accented symbolic ideals and generally ignored theorizing and researching deep-lying material interests—such as the historically derived racial privileges and unjustly gained wealth of white Americans and the unjust impoverishment of black Americans that resulted from centuries of slavery, legal segregation, and contemporary discrimination. Parsons and his colleagues generally ignored the national political interests that supported the persisting system of racism targeting Americans of color. They did not draw on the critical tradition of societal analysis offered by earlier sociologists like Jane Addams and W. E. B. Du Bois.

For centuries, white Americans have garnered their economic prosperity partially at the expense of African Americans. For example, during the Civil War, the US Congress passed the major Homestead Act, which provided access to productive land to many US families from the 1860s to the 1930s. An estimated 246 million acres of federal lands were provided by the US government to about 1.5 million homestead-ing families.[133] For the most part, African Americans were excluded from this program by racially discriminatory barriers, including white violence. As sociologists in the black counter-framing tradition, such as Du Bois and Oliver C. Cox had long made clear, there is much more to US racism than white prejudices or stereotypes. Material inequality along racial lines underlies the dominant racial hierarchy. Thus, one major weakness in structural-functional thought is the failure to assess the central importance of strong and conflicting socioeconomic interests in the foundational institutions of a society like the United States, interests that generate or link to the inegalitarian norms that are routinely acted upon in this society—as opposed to those norms that are asserted in societal rhetoric as being central (such as "liberty and justice for all"). Certain groups have distinctively different material interests and life chances than do others because the society has long been structured to benefit some of its members much more than others.[134]

Open and assertive support for structural-functional theories had begun to decline by the late 1960s. Indeed, today, few sociolo-gists explicitly use this theoretical perspective. In his classic book *The Coming Crisis of Western Sociology*, Alvin Gouldner described the crisis in sociology as involving the alienation of most sociologists from this structural-functional theory and a movement toward alternative theories, such as those of Erving Goffman, which encouraged a middle-range, social-problems approach that was more oriented to freedom and equality than to order.[135] To some degree, Gouldner was right, although his pre-dicted professional consensus on a more liberation and equality-oriented sociology has not yet developed.

ORGANIZED CHALLENGES TO ESTABLISHMENT SOCIOLOGY

By the 1950s, the expanding social science research for US military agen-cies and other mainline government agencies was being challenged by small groups of sociologists who emphasized the importance of a more critical perspective on US society and global society. For example, in the 1950s the Society for the Study of Social Problems (SSSP) was cre-ated by Alfred McClung Lee, Elizabeth Briant Lee, and other activist sociologists, as well as other concerned professionals and students. This group was concerned with giving legitimacy to progressive activism and research among social scientists, especially in regard to social problems.

They were concerned about protecting freedom of teaching and research in an era of enhanced political (anticommunist) censorship.

The SSSP is still influential in sociology today, with many progressive members committed to a sociology of change, although it has in recent years succumbed somewhat to the mainstream professionalization and instrumental-positivistic trends. Today, under the "In Pursuit of Social Justice" section on its official website, the SSSP chronicles some activism by its members. These include actions supportive of Frances Fox Piven against attacks from arch-conservative Glenn Beck (discussed in Chapter 1), opposition to anti-immigration congressional bills, opposition to legislative decriminalization of domestic violence, and support for academic freedom at public universities.[136]

One significant source of the critical sociology of recent decades has come from the aggrieved sectors of US society, those sectors from which earlier countersystem sociologists had emerged—white women and men and women of color. Other countersystem sociologists have come from the white middle-class sectors of the society, yet have sincerely taken up the concerns of those who are oppressed. In the late 1960s, the Women's Caucus and the aforementioned SLM were formed. At the 1969 and 1970 American Sociological Association national conventions, the SLM openly confronted the sociology establishment. It began the publication of *The Insurgent Sociologist* (now *Critical Sociology*).[137] The Women's Caucus, which became Sociologists for Women in Society (SWS) in 1970, has regularly pressed the ASA to take action to rid itself and its member departments of discrimination against women.

Also important in the 1960s was the Black Caucus, which became the Association of Black Sociologists (ABS). ABS's critical importance continues. For example, remarking on the year 2012, the ABS wrote: "We were reminded of the continuing significance of ABS ... as a support system, professional development network, scholarly community, and articulator of policy discourse. The re-election of Barack Obama occurred in the wake of new versions of old racist attacks, unprecedented restrictions on women's reproductive rights, and ongoing police brutality and homicides in communities of color across the country."[138]

Another group with restructuring goals is the Association for Humanist Sociology, which was created in 1976, again with the involvement of progressive sociologist Alfred McClung Lee. Lee argued that this organization is "one of several alternative sociological societies that are keeping the discipline alive, relevant, and exciting for faculties and students and useful for socially constructive efforts in our communities."[139] Proving its continued usefulness to such efforts, the Association is currently and actively supportive of social justice organizations such as the New Orleans Workers' Center for Racial Justice, which is committed to the power and participation of workers and communities across racial groups and industries; the Transformative Studies Institute (TSI), discussed in Chapter 9; Equality Florida, a statewide education and advocacy organization devoted to eradicating discrimination involving sexual orientation, race, gender, and class; and Sociologists Without Borders/ Sociólogos Sin Fronteras (SSF), discussed in Chapter 8.[140] Elected in an important write-in campaign, Lee was an outspoken and progressive president of the American Sociological Association in the 1970s, and his voice and progressive ideas remain influential today.

CONCLUSION

In an important 1978 book, Alfred McClung Lee noted that between 1905 and the late 1970s, the American Sociological Association, as a national association, had "never represented the needs and interests of American society generally or even many of the concerns of those working in the discipline."[141] He argued that the "ASA and its journals and other projects are still largely in the hands of entrepreneurs or 'research' institutes preoccupied with grants and contracts."[142]

Even with pressures from women sociologists, gay and lesbian sociologists, African American sociologists, Latino sociologists, Native American sociologists, Asian American sociologists, Marxist sociologists, and other progressive sociology groups, this is still too often the case in the twenty-first century.

CHAPTER 4

Sociology Today

Periodically, social scientists have argued that their disciplines are in "crisis." This is true for fields as diverse as economics, history, political science, and sociology. The recurring crises in the social sciences have been explained in a number of different ways. Some have bemoaned the breakup of their disciplines into too many uncoordinated specialties, whose diverse adherents often do not understand scholars in other social science areas.[1] In the case of sociology, some critics have argued that sociology is too much of a catchall discipline with no common consensus or integrating conceptual paradigm. Certainly, sociology has been the social science where, from time to time, issues not researched in other fields have been developed or housed. This has created significant and continuing intellectual diversity. Still, some suggest that without more integration and a professional consensus on core ideas, there will likely be a decline in sociology as a discipline.[2]

Degrees in Sociology

In the case of US sociology, some observers saw declines in undergraduate enrollments, PhDs awarded, and academic jobs in the 1980s era as signs of crisis in the field. The number of master's degrees in sociology hit its peak in the mid-1970s, at just over 2,000 a year, then dropped to about 1,200 a year by the late 1980s. The number of PhD degrees peaked at a little more than 700 a year in the late 1970s and decreased to about 500 a year by the late 1980s. The number of undergraduate degrees showed the same pattern. Several analysts took these declines as suggesting something more or less permanent about the declining status of sociology. However, by the early 2000s, the data no longer supported this sense of crisis in regard to degrees and jobs.

The number of college sociology courses recently taught each year has approached 50,000 annually. During the 1990s and early 2000s, the number of college students awarded BA degrees in sociology again increased significantly—from 15,993 in 1990 to 28,541 in 2006. Interestingly, this trend is opposite that for the field of economics, the social science often said to have the greatest national prestige. Over the 1990s, the number of BA degrees in economics actually decreased. Paralleling this significant increase in sociology BAs came an increase in MA and PhD degrees awarded in sociology—1,700 to 2,000 MA degrees and 550 to 600 PhD degrees each year from the late 1990s to the mid-2000s. However, after 2007, the number of graduate degrees in sociology decreased overall.[4] In 2009 the Task Force on the Master's Degree in Sociology noted in its report to the American Sociological Association Council (ASA) that "if the decline in the number of degrees awarded is any indication of the health of the Master's degree in sociology, it should be clear that the programs are not in the best of health."[5] Moreover, as the United States recovered from the Great Recession during 2010 and 2011, the unemployment rate for sociology baccalaureates was 9.9 percent, but still less than for graduates in political science, economics, and anthropology. Meanwhile, the *American Sociological Review*, the ASA's leading journal, has maintained its influence, with a greater citation impact score than all other flagship journals in the social sciences.[6] All and all, today sociology continues its contemporary influence, and especially among undergraduate students.

Because sociologists as a group have a less prestigious professional identity and have less intimate ties to powerful business and government interests than economists and political scientists, the field of sociology has sometimes had a tenuous position within colleges and universities. In fact, a major bulwark undergirding the development and institutionalization of US sociology since the 1960s has been undergraduate demand for college courses in sociology and majors in sociology. Undergraduate students are greatly attracted by the societal relevance of sociology courses and their content, such as crime, delinquency, family problems, racial matters, and poverty. Without this demand, there would likely be much less support for sociology departments in colleges and universities. Much sociology teaching is at the lower-division level, where the courses meet general education requirements or the need for service courses for other professional programs. Moreover, many of the PhDs from graduate sociology programs become teachers in sociology departments with heavy undergraduate teaching loads. Without the substantial undergraduate demand for courses at all levels of colleges and universities, there would be no large graduate sociology programs.[7]

The decline in students seeking sociology degrees during the 1980s did reflect a rational response to declining job opportunities for sociologists in the society. There was good cause for crisis talk among graduate-trained sociologists in the 1980s. Beginning in the late 1970s, sociologists and other social scientists faced a decline in the number of good jobs, especially in college settings, as the corporate disinvestment in parts of the US economy began to impact the public sector where most social scientists are located. This disinvestment was part of a larger societal trend. Although this employment situation has improved since the 1990s, there have been long-term effects. Thus, in many areas the character of numerous college teaching and research positions for sociologists and many others has changed. Since the 1970s there has been an increase in part-time and untenured faculty positions in many colleges and universities. The phenomenon of part-time work and temporary workers that has long been central in many areas of the US economy has now penetrated college and university employment.

In addition to the general US economic shifts, other explanations for the periodic "crises" in employment in sociology and some other social sciences have been cited. One change is the decreased funding for social science research. Funding for sociological research peaked in the 1970s. Cutbacks in research funds have periodically reduced the number of certain types of academic jobs, such as for graduate students and researchers on temporary research grants. Yet other analysts have argued that periodic difficulties in sociology and other social sciences are in part the result of a reduction in (especially more conservative) government policymakers' deference to social scientists for data on which to make important public policy decisions.[8]

A Changing Philosophical Climate?

In the mid-1990s, the politically conservative sociologist Irving Horowitz—who developed the social science magazine *Society* and was instrumental in developing Transaction Publishers—contended that in recent decades there had been "a huge shift from 'scientific' sociology to 'liberation' sociology. In this world, survey research, empirical verification, and so-called data-rich theory yield to a sociology in which lifestyle issues prevail and decisions about how to present the self come to prevail."[9]

Horowitz was here putting his own distinctive interpretation on the growth of more critical perspectives within US sociology since the

1960s. From marginal movements that challenged scattered professional sociology meetings in the late 1960s and early 1970s, critical sociology groups and organizations have blossomed with a range of perspectives that have increasingly achieved scientific maturity and intellectual relevance. Most conspicuously, however, conservative social scientists such as Horowitz greatly exaggerate the influence within mainstream sociology today of those who accent inequality ideas and conduct research on such important matters as institutional racism and sexism. We can speak to the marginalization of research on these matters within mainstream sociology from our own and our students and other acquaintances' experience with leading sociology journals, which are still mostly unreceptive to significant countersystem research seeking to explore deeply many class, race, and gender issues, especially using qualitative methodologies.

Indeed, sociologists like Horowitz are still lionized in some quarters. At the time of Horowitz's death in 2012, William Form, a former editor of the *American Sociological Review,* applauded him for "making a larger contribution to fundamental theory in social development and political sociology than any individual in the profession."[10] Carl Gershman, president of the National Endowment for Democracy, lauded him for his "empire of truth and information that *Transaction* has built."[11] The founder of the Free Press, Jeremiah Kaplan, called Horowitz "one of the most eminent social science publishers of our time."[12] Such accolades can surely only be fully understood if one also recognizes that Horowitz seems to suggest the notion of many conventional analysts, including those in the country's mostly white and male governing elites, that problems of institutional racism, classism, and sexism are no longer fundamental to the country's daily realities. However, as we have shown throughout this book, the extant social science data strongly suggest that this commonplace conservative view is quite misinformed.[13]

In contrast to Horowitz, who argues that the supposedly dominant liberation sociologists are too critical of the status quo, is liberal sociologist Monte Bute. Discussing contemporary sociology, Bute has recently noted the following: "There is no profession more insensitive to status inequality within its own ranks, or as inept at recognizing how taken-for-granted practices create and perpetuate this peculiar caste system. Sociology itself is in need of a populist insurgency.... I seek the demise of inequality within our field and the proliferation of a more populist sociology."[14] *Crème de la crème sociology* is the phrase Bute uses to describe what he sees as too much obscure scholarship and careerism at top-ranked sociology departments in well-regarded universities, in the governing circles of the American Sociological Association, and in major sociology journals like the *American Sociological Review* and the *American Journal of Sociology*. "This royal court has created estates of lords and commoners," explains Bute, "for both departments and individuals."[15] Instead of this conventional publishing and careerism, Bute assertively argues for a more "populist paradigm of practice" in US sociology:

1. Students are not means to an end but are ends in themselves. We take pride in teaching undergraduates, fostering a sociological imagination in students who may never take another course in the discipline.
2. We are public teachers, using all available venues to profess an edifying sociology to diverse communities of citizens.
3. We primarily practice the scholarships of integration, application, and teaching. Our priority is sharing these findings with students, well-informed citizens, and practitioners in the field.
4. Service to our home institutions, local communities, and provincial professional associations is a preeminent value. These local loyalties diminish the self-aggrandizing behavior of hyper-professionalism and contribute to the public good.
5. We maintain that sociology is not a career but a calling.[16]

For Bute, there is also the issue of acknowledging the deep activist roots of the sociology discipline that we have previously underscored. Thus, Bute urges an unearthing of grassroots activism going back to sociology's earliest founders. If we honor "our ancestors," including the likes of Anna Julia Cooper, Jane Addams, and W. E. B. Du Bois, future sociologists will more likely practice a citizen-friendly sociology.[17] As it now stands, Bute views himself as "an anomaly and an aberration," in the eyes of most sociologists. "Nevertheless," he explains, "my mission is to assist more sociologists and citizens to break free of 'The Matrix.' Too many of us live in a simulated reality analogous to the movie *The Matrix*.... Weber's two vocation essays capture scholarship and activism as I practice them. I am not really a professor as commonly understood. I profess sociology, it is not a career but a calling."[18]

Al Gedicks is another contemporary sociologist who argues that social science skills should be used to assist oppressed communities and social change. From his participation in the Vietnam antiwar protests at the University of Wisconsin in the 1960s to more recent work with Native Americans in opposition to multinational mining corporations, Gedicks unmistakably practices what he preaches. Assessing Russell Jacoby's commentary in *The Last Intellectuals* that "Radical sociologists may dream of revolution, but they bank on their profession," Gedicks recently commented that Jacoby significantly overlooks

> how many of us are involved in ongoing community struggles as researchers, advisers, advocates, grants writers, technical experts as well as participants. We write in popular magazines and the opinion pages of the newspapers, testify before legislative committees and governmental agencies, coordinate corporate shareholder campaigns, appear as guests on radio and TV talk shows, and even produce our own documentary video and film productions on struggles the rest of the media would prefer to ignore. This involvement hardly ever is recognized as academically meritorious or conducive to advancement and is often the cause of denial of promotion or tenure. Despite these drawbacks, the numbers of us doing "guerrilla research" or "participatory research" are growing steadily.... [In a] political era of social welfare cutbacks, attempts to roll back the gains of the environmental movement and scapegoat minority and immigrant groups for the nation's ills, this kind of sociological activism is needed more than ever.[19]

Contrary to Jacoby, Gedicks suggests that 1960s student activists mostly did not discard their political ideals. Rather, they adjusted to the academic situations they found themselves in and continued a pursuit of social justice. He even suggests that their shared thinking signaled a fresh approach to doing social science—a paradigm shift of sorts. Yet, Gedicks knows the difficulties of finding symmetry between a commitment to liberation sociology and to an academic career.[20]

As a case in point, in 1991 Gedicks was informed that the vice chancellor of the University of Wisconsin–La Crosse had received a letter from the governor asking for an accounting of his activities as a university professor and director of the Center for Alternative Mining Development Policy (CAMDP). A former employee of the Kennecott Copper Corporation, a mining company, was troubled by a foreword Gedicks had written for a book exposing a British mining giant's global attack on indigenous peoples and the environment. This employee said he had "never seen a publication with so many lies, falsehoods, innuendos and misleading 'facts.'" He asked the governor and university's board of regents if Gedicks was a professor at the University of Wisconsin, if this was the standard of research conducted at the university, and under what conditions educators could be fired.[21] Yet, Gedicks had no problem responding to the charges and documenting the claims contained in his foreword. After he provided information requested by the administration about his public interest work, his dean even congratulated him for "this excellent public service activity."[22]

Gedicks credits his success in balancing a commitment to liberation sociology and to an academic career to several factors:

1. He works in a supportive department that recognizes the attraction of liberation sociology and values the fact that he carries his activist experience into the classroom via courses on racial and ethnic relations, community organization, and environmental sociology.
2. His students welcome his observations from field experiences and his documentary films about ongoing social conflicts in communities throughout Wisconsin.
3. He has unfailingly scored high in department evaluations of professional and public service.
4. He has published in the popular media and in academic journals.
5. He is involved in the Wisconsin Sociological Association and is a book review editor for their journal.
6. The University of Wisconsin's administration has been supportive of his commitment to liberation sociology, granting him faculty leaves and awarding him tenure.
7. The American Sociological Association awarded Gedicks a Spivack Community Action Research Fellowship to support a sabbatical research project in which he has worked with the Sokaogon Chippewa to evaluate Exxon's mine permit application, thereby recognizing his work in enabling communities of color.[23]

Nonetheless, Gedicks recognizes that his ability to survive as a liberation sociologist "has not been without … costs…. I spend an enormous amount of time and energy keeping in touch with a grassroots movement and providing assistance where my expertise is most needed. It is a second career in addition to my academic career. At one point I had hoped to combine this with a family and kids, but not anymore. I don't see how I could find the time to do a good job in all these areas."[24]

The contemporary tensions between so-called committed sociology and scientific sociology are not new. We observed in earlier chapters how Robert Park and other leading sociologists made a determined and successful effort to move away from the more committed, activist sociology of early sociologists like Jane Addams and W. E. B. Du Bois to the "more scientific" approach, which developed into the detached instrumental positivism of much modern sociology. To take a more recent example of this, in 1975 the prominent sociologist Peter Blau wrote, "I have been concerned with the antisystematic, antitheoretical and antiquantitative biases that seem to characterize many members of SSSP."[25] He was referring to the Society for the Study of Social Problems (SSSP), which, as noted in Chapter 3, was an association created to resist the turn away from concern with social problems and social policy. Actually, the SSSP was founded to promote "a significant move toward scientific realism and away from the traditional scientific image sociologists once constructed for themselves in order to obtain legitimacy for their profession in university and in intellectual, political, and business circles."[26]

Who Are Sociologists Today?

What underlies the recurring complaints of too little concern with "rationality," too much focus on "subjectivity," and too much analysis of inequality issues in sociology? One reason for this view among some critics may lie in the changing makeup of those who actually do sociology in the United States. Over the past three decades, there has been a growth in the number of sociologists who are white women and women and men of color. These sociologists often raise new research issues and theoretical concerns.

Terms like *rationality* and *value-free* are still used as part of the methods talk in much mainstream social science, yet this language is itself reflective of group bias, in that it is often an ideological cover for the perspective held by the traditional interests long dominant in the social sciences. Interestingly, when white men were the most visible social scientists engaged in research touching on issues involving white women and people of color, their science was usually considered to be objective, value-free, and detached. Now that white women and people of color, once the "objects" of detached research, are active and visible researchers, they are often accused of doing "subjective" or "biased" sociology. The transformation of these objects of research into active practitioners of research has been central to the liberation trend in sociology that these critics lament. Thus, among many traditional social scientists, there is great concern over the increasing research interest in a broad array of relatively new issues, such as institutional racism and sexism, class exploitation, heterosexism, patterns of methodological and theoretical bias, and a variety of cultural issues. Moreover, the growing numbers of white women and people of color coming into sociology and the other social sciences, which has increased since the 1960s, have forced white men, who formerly faced little competition, to have to compete for academic and other employment positions with those formerly excluded.

In the 1960s, white men made up most of the sociology PhDs being awarded across the country; some 85 percent of the PhD degrees given in 1966 went to men, the overwhelming majority of whom were white. The percentage of women PhDs grew relatively fast over the 1970s and since then has continued to grow. Since 2000, well over half of PhDs in sociology were earned by women.[27] In addition, women have received a substantial majority of sociology BA and BS degrees since the late 1970s.[28]

Over this period there has also been a significant increase in sociologists of color. In the 1960s the percentage of PhDs, and also of sociologists generally, who were not white was quite small. By 1976, the year the number of PhD degrees in sociology reached a high point, whites still received most of the degrees, with scholars of color receiving about 8 percent. However, between 1976 and 2010, the portion of sociology PhDs awarded to black candidates grew significantly from 5.1 percent to 8.3 percent.[29] This percentage was much higher than in economics, psychology, and political science.[30] In addition, the proportion of Latinos in the total group of sociology PhDs increased from 0.9 percent in 1976 to 4.7 percent in 2010.[31] The share of the sociology PhDs received by Asian Americans and Pacific Islanders increased from just 1.8 percent in 1976 to 4.6 percent in 2010.[32] The number of Native Americans awarded PhDs is not available for 1976, but the percentage increased from about 1 percent in 1986 to 1.7 percent in 1996. Most recently, the percentage has declined to the point that the National Science Foundation reports only a group number for all the social sciences together (e.g., only twenty-nine Native Americans were awarded doctoral degrees in 2010).[33] The PhD numbers for sociology students of color are better than those for some other social science fields, and they do have the potential to increase more in the near future, for the recruitment pool has grown in recent years. Moreover, between 1995 and 2010, the number of students of color who earned BA degrees in the social sciences more than doubled, from about 15,000 to over 47,000.[34] The degree numbers have remained substantial since then.[35] It is likely that there will be even more female, African American, Latino, and Asian American sociologists in the future.

Interestingly, membership in the American Sociological Association declined from 15,000 in the early 1970s to 12,000 by the mid-1980s, but then began a slow increase to 13,708 as of 2010. A 2013 American Sociological Association (ASA) national meeting had 6,184 participants, which set the all-time attendance record.[36]

Additionally, increasing just the entry numbers of sociologists is not enough. In her 2006 SSSP presidential address, Claire Renzetti noted the serious mismatch between the percentage of the (mostly sociologist) SSSP members who were people of color and the fact that in that year, "as in many years past, all of the Society's officers were white. The Society's journal, *Social Problems*, has never been edited by a person of color."[37] The ASA has periodically faced similar problems, even to the point of its governing council rejecting in the late 1990s the first editor of color (and a distinguished editorial board of women scholars and scholars of color) ever to be nominated by the association's nominations committee as the sole editor of the *American Sociological Review*. Significantly, in her forthright 2006 address, Renzetti called on the SSSP membership to immediately "develop strategies for making SSSP a more welcoming professional home for sociologists of color, one in which white sociologists acknowledge their whiteness and the privileges that have historically accompanied it, but do not use it to dominate, dismiss, or disparage colleagues of color." Interestingly, since her address, the SSSP has had significantly more scholars of color involved in the association's leadership and on the journal's editorial boards.

If these demographic changes in graduate sociology degrees do become more fully translated into major structural and institutional changes, it is also likely that there will eventually be more white female scholars and scholars of color not only in associational leadership positions but also in chair, dean, and other administrative positions within academic institutions and managerial positions within private organizations. In this case, there will likely be ever more social science research on areas of interest to the communities from which these sociologists come. There is already evidence for this latter contention, though it is by no means at the dominant level suggested by some fearful white male commentators. Thus, in the year 2013, the Section on Sex and Gender; the Section on Race, Gender, and Class; and the Section on Racial and Ethnic Minorities were among the largest of the various research groups among sociologists in the ASA, although they were being challenged by yet other sociological sections. Consequently, in 2013 the growing Section on Culture (1,209 members) slightly surpassed the still large Section on Sex and Gender (1,174); the Medical Section (1,057) and the Section on Organizations, Occupation, and Work (1,022) overtook the still large Section on Race, Gender, and Class (1,004); and the Section on Political Sociology (901) overtook the large Section on Racial and Ethnic Minorities (869).[38]

This new gender and racial diversity in higher education will probably bring substantial benefits to all people, not just to the new entrants. In the United States, heterosexual white male scholars and administrators have long controlled most processes and institutions that develop academic learning, information, and knowledge. Yet, creative new ideas and data on long-neglected issues of social import often come from those traditionally excluded from mainstream processes and institutions. We have seen this in past eras, such as when Jewish American scholars were finally allowed substantial participation in US and European universities. Today, white female scholars, LGBT (lesbian, gay, bisexual, transgender) scholars, and scholars of color—the new "outsiders within"—have introduced much intellectual ferment into the study of traditional research topics, such as families, gender, and crime, and have opened up, in innovative ways, a range of newer issues such as institutional sexism, homophobia, and systemic racism. For example, in her pathbreaking book, *Black Feminist Thought*, African American sociologist and American Sociological Association past president Patricia Hill Collins has argued that a black-feminist theoretical framework is essential to developing a meaningful sociological understanding of women in US society, particularly African American women. Thus, she critically analyzes traditional stereotypes of black women, such as the old white racial framing of the docile mammy or the irresponsible welfare mother, and she demonstrates how such severely negative images undergird the system of systemic racism and white privilege.[39]

The black-feminist perspective, pioneered by early sociologists like Anna Julia Cooper and Ida Wells-Barnett (see Chapter 3), is hereby reinvigorated for contemporary sociology. For its long-term intellectual health, the field of sociology needs a regular infusion of new ideas and inventive research that expands its intellectual reach and depth.

INSTRUMENTAL POSITIVISM IN CONTEMPORARY SOCIOLOGY

Mainstream Positivism Today

In Chapter 3 we noted that before and during World War II there was a trend in the direction of a sociology less concerned with progressive change and reform and that was increasingly accenting statistical and survey research methods. The anticommunist crusades of the 1940s and 1950s placed sociology and indeed all US intellectual activity under a repressive umbrella of self-censorship.[40]

Since the 1950s, as discussed previously, many sociologists have worked to shape contemporary sociology into a field whose prestigious departments have often emphasized survey research, demographic methods, and quantitative analytical approaches to the detriment of other sociological research procedures. This type of instrumental positivism still typically involves the aggregation of survey data, the development of formal hypotheses, the adoption of specified falsification procedures, and the grounding of theories in conventional statistical measurements and data. Indeed, for many sociologists, the idea of "scientific methodology" has become largely equated with the application of statistical techniques to government census data or other survey data. Certainly, we do not oppose the use of quantitative methods in social science, a point to which we will return below. Our concern about contemporary versions of instrumental positivism is the way in which quantitative research methods have come to be seen by many social scientists as the only, or the most acceptable, way of doing "proper" social science—an approach to social science that is too often ahistorical and atheoretical and that downplays other important ways of generating significant social knowledge.

Qualitative research and analysis, such as focus group interviewing or ethnographic research in the field, have often been relegated by powerful elites in various social science fields to the unscientific or "softer scientific" category. In a conventional positivistic approach, propositional statements are accepted or rejected solely on the basis of a statistical evaluation of the evidence. Subjective factors in this type of research, such as the underlying assumptions and implicit biases of the researchers, are not ordinarily foregrounded or analyzed. By the 1970s, most major, and many other, sociology graduate programs had accepted this establishment quest for a quantitatively oriented, instrumental-positivistic sociology.

As with other such methodological systems, this approach to sociology is based on assumptions about how we know what we know and involves a set of metascientific underpinnings, a methodology, and some theory—all factors that are webbed together.[41] However, the mainstream tradition of instrumental positivism has often displayed a general lack of self-critical reflection on its underlying assumptions and other metascientific ingredients. Thus, even a quick look at the articles published in the ASA journal, *Sociological Methodology*, will show that only rarely have there been serious discussions of the social research process within a holistic and critical framework—of the interrelationships between mainstream methods, theory, and the role of underlying background assumptions and values in the research process.[42]

All research methods have their own languages. In the case of quantitative positivism, the language of research and presentation "pervasively reflects the foundational presumption of an objective world of concrete components that can be represented in terms of 'hard data.'"[43] The methods talk of quantitative positivism makes the social phenomena studied appear very substantial and coherent. Yet this substantiality and coherence is, at least in part, achieved through the use of conventional language and the interpretive framework of this type of research: "Method talk in the quantitative workplace conveys a deep commitment to systematically and rigorously representing a separate and distinct order of things without disturbing that order in the process."[44]

Whatever the methodological approach, the language used involves at base more than spoken or written words, because it entails categories of thought and the speaker's or writer's underlying assumptions. These underlying assumptions are often deeply embedded not only in cognitive processes but also in individual feelings or group-related emotions. This method's language has little to do with the truth or falseness of the facts being created in the research process. Indeed, all academic research disciplines are constituted by their errors as well as by their truths.[45] But the language of a discipline does have a lot to do with being "in the truth." As a rule, those wanting to do the "most acceptable" sociology must use the discipline's *mainstream vocabulary* and place their ideas and findings within the conceptual horizons enforced by the discipline's principal gatekeepers, such as the mainstream editors, editorial boards, and peer reviewers of certain major journals.

Nonetheless, the real social world is not so neat, and since research is done by fallible human beings, many extra-scientific factors necessarily intrude into sociological research on that world. From research on how hypotheses and theories are made, we know that they are often accepted before the evidence is in because they are in line with the researcher's background assumptions. Social science theories, methods of data collection, and the actual data collected are shaped by many of the same forces that mainstream social scientists study, yet these scientists are often unwilling to closely examine these forces as they pervade their endeavors. By its nature, the generation of ideas and theory is historical and social and riddled with underlying moral assumptions and collective values. "Every social theory has both political and personal relevance, which, according to the technical canons of social theory, it is not supposed to have."[46]

Funding Agencies and Instrumental Positivism

We noted in Chapter 3 the great increase in grant and contract money that became available to social scientists in the decades following World War II. In addition, the new social-welfare orientation of the 1960s and 1970s involved many social scientists in research studies for federal and state government programs, such as new anti-poverty programs. Some of these projects did come up with exciting new information and ideas for social understanding and change, although elite policymakers often ignored them. Over time this social science research for government agencies, with some notable exceptions, has generally become less reformist and/or more bureaucratized and conventional.

Over the decades, the increase in social science grants has created significant umbilical linkages to government agencies and private foundations. Generally speaking, enticing research grants have provided not only equipment and data materials but also research assistance— thereby supporting many graduate students, particularly at the larger "Research 1" universities. Sometimes, the grants have provided salary support for faculty members. Most of these major research grants in sociology and many other social sciences have been oriented to a quantitative positivism, which often makes use of surveys and census data. One reason for this is that since World War II, social scientists seeking research grants have typically found that the "hard science" methods of quantitative positivism are most acceptable to funding agencies accustomed to dealing with physical scientists and with a mathematical or statistical framing of scientific research (see Chapter 3).

Another probable reason for this situation is that much quantitative work in the social sciences has been in the form of a relatively atheoretical or hired-hand empiricism, which allows elite policymakers to more easily manipulate the research as they see fit.[47] Much sociological research done under government and foundation grants and under auspices of businesses has provided the knowledge that officials and other policymakers need to pursue the substantially undemocratic interests of elite social groups. This is clear in the case of market surveys done for corporations to ascertain consumer preferences and in the case of workplace surveys done for employers to enhance profitability at the expense of workers. In many research projects, social scientists have knowingly or unwittingly played a role in legitimating the problematic perspectives and actions of elite government and business interests.

It is mainly those research projects viewed as fundable by government and private granting agencies—and vetted by the usual reviewers, the mainstream scholars who generally function as gatekeepers—that get significant research support. To get substantial funding for social research, one must usually do research acceptable to government agencies and corporate-funded or other private foundations, which are typically oriented to the status quo or, at most, to modest reforms. Many social scientists' research goals have been shaped, often intentionally, to coincide with the establishment-oriented interests of the conventional bureaucratic benefactors. In seeking this funding, social scientists have usually fashioned themselves into grant-seeking entrepreneurs with the narrow scholarly goals and identifiable niches of inquiry that enable them to get grants. Thus, in major areas of sociological research, the accommodation to funding sources has resulted in a limited array of acceptable research topics being studied.

For decades now, we have had a situation of significant de facto restrictions on the types of social research funded by private and public agencies. To take just one critical area, in recent years very few major studies primarily involving qualitative methods, such as field studies involving ethnographies or much in-depth interviewing, have been funded by conventional agencies to study the everyday practices of racial and gender discrimination within workplaces, educational settings, and public accommodations—areas with major and continuing problems of such serious discrimination. Over recent decades the first author and his colleagues have done numerous field studies (several resulting in major books) on how racial discrimination works in everyday practice but have been unable to secure funding from the conventional governmental and foundation sources of funding for social science. Similarly, our review of the literature on gender discrimination has revealed no major field studies using in-depth interviewing or other qualitative research methods to study the range and character of everyday discrimination faced by women in the United States or other countries. Studies of such discrimination issues—other than a few involving demographic analyses and opinion surveys—are rarely funded by government agencies and leading corporate foundations. In recent decades numerous important qualitative research studies in sociology have been self-funded or funded by small grants from college faculty programs or a few progressive foundations.[48]

Not only individual researchers but also college and university settings have become closely tied to government funding and grants, which often carry important overhead (money) allocations to academic institutions where grant-supported researchers are located. This quest for outside funding has increased as many colleges and universities have suffered budget cutbacks at the hands of legislators or their boards of trustees. Coveting the prestige and overhead money—what universities charge to administer the grant—higher level administrators at public universities (ranging from the University of Georgia to the University of California) and private universities (from Harvard University to the University of Southern California) pressure their faculties to devote much energy to seeking outside grants. Indeed, some administrators go so far as to disproportionately hire just those who are likely to bring in large grants, often regardless of their teaching skills and scholarly promise. US colleges and universities are far from being the independent, pluralistic, unattached, and free-thinking organizations they often proclaim themselves to be. Increasingly, we see US colleges and universities run and managed as profit-seeking businesses.

Relying on Nation-State Data

We have noted several impacts from this often uncritical commitment in sociology and the other social sciences to an instrumental positivism and to working closely with governmental agencies and corporate foundations. Also noteworthy is the impact that the great social science reliance on data sources generated by official or establishment sources has on social scientific findings and development. (One major alternative is independent collection of data by social scientists in the field.) In fact, the data used for much mainstream social science analysis usually come directly from government sources, such as the Census Bureau, or from opinion surveys generated out of conventional research grants vetted and made by government agencies and corporate or other private foundations. Much sociological research involves extensive statistical analysis (and later reanalysis) of these survey and demographic data sets, both new and old.

Interestingly, US social scientists have often been critical of biases in government-generated data in other countries, such as those of the former Soviet Union or Communist China. Yet they much less often raise substantial questions about the political and economic biases in comparable data created by US government agencies—at least not in a fundamental and ongoing critical way. Various government and private agencies collect data on such items as military casualties, crime, family income and wealth, education, and migration. Studies have shown that some government agencies do not collect data that might put them in a bad light or that might be controversial (e.g., hate crime data). Sometimes, too, officials in local, state, and federal government agencies "cook" their data to fit their own bureaucratic or political ends.[49]

A heavy reliance on government grants and data can foster a general acceptance of the existing organization of, and data from, the government, yet such government data can be very problematic. For example, one study of police data on gangs and gang activities found that most of the criminal activities the police said were done by real gangs were only a small portion of the crimes police had included in their official "gang statistics." The researcher, Albert Meehan, concluded that social scientists tend to ignore the police and other governmental manipulation of such crime data: "Statistics generated by organizational personnel, for their own 'good' organizational reasons . . . , should never be treated as an indicator of events as they would appear to be to an observer."[50] Additionally, a leading criminologist, William Chambliss, has shown that many FBI and other police officials have periodically exaggerated the number of major crimes, including murders and assaults. He has summarized this way:

> In an effort to take a bite out of the budgets of other governmental agencies, the Department of Justice and its law enforcement bureaucracies, especially the FBI and the National Institutes of Justice, consistently inflate or bias reports of data on crime. These same federal agencies hand out lucrative research grants to criminologists who uncritically accept the Department of Justice's crime control perspective.[51]

All too often, establishment officials and politicians have played up these manipulated and exaggerated statistics for their political purposes, yet only a few social scientists have regularly and substantially criticized these distortions and political uses of government data. By accepting the data without recurring questioning, mainstream social scientists make a moral commitment to the persistence of certain types of government corruption, whether or not they consciously recognize it. They choose to reject the alternatives, which can include going into the field without large grants, collecting research data on neglected aspects of society, working locally with communities on research relevant to progressive goals, and doing countersystem research analyses significantly critical of the nation-state—all of which have been accomplished by many of the independent and countersystem social scientists we discuss throughout this book.

PROFESSIONALIZATION AND INSTRUMENTAL POSITIVISM

A Straitjacket for New Social Scientists

The professionalization of sociology over the past few decades has been distinctive. As with other social sciences, this professionalization is often characterized by sociology careers built around the methods and language of instrumental positivism, associated grant procurement, and research and teaching based on conventional statistical methods, usually with little consideration of qualitative research and critical-theory alternatives. Narrow professionalization has shaped the education and careers of too many new recruits coming into the sphere of the social sciences. Over the decades, much graduate student training in sociology has stressed the importance of instrumental positivism, including a too heavy emphasis on advanced statistical analyses. In fact, new graduate students are usually required to take several quantitative methods and statistics courses, while fully comparable in-depth training in qualitative research techniques—such as in-depth interviews, focus groups, and participant observation—is less likely to be required. A graduate or undergraduate education oriented to quantitative positivism is conventionally thought to help students, once they graduate, to get good jobs and to teach mainstream sociology—as well as, in many cases, to compete for grants and publish in conventional outlets such as mainstream journals.

In this process, the education of new social scientists is often corrupted. The savvy methodological critic Paul Feyerabend has castigated modern physical-science education as

> simplifying its participants: first a domain of research is defined. The domain is separated from the rest of history … and given a "logic" of

its own. A thorough training in such a "logic" then conditions those working in the domain; it makes their actions more uniform and it freezes large parts of the historical process as well. . . . An essential part of the training that makes such facts appear consists in the attempt to inhibit intuitions that might lead to a blurring of boundaries.[52]

All too frequently, the education of new social scientists also restricts their research efforts and interests by "simplifying" them as scientists, by narrowing the focus of their research imaginations. Needless to say, such an education can reduce their ability to contribute to the research necessary for building more just and sustainable societies.

Journals and Careers

Since the 1960s, quantitative analysis of survey data, census data, and similar materials has become dominant in the more prestigious sociology journals, usually to the point of minimizing other research styles and innovative data. New sociologists and other new social scientists are often pressured by their professors to adopt instrumental positivism as their main research style and to aim for presentations and publications that embed that conventional approach. If this commitment is made early, it may put the neophyte social scientist onto a research track that is unimaginative or narrow. The prestige of presenting or publishing instrumental-positivist research is typically high in the circles of those doing such research. Indeed, just a few such publications in mainstream journals like the *American Sociological Review* (*ASR*) (the profession's flagship and official journal) can substantially boost one's career in academia.

A few mainstream journal publications can elevate a scholar greatly in prestige in comparison to other researchers who may be more imaginative and prolific in other venues of publication. This is especially true for those who publish in specialty journals that deal with issues of great interest to formerly excluded groups, such as the journals dealing with gender, LGBT, racial, and class issues, in which female sociologists, LGBT sociologists, and sociologists of color often publish. Ironically, some specialty journals have a high rejection rate for research papers submitted to them, yet publishing in them does not confer the prestige granted by *ASR* publications. Moreover, a lack of publications in "mainstream refereed journals" can often have serious consequences when a faculty member comes up for promotion or when salary raises are distributed, especially at educational institutions that accent conventionally funded research. College-wide evaluation committees too often just accept the conventional rankings of mainstream journals as a substitute for a responsible judgment of the quality of a scholar's work when faculty records are evaluated for hiring, promotion, and salary raises.

Given the importance of prestigious mainstream journals to publication performance and professional evaluation, it is not surprising that there have been a number of controversies over the editorial makeup of the most prestigious journal, the *ASR*, since the 1970s. Periodically, numerous sociologists have protested the dominance of quantitative positivism in that and other major sociology journals. One factor in this dominance has been the increasing linkage of sociologists at major research-oriented universities to government and private granting agencies. In order to demonstrate success from such grants, there is a constant need for prestigious outlets in which to publish the results of the funded research. Thus, many of the sociologists who do this type of funded research have had a vested interest in making certain sociology journals remain very accessible to them and their research, even if this has meant a significant restriction in the publication of other important sociological research.

Although the *ASR* has had articles with an instrumental-positivist cast since its earliest days, the prose of the more quantitative articles was mostly essay-like until the 1960s. Some accent was on method, but it was usually a secondary concern. By the 1970s, quantitative-positivist methods, especially advanced statistical methods, became more central, and articles became less accessible to the general sociological reader.[53] Viewed narrowly, debates on the character of leading journals like the *ASR* seem to focus on what type of research should be featured in the journal and which editors should be at its helm. Yet, these controversies also reflect long-simmering tensions within the field over what social science theories and which research methods will be given full respect and attention.

There is yet another problem created by this mainstream journal dominance: If qualitative researchers do not use at least some of the talk (such as the language of hypotheses) or the apparatus (tables with numbers) of instrumental positivism, they may find it very difficult to get published in the prestigious sociology journals or even to get a hearing with a large audience of conventional quantitative sociologists. As a result, qualitative researchers seeking publication in mainstream journals are often forced to make some concessions to the quantitative-positivist framework.[54] Perhaps, even to be an employed sociologist in most US colleges and universities, one must accept, at least implicitly, some of the framework of instrumental positivism. To be heard by sociologists trained in this positivism, one often has to meet them at least partway, by using some of their methods talk and apparatus. Yet it is usually the case that instrumental positivists do not have others make a similar effort.

Article and Book Sociologies

One ironic effect of the bias and censorship operating in some major mainstream journals is the development of a "mainstream-journal sociology" and a "book sociology," often with important differences in style, methods, and subject matter. Since perhaps the late 1960s, articles in the prestigious mainstream journals have commonly focused on advanced statistical methods and have frequently mimicked the apparatus of natural science.[55] Significantly, words capture the nuances of human experiences better than numbers, yet the analytic or literary-quality essay seems to be dead as a genre in many mainstream sociology and other social science journals. As a result, the readership of these usually statistically oriented journals outside a modest group of specialized researchers is limited. Because advanced quantitative research usually does not sell well in book form, commercial publishers tend to look for alternatives—often a readable book using descriptive or qualitative research techniques.

Thus, in recent years, one of the best-selling introductory sociology textbooks—titled *Sociology* and authored by John Macionis (discussed later in this chapter)—draws heavily on book sociology and on nonsociological book sources, the majority of which do not use the statistical techniques favored in the prestigious sociology journals.[56] This and other major introductory sociology textbooks infrequently cite articles in the prestigious mainstream sociology journals. One reason for this is that the mainstream journals usually do not provide a significant in-depth analysis of numerous major societal events, developments, or crises of an era, a point to which we will return later. Not surprisingly, book-type social science research often provides a more accessible and contextualized source of data and interpretation for summary writing in sociology textbooks about the modern social world.

Sociology Is Not a Physical Science

One mistake of those who take the instrumental-positivist perspective too seriously is the assumption that the social sciences should be much like the physical sciences. Recall from earlier chapters the point that numerous positivistic social scientists have modeled themselves on the traditional image of the physical sciences, and thus have spoken of "the scientific method" as something separate from themselves and their assumptions. These social scientists frequently use an approach and logic that distances those studied from themselves.

Not surprisingly, those whom sociology usually studies, the "distanced" human beings, often have strong opinions about their lives and are able to routinely alter the social matrices in which they live.

Sociological research is different from natural science research in that sociologists study those who act to change the conditions being studied. As we have noted, there is a long tradition in sociology—going back to Addams, Du Bois, and Mead—that recognizes the important differences between a positivistic social science modeled on physical sciences and a social science sensitive to the distinctive character of human beings who are its subjects. Human beings develop intersubjective meanings and act on meanings they attribute to physical and social phenomena. They are interpreting subjects in interaction with one another—with individual and collective memories retaining and utilizing the accruing meanings over time. Thus, qualitative-humanistic social science may on occasion use some of the same methods as the quantitative-positivist social scientists, but the orientation toward the subjects and their under- standings, and an awareness of broader social issues, usually make the former approach quite different in its everyday practice from the latter.

Moreover, as we have previously underscored, it is not humanly possible to be neutral in the human sciences because there is "a moral relationship between the human beings studied and those who study them."[57] Edward Shils has underscored the point that a certain empa- thetic sensitivity appears to be important to the development of much insightful sociology. The central thrust of this sociology lies in the view that "all human beings possess a quality which entitles them to the respect and consideration of their fellows."[58] Social scientists are, of course, human beings and cannot escape being part of the human world they study. This research situation is much different from a scientist whose study of stars, minerals, or plants is much less intertwined with her or his own life.

The professionalization of sociology over the past several decades has frequently included a distinctive distancing of those studied. Ivan Illich argued that the mainline "professions" often become machines to extract money from those they study and serve without enabling them to act for themselves.[59] Reviewing the professionalization of social science research, Robert Blauner and David Wellman note some of its conse- quences: "According to this view, only the social scientist can define a suitable problem for research because he or she alone knows enough about the theories of the field and the methods by which theories are tested. In this model of science there is no place for the community-of-those- studied to share in the determination of research objectives."[60] Thereby, professional sociologists often disable those whom they research. Those preoccupied with being social science professionals may not listen care- fully to—or provide an outlet in their research reports for—the ideas and deeper concerns of those human beings they study, especially those who are socially subjugated and dehumanized.

Conventional Survey Research: Some Limitations

A positivistic theory agenda often attempts to "test" or "falsify" theories with "neutrally" collected data. This approach is highly suspect because all data collected by social scientists are theoretically channeled and situated from the beginning of the data-collection process. Countersystem sociologists reject a narrow instrumental positivism because "knowledge is not simply a reflection of an inert world 'out there' but is an active construction by scientists and theorists who necessarily make certain assumptions about the worlds they study."[61]

Underlying Assumptions and Methodological Individualism

Nevertheless, the fact-finding procedures of countersystem sociologists and conventional quantitative-positivistic sociologists may sometimes appear to be the same, for they both may use census and other official data or social surveys. Yet, viewed broadly, these procedures are not likely to be the same in practice, because the social scientists who use them have different perspectives and theoretical outlooks. To exemplify the way in which apparently similar procedures can become different methods when applied from divergent theoretical standpoints, let us briefly review the example of the measurement of "class consciousness," which has been a dynamic reality in Western societies since the Industrial Revolution.

Survey researchers have periodically tried to discern how class conscious North Americans are. In the 1940s, one opinion survey found that more than 80 percent of respondents identified themselves as "middle class." The conclusion drawn was that class was not a subjectively meaningful concept for describing the US social structure. Then social psychologist Richard Centers conducted another survey allowing the respondents to choose from "working class" and "middle class" and found that half chose the "working class" label for themselves.[62] Since Centers's study, data on the subjective dimensions and distribution of social class have regularly been collected using interviews, phone surveys, and voting data.[63]

Using the typical quantitative survey methods, contemporary social scientists have tried to study class identification and class-linked attitudes. The result from this body of mostly survey research is anything but the objective and neutral set of findings proclaimed by many advocates of quantitative-positivistic research. Measured this way, some researchers have found the presence of significant class consciousness among US individuals, whereas others have not. Furthermore, others have found class consciousness in their data but have actually denied it. As Rich Fantasia has put it, "Such differences have tended to reveal more about the preconceptions of the researchers than they have about any collective consciousness of class in the society."[64]

One common assumption of survey research can be seen in the typical focus on individuals responding in isolation. This methodological individualism involves an excessive emphasis on the isolated individual opinion-giver as the subject studied. Methodological individualism remains dominant in the social sciences because of the heavy use of survey and census data based on the interrogation of scattered individuals. The image of the human being here is of the individual respondent, often of a person giving views in isolation from family and community.[65]

This methodological individualism tends to ignore or downplay the omnipresent collective contexts of the creation of meaning. Taken alone, public opinion and demographic surveys cannot give an adequate portrait of important social phenomena because they typically do not provide much information about the broader contexts and interrelationships in which those surveyed arrive at their views and live their lives. Thus, in class-consciousness research, the collection of individual data is insufficient to assess the character and development of a collective class consciousness in a society. The way in which class consciousness and other human meanings are constructed in interrelationships involving two, three, or more individuals—or within the multiple social groups (e.g., families) to which individuals allocate their energies—is generally lost when using conventional survey research methods.[66]

A second limitation of much survey research is that it is conducted at one point in time, and responses to the survey questions are typically recorded "as fixed, static entities, minimizing any denotation of process, change, maturation, or ambivalence in consciousness."[67] This can be a problem because people may change the way they think or feel, commonly over short periods of time.

Yet another problem with survey research is that the realities being probed may be far enough below the surface that rather brief answers to similarly brief questions cannot tap respondents' often complex and nuanced views. Much of what we think we know as social scientists comes from these brief answers to brief questions, often relatively superficial queries framed from the viewpoint of middle-class researchers in relatively isolated university or corporate offices. The deeper realities of human thought, opinions, attitudes, and emotions cannot be probed by such relatively brief questioning. Most survey research is limited in that it ordinarily assumes that important attitudes, conceptions, feelings, and consciousness can be easily elicited in verbal or written responses to survey questions.

Survey questions on class-related issues are often "artificially decontextualized because they are abstracted from the class practices and social relations that give them meaning."[68] For example, even an apparently simple survey item, such as "income," can be problematical. When a survey researcher uncovers a positive statistical relationship between income and attitudes toward, say, the privatization of prisons (the higher the income of a respondent, the more support for privatization), the variable "income" is used to measure social status. However, when another researcher reports that "income" is negatively correlated with age (the higher the age, the lower the income), the variable "income" here also measures financial solvency and life support. In actual research reports, a measured variable (such as "income") may be ambiguous and problematic; it thus can be an indicator of different social realities that need much deeper probing to truly understand.

Social surveys need not be decontextualized, and they can be used for emancipatory purposes. We can go back more than a century to see an early example. Even Karl Marx once tried survey research and drew up an early social questionnaire, which was published in the French journal *Revue Socialiste*. Many copies were distributed to French workers' societies, socialist and social democratic groups, and newspapers. The questionnaire's preface asked workers to reply because only they could describe "with full knowledge" the problems of the workplace and "only they . . . can energetically administer the remedies for the social ills from which they suffer."[69] Marx's questionnaire did not ask for workers' attitudes, but instead requested them to actively describe in some detail working conditions, including wages, work hours, and safety. It used valuable open-ended questions, which today are usually considered to be too expensive (in time and money) to be included in most opinion surveys. Consider a few of his 100 questions:

> "If you are employed in a chemical works, in a factory, in the metal working industry, or in any other industry which is particularly dangerous, enumerate the safety measures introduced by your employer."
> "Are there shifts of children and young persons which replace each other during the hours of work?"
> "When work continues day and night, how are the shifts organized?"
> "Do you know any instances in which the Government has misused the forces of the State, in order to place them at the disposal of employers against their employees?"[70]

The open-ended questions were not designed just for research reporting, but rather to raise class consciousness and promote discussion among workers responding and to draw "an electoral program for the workers in connection with a coming election."[71] Marx was not just interested in workers' subjective appraisals of conditions; he wanted to promote group discussions about conditions as a way to inspire action. Workers' opinions did matter, but not divorced from meaningful action.[72] Here a survey was used for liberation goals—to promote critical conversations and discussions, thereby taking advantage of different individual levels of awareness and interest in working conditions. Such research-generated conversations can be an important tool for change. Clearly, the aims of fact-finding procedures, what their results mean, and what kinds of understanding they bring about are dramatically different for social scientists depending on their theoretical orientations and underlying assumptions.

Missing the Big Questions

Another problem with a too heavy focus in the various social sciences on opinion and census survey data, and on the advanced-statistical analysis thereof, is the restriction of much research to questions of relatively limited consequence for human societies. In many social science circles there is a serious neglect of a range of important issues that cannot be well studied with survey techniques or that are not likely to be funded by established agencies. For example, data on top corporate executives' attitudes and actions on critical social matters—such as on racial and gender discrimination in employment—or data on large landlords' discrimination against single women with children seeking rental housing have not been systematically gathered by mainstream social scientists. Much survey-oriented research focuses on relatively small-scale questions, and too often in isolation from broader societal issues. Thus, too many sociologists "have tended to scatter their attention."[73]

Of course, this approach is not limited only to those committed to variations on quantitative positivism. There is a more general problem of decontextualization in the social sciences. Many other social scientists, who may use an array of research methods, tend to study issues and problems in isolation from one another, from their historical context, or from the larger frameworks of class, racial, and gender stratification.

Official presentations of sociology in major handbooks frequently emphasize the need for standardization in the discipline and/or recommend more quantitative-methodological rigor as a way of dealing with sociology's allegedly low prestige in the academy and society. Yet the real problem is quite the opposite. Ted Vaughan has shown that several sociology handbook editors and commentators misunderstand the basis for the current marginality of much mainstream sociology to larger intellectual concerns.[74] The reason is not a lack of rigor but is because much sociological research has little relevance to major societal issues and needs. Sociologist Kai Erikson has asserted that a review of the issues discussed in leading sociology journals published over several decades would reveal that "many of the truly decisive happenings of our own time have passed with little or no comment from the sociological community.... [A future] historian would learn almost nothing about the pivotal events around which the flow of modern history turned."[75] Moreover, one empirical study of more than two thousand *American Sociological Review* articles published between 1936 and 1984 examined numerous major social and political events for five periods within this time frame—such as the Great Depression and McCarthyism. The study discovered that overall only one in twenty of the articles dealt with any of the major societal events of the periods examined.[76]

Walter Powell, former editor of the book review journal of the ASA, has noted the substantial difficulty he had in finding sociologists able to write about broader societal issues to review for the journal.[77] This may be, at least in part, a result of the more or less exclusive training many sociologists have received in instrumental positivism. A too-technical education may prevent social researchers from seeing the broad changes going on around them and from envisioning possible social futures. Such an ivory-tower education creates what Thorstein Veblen, an early US social scientist, once termed a *trained incapacity* (from higher educational programs) to see beyond a very limited area of immediate concern.

THE NARROWNESS OF SOCIOLOGICAL PERSPECTIVES

In addition to methodological narrowness in much modern social science, including sociology, there is a topical narrowness in many mainstream analyses. This narrowness can be seen in introductory textbooks in sociology, textbooks whose content and format are usually dictated by editors seeking to sell large numbers of books. Editors at textbook publishers often know little about the conceptual richness of sociology, but they are usually influenced by the early reviews of textbook manuscripts that come from teachers of sociology. The reviewers' comments persuade textbook editors that there is an established sociological canon, such as the three major theoretical paradigms noted below. As a result, the editors insist that these perspectives be featured in order for the textbook to be commercially competitive.[78]

For example, for some years, in numerous introductory sociology textbooks, one found a focus on three basic conceptual perspectives in sociological analysis, usually termed the *structural-functional (order)*, the *conflict*, and the *symbolic interaction* approaches. Until rather recently, most introductory textbooks provided a "balanced" approach focusing on these three perspectives. For example, one best-selling introductory sociology textbook is that of John Macionis, which has for some years emphasized these three theoretical paradigms.

Discussed first, the structural-functional (order) paradigm is said to have explanatory power for understanding how societies are socially integrated and to have had a significant influence on the recent development of sociology. A brief critique of this paradigm notes that it neglects "class, race, ethnicity, and gender, which can generate considerable tension and conflict."[79] This is an understatement. The domination of the structural-functional and related status-quo perspectives was so strong in US sociology from the late 1930s to the mid-1960s that there was little serious use of the extensive conceptual tradition of Karl Marx among US sociologists. Indeed, Marx's probing analyses of class and of capitalism as fundamental and oppressive in modern Western societies was long considered too radical for US academics, including most sociologists. Social theorists and analysts who pressed similar arguments about the fundamental character of gender and racial oppression were similarly marginalized during this period.

After discussing structural functionalism, current introductory textbooks often note a second and more recent conceptual paradigm, usually termed the *social-conflict framework*. Traditionally, this contemporary approach is said to have developed in response to the structural-functionalist approach. Viewed as influenced in part by Karl Marx, it helps students to understand social divisions and inequality. In the 2013 edition of his sociology textbook, Macionis, like other major textbook authors, suggests that this perspective has been criticized because it allegedly "ignores how shared values and interdependence can generate unity among members of a society." He also notes that some sociological critics see the social-conflict approach as often advocating explicitly political goals, thereby giving up the "claim to scientific objectivity."[80] Macionis did then note that those who support the social-conflict approach counter this criticism with the argument that all social theories have political consequences.

However, something important is omitted here: The social-conflict tradition actually arose much *earlier* than the structural-functionalist perspective in North American and European theorizing about society. In its influential US form, the structural-functionalist perspective was developed, in part, as a response to intellectual challenges coming from Marxist thinkers inside and outside (e.g., in unions) the major US colleges and universities in the 1930s. Marxist thought criticized the reality and impact of modern capitalism, whereas structural functionalism "did not so much justify capitalism (although it often did) as offer an explanation and understanding of its difficulties without condemning it."[81] Thus, the social-conflict perspective should be discussed as a serious conceptual perspective that emerged in Europe and the United States well before the structural-functionalist perspective evolved in US sociology.

A third paradigm, usually called the *symbolic-interaction paradigm*, is discussed by numerous textbook authors as different from the other two in that it gives much more attention to the details of everyday life than to the larger structures of society. It is often argued, too, that this perspective places too little emphasis on the structural factors in society. Such a commentary, however, ignores the fact that much symbolic inter-actionist research focuses on how social inequalities are created. Indeed, George Herbert Mead, one of the founders of symbolic interactionism, was a progressive activist and clearly recognized the importance of social inequality in his writings on US society. Also important in the symbolic interactionist tradition is the emphasis on social relations among individuals; an important corollary to this emphasis is the rejection of a methodological individualism. After presenting these three perspectives in the 2013 edition of his textbook, Macionis concludes that the three conceptual paradigms offer different sociological insights but that none is more correct than the others. As he sees it, "each paradigm is helpful in answering particular kinds of questions."[82]

The emphasis on just three conceptual perspectives is a major error in describing the state of the diverse theoretical and empirical field that is now sociology. Recently, this has been recognized by textbook authors like Macionis, who in the 2013 edition of his textbook does tuck in a gender-conflict approach and a race-conflict approach as subdivisions of the social-conflict approach. Still, numerous sociology textbooks contain no substantial discussions of the important critical-theory, feminist, antiracist, or humanistic conceptual traditions in sociology. Note that these critical perspectives cannot simply be subsumed under a general "social-conflict" perspective because they raise fundamental issues about social science as well as about society, including questions about the nature of social science theory and methods. Even textbook writers who give more attention to issues of social oppression in US society are often pressed by textbook reviewers or publishers to emphasize the "three basic perspectives."[83] Although publishers doubtless see themselves as following the desires of the teachers of sociology, their actions frequently restrict the knowledge available to students of sociology and the other social sciences.

The Alternative Tradition: Sociology Oriented to Change

Since the 1960s, North American social movements such as the feminist movement, gay rights movement, and the civil rights movement have underscored the reality that the long dominant, heterosexual white male social scientists have in their research and writings often left out or distorted the everyday realities of women, LGBT Americans, and people of color. Across the globe, anticolonial movements have demonstrated that Western social scientists have historically misrepresented the lives of non-Western peoples. And the union movements seeking to organize ordinary workers in many countries have regularly made it clear how such workers are frequently categorized, "othered," and oppressed by the policies and machinations of modern capitalism.

The 2011 to 2012 Occupy Wall Street movement in some 600 US communities, as well as in hundreds more communities overseas, has brought renewed attention to these practices of modern capitalism. A number of sociologist-activists have been studying or partaking in this important contemporary movement. Some have recently assessed questions concerning the significance and character of the movement in a special issue of *Sociological Quarterly*. In his contribution, the progressive University of California professor Richard ("Dick") Flacks explained Occupy's significance in terms of the "modes of social organization beyond capitalism" whose target and enemy are the predatory financial institutions. Flacks suggested there are strong links between Occupy Wall Street, the Arab Spring, the Chilean student protests, the student strikes in Québec, and other contemporary peoples' movements seeking greater freedom and social justice.[84] Columbia University sociologist Todd Gitlin, author of the important book *Occupy Nation,* has highlighted the significance of the "outer movement"—individuals who participate in the big marches but not in the general assemblies or other meetings.[85] We might note, too, Héctor Cordero-Guzmán, a Baruch College sociologist whose research on the movement is credited with bolstering the image of protesters as representing a cross-section of the US population.[86]

Flacks, Gitlin, and Cordero-Guzmán's contributions to a better understanding of the Occupy protesters bring to mind Gideon Sjoberg's words: "We must take great care to continually weed out the distortions and downright errors that social scientists have constructed about other peoples." This is particularly true for establishment-funded projects that are constructed "for administrative purposes (i.e., for social control), not to understand the other's definition."[87] The social movements of oppressed peoples have provided a recurring infusion of new insights and support for a progressive and liberating social science. In this book, we have stressed this liberation tradition in US sociology, which emphasizes social research and analysis for expanding justice and democracy.

Qualitative Approaches and Liberation Sociology

An underlying assumption of all critical analysis in social science is that one must look beneath the overt surface realities to understand well the often hidden realities of hierarchy and oppression. This probing for the hidden reality of power relations was a lesson taught well by Karl Marx, one of the first social scientists to analyze Western capitalist societies critically and in depth. In an 1843 letter, Marx suggested that the goal must be the "reform of consciousness not through dogmas but by analyzing mystical consciousness obscure to itself, whether it appear in religious or political form." Then he noted that the task for social scientists was the clarification of the "struggles and wishes of the age."[88] In his major writings, Marx showed how surface realities of capitalism, such as market-oriented trade in commodities and the money wage, disguised the important underlying realities of worker exploitation and class oppression.

Since the time of the early social scientists Harriet Martineau and Marx, the liberation social science tradition has been sensitive to the omnipresent realities of hierarchy and power. Thus, aware social researchers realize that their research and methods are affected by the power hierarchies of the society within which they work. As those power relations change, so, too, do questions about the collection of data on and interpretations of shifting societal realities.

Within the social sciences especially, the various dimensions and assumptions of qualitative research methods have been more systematically scrutinized than quantitative research methods. For example, many qualitative researchers have been aware, for some time now, of the Eurocentric bias of much anthropological research done in colonized societies across the globe. Hidden biases and domain assumptions in numerous areas of qualitative research have for some time been targeted, debated, and analyzed. Most have recognized that the instrumental-positivist triad of detached observer, distanced object, and "objective" scientific method remains highly problematic.

Recall from Chapter 2 that even in the physical sciences, to which social scientists have frequently looked for methodological models, the mechanistic Newtonian views of the physical world have given way to the Einsteinian idea of relativity—the idea that the character and description of physical phenomena depend on the reference frame of the scientific observer. Physical scientists such as Werner Heisenberg and Niels Bohr have made it clear that the scientist's measuring apparatus, the person doing the measuring, and the objects studied are closely interrelated and not independent of each other. Similarly, in social science the instruments of observation, the observed, and the observers are inseparable and intertwined parts of a larger holistic reality. The instrumental-positivist distinctions made among these are no longer tenable in the natural or the social sciences.

Using a variety of qualitative methods, social scientists can do research in everyday social worlds and make visible how people operating "in everyday life constitute, reproduce, redesign, or specify locally, what the institutional and cultural contexts of their actions make available to them."[89] There are different approaches in regard to field methods and theorizing in qualitative research. The array of field methods include, among other approaches, participant observation, life histories using in-depth interviews, and case studies using multiple methodologies, including social histories. Theorizing and interpretation can involve ethnomethodology, grounded theory, the interpretive case method, and the extended case method. The interpretive case method, often used by anthropologists, views microevents as expressions of the macrodimensions of a particular society. The grounded theory approach attempts to build new theories inductively from assessing several qualitative case studies. And the extended case method extends and reconstructs existing social theory by constantly examining its utility in explaining new qualitative research cases. In this latter approach, the current theory is laid out in advance and, if contradicted by data, is rejected or reconstructed for yet another testing with more field data.[90]

Qualitative Research and Countersystem Sociology

Although qualitative research methods and interpretive techniques need not be oriented toward the goals of a progressive or liberation sociology, they are so oriented more often than quantitative methods and techniques. From the beginning of the field, many sociologists have viewed their vocation as one of improving the world through field research. Though relatively conservative politically, Auguste Comte thought a positive investigation of the world could liberate human beings from the shackles that prior metaphysical thinking had imposed on them. Others linked a commitment to progressive social change to qualitative methods for observing the social world. Harriet Martineau not only translated Comte's work but also in the 1830s did the first qualitative field work in Western sociology. She was strongly committed to the abolition of slavery and the improvement of conditions for women and the poor in both Britain and the United States. Committed to improving French society, Émile Durkheim proposed the idea of studying social phenomena according to their consequences for human beings. For Durkheim, sociology was a moral enterprise and not a sterile exercise in data collection. Max Weber accented the need to study meaningful social action with regard to societal change. As we have seen in previous chapters, most founders of European sociology thought that sociology was a discipline to improve the world.

As sociology developed in North and South America, numerous early sociologists had a similar interest in changing oppressive societies for the better and in keeping a critical moral perspective intertwined with their social research and analysis. For example, sociology was apparently the first academic discipline in which researchers, albeit just a few, undertook serious studies of racial and gender inequality. It was one of the first where social researchers conducted serious research on class inequality. From the beginning, US sociologists in the liberation tradition have been among the sharpest critical analysts of society, as can be seen in early commentaries on racism by W. E. B. Du Bois, in the early analyses of class and gender inequality and of democracy by Jane Addams and her female colleagues at Hull House and the University of Chicago, and in the early analyses of gender relations and sexism by analysts such as Charlotte Perkins Gilman.[91] Although these analysts and their research were later marginalized within US sociology, the field of sociology provided some early support for their research and writings. Interestingly, these early sociologists combined various types of qualitative and quantitative (usually descriptive statistics) methodologies with a progressive and emancipatory approach to US society. However, they often used qualitative research methods, as most in this liberation sociological tradition do today.

One explanation for this reliance on qualitative research methods today is the high cost of quantitative research methods. Large-scale survey research, large-scale demographic research, and experimental research are typically intensively quantitative and relatively expensive. For several decades now, most of the social science researchers who have received significant amounts of research money from government agencies and large corporate foundations have been those committed to some type of quantitative positivism and usually to the status quo or modest reform therein. As we noted previously, researchers oriented toward a more progressive sociology have often had trouble getting significant grants, so they may make use of less expensive qualitative methods. But the explanation lies deeper than costs. More important than access to money for research are the theoretical and ideological assumptions (such as an acceptance of the status quo) underlying much instrumental-positivist research.

Another explanation lies in the character of the data-gathering itself. To take one major example, quantitatively oriented survey research often entails a restrictive instrumentalism in the way that interview questions are framed and the data are gathered and statistically analyzed. Respondents are typically given preformatted questions and answers to choose from. In contrast, much qualitative field research, such as participant observation or less structured in-depth interviews, allows those being studied to shape many of the issues and questions raised in the research—and, often, the direction in which the research proceeds. In this way, qualitative research frequently entails understanding how people think, act, and react. Qualitative researchers can garner new ideas and theories from listening carefully to their research participants' questions and interpretations.[92]

Although there is no guarantee that qualitative researchers will listen carefully to the developed interpretations of those whom they research, at least that opportunity is there, which it is not in typical survey, demographic, or experimental research. If one does qualitative fieldwork with those who are oppressed, listens carefully, and examines candidly their experiences and views, it is often the case that a more nuanced, perceptive, and critical perspective on society will emanate from that research—a perspective that may well be unacceptable to the contemporary elites of the society. Of course, as we have noted, some qualitative researchers do share substantially in the positivistic culture and, to varying degrees, constrain their observations and drape their analyses in the terminology of that conventional research culture.

Finally, to draw on a medical metaphor, most qualitative research is interested in discovering, identifying, and describing social "syndromes." A social syndrome is an interrelated pattern of numerous social "symptoms," and one well-studied case can be sufficient for understanding it. Quantitative research, in contrast, serves to map out the distribution of fewer and selected symptoms, usually called "variables." In quantitative work, assessing causal inference generally proceeds from findings of concomitant variation in individual traits. This abstracted process of causal inference conventionally follows a mechanistic Newtonian model of characterizing discrete objects moving in relation to each other according to their individual traits. For example, when some quantitatively oriented social scientists find a statistical relationship between "race" and "wealth" (inequality) variables for a country like the United States, they may draw the inference that "race is highly correlated with, or causes, wealth inequality." However, such researchers will have to go well beyond their quantitative data into speculation—or, preferably, significant qualitative research—in order to discover the dynamics of this relationship, its deep roots and long history, or what it means to have to "live it" constantly in everyday life.

Qualitative researchers are not encumbered by such rules governing quantitative methods, and they can more easily research the many and nuanced ways in which racial histories are closely linked to wealth inequality—and how wealth inequality causes racial inequality, or vice versa. They can explore how "race" is socially invented and examine its historical and contemporary ramifications in many directions, and they can better understand its textures and enfoldings. They can also probe and examine race's component parts—which encompass a large investment of energy and resources in maintaining white privilege, including great and continuing wealth inequality.

It is often the case that researchers using qualitative methods have opened up an area of research and understanding first, thereby allowing the possible use of selected quantitative methods to assist in the analysis. Moreover, even the best quantitative analysis usually requires outside insights—perhaps from qualitative research—to gain penetrating and cutting-edge understandings of the social life of human beings.

Research Techniques, Social Interpretation, and Moral Theory

A major consideration in adopting a particular research method to study social questions and issues should be choosing the method appropriate for the questions and issues at hand, rather than sacramental compliance with formulaic procedures. In fact, a major scientific rule is that the methods chosen should be appropriate to the object of study. Clearly, much survey research has contributed to our knowledge of the social world, and statistical analysis of various kinds has had its important place in contributing to this knowledge. There are, of course, quantitative researchers who use survey data in quite reflective and critical ways. Thus, we clearly recognize that the problem is *not* quantification per se but the too-frequently unreflective use of quantitative methods, including advanced statistical techniques, without consideration of the research's social context, societal relevance, hidden assumptions, probable uses, moral and ethical implications, and limitations in regard to probing deeper social realities of a given society.

How one collects and interprets research data is important. For example, recall the first empirical field study of black Americans, the 1890s field study by Du Bois published as *The Philadelphia Negro*. This pioneering study combined survey methods and descriptive statistical analysis with qualitative data and historical analysis of the community. Du Bois also joined social-theoretical interpretations of his data with a moral (human rights) reading.

In the research process, Du Bois made use of survey questionnaires to gather data to map out the conditions faced by working-class and poor Philadelphians, yet he was significantly limited by the institutional context for this research. The white men who commissioned his study were openly worried that "native stock" whites would be overwhelmed eventually by the "plague" of the urban black poor, whom they stereotyped as immoral and criminal. Du Bois was to conduct a sociological study of the black Philadelphians who were predefined by the white funders as a "social problem." The charge they gave to Du Bois was as follows: "We want to know precisely how this class of people live ... and to ascertain every fact which will throw light on this social problem."[93]

Working with these significant and racialized limitations, Du Bois ignored this paternalistic mandate to some degree. He spent many hours in the field interviewing some 2,500 households. Although he knew that his research manuscript had to be acceptable to the whites in charge, he worked into the final analysis sociological and moral interpretations that subverted the racist thinking of his day. He worked inductively, drawing generalizations from field data, and historically, profiling the background of Philadelphia's black population and its flight from the South. Webbing an antiracist analysis into his important monograph, Du Bois compared the black population with white immigrant groups just coming into the city—noting how the latter got a much better societal deal. Du Bois did not do much with the qualitative data at hand, such as the quotes from his interviews. However, he did detail the poverty of many black Philadelphians—and condemned their actions occasionally in moralistic terms—and offered what is likely the first major racial and class analysis of poverty and crime among black urbanites. His analysis was historically contextualized and sociologically nuanced.[94]

Although most reviewers of Du Bois's pioneering work have missed it, then and now, his concluding chapter used his survey and other social data to provide damning indictments of white racism as an underlying cause of the distressed black condition in the city. Du Bois closes his 520-page analysis of empirical data with a final section bluntly headed "The Duty of Whites." There he notes that whites may have "a right to object to a race so poor and ignorant and inefficient as the mass of Negroes; but if their policy in the past is parent of much of this condition, and if today by shutting black boys and girls out of most avenues of decent employment they are increasing pauperism and vice, then they must hold themselves largely responsible for the deplorable results."[95] Then he added an additional comment on the ethical responsibilities of white Americans: Racial discrimination is "morally wrong, politically dangerous, industrially wasteful, and socially silly. It is the duty of whites to stop it, and to do so primarily for their own sakes."[96] Writing in the first decade of empirical sociology in the United States, Du Bois combined survey and qualitative data with a sociohistorical analysis that was unafraid to combine social theory with human rights assessments of the need for social change.

Du Bois was a contemporary of the pioneering European sociologists such as Émile Durkheim, who also viewed moral interests as part of sociological research. A long line of sociologists from the nineteenth century to the present day have maintained a similar position. Indeed, over the past two decades a variety of sociologists have argued that moral issues should be part of sociological research and analysis. These include communitarians, such as Amitai Etzioni, who mix ideas from the conservative and progressive traditions, as well as critical feminists such as Dorothy Smith and world-system Marxists like Immanuel Wallerstein.[97]

Those working in the liberation sociology tradition today often accent moral and ethical concerns. They argue that social scientists have ethical obligations not only in regard to the rights of their research subjects but also in regard to all those who may be helped or hurt by the impact of their research.[98] They frequently note the impact of not doing certain kinds of much needed research as well. And they are the most likely social scientists to note the hidden moral assumptions underlying much traditional social science research, such as the utilitarian (e.g., cost-benefit) assumptions lying behind much evaluation and other policy research done by social scientists for government agencies.[99]

CONCLUSION

Liberation sociology assertively orients the decision on which methods, qualitative or quantitative, are to be used to the decision about what data are needed to build a better society and increase social justice. Social life is too complex for researchers to accept a methodological monolith, a reliance on only one type of social science method. We are certainly not arguing here that there is no room for mainstream quantitative research in understanding societal worlds or in developing strategies for liberating the oppressed majorities in many such societal worlds. There is, of course, much room for diversity of thought and methods.

Nevertheless, we must recognize that, over the course of the history of sociology, instrumental positivism has seized many centers of influence and far too much of the important resources within the field. This dominance must be challenged if sociology is to help build better societal worlds. As we have reiterated, central to the liberation sociology tradition is a constant looking for the hidden social realities usually missed by conventional researchers. As we envisage the future of social science, instrumental positivism must be replaced by research methods and interpretive procedures that provide deeper and more holistic pictures of important social realities, especially the continuing realities of human oppression. From our considered viewpoint, liberation sociology should draw on the tradition of such social researchers as Karl Marx and Harriet Martineau in their concern with not trusting the usual surface readings of a society.

Liberation sociology not only tries to find methods that voice the voiceless but also seeks to reveal how oppressive systems create voicelessness—and how governing elites create, maintain, and enhance such exploitative and despotic systems. Doing and publicizing research on the ruling class and the powerful bureaucratic structures it controls is of great importance for ongoing social science research, and such research requires more than conventional opinion surveys.

For example, using multiple research techniques and sources, progressive University of California sociologist Bill Domhoff has published numerous pioneering and nuanced research reports since the 1960s detailing what the ruling class is and how it rules. He is the author of *Who Rules America? The Triumph of the Corporate Rich*; *The Myth of Liberal Ascendancy: Corporate Dominance From the Great Depression to the Great Recession*; and *Class and Power in the New Deal* (with Michael Webber). Four of his books were named to the top fifty best-sellers list in sociology for the years 1950 to 1995.[100] Combining an individual-level analysis with a class-oriented viewpoint, Domhoff has demonstrated that individual capitalists and their close subordinates do rule in the United States, in part, by serving in top government positions. Emphasizing social and organizational networks, Domhoff has also shown the close linkage between land-interested businesspeople operating at the local level and those at the helm of major corporations.[101]

Domhoff is an innovative and critical sociologist who also makes use of the new online media. For example, his WhoRulesAmerica. net website focuses on how power is disseminated and exercised in the United States, building upon his *Who Rules America?* book. The book's subtitle, "The Triumph of the Corporate Rich," points to the wealthy few's political and economic conquests over the past few decades of their opponents—including organized liberals, labor unions, and environmentalists. As Domhoff writes, "The story of how the corporate rich won all the big battles is complicated.... [B]ut the short answer is through lobbying, open and direct involvement in general policy planning on the big issues, participation (in large part through campaign donations) in political campaigns and elections, and through appointments to key decision-making positions in government."[102]

At its best, liberation sociology frequently must develop adversarial methods to get at the procedures and secrets of top social elites and the onerous worlds they often maintain and to suggest ways of fighting back against this misery and subjugation. The countersystem tradition in sociology assumes that all social worlds are changeable—and that ordinary people, often with the aid of liberation social science, have the capability to change the world around them for the human ends of liberty, freedom, and social justice.

CHAPTER 5

Sociology in Action

Sometimes working with community activists, liberation-oriented sociologists have interactively developed concepts, methods, and practices to assist people in their struggles as well as to better understand and improve their everyday lives. In this and the next chapter we examine specific examples of sociological projects that are in this praxis tradition, most with a progressive or countersystem orientation. The examples are not exhaustive but illustrate the range of ways in which a type of liberation sociology has impacted communities, as well as the ways in which community activism has shaped liberation sociology in thought and practice. The first case we turn to is an example of the interaction between progressive community practice and a perspective that is essentially sociological.

MAKING LOCAL REVOLUTIONS: SAUL ALINSKY AND URBAN ALLIANCES

During the change-driven 1960s, as University of California sociologists Bob Blauner and David Wellman have noted, "many of the assumptions of the academic world were challenged by events both external and internal to campuses. There was a growing tendency for powerless and excluded groups to view academics and their activities politically, to criticize their relation to, and responsibility for, existing economic, social, and ideological commitments of social science."[1] Social action by many ordinary Americans was a major source of the pressure on social scientists to face the exploitative and inhumane realities of contemporary US society.

These 1960s movements were preceded by numerous similar movements in earlier decades, efforts that often laid the basis for the successful movements of the 1960s. We now turn to one of the principal community organizers and intellectuals in the history of urban activism and community struggle, activist and practicing sociologist Saul Alinsky (1909–1972). An intellectual activist who worked for and tried to understand the experiences of the oppressed, Alinsky founded the influential Industrial Areas Foundation (IAF) in 1940.

Alinsky's IAF evolved over time and has fostered much community organization across the United States. Indeed, the IAF currently has many affiliates that operate in numerous US states and in Canada, the United Kingdom, and Germany. With many field organizers, the IAF serves numerous coalition organizations linking hundreds of local groups and at least a million families. One IAF statement summarizes the organization's current goals and efforts: "IAF leaders and organizers first create independent organizations, made up of people from all races and all classes, focused on productive improvements in the public arena. IAF members then use those new political realities to invent and establish new social realities." The statement continues with a clear example of their contemporary efforts: "One new reality is the living wage movement in the United States. The first living wage bill was conceived, designed, and implemented by the IAF affiliate in Baltimore in 1994. The second bill was the work of the IAF affiliates in New York City in 1996. Since then, IAF affiliates in Texas, Arizona, and elsewhere have passed living wage legislation."[2] In 2009 the efforts of one such affiliate, the Rio Grande Valley (Texas) organization, garnered assurances from Cameron County, the City of Brownsville, and the Texas Southernmost Community College to increase the starting wages of all employees. In 2013, another affiliate, Austin Interfaith, won from the city of Austin a historic living wage ordinance requiring that any corporation in receipt of future taxpayer incentives must pay at least $11 per hour, the city-established living wage, or their normal wage, whichever is greater.[3]

Over several decades of building up the IAF organization, Saul Alinsky took some ideas from the sociological tradition and honed them as he became one of the more successful community activists in the Western world. From the beginning, a "thoroughly sociological perspective" underlay Alinsky's community organization.[4] Between the 1930s and 1970s, Alinsky created opportunities and procedures for local communities of the poor to do action research on social problems and act on that research to improve their communities. This community activism has, in turn, helped to stimulate a more activist social science.

Alinsky's ideas on community, organization, power, racial groups and crime, the poor, welfare programs, and social movements deserve an important place in the annals of sociological theory, analysis, and practice. As we will see later, Alinsky articulated these ideas in his books and speeches on community organizing, as well as in papers that he presented at the meetings of professional social science associations and charitable organizations.

Building New Organizations

Born in 1909 in a poverty-stricken area of Chicago, Alinsky was the son of Russian immigrants. He graduated from the University of Chicago in archaeology and applied for graduate work in criminology, where he encountered the ideas of urban sociologists. Soon thereafter, appalled by urban poverty and the growth of fascist movements of the 1930s, Alinsky abandoned the academic setting and began to organize poor immigrants in the community known as Back of the Yards, located behind the Chicago stockyards. The grassroots organizing transformed that community into a national model of effective organization against economic and political exploitation and discrimination. Alinsky and his allies pulled together a diverse array of groups, including union locals, bowling leagues, and ethnic clubs. The movement established better services in housing, public health, and welfare for poor residents. Alinsky's efforts focused on the development of community institutions and building community-based power, which enabled poor residents to act more effectively in the political arena and bring social change.[5]

Later on, Alinsky's organizing work and ideas brought him to the attention of other progressive activists and analysts in the United States and overseas. Jacques Maritain, a prominent French philosopher, was impressed with this work and argued that the achievements of the Back of the Yards movement "opened a new road to real democracy."[6] Maritain identified Alinsky as one of two major social revolutionaries in recent times. His other choice was Eduardo Frei, the president of Chile from 1964 to 1970, a man whose administration claimed to implement a program of far-reaching reform. Indeed, communicated through progressive Catholic sources, Alinsky's ideas were also influential in politics in South American countries like Chile.[7]

Using Creative Tactics

In pursuing community change, Alinsky's tactics were creative and irreverent. He sometimes said that revolutionaries should enjoy revolutions—and that such an approach expands participation. For example, in a Rochester campaign to improve conditions in poor communities, Alinsky came up with irreverent proposals. "One suggested tactic was to buy one hundred tickets to the opening performance of the Rochester Symphony Orchestra, a cultural jewel highly prized in the city." These tickets were to be given to residents of poor communities, who would be hosted at a dinner party where the sole food item would be baked beans. "In the end Alinsky never carried through on the tactic, but the threat alone accomplished much."[8]

From the 1940s to the present, the Alinsky tradition of community organization and citizen participation has had a significant impact. Over time, organizations similar to Back of the Yards have been created in several US cities. In the late 1960s, the US Conference of Catholic Bishops initiated the Catholic Campaign for Human Development (CCHD), "a crusade to organize associations of poor Americans to exert economic and political power on behalf of their communities." The CCHD has become an official arm of the US Conference of Catholic Bishops. By 2008 the Catholic Church had spent several hundred million dollars on the campaign. Among its efforts on behalf of low-income Americans has been pressing for more than 100 living wage ordinances, which have so far generated three-quarters of a billion dollars in new wages for modest-income workers in various cities and counties.[9]

Recently, this organization has come out in support of the Justice for Immigrants Campaign, conferring $1 million in special grants to develop broad immigration reform. In an effort to tackle overlooked aspects of poverty, such as a flawed criminal justice system and family life, CCHD has awarded more than $2 million as part of its Strategic National Grants Program.[10] In 2013 the *National Catholic Review* reported that during the past year, CCHD gave more than 214 grants valued at about $9 million to community and economic development organizations committed to providing low-income citizens with a means "to knock down" the "walls" of poverty. Nonetheless, John Gehring, writing for the *National Catholic Review* has noted the following:

> While CCHD has earned national kudos for its essential work over more than four decades, the campaign is also dogged by an increasingly aggressive network of opponents who claim the anti-poverty initiative funds groups that promote "abortion, birth control, homosexuality, and even Marxism." ... Many of these same groups also target the bishops' international development arm, Catholic Relief Services.... When opponents claim that C.C.H.D. is simply a vehicle for an activist liberal agenda, I'm always reminded of the famous quip by the late Brazilian Archbishop Helder Camara: "When I feed the hungry, they call me a saint. When I ask why they have no food, they call me a Communist."[11]

Overall, the CCHD has been greatly influenced by the ideas and work of Alinsky and his urban organizations for community change.

Other movements for change have been linked to Alinsky's ideas and work. Cesar Chavez, longtime leader of the US farmworkers' movement, was hired by Alinsky as a staff member of the Community Service Organization (CSO) in 1953, an action that initiated Chavez's important career as a community organizer.[12] Founded in the late 1940s, the CSO was an organization devoted to the expansion of the political rights and economic opportunities of Mexican Americans. In 1962 Chavez left the CSO and moved to California to begin his efforts to organize a farmworkers' union, which was eventually successful in improving conditions for farmworkers. In a 1984 interview, Chavez noted, "We took [on] the growers as a union but it was really a community organization.... The foundation for the union was laid by the CSO through Alinsky's perception of power and how to strategize for power and Fred Ross's [an Alinsky ally] organizing techniques on how to put people together and make them work together."[13] The union's most successful tactic, one that farmworkers still use, was to launch food boycotts to supplement strikes, slowdowns, and picket lines. Significantly, in 2010, *Organize! The Lessons of the Community Service Organization*, a film on the history of the CSO, premiered nationally on US television. Viewers got to see how poor immigrants were able to move into the mainstream of US society via the CSO's and related legislative campaigns, voter registration drives, and progressive lawsuits.[14]

The best-known umbrella organization associated with Alinsky is the IAF, the national organization that he founded. Over the decades, the IAF has trained many organizers, and it currently serves hundreds of local groups and hundreds of thousands of families in numerous states and overseas. Today, the IAF is "the center of a national network of broad based, multiethnic, interfaith organizations in primarily poor and moderate income communities."[15] Typically, these local organizations are broad coalitions, which include an array of local churches; synagogues; mosques; unions; schools; and environmental, health, and civic organizations. These coalitions get local organizations to listen to, and learn from, each other—and then work to develop coordinated strategies to get local decision-makers to sit down with them to make meaningful changes in community conditions and services. IAF groups work to establish and renew local democracy by empowering citizens through participation and political action.

One IAF organization is the South Bronx Churches (SBC). Founded in the 1980s, the SBC has built a coalition of several dozen churches and politicized many citizens to challenge the local political leadership. The group has petitioned for better schools and affordable housing and won improvements in hospital services. They have challenged the New York City Housing Authority (NYCHA). NBC's *Dateline* aired a story on SBC and the rest of the Metro IAF in 2014, documenting the groups' successful attempts to force the NYCHA to clean up mold and moisture that cause asthma in its many housing units. Their organizing work had led to an important legal settlement with NYCHA and the city of New York that brought important housing changes.[16]

In Texas, the IAF has helped build several successful organizations, including Communities Organized for Public Service (COPS) in San Antonio—one of the more successful such community organizations in the United States. In the 1970s, Ernesto Cortés, an organizer trained by the IAF, was invited to help the Mexican American community inventory its needs and plan action. Using the parishes of the local Catholic church as organizing units and securing aid from the national CCHD, the Alinsky-shaped organization adopted both electoral and confrontation tactics. It thereby secured concessions from the city's traditional white leaders and elected a more representative city council, one with more Mexican Americans on it. Today COPS continues to develop job training programs and to seek significant improvements in local educational systems in San Antonio.[17] In addition, COPS currently identifies family unity, immigrant integration into society, due-process protections, and humanitarian values as priorities for US immigration policies.[18]

COPS and similar Texas organizations constitute a statewide network and have brought together Mexican American Catholics, African American Protestants, and white Protestants to work on issues of common interest. Across the country, various multiracial coalitions work for political candidates, yet they are often temporary formations with cooperation restricted to those at the top. In contrast, the Texas IAF organizations bring together groups that include more than just organizational representatives—such as grassroots people—and unite all participants around a common agenda and commitment.[19]

Mark Warren, a sociologist who has studied the work of the IAF in Texas, has attributed the success of this interracial cooperation to three factors. The first is that, while Latino, black, and white leaders are united in a single organization, considerable autonomy is allowed to the different groups and neighborhoods. A second factor is that the IAF organizations "follow a consensual issues strategy that avoids divisive campaigns and frames issues in a nonracial manner."[20] The third factor is that IAF "taps the religious culture of its social capital base to provide trust for the initial establishment of multiracial organizations and a common identity to sustain cooperation."[21] This has allowed IAF organizations to frame issues in terms of religious and family values. Stanley Ziemba has noted that Alinsky's social-analytical and activist "principles and tactics continue to be employed by community groups across the country, and scores of community organizers he trained personally or inspired continue to strive to make his dream a reality."[22]

THE THINKING OF SAUL ALINSKY: LIBERATION SOCIOLOGY IN ACTION

A Practicing Sociologist

Although trained as an archaeologist and a criminologist, Alinsky was often called a sociologist in the media when he was actively involved in bringing changes to communities, and he accepted that appellation. Various scholarly commentaries, then and recently, have noted the importance of certain sociological ideas in his thinking, including those that guided his organizing. He understood how social problems were rooted in deep-seated structural realities of racial discrimination and impoverishment under a capitalistic economic system. Alinsky's success as a community organizer was based on an insightful understanding of local communities, which was based in part on sociological concepts drawn from his course work in the University of Chicago's department of sociology. Alinsky took sociology courses in the 1920s and 1930s when the sociology department was the country's most influential and a national center for urban social science research.[23]

In the 1920s Robert Park and his associates at the university asserted their view of the city as a laboratory for research. Drawing on urban fieldwork and ideas of earlier women sociologists—though rarely acknowledging the fact—the sociologists at the University of Chicago developed a distinctive approach for studying urban communities, one that Alinsky drew from in building his ideas. For the Chicago sociologists and Alinsky, the city was not only a geographic entity made of streets and buildings but also a matter of customs, organized attitudes, and sentiments.[24] From this perspective, neighborhoods were "natural areas," the organic living units of a metropolis. The neighborhoods had distinctive formal and informal organizations according to the particular social, economic, and political needs of their populations. A crucial idea in this vision of the city is that neighborhoods are not detached but are parts of a larger social structure of the metropolis and are thus affected by social forces at play in that larger context.

Parting Company with the Chicago Sociologists

In his thinking and sociological practice, Alinsky parted company with the Chicago sociologists of the 1920s on at least one key assumption. Unlike many of them, he wanted to bring major social change in urban communities by sociologically informed activism. By the 1920s, most Chicago sociologists viewed these communities as evolutionary worlds that changed slowly through long-term effects of broad social forces. As we have previously noted, most were moving away from the commitments of even earlier sociologists to substantial reform and societal change. Recall the discussion in Chapter 3 on how the white male sociologists at the university ignored or downplayed the earlier field research of the white female sociologists (and some black sociologists) and their support and action for substantial reforms in urban areas.[25]

In contrast, Alinsky's conceptual world envisioned great community changes brought about by purposive human action. Although Alinsky sometimes criticized what he saw as the timidity of the urban social workers in the settlement houses, his thought was much in line with the thinking of Chicago's earlier sociologist of the poor, Jane Addams. Although the full development of this liberation sociology, and certainly of major societal reformation, remains to be accomplished for the United States, Alinsky is one of the sociological pioneers who has pointed the way to such a liberation framework.

Human Dignity and Social Activism

When Alinsky met Jacques Maritain, a leading French humanist and philosopher, in the 1940s, they both had developed a distinctive system of ideas about human nature. The Jewish leftist from Chicago and the Catholic philosopher from France became friends, and they shared the same views on the humanity of ordinary people. From the 1930s forward, Maritain broke with conservative thought within the Catholic Church and called on Catholics to develop a stronger social conscience. During the 1930s, when the church was supporting reactionary monarchies and fascist regimes, Maritain took a progressive position within the church.[26] Thus, in some ways he was an early forerunner of what would later be termed *liberation theology*. As a humanist, Maritain pressed for the recognition of the dignity and rights of ordinary workers, of the common people.[27]

At home among social philosophers, Alinsky shared his friend's faith in common people. He developed his own ideal type of the "radical" with this orientation in mind. At the most general level, such a radical is a person who has a deep feeling for other people—in contrast to most liberals and conservatives whom Alinsky thought feared, distrusted, or tolerated the poor. Yet he did not idealize the oppressed:

> I do not think that people are specially just or charitable or noble because they're unemployed and live in crummy housing and see their kids without any kind of future and feel the weight of every indignity that society can throw at them, sophisticated or nakedly. Too often I've seen the have-nots turn into haves and become just as crummy as the haves they used to envy.[28]

Alinsky's sociological acumen comes through clearly in such penetrating social analyses.

The Idea of Democracy in Action

In his classic book *Reveille for Radicals*, Alinsky develops a historically informed sociological analysis. He explains that in early US history, the term *democrat* was often a synonym for *radical*. About these early democrats, Alinsky writes: "They fought for the right of men to govern themselves, for the right of men to walk erect as free men and not grovel before kings, for the Bill of Rights, for the abolition of slavery, for public education, and for everything decent and worthwhile."[29] As he sees it, activist radicals can be found throughout this country's history. Unlike many other commentators on early US history, Alinsky singles out perhaps the most radical democrat among the founders, Thomas Paine, who fought to abolish monarchical oppression and African slavery. Reviewing later history, he notes the many Americans who ran the Underground Railroad and the numerous labor radicals who secured the workers' right to organize. Radicals "are to be found wherever and whenever America moves close to the fulfillment of its democratic dream."[30]

Alinsky anchored his ideas and methods explicitly in democratic ideals:

> Democracy is a way of life and not a formula to be "preserved" like jelly. It is a process—a vibrant, living sweep of hope and progress which constantly strives for the fulfillment of its objective in life— the search for truth, justice and dignity of man. There can be no democracy unless it is dynamic democracy. When our people cease to participate—to have a place in the sun—then all of us will wither in the darkness of decadence.[31]

Democracy, seen as active citizen participation, is a means to change society. To achieve it, Alinsky argues that radicals must work at "the awakening of our people from the abysmal apathy which has resulted in the decay and breaking down of a large part of those few ideals which mankind has desperately clung to."[32] Community-based organizations of people participating democratically are a way to emancipation.[33] By means of this democratic participation, the people "become informed, educated, and above all develop faith in themselves, their fellow men, and their future. The key is for them, the people, to have the opportunity and power to implement their decisions."[34]

For Alinsky, democracy is not just an end in itself. As he put it in his book *Rules for Radicals*, "it is the best political means available toward the achievement of these values."[35] By these values he meant freedom, equality, and justice. Alinsky was constantly concerned with the moral character of human life, and especially with showing the have-nots how to take illegitimate power away from the haves.[36]

Activist Organizations: The Broad View

Alinsky reacted against conceptual approaches that isolated problems from their social contexts to understand them. In this manner, he thought along the holistic lines of earlier activist sociologists like Addams and Du Bois. Problems such as those of delinquency and crime should not be understood as separate social problems; they are both facets of the larger problem of social inequality. He began his sociological and community-oriented writing in the 1930s. In 1934 Alinsky published his first sociological article, titled "A Sociological Technique in Clinical Criminology." There he argued that to communicate with and research those in trouble with the law, one should use the "vocabularies characteristic of the inmate's community."[37] Moreover, in 1937 he presented an important paper at the American Prison Association in which he showed the close relationship between the capitalistic system and the individualistic approaches common in mainstream criminology. He sent the paper to C. Wright Mills, who thought it was a fine paper and congratulated Alinsky on his sociological "radicalism," radicalism here in the sense of going to the "roots" of societal problems.[38]

In Alinsky's view, unemployment, disease, undernourishment, demoralization, and crime are parts of a larger societal picture and are not separable social problems.[39] This holistic view of social problems led Alinsky to develop broad activist organizations that were not organized just to deal with one community problem such as troubled youth. As he saw it, citizens narrowly organized to deal with one local issue will often abstain from other controversial efforts when those efforts are needed to meet squarely larger social issues and to courageously rebuild local communities. The purpose of organizations of the poor is to battle all social forces that create poverty and inequality in cities.[40] As he put it in writing about the Back of the Yards movement, local change-oriented organizations should be "completely cognizant of the place of their community in the general mosaic of communities which make up their nation."[41] Radicals have traditionally seen the labor movement as the way to bring economic justice and human betterment, but when he examined the movement, he found it often wanting. Unions and other local organizations should look at the world through the lens of what some sociologists have called the "total social phenomenon."[42]

Alinsky's argument for local organizations having a citywide vision and for unions developing a broad set of social goals is similar to the view of the social world of leading European sociologists. Consider, for example, Marcel Mauss, Émile Durkheim's socialist nephew. Mauss argued that social phenomena are not just economic, religious, familial, political, and the like, but that all these dimensions are aspects of the same social whole. Social life does not take place divided into these neat categories but rather all at one time and all together. Recall our discussion of Marx's dialectical perspective. He, too, insisted that social phenomena come with many dimensions embedded into one comprehensive whole. For Alinsky, as for Mauss and Marx, social life is always a holistic and constantly interconnected phenomenon.

Respect for Racial and Ethnic Diversity

One of the harshest criticisms made by Alinsky in regard to labor unions was his disapproval of the white-male-led labor movement's attitudes and practices toward workers of color. Like corporations, most labor unions then practiced racial discrimination. Some unions excluded African Americans by explicit provisions, whereas others did so informally. Alinsky condemned these practices as destroying the possibility for effective coalitions across key social groups.[43]

In his astute organizing book, *Reveille for Radicals*, Alinsky develops the idea that the people of the United States are as socially diverse as any people on the planet. He adopts a broad sociological view of the country's diversity: US residents represent a bridge between the narrow nationalism of the past and a new humankind, a people of the world. Yet, although many people claim to fight against racial and ethnic prejudices, they are often rather prejudiced themselves. Assessing the perspectives of a broad range of Americans—from Irish Catholics and white Protestants to Jewish Americans, African Americans, and Mexican Americans—he draws on historical data to argue that they all have their prejudices and inconsistencies in regard to yet other groups. From this standpoint, he then calls on all groups to join a coalition against intergroup hostility, inequality of opportunity, economic insecurity, and educational inequality. Once again, a holistic sociological view is aggressively asserted.

Capitalism and Left Analysis

Although Alinsky repeatedly declared that he was not a Marxist, he did agree with Marx that capitalism had failed and that economic control in a capitalist country like the United States is associated with substantial political power. To achieve full human emancipation and realization, modern capitalism has to be effectively overcome. Like Marx, Alinsky suggested that this would not happen through evolutionary change but rather through collective and purposive action. Alinsky wrote about and worked to accumulate significant power in the hands of the community organizations of common people—not just workers but much larger groups of ordinary people.

Alinsky and the many community activists his organization has trained over decades see much left-wing analysis, both that of social scientists and that of general commentators, as too abstract and removed from the everyday life of ordinary people. Traditional leftists look too much to the white male workers in the working class for change. Supported by activist theorists like Alinsky, community activists often argue that successful social movements must cross traditional class and racial lines.[44] In contrast, critics on the left have often viewed the IAF-inspired community and other populist movements as too grounded in religion and ethnicity and as too localized and parochial; community movements are viewed too focused on individual and family consumption and not enough on the worker-capitalist struggle.[45]

Alinsky and the Settlement House Approach

Alinsky had a critical view of traditional social work and settlement house approaches to the poor, even to the point of some harsh attacks on women activists who had helped spread the settlement movement in Chicago and other cities.[46] Indeed, reflecting the sexist thinking of his day, Alinsky was skeptical about women doing effective field organizing.

Alinsky's organizing approach differed from the approach of many women activists, including those who had founded the settlement house movement (see Chapter 3). The most famous of these settlement houses was Chicago's Hull House, founded by sociologist-activists Jane Addams and Ellen Gates Starr. These settlement house activists were pioneers in efforts to improve the lives of the poor of numerous cities, including Chicago. They pressed successfully for better public services for the poor and often worked for radical reforms in regard to workplace and labor conditions, the protection of children, immigrants' rights, and women's rights.

This settlement house work by these women sociologists and activists was already well developed in Chicago when Alinsky started his Back of the Yards organizing. Yet, he and his fellow male organizers tended to overlook this history and to view the women as do-gooders mostly doing charity work, rather than the type of adversarial sociologist-activists whose research-based activism could and did accomplish real social or political change.[47]

Alinsky accepted the idea of political power being a zero-sum game. As Randy Stoecker and Susan Stall have noted, he believed that "you either have more of it or less of it, and if you have less the only way to get more is to take it from someone else. Alinsky was adamant that real power could not be given, but only taken."[48] As a result, Alinsky directed his organizing of poor urbanites toward singling out a few elite targets and isolating them from other parts of the elite. In contrast, the women settlement workers and sociologists did not accept the idea of the zero-sum game in organizing the poor. They saw power as more or less unlimited and accented the creation of "co-active power," which was "based on human interdependence and the development of all within the group or the community through collaboration."[49] From the women's holistic perspective on organizing, the empowerment of the poor entails developing their self-confidence, building up their individual and collective skills and resources, and enabling them to develop a critical view of their social and political environments. Cooperative organizing builds lasting communities and is more effective than an in-your-face adversarial approach.[50]

As Stoecker and Stall see it, the Alinsky approach emphasizes conflict, opposition, and winning, which tend to be the traditional masculine-role approach. Many men are taught to be aggressive and competitive and to deal with confrontations head-on, while women are more likely to be taught connectedness and relationship building. From the women's perspective, sensitivity to others and to building relationships is centrally important in organizing and coalition building. Clearly, in particular local situations, the two approaches can be complementary and can be combined for more effective local efforts to bring social and political changes.

Alinsky and Organized Labor

In his sociological perspective, Alinsky had a critical view of organized capitalists and organized labor. Both are groups that accumulate economic power ordinarily used for their own ends, not those of the larger community. A successful change strategy requires a move away from the "jungle of laissez faire capitalism" to one where broader human values are relished.[51] The control of production facilities by a small capitalist class is injurious for the masses of people because it brings about a concentration of social and economic power that prevents a democratic and egalitarian way of life. Alinsky developed a critical analysis of the labor movement as being too dependent on capitalism. Organized labor is not the likely vehicle to achieve a more democratic society because it too fully participates in that capitalistic system. Because it is predicated upon bargaining between employers and employees, the union movement envisions only, or mainly, an employer-employee type of society. Ever the sociologist, Alinsky used empirical instances from the history of labor and business to support his critical view that organized labor has often sought "to secure its own interests at the expense of both technological progress and the general public."[52]

However, the capitalistic system is basically responsible for much pain and oppression. There is too much focus on money, profits, and wages. In contrast, true radicals "want to do away with economic injustice, insecurity, unequal opportunity, prejudice, bigotry, imperialism, all chauvinistic barriers of isolationism and other nationalistic neuroses. They want a world where life for man will be guided by a morality which is meaningful—and where the values of good and evil will be measured not in terms of money morals but in social morals."[53] Clearly, this moral community cannot be fully accomplished under modern capitalism with its heavy accent on individual or corporate profit.

Yet, in spite of his stinging sociological critique, Alinsky was generally in favor of unions, because many radical activists could be found there. Even with their weaknesses, many unions have more democratic participation than most other US organizations.[54] Radicals, he contended, must work to change the philosophy of the labor movement into one "whereby it will clearly recognize that the welfare of its constituents does not depend solely upon an improvement in economic earnings but upon a general improvement of all of the standards in the life of the worker."[55] Thereby, Alinsky proposed that the labor movement help build a broad people's organization that could bargain aggressively and effectively beyond the factory gate.

Gaining Power by Conscious Action

For Alinsky, and most of his followers today, a major aim of people's organizations is to become powerful so that they can sit at the same political table with established elite decision-makers and achieve their community goals. Goals are defined in a commonly agreed upon program of principles and action. This is the opposite of welfare-state programs, which are usually designed to fit people into their oppressive situations. People should not be "adjusted," Alinsky wrote, "so they will live in hell and like it too." He adds that many "apparently local problems are in reality malignant microcosms of vast conflicts, pressures, stresses, and strains of the entire social order."[56]

In Alinsky's sociologically informed perspective, communities do not develop a strong political identity as a result of unintentional actions, but rather as a result of a conscious response to common political-economic enemies. This is why Alinsky developed strategies to use the often-negative responses of city officials and local media to build community identity and action. The identification of common enemies, who responded negatively, enabled local communities to overcome to some degree their racial, ethnic, class, and religious differences in seeking to better social conditions in their communities.

Alinsky's Legacies

Saul Alinsky put his education in urban sociology to good use for community change. Over his lifetime, he was a practicing sociologist with strong connections to the sociology discipline. He had contacts with numerous progressive sociologists, such as C. Wright Mills and Robert Lynd, with the latter serving on the IAF board when he was a sociology professor at Columbia University.[57] Indeed, in the 1950s, Alinsky was asked to teach a sociology course on social disorganization at Catholic University in Washington, DC.

Alinsky was active as a community organizer and sociological theorist of citizen action. He viewed cities from a strong sociological perspective and constantly encouraged community leaders to set local struggles within a broader conceptual and action framework highlighting a range of social justice goals. This broader view fostered a better vision of community futures and facilitated successful coalitions for community improvement across otherwise divisive lines of race and religion. Some groups have used the sociologically informed perspective of Alinsky to develop action research projects supporting relatively radical political agendas. In this fashion, sociologically oriented research has helped to change the social or political face of numerous US communities.

Beyond his impact on community organization and movements, Alinsky has had a significant impact on social science research and thinking. We did a computerized search of the Social Science Citation Index database and found hundreds of citations to Saul Alinsky's books and other publications. (These are citations in articles in social science journals only and do not include his likely many citations in progressive magazines or social science books.) Alinsky's ideas and actions are cited in research and commentary articles in journals as diverse as the *Journal of Social Issues, Human Relations, Human Organization, Crime and Delinquency, Theological Studies, Urban Life, Social Science Quarterly, Social Science and Medicine, Community Theory, Journal of Urban History*, and the *Sociology of Sport*.[58] Clearly, Alinsky's action-oriented ideas continue to inspire many social scientists and other researchers and community activists.

Alinsky's ideas have been consequential for those working in the progressive sociology tradition, including the authors of this book. Indeed, we all read Alinsky's books early in our careers and were influenced by his efforts to dovetail sociological ideas and research with efforts to bring progressive societal change. Other social scientists have noted the influence of Alinsky's writings, or of participation in IAF organizations, in their own personal development toward community activism or toward a liberation sociology perspective.[59]

In August 2008, when Barack Obama received the Democratic nomination for the US presidency, Saul Alinsky's son, L. David Alinsky, wrote about some of the continuing impact of his father's model for organizing on Obama's political campaign:

> The Democratic National Convention had all the elements of the perfectly organized event, Saul Alinsky style. Barack Obama's training in Chicago by the great community organizers is showing its effectiveness. It is an amazingly powerful format, and the method of my late father always works to get the message out and get the supporters on board. When executed meticulously and thoughtfully, it is a powerful strategy for initiating change and making it really happen. Obama learned his lesson well. I am proud to see that my father's model for organizing is being applied successfully beyond local community organizing to affect the Democratic campaign in 2008. It is a fine tribute to Saul Alinsky as we approach his 100th birthday.[60]

Nonetheless, the fact that the creative sociological analyses in Alinsky's articles, addresses, and books are not included in most sociology textbooks—either in the theory or in practice discussions—yet again suggests an ingrained resistance to sociologically oriented activism within most mainstream traditions of sociology.

ACTIVIST SOCIOLOGY: A COLLEGE SETTING

Sometimes high school or college students, convinced of the need to build a more just and egalitarian United States, seem a bit overwhelmed and ask, "But what can one person really do to bring change?" Unquestionably, Saul Alinsky, like his activist-sociology predecessors Addams and Du Bois, made a difference as an individual, a person committed to progressive and positive changes in the conditions faced by the poor and oppressed. Let us now briefly examine the example of another bold sociologist who has more recently made a real difference in the direction of building a more just and egalitarian society.

Fighting Racism: Making a Difference

In the mid-1990s, Noel Cazenave, a young sociology professor at the University of Connecticut, decided to teach a course specifically on "white racism," for which one of our books was to be a textbook.[61] Cazenave proposed it first as an experimental special topics course.[62] The sociology department approved it, but from the beginning, Cazenave had difficulty in securing approval from his college's Committee on Curricula and Courses. In October 1995, he was told by the chair of the college committee that his course proposal was tabled and that some white faculty members were "jumping up and down about the course title."[63] At a meeting two weeks later, the course was again tabled. There were long discussions in the meetings about this course proposal. Such debate was unusual since most experimental topics courses were routinely approved. According to reports from committee members, some on the committee wanted the title to be watered down, and in the second meeting "questions were raised about the appropriate subject matter of sociology and about the legitimacy of sociology as a discipline." One member of the committee was quoted as saying the title was a "derogatory term."[64] (Of relevance in understanding these events is doubtless the fact that Professor Cazenave is African American and that the committee had no African American members.)

Before the third meeting of the college committee, the chair received numerous letters and messages from the campus and from around the country in support of the course. This time the experimental course was approved by voice vote, with some expressed opposition. Interestingly, the local mass media now got involved, yet did not focus so much on the academic freedom issue as on the fact that the course had been approved. Some university committee members were cited in a local newspaper as having negative views of the course. They said "the course is itself racist" and "offensive to whites because it implies that whites are morally defective."[65] The next step was for the course to be approved by a faculty meeting of the College of Arts and Sciences, ordinarily a routine matter. Again, there was strong vocal opposition from some white faculty, and the vote was close, but in favor of allowing the course.[66]

Even though this was just one experimental course, it got considerable political and media attention. On and off campus, whites tried to end the course. One white professor argued that "Cazenave clearly has an agenda that has no place in a university that should be a house of dispassionate inquiry."[67] Another professor, who voted against the course in the committee, was quoted as saying that any course with a racially inflammatory title would have stirred debate. Not surprisingly, local politicians weighed in on the matter. The course's "title alone is an example of racism and discrimination," fumed Connecticut state Senator Louis De Luca in a letter to the university's president requesting that the course be eliminated.[68]

Campus and state newspapers in this supposedly "liberal" northern state gave the issue considerable negative attention. A commentary article in the *Hartford Courant* by Laurence Cohen, the director of the Yankee Institute for Public Policy Studies, attacked the course as symptomatic of the "peculiar and ill-conceived" courses that "lurk in black studies, women's studies, and sociology departments across the land." After hearing Cazenave lecture on the controversy, Cohen even wrote that his own sources at the university said Cazenave had a "racial agenda so strongly implanted in his psyche that you want to jump across the faculty lounge and strangle him."[69] National papers were more cautious. The *Chronicle of Higher Education*, the major national education weekly, featured what it called a "skirmish." The *Chronicle's* coverage opened with this sentence: "If Noel Cazenave had called his new course 'Racism in American Society,' it probably wouldn't have set off any alarms."[70]

Cazenave did not let this swirl of criticism deter him. He wrote carefully reasoned articles for the newspapers and gave local community lectures explaining why this type of sociology course was very necessary to improve the social health of the United States. He also spoke at other universities and at professional social science meetings about the course and its opposition. In one lecture, he explained why he wished to teach this course: "Why do it? Why risk the danger? Because it's there! White racism exists. Only through breaking the yolk of denial of the existence of white racism can we begin to address the problem. As long as white racism remains an invisible and a forbidden topic, it is virtually impossible to ameliorate."[71] The hostile white reaction to the course, he noted, offered a case history "on the militant refusal to not only acknowledge the existence of white racism in this country, but to even allow the words 'white racism' to be spoken." One conclusion Cazenave drew from his experience is that "we should organize to have white racism courses taught in every school in America."[72]

Researching the Protests

In a later research paper on the course-related events, Cazenave and his colleague Darlene Alvarez-Maddern offered an even deeper sociological analysis. They suggested that the course controversy was an instance of symbolic conflict that "occurs when groups compete over the language used in the discourse."[73] The struggle over the course showed how racial symbols are often linked to ideological power. The authors carefully examined statements that were critical or supportive of the course, statements in newspaper articles and commentaries, cartoon editorials, and letters to editors, as well as commentaries on the Internet, anonymous materials placed in Cazenave's department mailbox, and notes taken at the college's curriculum committee meetings. The data on those who opposed the course on the campus showed that opposition came exclusively from white male faculty members: "No published criticisms of the course were made by European-American female faculty or students, or by faculty or students of color of either sex."[74] Since the committee had more professors from the natural sciences than from the social sciences, one might speculate that opposition to the course came from "hard scientists" critical of social science methodology and concepts. However, as Cazenave and Alvarez-Maddern indicate, this was unlikely to have been the main source of opposition because other social science courses were routinely approved. In addition, some of the course's most vocal critics were not natural scientists.

The largest categories of criticism of the course were (1) that it had a racially offensive title and (2) that it was inflammatory and racially divisive. The first type of criticism suggests the notion that the "White Racism" title is offensive to whites, while the second type of criticism contains a claim that the title would worsen "racial relations" among different groups. One letter from the president of a manufacturing company began with "I am personally insulted." Interestingly, his letter about this alleged insult concluded with an insult of his own: The writer noted what he saw as the low "IQ" of the substantially black jury that acquitted O. J. Simpson of murder. Other whites attacked sociology professor Cazenave personally by calling him "nutty" or attributing the course to an agenda of leftist propaganda.[75]

In addition, significant positive commentary came from some campus sources. One student responded that he did not feel offended because the course was about racial structures deeply rooted in this country. One professor who wrote to the curriculum committee noted: "Several weeks ago a US president gave a speech in Texas calling for all Americans to work hard to combat—you guessed it—'white racism.'

Perhaps the first step in combating it is to name it."[76] Other arguments in favor of the course addressed the educational benefits from teaching a subject that badly needs to be addressed, cited the appropriateness of the course for the sociology curriculum, and noted the course's carefully conceived format. Moreover, the department of sociology at the university passed a set of resolutions, one of which stated what should have been obvious: "Naming the problem of white racism is not equivalent to claiming that all white Americans are racists, nor does naming the problem express racism or animosity."[77]

In their research presentation, Cazenave and Alvarez-Maddern noted that their focus on racial discourse and commentary neglected the local context and power relations responsible for the course's eventual approval. In the end, the support of the students and the sociology department faculty was important. However, "the ultimate department consensus," wrote Cazenave and Alvarez-Maddern, "did not emerge quickly, easily, or naturally. In some instances, it was forged through intense internal conflict."[78] Also important was a carefully researched, positive article in the major local newspaper, the *Hartford Courant*. The article was written by Frances Grandy Taylor, a reporter who interviewed opponents of the course, attended class lectures, and talked with students enrolled in the course. After this well-researched article appeared, opposition to the course dissipated. It was clear from the article that the sociology course was very solid and scholarly.[79]

Action-oriented sociologists often take into account the larger contexts. Cazenave wisely took the issue outside the University of Connecticut, something that irritated some social science colleagues. "While there was more of an element of risk in taking the issue off-campus, it was feared that otherwise, the matter might be settled by a group of largely affluent, European-American male faculty members who were unlikely to have experienced white racism, or any other form of social oppression."[80]

Later Events

In February 1997, the White Racism course was approved as a permanent course without further conflict, and later, at the request of graduate students, Cazenave began teaching a graduate seminar on the topic. To meet the undergraduate demand for the course, in the spring of 2000 the class was offered as an interactive distance-learning course televised to regional campuses of the University of Connecticut. Clearly, there was demand for candid discussion about the problem of and solutions for white racism. Cazenave has continued effective teaching on the subject.

This success story in activist-scholar sociology required the courage and superior scholarship of a committed sociology professor. It required an educational strategy aimed at opening the debate on racism issues in the larger community. White racism is a "significant social phenomenon and a major social problem which has devastating consequences for many people in modern societies. Neither the structure nor the dynamics of these societies can be understood without understanding white racism."[81] In developing his course, Cazenave was aware that, although racial prejudice is a widely accepted field of inquiry, systemic white racism and its many dimensions are not. He had reviewed the American Sociological Association's publication on teaching racial and ethnic relations and found that the only course among three dozen featured in this important teaching resource that had the words *white* and *racism* in its syllabus was his own.[82] The titles of the conventional sociology courses there revealed a strong tendency to focus on the victims of racial oppression rather than its white perpetrators.

As with all examples of liberation sociology, there was a significant personal cost. In proposing the course, Cazenave became the target of strong personal attacks and intense scrutiny by his colleagues and administrators. His teaching was publicly commented upon and criticized by a broad array of students, colleagues, and journalists. In many ways, he became the messenger who was blamed for the message. Like W. E. B. Du Bois long before him, Cazenave was operating as an "organic intellectual," a scholar-activist representing the interests and concerns of those directly oppressed by US racism.

We should underscore the point that cases like those of Professor Noel Cazenave raise the issue of personal and career risks that scholar-teachers take in doing liberation sociology and other emancipatory social science. From one point of view, these risks may seem rather daunting, thereby discouraging some younger or newer teachers and scholars from doing this important teaching and research. However, in the Cazenave case, as in others like it, a major and necessary way to counter such risks emerged: finding an important local or national network of experienced scholar-teachers and other colleagues who can provide significant support and mentoring to assist in these campus and disciplinary struggles. Most liberation scholar-teachers need to find colleagues across disciplines in their college settings or in departments in other colleges and universities with whom they can talk about their problems and from whom they can get moral support and significant ideas for strategies to counter those trying to limit their academic freedom, such as racially or politically reactionary activists and politicians who have periodically tried to stifle discussion in US colleges and universities.

Making a Difference: A Community Setting

Working with Immigrant Activists

Let us now consider a sociologist working for liberation sociology goals outside an academic setting. Operating in a rural area near San Jose, California, the organization called ¡Vote! is nonprofit, nonpartisan, and community based. Its members have included many immigrants to the United States and their family members. Among other goals, the organization works for expanded citizenship and better job opportunities in various areas of California. Founded in the 1990s in response to California's Proposition 187, which tried to restrict immigrants' use of social services, this citizenship project was created by Mexican American farm and cannery workers active in the movement for union democracy and racial justice. The movement initially focused on union members, but the activists soon realized that immigrants too needed assistance, for they were facing exclusionary welfare and immigration laws. Thus, !Vote! expanded to organize and serve the larger Latino communities.[83]

Also known as the Citizenship Project, ¡Vote! has been affiliated with the Community Studies Program at the University of California–Santa Cruz. Paul Johnston, a sociologist, was brought in as a researcher and executive director for the group and developed a staff of Mexican American organizers.[84] With this staff, ¡Vote! has run several important community service projects, including a naturalization campaign helping thousands apply for citizenship and a Freedom School where citizens-to-be can learn English and study for citizenship and participation in public life. ¡Vote!, the name of the project, refers to campaigns to educate and mobilize voters. In addition, a strike-support program has helped the labor movement fight for a better economic future for local communities.[85]

Sociological Reflections

Johnston's extensive involvement in this type of sociological practice is another example of how one sociologist can make a difference. He has provided autobiographical details. "This experience," Johnston noted, "has convinced me of the viability of this model of sociological practice, and has led me to begin envisioning a form of training and a model collegial organization (an alternative to the pre–information age university department) which would support and promote it. I hope someday to help build such an institution."[86] In our interview with him, Johnston reported that he began to study social theory intensely "through reading and practical work, at the same time that I dropped out of Stanford as a freshman at the height of the Vietnam War (on the occasion of the invasion of Cambodia, the Kent and Jackson State shootings, my moral revulsion [in regard to] student deferments for kids like myself, a particularly distasteful experience with my advisor and teacher William Shockley, and an interest in working for the United Farm Workers)."[87]

Some years later, Johnston returned to college and enrolled at the University of California. His intention was "to return to practical work, better informed or at least more confident of my understanding. It didn't sink in for several years that I was being trained to be a professor."[88] Johnston took a job at Yale University, but after being promoted to associate professor he grew restless. He returned to California right after the passage of Proposition 187 to start "a mode of scholarly practice in which research and writing would be combined with participation, rather than with teaching."[89] Like Alinsky and Cazenave, Paul Johnston's research and activism are grounded in an understanding of the importance of social justice. He has described his general view:

> I learn best about a phenomenon (usually, because of the nature of my research, an organization or a social movement) by participating in it, working on it, acquiring an almost tactile feel for it in the same sense that we know our clothes by wearing them. . . . I am well aware of the dangers that involvement poses to scholarship; I understand, however, that we are all always participants in the settings we study even when we imagine that we are not, and that an essential avenue to insight is analysis of the effects of our participation on the questions we ask and neglect to ask and the things we see and fail to see. I believe that the best empirical research and theoretical work can come from engaged researchers who struggle with their own bias. But I confess that though I am fascinated, obsessed, addicted to that purely scientific challenge of understanding social processes, my main motive for doing sociology—both scholarly and practical—is a commitment to social change.[90]

New Destinations: More Immigrant Projects

Let us next consider a sociologist working for liberation sociology goals in Chicago, a city with an enduring history of immigrant activism, including being the first municipality to hold a massive march on behalf of Latino immigrants in the mid-2000s and one of the first with a church that offered sanctuary to undocumented immigrants confronting deportation. [91] A sociology professor at the University of Illinois, Nilda Flores-Gonzalez is codirector of New Destinations in an Old Gateway. An ongoing research study, the project analyzes how localities in the

Chicago area have responded to high levels of immigration from Latin America over recent decades. Flores-Gonzalez and her social science associates have explored how different immigrant destinations—for example, cities, suburbs, rural areas—experience and deal with new immigrants; how various localities experience similar or dissimilar policy-making processes; how proximity to a traditional immigrant gateway impacts policy in new destinations; and how local, regional, and national government and non-government actors participate in local political processes to influence policy in these new destinations.[92]

Flores-Gonzalez is also codirector of the Immigrant Mobilization Project, a collaborative research effort aimed at providing a multidisciplinary analysis of recent immigrant rights rallies in Chicago, and more generally, of the immigrant rights movement in the city and its connection to the national movement.[93]

In view of the demographic and political significance of immigration issues affecting millions of undocumented workers and their families, and the unique character of this immigration rights activism in a population that some have routinely deemed to be disengaged, Flores-Gonzalez's work offers considerable social insights. Her work reveals the social roots of the immigration rights movement and the public policy consequences of this activism and highlights emerging Latino political goals and concerns.[94] Flores-Gonzalez has contributed considerably to sociological understandings of differences in local immigration policies across the United States, including anti-immigrant policies that are periodically ruled as unconstitutional by US courts.

Immigrant Families in Crisis

Similarly, social scientist Leah Schmalzbauer is dedicated to researching contemporary immigration issues and working for a more socially just world. "It's an interesting time in Montana to study immigration," she explains. "The fastest-growing immigrant communities in the United States are in the West, Midwest and Southeast. Jackson Hole, Wyoming, actually has the fastest growing Latino community in the country in terms of percentage growth."[95]

Schmalzbauer, a professor of sociology at Amherst College, has seen her work cited in the *New York Times* and the *International Herald Tribune*. She focuses her research on immigrant families in crisis. Her book *Striving and Surviving* was the first daily-life study of undocumented immigrants and the first transnational analysis of Honduran families. Based on data she collected in Honduras and the United States from in-depth interviews, participant observation, diaries, and focus groups, *Striving and Surviving* focuses on the experiences and prospects of migrant labor in the United States, particularly as it concerns the "American dream." It also explores the ways in which immigrant families negotiate their difficult caretaking responsibilities, both financial and emotional, while struggling and surviving in a transnational space.[96]

Her second book, *The Last Best Place*, draws on years of ethnographic research on Mexican migrants' gendered experiences of legality in rural Montana. "Montana presents labor migrants with unique challenges," she explains. "Limited or no translation services in public schools, hospitals, jails and social service agencies, the impossibility of anonymity in one of the 'whitest' states in the country, and vast mountainous terrain that is difficult to traverse, all contribute to the construction of migrant legality." She shows, too, how many immigrants "are members of mixed status families, in which one or both parents are unauthorized and their children are citizens, [and how this] presents additional challenges."[97]

Explaining her path to activist sociology, Schmalzbauer told us that she grew up in a tight-knit family. "My mom instilled in me a strong sense of social justice," she explains. "Having grown up on a poor farm in rural Minnesota, my mom was determined that her children would know a bigger world and that they would understand the inequalities that exist within it. She was very firm in her dictate that we would learn to speak Spanish, that we would recognize our privilege, and that we would use whatever privilege we had to work for a more socially just world."[98]

Schmalzbauer attended the University of New Hampshire, where her Spanish professor taught her about US involvement in the civil wars in Central America. She was outraged by the role the United States was playing in the terror there and joined the Progressive Student Network. Through her student activism, she became connected with the New England Central America Network and the Nicaragua Network. She became their student representative in 1990 and traveled to Nicaragua on peace delegations. When she graduated, she was hired as the Nicaragua organizer for the New England Central America Network (NECAN).[99]

As the wars in Central America wound down and US policy shifted to economic intervention, NECAN reworked its mission to focus on the impact of economic austerity and neoliberalism on poor people throughout the Americas. NECAN joined forces with ARISE for Social Justice, a domestic anti-poverty organization in Massachusetts. Among the most transformative experiences of Schmalzbauer's life was traveling to Central America with activists from ARISE and witnessing the immediate connections that sparked between poor and working class activists from the United States and Nicaragua. Many of their issues were similar. "It was my first realization that globalization was upon us," she said.[100] Moreover, in 1996, Schmalzbauer was hired to reach out to the growing Latino immigrant community in Minneapolis and

Saint Paul to participate in welfare reform education. This was the first time she had worked with an immigrant community. "What I realized through my work in Minnesota," she explains, "was that the immigrants I was getting to know from Central America were fleeing the wars and economic policies that I had struggled against when I worked for the Nicaragua Network. Immigration was a part of the legacy of military and economic intervention."[101]

These diverse experiences, and a love of teaching, led Schmalzbauer to pursue a PhD in sociology and write a dissertation on an immigrant rights group (Proyecto Hondureño). She recounts thus:

> In 1997 I began a PhD program in sociology at Boston College (BC). I had never taken a sociology class, but sociology seemed to encompass my passions. Boston College was an amazing place to be. The theme of its sociology program is "Social Economy and Social Justice: Gender, Race, Class in a Global Context." There I met sociologists who were committed to social justice. Juliet Schor, Bill Gamson, Charlotte Ryan, Stephen Pfohl, Charlie Derber, and Lisa Dodson were incredibly influential in my graduate training; all professors whose work was overtly political and engaged. I credit Boston College with training me as an activist sociologist. Not only were my professors at BC prominent scholars, they were incredible teachers.... I absolutely love to teach and I love to do research. I use a social justice lens for both. My research is ethnographic and community-based.[102]

ACTIVIST STUDENTS: CONNECTING CAMPUSES AND COMMUNITIES

The United Students Against Sweatshops

United Students Against Sweatshops (USAS) is a grassroots organization run entirely by sociologically informed college students and other youth. According to the USAS website, they "envision a world in which society and human relationships are organized cooperatively, not competitively. We struggle towards a world in which all people live in freedom from oppression, in which people are valued as whole human beings rather than exploited in a quest for productivity and profits."[103]

With affiliated locals on more than 150 campuses, the USAS is the largest youth-directed, student labor campaign organization in the United States. As in other countersystem projects, the USAS's mandate is premised on a desire to change to make a societal difference. In collaboration with supportive social scientists and worker and community organizations, USAS affiliates run local and nationwide campaigns for economic justice, while educating students using social science data on the negative effects of the rising dominance of corporations in the globalized economy and on the intersectionality of identity and social justice issues with the realities of labor movements. They prepare tens of thousands of new activists to be skilled organizers, researchers, and campaigners in labor and social justice organizations. According to its website, "the USAS is committed to building the next generation of progressive leaders who will be at the forefront of labor and social justice struggles. In carrying out this mission, we actively practice the principles of collective liberation to prioritize the development and mentorship of students of color, working class students, mixed-race students, women, transgender, queer and differently-abled students."[104] The USAS is a good contemporary example of how informed students and other youth can make a real difference in the direction of building a more just and egalitarian society.

CONCLUSION

In Chicago, and eventually in many other cities, Saul Alinsky made a major difference in the progressive cause as an individual activist committed to change—progressive and democratic change for all Americans, especially those Americans who are poor and oppressed. Using sociological ideas tested thoroughly in activist practice, and working with other organizers and the poor themselves, he succeeded in significantly improving the lives of many in poverty-burdened communities across the country. Alinsky was strongly committed to a society where people's class, racial, and ethnic backgrounds do not bring social oppression. Today, he remains an example of how one individual committed to sociologically informed activism can make a major difference in expanding democracy and social justice.

As we have seen, Alinsky's example is not unique. In a savvy book on participatory action research, titled *Building Community: Social Science in Action*, the social science editors note how Alinsky's critique of academic relevance can be a starting point for discussing the alternative route for social scientists concerned with working with local activists to create healthier communities. One can see the inspiration of Alinsky in their stated perspective:

> Traditional academic-based research does not always have the betterment of a particular community in mind, nor is it consistently concerned with finding ways to improve the quality of life for those

in society who do not have a fair share of their nation's wealth....
The purpose of this book is to present an alternative route to gaining
a better understanding of the world around us.[105]

As individuals and as groups, liberation social scientists can take
effective actions to challenge established ways of thinking about society
and established ways of oppressing others. As we have seen, one young
sociologist, Noel Cazenave, was willing to take some risks in order to
assert his right of freedom of thought and to choose a college course's
subject matter. Sometimes academics are seen as isolated from the real
world in their ivy-covered towers. Yet, the real world is ever present
there, and some sociologists have had to make very significant sacrifices
to bring the practice of liberation sociology to their own institutions.

Similarly, Paul Johnston left a secure life at Yale University and put
concern with making sociological understandings relevant into practice
by directing an organization devoted to the expansion of the rights
and the improvement of living conditions for some of the poorest of
Americans. Johnston did not give up the principles of good sociological
research. He continued his sociological research and published in scholarly and popular outlets. He is well aware of the dangers that community
involvement imposes on scholarship, but he is more concerned that all
social researchers recognize that they are participants in settings they
study. Especially important in Johnston's autobiographical comments
is his view of the importance of researchers' decisions on the questions
they ask, and neglect to ask, and on the things they see and fail to see.

In discussing the work of social scientists Nilda Flores-Gonzalez
and Leah Schmalzbauer, we see clearly what Johnston means. In a climate where local government reactions to increased immigration run
the gamut from creating integrative and inclusive policies to creating
highly restrictive and exclusionary policies, activist-researchers Flores-
Gonzalez and Schmalzbauer effectively represent the important concerns
and interests of US communities that have mostly been excluded from
the support of US political elites and from the analyses of mainstream
social scientists.

Finally, as we have seen, in pursuit of its mission, the USAS's
organizing philosophy embraces solidarity, collective liberation, grassroots democracy, and pluralism. The USAS suggests that a solidarity
framework unites allies fighting on diverse fronts toward similar purposes. The group promotes collective liberation because it believes that
the student-labor solidarity movement is part of a greater struggle for
global justice. Drawing on social science research and activist researchers,
this important student group supports the self-organization of working
people to fight for better working and living conditions in the form of

grassroots organizations such as unions and other democratic organizations.[106] These youth and students are willing to take risks in order to shed light on oppressive working conditions, providing an important example of how students committed to sociologically informed activism can make a major difference in expanding democracy and social justice.

CHAPTER 6

Doing Liberation Social Science

Participatory Action Research Strategies

The social science research strategies variously called *action research*, *community action research*, *participatory research*, and *participatory action research* (PAR) commonly engage social scientists with people in local communities. These researchers usually take issue with the main tenets of a detached social science and work directly for the betterment of human society. Today, there is a great diversity in this type of applied social research, which has spread dramatically across the globe. In this chapter we explore some of these research strategies.

DIMENSIONS OF ACTION RESEARCH

Conceptually, one can distinguish between three dimensions of participatory research—its goals, its sources, and its trajectory over time. There is a significant range of goals in what is called *participatory* or *action research*. One can visualize the goals on a continuum. At the conservative end, there are large corporations, corporate foundations, and governmental bureaucracies that sometimes use participatory research as a device to get people at the grassroots to comply with the profit-making or other establishment goals of these organizations. Examples of this are the agricultural "research" projects in postcolonial nations that are set up by chemical companies, or their foundations, to get peasant farmers to use agricultural chemicals such as pesticides and fertilizers in local farming. In these cases, the participatory aspect, such as bringing in peasant farmers for feedback, participation, and education, is often a ruse to make more profits off expanded sales of agricultural chemicals. There is little interest in helping local people determine what their problems—and local solutions—might be, and in recognizing their central participation in the decision-making.

As one moves from the conservative end of the continuum to the more progressive end, there is an increasing level of concern with democratic and liberation goals. Participatory research aimed at expanding the participation of people in research directed at their self-defined needs is growing across the globe—with a lot of diversity in its application. Social scientists are making much use of participatory action research to serve and learn from an array of grassroots people's organizations. These researchers are often re-creating social science in new and innovative ways.

In our review of the literature, we have found several sources of participatory research projects. These include local community activists, an activist social scientist coming from the outside, progressive organizations outside local communities, and a corporation with a limited economic interest. In many cases, action research is generated by activist leaders or community organizers who come to social scientists seeking their help in researching local community problems and their possible solutions. We will examine several examples of this type later in the chapter. Yet another source for these participatory projects is an activist sociologist coming to a community with ideas for localized research that will be of use to the community in defining its problems and their solutions. We see an example of this in the work of a leading South American sociologist, Orlando Fals-Borda, in a later section.

An additional source for participatory research projects is when a progressive organization comes to a local community and to social scientists seeking to get them both to join in efforts to deal with local community problems. In some cases, the progressive organization doing this stimulation of research is new and has emerged in connection with recent movements for democracy, women's rights, or indigenous people's rights across the globe. In other cases, older nongovernmental organizations (NGOs) have moved in a more progressive direction and are currently working to stimulate research oriented to local community needs. A fourth source of participatory research occurs when more conservative organizations, such as the aforementioned chemical companies, seek to use participatory research to pursue their own political or economic goals, such as expanded profits.

Another dimension of participatory research projects encompasses the varying trajectories of community projects once they are under way. The point of origin clearly affects the trajectory. Some participatory action research projects seeking corporate goals are successful, whereas others fail because they are not seeking the self-defined interests of the communities involved. However, even those projects seeking corporate goals by involving local people, such as peasant farmers, in some type of participatory research sometimes manage to generate radical protest movements farther down the line. Once local people are organized for a limited purpose, they have frequently used their new community organization to seek more radical goals. This is an example of the social science concept of "unintended consequences."

HISTORICAL PRECEDENTS FOR PARTICIPATORY RESEARCH

William F. Whyte once edited a much-cited volume reviewing different participatory projects. Those projects range across the aforementioned continuum, with the degree of community input into the research projects varying significantly. In an opening article, Whyte and his colleagues note that it is possible to achieve good scientific knowledge and provide action-oriented solutions to concrete problems at the same time.[1] Whyte and his colleagues trace the origins of participatory research to three historical influences. The first is the traditional methodology of social anthropologists and sociologists who have involved insightful local informants as active participants in their field research projects in particular communities. These researchers have often discussed with their informants the interpretation of the societal processes being observed.

A second influence on the development of participatory action research is the corporation-fostered study of workers' participation in workplace decisions, such as Quality of Work Life (QWL) programs. These QWL programs have often focused on humanizing some aspects of the workplace, on the assumption that a better quality of work life increases productivity and loyalty to a company. In the area of agriculture, the recognition that new high-yield varieties of crops developed by scientists were predominantly benefiting large farmers led to an interest on the part of some governmental agencies in incorporating small farmers into research and development projects. A third line of influence in the development of participatory research is the emergence of the systems-theory framework that since the 1950s has been applied in organizational research, such as that attempting to understand how workplaces can better integrate human and technological factors.[2]

In Whyte's edited book, there is some discussion of applied research with community cooperatives, but most of the book's examples focus on establishment organizations. The emphasis is on enhancement of the applied use of social science for existing private and public organizations.[3] There is relatively little discussion of participatory research projects that try to empower communities of the socially oppressed that are unorganized or just beginning to organize in nontraditional ways.

EMPOWERING THE POOR

Participatory action research with a strong emancipatory cast has other historical and regional roots, which the authors in the Whyte collection generally neglect. Indeed, one needs to go back to the beginnings of US sociology to find the ultimate roots of participatory action research. As we described earlier, in the United States activist sociology was pioneered in the 1890s by the mostly female sociologists working out of Hull House in Chicago. These female sociologists did the first extensive sociological research in local urban communities, and as activist researchers they provided their field and demographic research studies to local residents for their information and input.

Moreover, since the 1950s, renewed efforts directed at participatory action research on behalf of the poor have been generated in postcolonial countries, especially in Latin America, where a growing number of important links have been established between researchers and grassroots movements. In this research tradition, people in local communities define many research questions, control much of the research process, have substantial access to research results, and decide on much of the use of research results. The generation of knowledge in this action research usually becomes a source of group and individual empowerment. Knowledge ceases to be the private turf of professional experts and political elites.[4]

A crucial impetus for participatory projects is the provocative perspective of the Brazilian educator Paulo Freire (see Chapter 1). His seminal ideas have reached an international audience of educators, social scientists, and other scholars and community leaders. Freire pressed the idea of establishing a two-way dialogue between the researcher and the people researched, thereby overcoming the traditional subject-object dichotomy in social science research. The accent is on close ties between researchers and community members, with no necessary tie to the academic setting. These participatory research sociologists work with an awareness that there are many sources of knowledge and that knowledge is indeed power. People's empowerment and what Freire called "conscientization" are major goals of participatory action research. Recall from our earlier discussion of Freire that *conscientization* means the creation of an awareness among people—a pedagogy of how oppressed people can liberate themselves.[5]

This empowering research often contrasts significantly with traditional social science research. In one traditional "professional" model of social science, "there is no place for the community-of-those-studied to share in the determination of research objectives."[6] As sociologists Blauner and Wellman have noted, academically oriented social scientists tend to respond to the interests of fellow social scientists: "The theories, the interests, and the very concepts with which we work respond to the dynamics of increasing knowledge within our individual disciplines and professions, as well as to fashions and status concerns. The life problems and needs of the communities-under-study affect the scholar only indirectly; they are rarely the starting point for theory and research."[7]

The empowerment perspective attempts to involve ordinary residents in the local community, who not only have needs that should matter to social scientists but who also can do important social theorizing. Ideas, theories, and methodologies of social improvement and empowerment are not ordinarily part of the frame of reference of mainstream social science, and they must be added to that frame of reference if social scientists are to assist in creating a better world.

ACTION RESEARCH: THE WORK OF ORLANDO FALS-BORDA

We will now turn to some major examples of participatory action research (PAR) in the empowerment tradition. Orlando Fals-Borda, a leading Latin American sociologist, was one of the first to engage in participatory action research on behalf of the poor. He pioneered in action research strategies. His methods have sometimes been criticized by mainstream sociologists, and for a time his research alliances with peasant movements in Colombia even led the US Department of State to refuse him entry visas to the United States.[8]

In 1955 Fals-Borda published a pioneering book called *Peasant Society in the Colombian Andes*, a study that he completed without institutional sponsorship and that was the first major empirical sociological research done in Colombia.[9] Over the next few decades, he honed new participatory research strategies working with poor Colombian farmers. For example, in an Andean study, Fals-Borda and his research team examined the development of a rural community. At the time, he was chair of a university sociology department and head of Colombia's Ministry of Agriculture. This project involved community action in a rural Andean community of seventy poor families, a community whose younger generations were leaving. In the 1950s, the local school was in a dilapidated building with few windows. Since the municipal authorities did not respond to calls for repairs, the local people organized bazaars and gave the money collected to the authorities, who still did little. At the same time, urban growth and technologies were creating some new values and often undermining such traditional cooperative practices as "brazo prestado" (the borrowed arm), in which labor contributed to a neighbor's project was repaid later. In his report on the research project, Fals-Borda commented, "The new values being adopted seemed to destroy the old social structure without offering any apparent compensation or alternatives to a new integration."[10] Under these conditions, the apparent apathy of the local people made it seem impossible to solve the problems of the community without outside agency.

After doing research in this rural community in the late 1950s, three change agents—a rural sociologist, a social worker, and an architect—decided to help the community meet its own defined goals. By providing the community with the results of the sociological research—which included a demonstration of the people's concern for a better school—these researchers were able to spur a local community meeting. All residents attended, and the social worker and the sociologist helped to facilitate discussion. When the mayor came to understand the strong concerns of the people for a school, he offered to provide building materials if residents supplied the labor. A newly created community organization elected its own board of directors to represent the community. An important step was the appointment of a treasurer, who would keep the money collected within the community and thereby increase the confidence of the people. After the new school was completed, numerous community activities and organizations were developed, thereby strengthening the local community.[11]

A striking difference between Fals-Borda's research report on the project and more traditional sociological reports is that it contains a large section of photographs of local people and of places in the community. It includes the inaugural minutes of the community's organization and a report from the treasurer. This type of research publication is not only a contribution to sociological knowledge but also an important historical record for use by people in the community.

In his monograph on the community project, Fals-Borda reflects on his research experience and discusses sociological theories of group dynamics. Successful community action, he notes, is the result of a community taking charge of its problems and organizing to solve them through the development of local and external resources. One principle here is "social catalysis," the process of change that develops because of the presence of action agents who ensure that the new democratic approach proceeds, certain mistakes are avoided, and latent community needs become explicit. Social-catalytic agents can facilitate community stability. In this case, a sociologist was one important catalytic agent. The stimulus for community action initially came from outside, and the outsiders gradually received recognition from local church and municipal leaders. More importantly, they gained the trust of the local residents. Contact with agents of change, who became trusted, was significant in launching a process of community change. Local groups without active change agents like Fals-Borda or Saul Alinsky (see Chapter 5) often fail. However, the catalytic agents cannot be effective if they become "the experts." The programs initiated by the change agents are successful only because they help train new leaders for the local community. These new leaders then "become the yeast that rises the whole dough, adopting the catalytic qualities that the external change agent had so that they can continue the work and take initiative and responsibility."[12]

Recent Research and Activism

In more recent decades, Fals-Borda continued to pursue PAR methods and strategies in innovative ways. Indeed, in 1985 *Siglo Veintiuno, Editores*, an influential publisher of social science literature in Spanish, published a book by Fals-Borda on social knowledge and people's power. This is, in effect, a handbook for PAR in postcolonial countries.[13] In contrast to Whyte's handbook, Fals-Borda's is much more clearly about PAR as a methodology and strategy for local and popular empowerment.

Fals-Borda reached broad audiences with his PAR ideas through his active presence at many meetings and conventions across the South American continent. In 1977, his presentations at the World Symposium on Participatory Action Research in Colombia served to systematize his PAR methodology. His presence at the World Assembly of Adult Education resulted in a book on participatory research that has been highly influential in Latin American countries.[14]

In addition to this PAR work, Fals-Borda became an important sociologist of education with influence in many countries of Latin America and elsewhere. In Latin American countries, personal presentations at meetings, symposia, and conventions, as well as other forms of face-to-face scholarly communication, are far more important than in the United States and Europe, where written publications are generally regarded as more important. Indeed, one idea for liberation sociologists in the United States and Europe is to expand the strategies for research presentation to include many more interactional settings for ordinary people. In Chapter 1, we noted one US example of such interactive work by Project South, the Atlanta-based organization strongly committed to extensive popular education for low-income communities.

Rethinking the Research Process

Fals-Borda's participant observation and action at the grassroots level came to shape his scholarly view of the research process. For him, "the results of participatory research are open to validation and judgment like in any other discipline, not only by fellow scholars and bureaucrats—who are now in a rampage to co-opt it—but also by the opinion of the subject peoples themselves."[15]

Similarly, Fals-Borda's presentation of his research broke new ground. In the 1980s, he published four volumes of sociological and historical research on the coastal region of Colombia. He dedicated Volume 4 to "the resurgent grassroots movements struggling for life, democracy, and peace, because they will be able to save Colombia if they stick to their historical destiny: to replace the current ruling classes whose devastating and egoistic performance is once again laid bare in this volume."[16] In this study, he traces a Colombian region's social history, from pre-Columbian times to the 1980s. Significantly, the four volumes present research information in a different and innovative format. On the left-hand pages of the books are historical accounts and empirical descriptions, while on the right-hand pages are concepts, theoretical interpretations, sources, and methodological discussions of what is on the left-hand pages. For example, on one left-hand page, there is a brief story of how several Native American groups were exterminated or conquered by the Spanish and how their lands were occupied. On the right-hand page, we learn that the main workforce, which produced the wealth of the conquering Spaniards, was made up of enslaved Africans. The direct and indirect destruction of the Native American population was so complete that the Spanish exploiters could not use their labor by the late sixteenth century.[17]

"Commitment" and Participatory Action Research

Articulating his view of participatory action research, Fals-Borda reported that he initially used traditional research techniques, such as participant observation, without being fully aware of their epistemological implications. In traditional academic research, "participant observation" has meant that sociological researchers observe but do not get fully involved in the processes observed.[18] In contrast, Fals-Borda began developing by the 1960s the concept of commitment, the idea that participatory social scientists should work to transform an intolerable society into a humane one. The practice of sociology should be focused on the needs of people who are victims of social exploitation. In thinking through the implications of his own research, Fals-Borda did not find his PhD training in sociology of much use—a frequent report of many sociologists doing participatory action research—and thus did not resort much to Western academic techniques in developing his understandings of community research. Indeed, for new ideas he sought out Latin American and Native American thinkers, though few of the latter's perspectives have survived centuries of Western colonial onslaught.[19]

Very influential in the case of Fals-Borda and fellow sociologists were yet other intellectual stimuli from postcolonial sources. During the 1960s and 1970s, Latin American researchers linked to the United Nations Economic Commission for Latin America came up with what came to be called *dependency theory* to explain societal structures in South American countries. This was the first theory to break with the notion that the so-called backwardness of postcolonial countries was due to the social, economic, or cultural inferiority of the people in those countries. Instead, the realities of economic underdevelopment across the globe were now set within the framework of the capitalistic world system—one in which the more industrialized countries at the center intentionally *created* economic dependency in less industrialized countries on the periphery. As Fals-Borda has noted, this was the "first cry of Latin American intellectual independence from the traditional colonialism that has characterized our elites."[20] As Latin American social scientists began to break with older patterns of European-influenced thinking, they joined a reworked Marxism, a dependency theory configured to their own political-economic conditions.

For example, during the 1960s, Pablo González Casanova, a Mexican political scientist, expanded the traditional Marxist concept of exploitation and made it applicable to the economic complexity of agriculturally oriented Latin American societies. Fals-Borda and his colleagues were also influenced by the work of Paulo Freire in regard to many aspects of popular education. Yet another critical influence was the activity of Camilo Torres, a Catholic priest and academic social scientist who died with Colombian guerrillas fighting for social change. Clearly, the Latin American perspective on participatory action research is different from that highlighted in the often more managerial, applied-research tradition that is emphasized in the aforementioned edited volume by William F. Whyte.

In 1985 Fals-Borda gave a keynote address at a Southern Sociological Society meeting in the United States. There he described how research for social justice by researchers in the Northern and Southern Hemispheres was beginning to converge. Latin American and other postcolonial researchers had had a lead over US sociologists, but the latter were beginning to catch up. "Participatory researchers in the Third World," Fals-Borda told his audience, "contributed to this merger with a version of 'commitment' which combined praxis and phronesis, that is, horizontal participation with peoples and wise judgment and prudence for the good life." He continued by noting that he, an activist sociologist, had worked hard "in the service of peasants and workers' struggles, which meant a clear break with the Establishment, plus an active, sometimes dangerous search for social justice there."[21] Indeed, he was actually imprisoned several times with those whom he had served.

In his US address, Fals-Borda added this personal note about being an activist sociologist:

> But I could not consider myself a scientist, even less a human being, if I did not exercise the "commitment" and felt it in my heart and in my head as a life experience, *Erfahrung* or *Vivencia*. This methodology became an alternative philosophy of life for me and for many others. There is no need to make an apology for this type of committed research. Nearly everyone knows that PAR combines qualitative and quantitative techniques. It utilizes hermeneutics, literature, and art according to needs. And it joins with action simultaneously. There appears to be now ample agreement that PAR can serve to correct prevailing practices in our disciplines which have not been altogether satisfactory or useful for society at large.[22]

In recent decades, many sociologists and other social scientists in North America have recognized Orlando Fals-Borda for his pioneering efforts in participatory research.

Note, too, that Fals-Borda viewed participatory action research as usefully combining qualitative and quantitative research methods. By itself, quantitative research can rarely produce deep understandings of the social world. In addition, the intellectual ferment and community from which Fals-Borda's participatory action research emerged are different from other forms of applied sociology. The main reason for this is the close connection between the researchers and communities of the aggrieved. Indeed, it is the pressures from the oppressed that, directly or indirectly, generate this type of participatory action research.

Some observers have seen in the increasing funding of participatory research approaches—mainly by Western nongovernmental agencies and certain private foundations—a new form of northern "co-optation" of southern nations. Indeed, participatory development, sustainable development, and human rights, feminist, antiracist, and other critical actions against the societal status quo "have been relentlessly subjected to efforts at co-optation and domestication."[23] Yet, this does not mean that this funded research is necessarily co-opted in all features by its corporate and bureaucratic funders, since participatory research, once inaugurated by means of extensive community participation, is hard to contain. Local people, once organized, may move their organization in the direction of more radical goals, such as expanded political democracy, than its funders ever conceived.

PARTICIPATORY ACTION RESEARCH AROUND THE WORLD

Patients Shaping Research: A Chilean Project

In regard to action research, Chile is an important country to examine because of the extensive involvement of sociologists in such research with a variety of people's organizations. This participation has varied with the ebb and flow of the democratic institutions in that country. Ironically, in the 1960s, Chile was the location for one of the largest research projects ever involving sociologists, a multimillion-dollar research project called Project Camelot, which sought to study groups engaged in popular dissent against the country's sociopolitical structure. This reactionary research effort was designed in the United States to measure the potential for insurgency among the people and to reduce or eliminate these progressive people's movements. The head of the project was a US social scientist, and several other US and Chilean social scientists, including sociologists, were heavily involved in the large-scale undertaking. During the cold war with the former Soviet Union and its allies, the US government had an overt goal of destroying numerous popular movements across the globe, movements it fantasized were allies with the Communist bloc in Europe. Fortunately, Chilean social scientists and university administrators were successful in the battle they waged against this misguided research project.

One of the authors, Hernán Vera, has done participatory action research in Chile. He carefully studied the quality of the performance of medical clinics providing important services to the poor. The inauguration of the project stemmed from the progressive managers of the medical clinics, who, during the redemocratization of Chile in the late 1980s, were running clinics with substantial input from those poor Chileans whom they served. Since the managers of the clinics had initially defined the project as a probing self-analysis, Vera decided to present the staff and the managers with the strategy of participant action research. In this research plan, the people served by the clinics and the medical staff would all participate directly, if in different ways. Initially, participatory procedures were difficult to implement because the physicians, nurses, and midwives expected the kind of scientific research they had learned about in their own training. Early in the process, one of the clinics' physicians expressed the view of most of the medical staff that the sociologist should not involve the staff but should proceed with conventional questionnaires and methods of reporting: "I do not ask patients to make decisions," and "You should not ask us to make yours."

Gradually, the terms of this participatory research project were negotiated between the staff and the sociologist, with the staff voting on each aspect of the research. In weekly meetings, they were presented with concrete ideas for the research project, and they became a reservoir of innovative ideas that greatly improved the research instruments and procedures used by the sociologist. There were some immediate benefits for the clinics' personnel and operation. In organizations like these, frequent staff participation in research decisions—including participation in designing interview protocols, in selection of interviewers, and in commenting on drafts of the research report—served to allay fears among the medical personnel that the project was only a managerial effort aimed at greater control of them.

At this stage, the research was participatory for the staff, but not yet for the patients. Soon, however, Vera began to involve the poor Chileans served by the medical clinics as well. They were interviewed using a series of open-ended questions designed to allow them flexible input, and they also participated in focus groups—group interviews that allowed for interactive expression and creativity. Substantial benefits accrued from this part of the participatory action research. The medical practitioners now came to see how the patients actually felt about the services provided. From this comprehensive participatory research process, the medical staff gained a better sense of what needed to be improved. Given this success, the innovative participatory methods spread to other medical clinics across the country. One physician who had witnessed the patient focus groups was so elated at the results of the research technique that he argued that this focus group technique should be taught in medical school as an essential communication tool for medical practitioners.[24] Interestingly, this is an important idea that has yet to be developed in the medical school settings of the United States.

For the most part, the clinics' patients were disenfranchised low-income women served by a weak health care system that never consulted them about their needs. The open-ended interviews and the opportunity to exchange ideas with other women in focus groups were liberating for these women. Indeed, the research-oriented focus groups were sometimes transformed into workshops and community action groups. For example, one focus group, consisting of a dozen low-income women, eventually became a local action group working to inform pregnant women in a neighborhood of the need for early medical checkups. Clearly, sociological research, conducted in an effective emancipatory mode, can help create more democratic social, economic, and political systems across the globe.

Community Action Research in Mexico

In 1973, sociologist Maria Sanchez began conducting research for her dissertation in Mexico's poverty-riddled Sierra Norte de Puebla region. Spending her first year learning about indigenous life, she studied kinship rituals, the power structure, and the economy. She gradually became friends with local families. In a later discussion of the research project, Sanchez noted that "her initial goal was to collect information for her dissertation, but her interactions with the villagers persuaded her to give her academic concerns secondary priority."[25] Soon she persuaded a group of urban friends, some social scientists and some members of religious groups, to join her as a live-in team working with the indigenous people in the town of San Miguel, in a mountainous region populated substantially by indigenous people. This was a poor region whose economy was centered in corn and coffee production.

From the start, Sanchez and her team were involved in a participatory action research project. The outside team of activists and researchers met interactively with the local villagers weekly to plan action, with Sanchez presenting research results and villagers and team members proposing community projects. The villagers proposed such programs as first-aid courses, vegetable gardens, and the creation of a handicraft group. Gradually, rural-urban, racial-ethnic, and class barriers between the researchers and the people were somewhat broken down. Working together, the team and the villagers gathered research data and significantly improved local living conditions. A regional agriculture co-operative was formed, which built a farm and served as an agricultural experiment station. A Study and Educational Promotion Center was founded. Eventually, roughly half the community's families were participating in the various projects and activities.[26]

However, some political authorities, some rural teachers, and the local oligarchy were opposed to this new type of participatory teamwork. Officials in governmental agencies, political parties, and the church tried to co-opt the community movement, but unsuccessfully. The activist research team was accused of being "foreigners" with no respect for established authority, but the community strongly defended them.

Over more than two decades, the participatory research project greatly benefited the local community. Three local peasant leaders put it this way: "We have seen that change has been taking place. Critical thinking abilities have increased. We do not allow people to impose their ideas any more. We all have the right to express our own ideas. People are participating in San Miguel because they have seen more than promises."[27] In addition, the team of activist researchers felt important goals had been achieved, including much reciprocal learning:

> Through our twenty-year experience we, as team members, have witnessed the capacity of community members to question their own knowledge and to theoretically reconstruct it.... One of the most valuable things *we* have learned during these twenty years is the importance of reciprocity in research, learning, providing service, liberating.[28]

Over time, the activist sociologist Sanchez and her team members developed a strong appreciation of local knowledge and folk wisdom and a respect for traditional community ways. As the researchers saw it, the university community could benefit from the popular education of its researchers. In this participatory research modality, community changes are not imposed from above. This goal requires vigilance in regard to the ethics of the relationship between community members and researchers.

Action Research in Tanzania

Another example of liberation sociology helping ordinary people is the project of social researchers Rakesh Rajani and Mustafa Kudrati, who researched the conditions of street children in Mwanza, Tanzania. Working with a nongovernmental organization (Kuleana) and financed by UNICEF and the Population Council, these sociologically oriented researchers sought to develop reliable knowledge about the children of the streets, especially about their sexual activities and related health consequences. The goal was to devise effective social programs for the street children.[29]

Rajani and Kudrati approached this research with a human rights perspective and have noted that "building relations of mutual trust and respect with street children lies at the heart of conducting effective research and promoting healthy sexual behavior."[30] Their research priorities were driven substantially by the children's concerns. The children participated in regular, candid, and in-depth discussions about sexual practices with researchers and the organization's staff. When the research was launched, the risk factor in HIV infection among street children was derived mainly from the necessity of them selling sexual favors to exploitative adults. However, the research pointed to the importance of children's sexual expressions with each other as another risk factor. A baseline set of data on each child's past and present was collected, and the children's experiences and views about sex were shared in discussions in a variety of structured and informal contexts such as classrooms, theater performances, and impromptu interactions with the children.[31]

In their research report, Rajani and Kudrati note the difficulties in trying to help the street children develop healthy lifestyles. They argue that researchers and staff members should avoid autocratic and paternalistic programs, which are usually doomed to fail. They suggest that "children and adolescents are also sexual beings, with feelings of desire and connection, curiosity and lust. Sexuality and the license to deal with sexual feeling are rights and responsibilities for children as much as for anyone else. In denying this, adult-run NGOs may be doing the greatest disservice to the children and young people they aim to serve."[32]

As a result of this consultative and participatory research, the children got better health and education programs, which were substantially designed based on knowledge gained in the research. The research also facilitated the establishment of training programs producing a more knowledgeable staff to run programs. Staff members who work with street children have received training to act in nonpatronizing ways. In this case the social researchers became human instruments at the service of poor and oppressed children. The decisions required to conduct the research were still made in the best social science terms, but with an explicit awareness that the interests and concerns of the oppressed should drive the research.

Participatory Research in Germany

European social scientists have made important use of participatory action research. Peter Mettler and Thomas Baumgartner conducted a future-oriented participatory experiment that sought to make the shaping of ongoing technological developments more democratic. Financed by the Ministry of Labor, Health, and Social Affairs of North-Rhine-Westphalia in Germany, these sociologists persuaded ninety local residents from different parts of the region, different social classes, and different ethnic groups to attend several days of intensive group discussions. The aim was to test a new framework—called the Participatory Delphi Procedure for Future-Oriented Interdisciplinary Policy Planning—aimed at developing new decision-making procedures that fully take into account the social and environmental consequences of scientific and technological advancements.[33]

The citizens met in several groups and became the "experts" on daily life in regard to three possible scenarios that were presented to them. These scenarios were constructed by the researchers based on three different logics of societal development, each involving certain technologies and work arrangements. Participants were asked to imagine what their society would be like in the year 2020 and to describe it in detail. For example, work in Scenario A is seen as compensated activity in a dependent relation to the employer, much as it is today. But the Delphi participants were to envision a shorter (25–30 hour) workweek by the year 2020. In this scenario, housework and other modes of labor were regarded as less useful activities. They were asked to evaluate this futuristic scenario.

In Scenario B, a broader view of work in the future was asserted. Work was viewed as an important part of life, one that comprises all activities in the economy, society, and private household realm. The different work activities, including housework, were to be of equal value. Participants were asked how they would see such equality of work efforts.

Then, in Scenario C, the image of work was one of achievement entirely determined by the multinational corporate sphere: "The organization of labour is strictly hierarchical and work hours are strictly determined by production necessities with shifts and Sunday work."[34] In this scenario the present work arrangements would more or less persist, but all under the control of a multinational managerial elite. In this project, various research procedures were used, including the assessment of the future-oriented scenarios and role-playing exercises. For example, the social science researchers introduced the idea of a film studio in which the group participants imagined themselves as the stage managers and the research team as the actors that the former had to tell how to act in a particular scene.

Most research participants indicated that they had not thought much about the future. The participants, and by extension other citizens, had not yet noticed the lack of future-oriented planning by their government. The citizen participants admitted that they were not innovative with regard to new technologies and work arrangements and that although they were interested in new knowledge, they could likely assimilate a limited amount. Nevertheless, they wished to see improvements in the way scientific and technological knowledge about future work and economic arrangements are communicated and implemented.

This large-scale use of participatory research methods is emancipatory in that its investigations furthered substantial participation by ordinary citizens in regard to critical decisions about their future. Without projects such as these, such decisions would likely be made only by a wealthy elite, and mostly outside of the democratic political arena. Such important decisions can set the life conditions for people for generations. With the people's participation in these determinations, the environmental forces cease to be seen as obscure and determinant, but as socially invented life conditions. Like the projects in Colombia and Chile, this participatory research project provided democratic ways of discovering and producing new sociological knowledge, which, in turn, could be used to bring both a better standard of living and a more democratic way of living.

Applied Research in Norway

We now note one example of a more conventional type of applied sociology, in this case an example that assisted corporations in profit development but that also had a significant democratic impact. The case we consider is applied sociological research in the international shipping industry.[35] During the 1960s, the Norwegian shipping industry was undergoing major changes because of a shortage of seafarers, which was mainly due to competition from onshore jobs that offered a better quality of life. The idea of action research developed when social science consultants began to examine how to bring participatory research to bear on increasing workers' involvement in work planning and supervision in the shipping industry. In their conceptualization of the change process, these social scientists focused on what they termed the *action cycle*: the series of steps one goes through once a problem and the factors that may influence its solution are identified. These action-cycle steps involve the formulation of proposed changes and a plan to implement them, the initiation of the changes, the assessment of changes and methods used, and the further diffusion of the changes.

A contact group was created, including representatives from workers' unions, the shipowners' association, and government directorates. Researchers from the Norwegian Work Research Institute (WRI) participated in the numerous group meetings that took place over several years. The meetings were "an open forum for exploring options, confronting differences, and clarifying—if not endorsing—organizational principles."[36]

The WRI researchers also assisted a shipping company whose ship *Mistral* had been chosen to conduct the first trials of greater worker participation in everyday decision-making. The seafarers selected as the crew visited work sites where experiments had been done in other industries to learn from workers, union officials, and managers about issues they were likely to face. On the *Mistral*, significant crew involvement in work planning and supervision was implemented. A common recreation room for officers and crew was established, together with a new personnel planning and salary system designed to enhance crew continuity. Democratic input was encouraged. After a year, the project was evaluated and found successful at the ship and the firm levels.

A third major experiment was launched aboard a ship of a different company. The three experiments showed that democratic crew arrangements were feasible and cost-effective. Eventually, the innovations introduced in these ships were diffused to other ships, and active participation by crews and trade unions in decision-making was extended. By the 1980s, this tradition of group participation and experimentation within the Norwegian shipping industry was firmly established.[37]

Indeed, since then a number of the Norwegian innovations have spread to fleets of other countries. In this case, the participatory research projects were large-scale and involved private corporations, as well as unions and government agencies. Although corporate profitability was sought and enhanced in the process, the corporations were forced to consult directly with unions and thus to involve their workers more centrally in decision-making. Worker satisfaction with their work lives on these ships increased. The results in Norwegian shipping were liberating for the crews, which became more directly involved in work planning, supervision, the development of recreation facilities, and the salary system.

ACTION RESEARCHERS IN CANADA

The Manitoba Research Alliance

The sprawling inner city of Winnipeg, Canada, is characterized by poverty and its associated problems—unemployment, inadequate housing, low levels of education, family instability, and crime. In these respects, it is typical of the spatially concentrated and racialized poverty entrenched in urban centers across North America—except that in Winnipeg, those most predominant among the urban poor are indigenous (First Nations) people. Of the major cities in Canada, Winnipeg has the highest density of indigenous people, representing 10 percent of the total population.[38] While 20 percent of Winnipeg city households are officially living in poverty, that figure is 40 percent for inner-city households. For indigenous households, the figure is much higher.[39]

At the same time, Winnipeg's inner city is home to a large number of creative and effective community-based organizations (CBOs), many led by indigenous people, especially indigenous women. This contradiction—many deep, poverty-related problems but a wealth of creative and effective CBOs—is a significant feature of the inner city.[40]

Many CBOs and their leaders are active members of the Manitoba Research Alliance (MRA). This important alliance has been engaged in producing original social science research that is rooted in the experience of, and accountable to, the local community. The MRA aims to build local capacity, produce concrete deliverables for community organizations, impact public policy, and contribute to knowledge that will help other communities. Its work draws on a range of social science theories to explain the structures and forces that marginalize people and reproduce poverty—including feminist, critical, and postcolonial theories. The MRA accents the holistic approach embraced by its community partners and seeks to reveal the class, racial, gender, generational, and other dynamics of the area as they contribute to the ongoing social subordination of indigenous and other inner-city people. They also seek out workable solutions to the complex problems these oppressive social dynamics produce.[41]

The MRA is mainly comprised of university-based researchers from a range of disciplines (sociology, indigenous studies, economics, and political science), provincial government departments and agencies, and community organizations. Community partners include a diverse range of organizations, including First Nations organizations, community economic development organizations, youth-at-risk agencies, neighborhood associations, and prisoner advocacy groups. The MRA's research is community-driven. First Nations and inner-city organizations play a central role in all aspects of the Alliance's work, including identifying what is researched, who is included among researchers, and the forms in which research findings are made available. The academic members of the team do not purport to be "experts" who tell communities what they need. Rather, they follow the lead of other liberation sociologists in their belief that people who are oppressed have valuable standpoints and experiential knowledge that are key to understanding their circumstances and making change. Theirs is a genuine community-university research partnership, the strength of which was recognized recently when the MRA was the recipient of a prestigious international award from the Community-Campus Partnerships for Health.[42]

As in other examples in this book, the MRA's research approach is contrary to what has often been the case in much academic research. The MRA is committed to a two-way flow of benefits and to research outcomes that directly advantage the communities with which it works.[43] The MRA has been successful in securing large Social Science and Humanities Research Council of Canada grants, including a grant to do research under the title "Partnering for Change: Community-Based Solutions for Aboriginal and Inner-City Poverty." This project will investigate through time the impact of promising community-based solutions to racialized poverty in order to determine how they can be expanded and made sustainable at the larger institutional and public policy levels. The MRA organizes its research efforts into four streams: justice, safety, and security; housing and neighborhood revitalization; capacity building, education, and employment; and community economic development. Within each stream, research projects are conducted by community partners and university researchers working together. The purpose is to try to understand Winnipeg's inner city "from the inside" as much as possible and to do social science research that contributes to positive transformation of these communities.[44]

More specifically, in the justice, safety, and security stream, the MRA has conducted research examining safety at the neighborhood level, as understood by those in inner-city neighborhoods.[45] It also explores the street sex trade from the standpoints of those involved[46] and locates indigenous gang members and their involvement in the drug trade in the context of contemporary neocolonialism.[47] In the housing and neighborhood revitalization stream, the MRA has examined indigenous forms of community development and worked closely with community members to conduct detailed examinations of everyday life in public housing projects.[48] These studies have led to significant tangible benefits in at least one housing project.[49]

In the capacity building, education, and employment stream, the MRA has delved deeply into indigenous educational issues and approaches to education that have proved to be successful where mainstream approaches have not.[50] The MRA has worked with inner-city community partners to develop finely tuned means of evaluating work done by CBOs that involves forms of capacity building that are missed by mainstream methods.[51] In the community economic development stream, the MRA has conducted ethnographic studies in a number of indigenous communities[52] and is working on a large project aimed at constructing a history of indigenous people's development of inner city CBOs.[53] This history is largely unknown, and bringing it into the light of day through video-taped interviews with elders and a collection of written material will assist in reconstructing the negative image, stigma, and stereotyping of First Nations people in this racially segregated city.

The MRA's research is deepening an understanding of Winnipeg's inner city and of Canadian and US inner-city issues. This is the result of good sociological and other social science scholarship that directly involves communities researched. Beyond that, the MRA's research efforts are aimed at issues with social justice implications. Moreover, because of the way the MRA functions—a shared process combining people from universities and low-income and racialized communities—it is building bridges and finding solutions in a deeply segregated city. The research is contributing to the production of a range of tangible and positive outcomes.[54]

As a result of the MRA research, social science researchers have become aware of two important and often misunderstood themes. First, the spatially concentrated, racialized poverty that prevails in the inner city is deep and complex and not at all susceptible to single or short-term solutions. There are no easy fixes for a complex set of structural problems. But secondly, there are solutions that do work. The MRA has identified, studied, and written about many. Poverty can be solved, but doing so requires significant public investments, intelligently directed at strategies shown to work well and consistently applied over a generation or more.[55]

Digital Stories: First Nations' Women Explore the Legacy of Indian Residential Schools

In 2008, Canadian prime minister Stephen Harper's official apology to former students of Indian residential schools acknowledged that the "policy of [forced] assimilation was wrong [and] has caused great harm ... [Children were] inadequately fed, clothed and housed ... All were deprived the care and nurturing of their parents, grandparents, and communities." Harper accepted that the legacy of Indian Residential Schools "has contributed to social problems that continue to exist." While social researchers have conducted many studies on the consequences of these residential schools for indigenous students, few of these have concerned the impact on children of survivors. These residential schools produced disconnection and emotional distance from family members, home cultures, language, community, and traditions, usually leaving former students with painful memories too difficult to share with their children.[56]

Prairie Women's Health Centre of Excellence (PWHCE), an organization dedicated to improving the health status of Canadian women and whose doors closed in 2013 as government funds supporting it were discontinued, was responsible for a ground-breaking study that focused on children of survivors. It used digital stories, with personal narratives and still images, video, and music characterizing an individual's testimonial.[57] This cutting-edge qualitative research brings to mind the innovative field work of early sociological researchers like Jane Addams, who represented the concerns of communities generally excluded from the political interests of elites and mainstream academics. In the custom of organic intellectuals, indigenous peoples' digital stories reveal intellectual traditions with potential to disrupt colonial narratives of history, identify injustice, honor resistance, and imagine a more just society.[58]

The research report documents the resiliency of residential school survivors and how they passed their determination to their children, grandchildren, and future generations:

> Many mothers passed on their abilities to deal with crisis, to survive extraordinary and everyday struggles, even though they had limitations, and to love in the ways they could.... When we add these women's stories to the stories of many other Aboriginal women, men, Elders and children, it forms the knowledge to counter ongoing legacies of "civilization" and "assimilation." The wisdom and awareness about inter-generational effects of residential schools resides in the collective and individual experiences, memories, bodies and spirits of women and other First Nations people.[59]

PARTICIPATORY ACTION RESEARCH IN THE UNITED STATES

In the United States, much participatory action research has dealt with environmental issues, education, health care, racial and class diversity, and community control. Sociologists have been central participants in the expansion of PAR strategies across the United States.

Action Research in Housing: Milwaukee

In Milwaukee, several sociologists have worked with the local Fair Lending Coalition in a participatory action research relationship. This coalition is a multiracial, inner-city organization with representatives from churches, unions, civil rights organizations, and community groups. Led by a racially diverse board, the coalition worked with Gregory D. Squires and other social scientists then at the University of Wisconsin–Milwaukee in order to bring change in local banks' investments in the central city of the Milwaukee metropolis.

Prior to this effort, the city of Milwaukee had experienced a high ratio of black-to-white rejection rates in home and small-business loans. Drawing on federal statutes requiring financial institutions to disclose local lending practices and to be responsive to needs of moderate-income communities in their areas, the coalition negotiated numerous community investment agreements with local financial institutions, thereby securing commitments to make millions of dollars in new loans in formerly redlined neighborhoods. Working closely with the coalition groups, local PAR sociologists did research on lending practices, which showed high loan rejection rates for low- and moderate-income communities. The data also showed which lenders had a low number and percentage of their loans in areas with poor residents and residents of color. These data on income and racial barriers enabled the coalition to press lending institutions to provide commitments for new loans in these seriously underserved communities.[60]

Although it went out of business in the late 1990s, during its lifetime the coalition was effective because of its broad community representativeness and its close collaboration between housing activists in the community and the sociological researchers in the university. As the researchers have noted, "research, in the absence of effective organizing, would become little more than an academic exercise. And the organizing, without a strong research foundation, would be far less effective."[61]

The Participatory Budgeting Project

"These are our weapons" is an assertive chant of some contemporary social movements in Spain. "When you hear it, you are supposed to raise your hands up in the air," writes Gianpaolo Baiocchi about the contemporary Spanish movement to protest the evictions of people who cannot pay the mortgages on their homes.[62] Informed by critical sociological theory and accenting the importance of civic engagement, Baiocchi, a sociology professor at New York University, has increasingly become immersed in projects on knowledge production: "Several of the projects I have been engaged in have been collective, and across career stage. I like to think they are democratic. . . . [W]e try to run them more like anarchist collectives than along the Principal Investigator/Research Assistant model."[63]

An engaged scholar-activist, Gianpaolo is one of the founders of the Participatory Budgeting Project (PBP), whose mission is the advancement of urban democracy primarily in the United States and in Canada. Based on the belief that people have valuable knowledge regarding their own needs and that smarter political decisions are made when the knowledge of local people is sought, this nonprofit organization gives ordinary people real power over real money that is collected. Recognizing that people with more power and money tend to participate more in politics, the PBP engages marginalized communities, such as low-income individuals, people of color, and youth. Working diligently with grassroots groups to produce inclusive processes, PBP draws on local feedback and professional insights to thoroughly assess its social program work and active budgeting for programs.[64] Funded projects for the communities have included bike lanes, a community garden, a new ultrasound system at a hospital, heating stations and benches on train platforms, playground improvements, new technology at schools and libraries, a community composting facility, a Meals on Wheels delivery van, and streetlights.[65]

More Action Research: Chicago

In Chicago, another group of sociologists and community activists—initially coordinated by Philip Nyden, a sociologist at Loyola University, and Josh Hoyt, then executive director of Organization of the Northeast (ONE)—used sociological research to shape efforts to improve the lives of the moderate-income residents in two Chicago lakefront communities. The residents of these areas are very diverse in racial, ethnic, and class terms. ONE, the name of an umbrella group headed by an elected board drawn from about eighty organizations, is dedicated to maintaining stable racial-ethnic diversity in housing and to improving the housing and socioeconomic conditions of local residents. Since the 1990s, ONE has organized strategy teams to work on issues of education, housing, jobs, and economic development. In a series of field research reports, local sociologists have assisted ONE activists and community residents to better understand what is happening in their area and to formulate progressive strategies for change.[66]

In 1990, ONE began organizing tenants in ten apartment buildings constructed with major financial assistance from US Department of Housing and Urban Development (HUD) low-interest loans. The large apartment buildings, housing many of the area's tenants, were supposed to provide below-market-cost housing to low-income families. However, the owners used a loophole to convert some buildings to market-rate apartments, sharply reducing reasonably priced housing in the area and likely increasing owners' profits. Working with ONE, action-oriented sociologists conducted interviews and surveys with tenants and found that there was substantial racial-ethnic diversity in the buildings and that this affordable apartment housing was a key base on which families built stable and self-sufficient lives. Although the study did identify tensions between renters and homeowners, it found much satisfaction among the residents with a residential area where relations between diverse racial and ethnic groups had stabilized. The joint effort between community activists and social researchers was successful in keeping several of the buildings in the uptown area affordable for low-income residents. More recently, however, there have been renewed threats to the buildings, including a reduction in the availability of certificates used to subsidize rents and the expressed desire of new middle-class residents to force out the low-income residents. Nonetheless, ONE has continued pressing to improve the lives of people in this part of Chicago.[67]

ONE continues to live up to its reputation as a first-rate community organization. In recent times, it has united with other Illinoisans in a Fair Economy Illinois coalition and met with state legislators to discuss the need for corporate tax transparency.[68] In 2013, ONE members joined other concerned Chicagoans at the Grassroots Collaborative's Take Back Chicago public meeting, where they discussed plans to launch a progressive agenda to challenge city and state policies that abandon middle- and low-income families in favor of wealthy corporations. ONE secured commitments from city and state legislators on matters such as school closures, a graduated income tax, the closing of mental health clinics and other service cuts, a community affordable-housing plan, and raising the minimum wage.[69]

In this participatory action research, the trust built up between the team of social science researchers and the community activists led to a longer-term collaborative research project, which resulted in research reports on the nature of business in the community, on tenant organizing, and on youth and family issues. These reports had some impact on local policymaking, for they showed community residents as well as funding agencies, officials, and newspaper editors that these highly urban areas had relatively stable racial-ethnic relationships, with different groups actively cooperating to improve local conditions. The sociologists' reports showed that community organizational struggles were often effective in marshalling resources and bridging to progressive change. The research studies also provided knowledge and skills for staffs of the community organizations. Significantly, it was the trust and respect that the sociologists gained from community leaders and residents that made the collaborative relationship work.[70]

Given the sharp increase in predatory and exploitative lending by various banks and mortgage companies, and the resulting major housing crisis of 2006 to 2009 in what is called the subprime mortgage market, we should add a note on the growth in community groups and national organizations seeking major changes in this mortgage industry. Sometimes advised by sociologists and other social scientists, the (now-defunct) Association of Community Organizations for Reform Now (ACORN), the National Community Reinvestment Coalition (NCRC), and the National Fair Housing Alliance (NFHA) have assertively pressed for better mortgages and financing for moderate-income Americans who have faced much discrimination at the hands of the financial services industry for many decades. In a summary report, sociologist Gregory Squires notes, "NCRC estimates that more than $4.7 trillion in new loans have been secured for low-income and minority markets, largely in response to community organizing efforts."[71]

ACORN died as an organization in 2010, soon after it had helped millions of mainly low-income citizens apply to register to vote in 2008. In the wake of that voter registration drive, the organization came under vicious attack from arch-conservative operatives for an alleged misappropriation of its funds. However, a report released by the non-partisan

Congressional Research Service in 2009 found no such misappropriation of its federal funds and no efforts at improper voting after its 2008
voter registration drive. In addition, the report's architects raised issues
concerning the constitutionality of a government-wide funding ban
for ACORN and concluded that filmmakers who conducted a widely
publicized "sting" operation against ACORN likely broke the law.[72] To
its very end, ACORN made a difference. In its final five years, it assisted
families with 150,000 free tax returns and consequently, $190 million in
tax refunds. ACORN's legacy is that it was the United States's leading
community organization of low and moderate-income families, working together for social justice and stronger communities from 1970 to
its end.[73]

The scale of the major crash in the mortgage and lending markets
in recent years indicates that much stronger coalitions of such activist
groups, perhaps with significant social science research assistance, will be
necessary to deal with persisting and severe housing problems faced by
low- and moderate-income Americans. The NCRC does remain active.
In 2014 its president made the following comment:

> We applaud President Obama for focusing on income inequality
> and the importance of upward mobility in his State of the Union
> address.... A trend in this country has emerged which is in essence
> a war on poor and working people.... Housing is a central issue in
> this fight.... Homeownership is the single most effective path to the
> middle class.[74]

The NFHA also remains active. In 2014, on the heels of the Utah
state Senate's plans to table an antidiscrimination bill protecting gays
and lesbians under the state's existing housing laws, the NFHA called
for the state legislature body to keep the bill alive:

> Today, Utah's housing and employment law does not protect all
> people, and leaves the door open for landlords and other housing
> providers to deny housing choice to people based on their sexual
> orientation or gender identity rather than on objective qualifying
> standards. This is not the American way of equality and fairness. All
> people deserve the right to equal access to housing.[75]

Sociologists and Environmental Racism

Sociologists have worked on a variety of environmental issues with local
community groups. Sociologist Robert Bullard and his associates have
done much important research assisting several local groups facing

serious environmental hazards. As an organic intellectual representing excluded people of color, Bullard has worked hard to make their concerns about the environmental degradation of their communities public. In the 1970s, he and his students at Texas Southern University examined the pattern of waste facility siting in Houston, Texas. They found that from the early 1920s through the 1970s, all city-owned landfills and most incinerators were located in black neighborhoods. A local community group, the Northeast Community Action Group, used the sociologists' findings of racial discrimination in their political efforts to bring positive changes. They succeeded in forcing a change in state permitting require-ments for waste facilities and in getting the city council to restrict the location of future waste facilities.[76]

In addition, Bullard did research for a Louisiana group, Citizens Against Nuclear Trash, which was trying to stop the location of a pri-vately owned uranium enrichment plant in the middle of rural black communities. This research showed discrimination in the choice of the site for this hazardous plant—a working-class community that was 97 percent black. Community groups pressured the Nuclear Regulatory Commission (NRC) to look into environmental justice issues, but the final environmental impact statement only dealt briefly with these hard environmental questions.[77] Even the Environmental Protection Agency (EPA) criticized the NRC report as inadequate and recommended additional study of environmental impact. Presently Bullard is dean of the Barbara Jordan-Mickey Leland School of Public Affairs at Texas Southern University in Houston. Using a community-based participa-tory research approach, and providing support services on an array of environmental justice and related issues, a research center there strives to include populations and communities in environmental decision-making who are at greatest risk of environmental and health challenges.[78] Moreover, Bullard has been instrumental in creating and spreading the important concepts of "environmental racism" and "environmental justice," and has coauthored or coedited numerous books dealing with these major policy issues.[79]

Bullard's award-winning book *Dumping in Dixie: Race, Class and Environmental Quality* is a standard text in the environmental justice arena. Two more recent books are *Environmental Health and Racial Equity in the US* and *The Wrong Complexion for Protection*.[80] Under-standably, *Newsweek* magazine has named Bullard one of the thirteen environmental leaders of the twenty-first century.[81]

Robert Bullard is a major example of the way in which a liberation sociologist can have significant and lasting positive influence on future generations of activist-scholars. As an undergraduate, David Naguib Pellow, a University of Minnesota sociologist who has now published extensively on environmental justice issues in communities of color, contacted Bullard. Bullard told him about the environmental justice movements' activities and became a mentor to Pellow. Mentors of color were central to Pellow's development as a liberation sociologist. "It was great ... psychologically, because I could envision my work as a career, and I was able to model myself after them, knowing I could make an original contribution as I read their books." From the likes of sociologist Bullard, Pellow grasped the importance of being accountable to the local communities in which he works.[82]

Acknowledging that one cannot remain dispassionate even though accuracy and objectivity are imperative to the sociological craft, Pellow traces his commitment to liberation sociology to his childhood in the southern United States. While he cites the racial, industrial, and natural histories of the South as factors that influenced his liberation sociology, his parents also encouraged him to include his liberal political views in his work. "I am a Southern man, so I never saw any shortage of social inequality, but I was lucky to have access to natural environmental amenities.... My parents were involved in the civil rights movement ... and they were role models for turning out students who would go on to do work in their communities."[83]

Pellow considers the highpoint of his career so far to be the support he received from the people in the community organization featured in his book *The Silicon Valley of Dreams*. With coauthor Lisa Sun-Hee Park, he examines environmental racism within the context of immigrant patterns, labor markets, and the historical arrangements of colonialism, arguing that one cannot understand the global economy without considering the role workers of color play in the electronic industry's toxic work environments.[84] Affirmation from community activists, who used information from the book to raise funds and boost their legitimacy, is precisely what Pellow means when he speaks about the importance of being accountable to communities. "All too often academics don't have to make a case for what they do, and that can lead communities down the wrong path. We all need to be questioned," he explains.[85]

In addition, Pellow, again with Lisa Sun-Hee Park, published *The Slums of Aspen*, based on comprehensive fieldwork (including observations, interviews, and archival analyses of documents) in the Aspen, Colorado, resort area. Focusing on low-wage immigrants mainly from Latin America, who work in the service and leisure industries there, the authors examine connections between environmental crises, immigration, social inequality, and racial privilege:[86]

> For more than three decades, scholars have presented evidence that low-income and minority communities face greater threats from

pollution and industrial hazards than other groups. While these studies reveal the hardships and crimes associated with environmental inequality, fewer studies consider the flip side of that reality: environmental privilege. Environmental privilege results from the exercise of economic, political, and cultural power that some groups enjoy, which enables them near exclusive access to coveted environmental amenities such as parks, mountains, and open lands.[87]

Pellow's research serves to persuasively demonstrate that social science's mostly indifferent approach to "the connection between humans, the environment, and communities of color" is irresponsible and outdated.[88] He strives to create a sociology more responsive to audiences outside academia, and the daily experiences of socially subjugated peoples are a central focus of his scholarship and activism: "I've been active in social and environmental justice work for more than 20 years and that experience shapes my teaching, student mentoring, and research every day because those three things are ultimately done for the purpose of achieving a world that is more socially just and ecologically sustainable."[89]

Another activist sociologist, Daniel Faber contributes greatly to the ever-widening scope of environmental justice scholarship. A sociology professor and director of the Northeastern Environmental Justice Research Collaborative, Faber focuses his research on such areas as political economy and crisis theory, environmental sociology and policy, and globalization. His most recent work is concerned with problems of environmental injustice in the United States. Faber has produced major research reports related to environmental justice, including *Green of Another Color*, which assesses relations between US foundations and the environmental justice movement. Faber is a board member of the Alliance for a Healthy Tomorrow, a coalition of scientists, health professionals, environmental advocates, and labor unions working for a precautionary approach to environmental policy in Massachusetts. He has recently worked on a report on climate justice, ecological refugees, and equitable policy approaches for dealing with global warming.[90]

The idea that people are not polluted equally is a fundamental tenant of his research and associated activism. In his book *Capitalizing on Environmental Injustice*, he explains environmental justice concerns as necessarily involving a merging of previously independent social movements: the civil rights movement, the occupational health and safety movement, the indigenous lands movement, the environmental health movement, the human rights movements, and the immigrants' rights movement. These outwardly disparate movements have a mutual underlying cause: concerns about capitalistic profit orientations.[91] Faber continually seeks to look at environmental injustices as experienced by people of color; farmers and rural families; working-class whites; and indigenous peoples, peasants, and farmworkers—in Central America and the Global South generally. His own background reportedly plays a profound role in his passion for environmental justice. He was raised in a family committed to civil rights. Growing up in Kentucky, he was regularly exposed to the major injustices facing poor families in there and in other parts of Appalachia, particularly those connected to farming and the strip-mining for coal.[92]

Action Research on Violence against Women

In 1986, the Rainbow House, a center for battered women in Chicago, began a violence prevention program. This included programs for high school students on the patterns of male violence in US society. As these activists realized that children's attitudes toward violence were learned at a young age, they developed programs for ever-younger children, including a plan to instruct the teachers of children in conflict resolution. A Rainbow House Institute for Choosing Non-Violence was established to facilitate programs teaching about the pervasiveness of societal violence and about nonviolent ways of countering it. Numerous Chicago organizations and agencies have used the nonviolence training programs of the institute to the present day. At one point in its development, the director of Rainbow House asked sociologist Nancy Matthews of Northeastern Illinois University to help design a research program to evaluate the training program at the institute.[93]

A key goal of the collaborative research project was to assess the effectiveness of nonviolence training programs at Rainbow House by means of qualitative social science methods. Other goals included building more ties between the bold new antiviolence program and key local leaders and funders, as well as the general public, and exploring the utility of a new site-intensive approach to nonviolence training. The sociological researcher, Matthews, "conducted observations of trainings followed by interviews with individuals and groups about the perceived effects of the training, and observations of interactions at the site."[94] Many participants in the training programs reported that they had become desensitized to societal violence and that the programs resensitized them to the seriousness and pervasiveness of this societal crisis. The Rainbow House staff learned from this research about how people react to violence in their everyday lives, including how they cope with the stress and how they contribute to violence by becoming desensitized. The research also generated expanded discussions across racial, ethnic, and other community lines, thereby facilitating community building. In this case, the goal of reducing violence in urban communities was furthered by intensive collaboration between a community group and an activist sociologist.

We should add that in recent years numerous female sociologists and other female social scientists, as well as some male social scientists, have developed a now significant body of field research on the violence faced by women in society, not just in the United States but across the globe. Indeed, in the 1990s an important new international, interdisciplinary journal called *Violence Against Women* was started, one that has explicitly encouraged traditional academic researchers as well as clinicians, practitioners, poets, and activists to submit material for publication.[95]

CONCLUSION

In this and previous chapters, we see a number of important lessons in the action research projects. Community-oriented, collaborative research often takes time to develop fully. The social scientists involved must be flexible enough to fit into an ongoing collaborative process. From the viewpoint of community residents and activists, participatory action research can demystify research and policy-making by academic "experts" and can create an environment that welcomes new community participants to the research process. It provides a collaborative and more democratic way to develop social policy and has helped to build networks of community activists and projects in many cities. Participatory action research tends to use limited resources effectively and to build new research capacity in communities. Moreover, participatory action research has theoretical, empirical, and personal rewards for the researchers that come from assisting in positive community changes.[96]

Interestingly, as one can see in numerous examples in this book, much progressive sociological research now is conducted by researchers from the less elitist colleges and universities, where the pressures to do abstract-empirical, instrumental-positivistic research may not be as great. Some of the less elitist colleges and universities (and some non-university think tanks) appear to have developed much more extensive relationships with progressive community activists and organizations. Increasingly, this has meant the creation of new networks of knowledge production. Indeed, these college and university settings have also generated some of the most important alternative and countersystem sociological thinking about the operation and character of US society.[97]

In addition, much of the impetus for participatory action research has come from the efforts of scholar-activists in postcolonial countries to reduce or end various forms of social oppression. Recall Orlando Fals-Borda's comment that he could not be a scientist, much less a human being, and remain uncommitted in sight of human injustice and suffering. In participatory action research, social scientists are still under the broad oversight of some of their disciplinary peers but must additionally submit their work to the full review of the people they are trying to serve.

Moreover, the method of participatory research varies greatly in its application. Sometimes it refers only to the presence of a few open-ended questions in the research instrument being used. For example, one international health organization advertised a "woman-friendly" program that contained a participatory research component consisting only of a few such open-ended questions. Much other participatory action research involves those researched in key decisions on what is researched, how it is researched, and how it is reported. Between these two examples, there is a range of research projects in which those being studied participate to varying degrees in the social science research process.

Today, participatory action research has extended throughout the world, though its use in the industrialized world has not always been faithful to a commitment to end social oppression. Moreover, as Davydd J. Greenwood and Morten Levin suggest, "the racially oppressed, the homeless, the drug addicted, the abused, and the illiterate in the north are oppressed, as are the workers in factories run by executives who use participation as a cover-up for speed-ups, downsizing, and union busting, as are middle managers who are being replaced with cheaper labor that is more easily manipulated. Oppression is oppression everywhere it is found, south or north."[98]

As we have seen, many participatory action researchers are concerned with finding progressive solutions for the problems of real people in everyday settings. This accent on *solutions* is an important virtue of participatory action research, including that in the United States. Oddly enough, in US colleges and universities, we have numerous courses on social problems but very few on social solutions.[99]

This persisting skew in US sociology is problematic and discourages many, including new or younger, social scientists from getting involved in community-related research with a clear solution focus. Fortunately, the numerous participatory action researchers are helping to change this view. In the twenty-first century, solutions will be central to the social science research process, if only because of the many current threats to human civilization over this century. As a rule, participatory action research involves the social researcher in the lives of those people being researched. At its best, participatory action research involves those researched in both the decision-making and the interpretation phases of the research project. Such an approach does not view the people studied as passive but helps to empower them to bring significant change in their own lives and communities.

CHAPTER 7

Liberation Theory and Liberating Action

The Contemporary Scene

Meaningful social diversity is a key aspect of the theories and perspectives developed by countersystem sociologists. This is not surprising, given that this way of practicing social science aims to create a sociology for those who struggle for their liberation from various types of societal discrimination and oppression. The methodological and conceptual needs of emancipation struggles are multiple and varied. In this chapter we turn our attention to some contemporary theorists engaged in critical social theory, those social scientists who choose to centrally elaborate theories that aid in action to build a better social world. We illustrate here how liberation sociologists have integrated social theory, research, and activism in their everyday lives.

ABSTRACTIONS FOR WHAT?

Generally, the theorizing of liberation sociologists is different from much conventional theorizing that proposes abstractions to explain social relations as if these abstractions were neutrally and naturally generated ideas. Recall that C. Wright Mills used the term *abstracted empiricism* to designate a style of social theorizing (or lack thereof) that has been commonplace in the social sciences from at least the 1930s to the present. In the case of abstracted empiricism, theory becomes the collection of low-level generalizations—generally "variables useful in interpretations of statistical findings."[1] As we saw in Chapter 3, those working in this social science style tend to view answers to opinion surveys and censuses as the best data, data often to be manipulated statistically to seek relations among variables. This usually results in assertions of statistical proportions and relations that are considered to be empirical tests of abstract ideas and conceptions.

Another theory style criticized by Mills is the development of "grand theory," as exemplified in the work of Talcott Parsons and his associates. Such grand theory entails speculative attempts at constructing all-encompassing taxonomies of societal phenomena. In the era after World War II, Parsons's teachings "were dogmatic and elitist, useful both to the obscurantist and the managerial."[2] In an important book, *Toward a General Theory of Action* (1965), Parsons and Edward Shils wrote that "the theory of action is a conceptual scheme for the analysis of behavior of living organisms. It conceives of this behavior as oriented to the attainment of ends in situations, by means of the normatively regulated expenditure of energy."[3] For them, good social science theory has three functions: (1) to "aid in the codification of our existing concrete knowledge" understood as "unifying discrete observations under general concepts"; (2) to be a guide for good research; and (3) to help control "the biases of observation."[4] These seem like reasonable goals, but in reality whose observations were Parsons and Shils seeking to codify? On reviewing the index of this influential book, one discovers that such leading and critical sociological theorists as Karl Marx, Jane Addams, Thorstein Veblen, W. E. B. Du Bois, Oliver C. Cox, and C. Wright Mills are *not* even cited there.

Parsons and his associates were shaping the then-dominant structural-functionalist framework in the direction of the ideas of Émile Durkheim and Max Weber, both of whom were constructed conservatively as forerunners of a sociological theory of social consensus and a social system that they were proposing. The more progressive ideas and proclivities of Durkheim and Weber (see Chapter 2) were generally left out of the influential structural-functionalist analysis. From the 1930s to the 1960s, Parsons and his associates made little use of the ideas of such probing critical theorists as Karl Marx. Indeed, Alfred Marshall, Vilfredo Pareto, Émile Durkheim, and Max Weber were the key figures examined in detail in what is perhaps Parsons's most famous work, the 1937 book *The Structure of Social Action* (see Chapter 3). Parsons saw in the ideas of these scholars a convergence in the direction of a new "voluntaristic theory of action."[5] This generalized theory successfully accented the importance of traditional values and social rituals in human societies as opposed to the older utilitarian, means-ends, economic interpretations of societies. Parsons's grand theory thus made some important contributions in bringing certain neglected aspects of social life back into the theoretical discussion, yet his attempts to develop social theory were usually at a very abstract level and made use of much obscure jargon.

By not drawing significantly on the more critical theoretical and empirical analyses of Western societies, Parsons and his colleagues left out a serious consideration of hierarchy, oppression, and ongoing intergroup domination, such as that found in racist, sexist, heterosexist, and classist arrangements. By doing this, Parsons helped to shape the future of US sociological theory in a direction often more or less supportive of the oppressive status quo.[6] A generation or two of graduate students were thereby shielded from most of the critical tradition in social science theory and analysis.

As a point of contrast, consider how the black feminist scholar bell hooks (Gloria Jean Watkins) has described her theorizing efforts in the area of contemporary feminism: "Writing progressive feminist theory was so compelling precisely because we knew that the work we were doing, if at all useful, would have a meaningful transformative impact on our lives and the lives of women and men both inside and outside the academy."[7] Compare the distancing vocabulary of "living organisms" and "expenditure of energy" that Parsons used to refer to human beings with the active "we," "useful," and "impact" language of bell hooks. Also compare the grandiose aim of abstract knowledge assembly on living organisms in Parsons's analysis with bell hooks' aim of theorizing in order to have a "transformative impact" on actual human lives.

Liberation theorizing aims at human emancipation through the development of "knowledge that helps persons locate their experiences, discontents, and troubles as aspects of processes that are subject to human intervention and transformation."[8] As Mills put it, this theorizing involves a sociological imagination that allows people "to grasp what is going on in the world, and to understand what is happening in themselves as minute points of the intersections of biography and history within society."[9] Liberation theorizing also means reflecting on the methodological and normative principles governing the contemporary practice of sociology.

IMPLICIT THEORY AND EVERYDAY EXPERIENCE: OPPRESSION IN BUREAUCRATIC SETTINGS

Emancipatory sociological theories are important to those engaged in transforming the world into a more just place for two principal reasons. First, theories are like looking glasses that allow us to read social reality.

Theories can render important aspects of social reality, the "facts," visible while hiding other aspects of reality. We place "facts" in quotation marks here because what these facts are—and what they are called—will vary with the social science theory being used. Second, the decision that one solution and not another—or one result and not another—is what is needed to bring desired change typically depends on the social theory chosen. In this way, social theories can become linked to action; they are "ideas to think with" about troubled times and realities. Ultimately, most human interactions, whether orderly or conflict-riddled, are based on some type of social theory, whether or not we are aware of that theory.

Although we are usually unaware of the intricacies of the thought processes that lead us to our choices of frames, perspectives, and strategies, few of us will claim that we act without thinking. Sociological theorizing is the systematic thinking behind and interpretation of what social scientists and others observe and discover and behind the actions they take in application of discoveries. Systematic theorizing in social science is, typically, different from everyday thinking in that it ordinarily involves more detailed analysis, greater rigor, more reflection, and more attention to current and historical contexts.

Nevertheless, there are some important similarities between systematic theorizing and everyday theories. Often the latter are the beginning of the former. To illustrate the process of everyday theorizing and the impact it has on our understanding and actions, consider this hypothetical case of a college professor whose salary is considerably lower than that of a male colleague who performs work identical in nature, effort, and responsibility to hers. Initially, she was shocked and angry to find this out, since this male colleague was hired some years after her, and she had actually trained him for his current job. And she has continued to help him on a regular basis. "Why is this happening to me?" she asked a group of coworkers over lunch. This type of question—*Why is this happening?*—is one that frequently initiates the search for a specific or generalized explanation in everyday life, as well as in the practice of social science.[10]

One of her colleagues advanced the idea that the disparity in her salary had to do with the sometimes-biased ways in which her department "chairman"—the title still often given to academic middle managers—made some salary decisions. Her colleague added that the explanation may be "in the evil in this man's heart." Expanding on this idea, her colleague added that "he often gives salary raises and other privileges to his friends instead of rewarding objective merit." On hearing this, a female colleague who was present in the group noted that not all the fault should be placed on this chair. The favored male colleague is well known for being obsequious, in a manner that has earned him a place in the chair's inner circle, an "ole boy" network that runs this particular department. A third colleague agreed but argued that the critical thing to observe is that this network is composed exclusively of white men. The problem, in her view, was not in the ill will of the chair, but in the different way in which men and women are differentially allowed into decision-making networks in most college and corporate bureaucracies. Thus, she argued, the lower salary of the better-qualified female professor had to do with "institutional sexism." Moreover, since the latter person was a woman of color, it was proposed, too, that some racial bias was likely present, not just in the chair's discriminatory practice but also in the institutional discrimination built into managerial inner circles at most historically white colleges and universities. "These are well-established ways of doing things, of thinking about people, and of feeling toward what they deserve because of what they are perceived to be able to do, and not do, well," this female colleague added.

This third explanation captured the imagination of the group around the table, whose members then came up with a number of other examples of similarly unfair situations affecting white women and people of color. Take some examples drawn loosely from several incidents of which we have heard: A woman faculty member was passed over for an appointment in spite of being better qualified, and another had spent many more years in a lower rank than men typically spent. Additionally, women faculty members in many departments have reported that they are asked to perform too many of the dead-end tasks that typically do not lead to significant salary rewards and career advancement.

Moreover, in the case we began with, yet another woman faculty member commented on the disproportionate burden that women, including women faculty, ordinarily bear in the US family. The woman being discussed may have had less time for research and publication because she had the greater burden of child care in her family. Finally, someone called the group's attention to the possibility that the woman faculty member being discussed might not be an isolated case and that men in their college were probably paid more than the women there for the same work. Further study disclosed that, in fact, women were making on average less than men made for the same teaching and research activities. Once again, institutional sexism was likely evident.

In this plausible example of a woman faculty member facing problems in a college department, it is clear that, although the various explanations contribute to understanding, some are more useful than others in probing beneath the surface to interpret what is going on—and to learn what might be done to correct the situation. The explanation that the situation is a result of the "evil in the manager's heart" is, of course, very difficult to verify. This explanation identifies the cause of the problem as one that is difficult to remedy. The next explanation—that part of the blame should be attributed to the active influence of the better paid male faculty member on the chair—can be verified through observation and comparison, yet it is not clear what corrective action could be exercised. The third explanation, or explanatory theory, does not contradict the previous ones and can be more easily verified with numerous empirical observations of similar cases. In many real-life situations like this, the recognition of a certain institutionalized pattern of discrimination against women faculty has led a female faculty member to consult a lawyer and sue her college or university for redress.

THEORY TO CHANGE THE WORLD

The Prophetic Tradition

A crucial element of much liberation sociology thinking is the ancient belief of numerous prophetic traditions that the world can be changed in fundamental ways through intentional human effort. This old ideal has some deep-lying religious roots. In the West, some attribute its origin to early Judaism.[11] A number of analysts of US social science have distinguished between what they call the prophetic and the priestly traditions of social science. Robert Friedrichs has noted that the prophetical tradition in sociology speaks of human alienation—that is, "from one's untapped creative resources and an estrangement from the bonds of community with one's fellows."[12] Prophetic sociology calls for freeing human beings from this human-imposed alienation. This belief in major human change informs all liberation sociologies and, to varying degrees, progressive thinking in other social science specialties and numerous professions. Indeed, the liberation theologies or progressive worldviews of people in Latin America, Africa, Asia, as well as of those of Jewish, Latino, Asian, Native American, and African American descent in the United States usually share in this fundamental assumption about human change.

Critical Social Theories

In this chapter we cannot review the full range of social science theories currently in use. We will discuss instead some of the conceptual frameworks termed *critical social theories*, those that involve theorizing what is particularly useful for human emancipation and liberation from societal oppressions. Whereas some postmodern analysts have called for an end to social theory, we see this view as out of touch with everyday human reality. Whether we like it or not, most human action is embedded in explicit or tacit social theory. Indeed, there are many social science analysts intent on developing useful versions of critical social theories. One of the exciting developments in recent years has been the emergence of an array of critical theories in both the humanities and the social sciences. A recurring theme among these critical theorists is that of social domination, subjugation, and oppression. Most of these analysts seek the liberation of human beings from these dehumanizing and oppressive societal circumstances.

Introductory sociology textbooks have periodically designated the structural-functionalist, the social-conflict, and the symbolic-interactionist perspectives as the three most important sociological paradigms. However, these paradigms do not capture the richness of contemporary theory in sociology and related social sciences. For the purpose of assessing a sociology of liberation, we will distinguish between instrumental-positivistic approaches to theory and critical approaches to theory. These differences are fundamental. They distinguish among social scientists in terms of how they claim to know what they know—their fundamental assumptions in regard to what they see as the scientific method and their ultimate aims in doing social science.

Critical social theorists seek to bring about awareness in individuals and their groups so that they can overcome the social oppression in the world around them. To bring about this awareness, one needs to be involved in a recurring dialogue with the human subjects of research and not just in a distancing observation or experimental manipulation of observed objects. In contrast, instrumental-positivistic science seeks a neutral way of learning about the world, a way to produce knowledge that is not tied to any particular self. When transferred to social science, this attitude makes society into scattered, neutral pieces of information—into raw data to be observed from the outside.

Today, the expansion of social science theory has numerous branches, including feminist theory, queer theory, postmodern theories, antiracist theories, European critical theory, critical criminology, and critical legal studies, among others. What these perspectives have in common is that they start from the belief that all human beings are "potentially active agents in the construction of their social world and social lives."[13]

THE CRITICAL THEORY OF THE FRANKFURT SCHOOL

One of the oldest critical theory traditions is that of the "Frankfurt School" in Germany. Sociologists and other social scientists associated with the University of Frankfurt have had a major impact on liberation-oriented theorists since the 1920s, when the Institute for Social Research at the University of Frankfurt was founded. A group of Marxist intellectuals established the institute as a research organization. Its critical and radical orientation, and the fact that most of its members were Jewish, led to serious attacks by fascist forces in Germany, and the institute was forced to relocate to the United States in 1934. In 1949 the institute and its members were able to return to Germany. Its members sought to synthesize a large number of social science and humanities disciplines, to integrate theory and empirical research, and to overcome the isolation of traditional social theory from practical uses. They were critical of orthodox Marxism, too, but did not reject its ambitious project, which was "the ultimate unity of critical theory and revolutionary practice."[14]

The scholars in the Frankfurt School developed major critiques of capitalistic ideology and culture for a growing audience of intellectuals and students across the globe. The participation of the working class in European fascist movements before and during World War II led them to argue that "the struggle for socialism could not be carried on successfully unless the working class developed a 'conscious will' for a liberated and rational society. It was the responsibility of intellectuals to produce the critical and liberating ideas which might eventually shape the working class' conscious will."[15] The Frankfurt School's concentration on class-linked social exploitation and domination has long made their writing inspiring to many liberation-oriented social scientists across much of the globe.

Theodor Adorno and Max Horkheimer

Among the best-known members of the Frankfurt School are Theodor Adorno and Max Horkheimer. In their important book *Dialectic of Enlightenment*, they examined problematic ideas of eighteenth-century European Enlightenment thinkers. The aims of the Enlightenment thinkers were mostly reformist, not radical. Their intellectual program was not to launch a radical break with a reactionary past by fully enabling ideals such as freedom, liberty, and equality, but rather to achieve "the dissolution of myths and the substitution of knowledge for fancy."[16] Unfortunately, Enlightenment thinkers sometimes paved the way for new forms of social domination under the growing capitalist bourgeoisie, with its strong scientific commitments. In theory, at least, scientific thought was supposed to improve the welfare of ordinary folk, but too often it created more effective ways of dominating them. The major advantages of the late eighteenth-century political revolutions and of expanding and imperialistic capitalism usually accrued to European elites and upper-middle classes. Whether evolutionary or revolutionary, societal changes are not necessarily progressive.

Thus, in Germany, long considered one of the most civilized societies, a far-right totalitarian (Nazi) state with advanced technological development emerged in the 1930s—substantially out of political turmoil provoked by economic depression. As Adorno and Horkheimer remind us, the possibility of a rationally organized and free society lies not in faith in some natural force of progressive change but in the determined efforts of human intelligence and organizations guided by a critical and democratic vigilance.

The Current Generation: Jürgen Habermas

Jürgen Habermas is an important contemporary sociologist, one who wears the theoretical mantle of the Frankfurt School. Very productive, Habermas began to have an impact in the English-speaking world when his book *Knowledge and Human Interests* was translated into English in 1971.[17] Habermas's theorizing covers the social sciences as well as ethics, law, literary issues, and communications, and shows a recurring concern with the emancipatory ideas of Karl Marx, the need to overcome positivism in social science, and the obligation to create critical social theory relevant to modern societies. His main critique of traditional social science theory is its tendency to interpret the world too narrowly and usually within the confines of physical science and its accompanying technologies.

Habermas notes two tendencies in contemporary social theory, what he terms the *empirical-analytical* (instrumental-positivistic) orientation and the "historical-hermeneutic" (dialectical-interpretive) orientation. This empirical-analytical orientation generally uses controlled observation of behavior, "which is set up in an isolated field under reproducible conditions by subjects reproducible at will." In contrast, those working from a dialectical-interpretive approach examine "the situational consciousness of acting individuals themselves" in their social life-worlds and explore sociologically the meanings articulated therein.[18]

Representatives of both orientations can use the idea of a larger social whole within which particular observed phenomena are situated. Yet, the instrumental-positivists may rely on the idea of a social system, an organic entity of mutually related elements. We see this idea in the work of sociology's structural functionalists, as previously discussed. The purpose of this type of research is to specify the manner in which system components, often viewed as certain operationally defined "variables," react or relate to each other. This social scientific research lends itself to use for established bureaucratic administration. Scientifically accurate predictions are supposed to be based on theories that deal with observed objects that have lawlike patterns.

In Habermas's view, social systems are in reality not neatly law-like repetitive systems because social systems of human beings always "stand in historical life-contexts." At best, the often useful findings of instrumental-positivistic research relate only to parts of real social systems, and conventional research techniques typically cannot demonstrate how a particular societal phenomenon relates to the societal totality.[19] Habermas is also critical of the positivistic notion of value-neutral research. As he sees it, this value-neutral claim is only a way to avoid openly discussing the problem of how, by whom, and for what purposes the social research is actually conducted.

Habermas is critical of much postmodernist thought, a tradition we discuss below. He sees today an implicit alliance of postmodernist conservatives with older premodernist conservatives and neoconservatives. The newer conservatives, among whom he places Georges Bataille, Michel Foucault, and Jacques Derrida, claim that they have discovered the idea of a "decentered subjectivity"—that is, that individual agency is no longer a basic assumption necessary for analysis. This decentered subjectivity is "emancipated from the imperatives of work and usefulness, and with this experience they step outside the modern world. On the basis of modernistic attitudes, they justify an irreconcilable antimodernism."[20] Moreover, neoconservatives in US social science have observed the "decline of substantive reason, the differentiation of science, morality and art, the modern worldview and its merely procedural rationality, with sadness and recommend a withdrawal to a position anterior to modernity."[21]

The neoconservatives, among whom Habermas places the sociologist Daniel Bell, "welcome the development of modern sciences, as long as this only goes beyond its sphere to carry forward technical progress, capitalist growth, and national administration."[22] As Bell sees it, late capitalism is a postindustrial society, one that is moving beyond the old industrialization, such as that of steel and automobiles. What he sees as a democratic populism of the current era has a desire for "wholesale egalitarianism" that insists "on complete leveling," and these egalitarians are seeking to get rid of the ideas of individual merit and rewards for personal achievement.[23] The development of a critical theory and science that deeply question the status quo is not seen as valuable by these neoconservative social scientists, who seem wedded to the many social inequalities still created and maintained by contemporary elite decision-makers.

The critical theories of the Frankfurt School have roots in the Marxist tradition. However, the influence of Marxist thought in European and US social science was greatly reduced between 1917 and the late 1950s, for two major reasons. One was the political dominance of Soviet Marxism, "which pushed other versions into a marginal position ... with the result that they were, generally speaking, little known and largely ignored."[24] The second, and more important, reason was the fascism and anticommunism in many Western countries, including Nazism in Germany and protofascist movements such as political anticommunism and McCarthyism in the United States. In most countries, only a few brave intellectuals and community activists dared to work with Marxist or neo-Marxist ideas during this long period.

Since the 1950s, Marxist scholarship has been going through a process of renewal and reinterpretation, especially in Europe. Although theorists like Habermas and Herbert Marcuse have been consistently critical of Marx and abandoned some of his ideas, they nonetheless have accepted much in his dialectical and historical approach to understanding society. The dialectical and historical perspective generally accents the important idea of social totality. The idea of the social whole must be grasped by ordinary people if societal emancipation is to occur.[25] In Marx's thinking, *totality* refers to the ways in which the social whole, such as a capitalist system, can be seen impacting each of its parts (see Chapter 2). The societal totality is always there, in this sense. There are no fixed boundaries, and the interconnectedness of the social world is central to Marx and to later interpretations of European critical theory.[26]

Communication and Liberation

Habermas is a strong advocate of the idea of societal progress and the *critical* use of human reason. His optimistic view includes the idea of an increased interactive dialogue among people across many groups and societies. He calls this a theory of "communicative action."[27] Habermas views the macroeconomic structures of bureaucratic capitalism as routinely burdensome for the worlds of human action. In a modern capitalist society, these macroeconomic structures crash in on the everyday worlds of people, thereby "colonizing" these life worlds.[28] They constantly create the everyday mechanisms of social exploitation faced by ordinary people as they live, work, and consume.

In US sociology, *symbolic interactionism* is the common term for theories that call attention to the role that meaning and communication play in everyday life. However, symbolic interactionism is often concerned with situations in which actors negotiate to "mutually fit their interpretations in order to coordinate their actions."[29] Although there are aspects of symbolic negotiation in communication processes, the latter involve much more than symbolic negotiation. Habermas's theory of communicative action is founded on the distinction between instrumental action and emancipatory communicative action. We engage in instrumental actions to achieve anticipated goals under given conditions with available means. A commercial advertisement is a one-way communicative device, an instrument typically designed to achieve the goal of persuading people to consume.

In contrast, *communicative action* is more democratic and is about conveying messages to others who actively interpret the message and then interact with and talk back to the first actor. Success, in this case, consists of the actors mutually understanding each other and agreeing how the messages should be interpreted—and on how each should act. The primacy of the communicative mode is a major theoretical insight of Habermas's general theoretical framework. "Communicative rationality," Habermas writes, "carries with it connotations based ultimately on the central experience of the unconstrained, unifying, consensus-bringing force of argumentative speech, in which different participants overcome their merely subjective views and, owing to the mutuality of rationally motivated conviction, assure themselves of both the unity of the objective world and the intersubjectivity of their life world."[30]

Thus, these democratic communicative forms of discourse, language included, can be emancipatory. Habermas identifies elements of an emancipatory social theory, one that works as a "frame of reference for distinguishing between 'what appears to be' and 'what is,' so as to eliminate institutional domination."[31] His theory relates to George Herbert Mead's ideas about the social self and to Émile Durkheim's theory of the linkage of sacred rites to the realm of the secular (see Chapter 2). Amplifying their views helped Habermas to provide a "double-edged theory of communicative behavior, evolutionary and procedural."[32] Moreover, for Habermas, the idea of communicative rationality serves as a basis for a theory of modernity, a theory of social evolution, an ethics of discourse, and a theory of language.

A crucial aspect of communicative reason is that it "does not simply encounter ready-made subjects and systems; rather, it takes part in structuring what is to be preserved. The utopian perspective of reconciliation and freedom is ingrained in the conditions for the communicative sociation of individuals; it is built into the linguistic mechanism of the reproduction of the species."[33] Thus, in our terms, Habermas is proposing that communicative reason—active interpersonal discourse in its most uncorrupted democratic form—is emancipatory. His theory allows for a moral reading of the world that accommodates the aim of dramatically changing the world, and it is flexible enough to use with various democratic projects.

Nevertheless, one problem with his theory is that its principal level for analysis is the society taken as a whole. In trying to shed light on the relationship between social conditions and individual freedom, Habermas implicitly theorizes about an undifferentiated public, about individuals struggling to free themselves from the social and cultural constraints that compel their behavior. Some theorists of democracy have raised serious questions about this assumption of a *homogeneous* public in this theory of communicative action. Instead, they underscore the persisting significant divisions and diverse languages of class, race, heterosexuality, and gender that constantly interfere with goals of increased societal communication and democracy. Clearly, such limitations invite a thorough revision and extension of this theory of communicative rationality, which is in our view an innovative start toward conceptualizing a better social world.

Impact on the United States

The penetration of European critical theory into US sociology has occurred rather slowly. During the 1960s and 1970s, the critical turn in US sociology was only modestly influenced by these creative European sources. More important in challenging the dominance of a too-quantitative, instrumental positivism was the work of interpretive scholars and theorists like innovative sociologist Erving Goffman. For example, the study of public place interaction was pioneered by Goffman and his students, who gave much attention to the meaning of microlevel interaction between strangers in public places. Goffman was perceptive in examining interactive rituals, such as deference rituals between people seen as superior and inferior. Obsequious words and gestures, such as the etiquette of racial relations in the South during legal segregation, were a type of deference ritual, which "functions as a symbolic means by which appreciation is regularly conveyed to a recipient."[34]

With much new sociological insight, Goffman described other subtle dimensions of social behavior, such as the distinction people make between their actions in the frontstages and the backstages of their lives.[35] Goffman, and other interpretive scholars like Harold Garfinkel, helped US social scientists see the importance of the everyday symbolic interaction and recurring interpersonal meanings. Although the latter too often ignored the larger structural realties around the everyday "micro" events, these US innovators did help to stimulate more interest in the critical sociologies of European scholars like Habermas and Marcuse. Today we see a more frequent use of European critical theory in US social science, especially by those concerned with systems of social oppression.

Contemporary Feminist Thought

Among the important critical theories, contemporary feminist theories stand out for their dynamism and growing contributions to understanding society. Feminist theories generally assess the situations and experiences of women in male-dominated, patriarchal societies. They view women as central *subjects* in the investigative project—that is, they seek to see society and societal change from the vantage point of women. In feminist analyses, there are well-developed conceptual frameworks targeting key aspects of gendered oppression and liberation. A feminist framework is often "critical and activist on behalf of women, seeking to produce a better world for women—and thus, it argues, for humankind."[36] Beginning with the intellectual and activist efforts of feminist pragmatists like Jane Addams, Charlotte Perkins Gilman, and their many female (and some male) colleagues in the late nineteenth and early twentieth centuries (see Chapter 3), feminist thinkers have brought to critical social theory a major concern for the cognitive underpinning of oppression and for the negative emotions, feelings, and attitudes that also underlie contemporary oppression—as well as for strategies of resistance that encompass counter-emotions by means of consciousness-raising, a major resistance strategy. Consciousness-raising includes self-inquiry into one's own attitudes as well as active dialogues with numerous others.

Feminist scholars and researchers in sociology and other disciplines work to broaden their academic disciplines and to rework the fund of disciplinary knowledge in terms of the experiences of women. Within the discipline of sociology, feminist concepts and approaches are gradually beginning to have a general impact. Feminist sociologists such as Judith Stacey and Barrie Thorne have noted that today the fields of economics and political science are still more masculinist than sociology, whereas anthropology and history have incorporated some feminist ideas into the mainstream of their disciplines. They view sociology as falling in between, with feminist ideas beginning to have important impacts. Stacey and Thorne also accent the extent to which feminist ideas are having a transdisciplinary impact on academic life, such as in feminist critiques of androcentric social structures and of the Enlightenment concerns with separating mind and body, nature and nurture. They note that "many academic feminists are now involved with overlapping, interdisciplinary, interpretive communities, such as ethnic studies, queer theory, critical theory, and cultural studies."[37]

When the major sociology journal *Social Problems* staged a twentieth-anniversary celebration to commemorate the publication of one of Stacey and Thorne's groundbreaking articles, the authors asked,

"Who could have imagined that so many fine feminist minds would still want to bring such surprising, creative gifts to the gathering?"[38] Many did, including sociologist Christine Williams, who focused her comments on Stacey and Thorne's 1985 critique of the co-optation and containment of feminism within sociology. Williams—agreeing that functionalism, quantitative methods, and Marxism have been barriers to feminist progress in the past—argues for critical engagement with these academic arenas by feminists. "From my vantage point as the former editor of *Gender & Society*," she explained, "it seems critical that we maintain the institutional foothold we have achieved.... We need to continually reinvent ourselves to insure our relevance to researchers, students, and activists. Engaging with our former enemies should be part of this effort."[39]

As we have seen in the work of the early feminist pragmatists, feminist theories have long been interdisciplinary and still make much use of perspectives as diverse as social psychology, psychoanalytic theory, Marxism, democratic socialism, postmodernism, and cultural studies in order to interpret and understand the realities and meanings of gendered structures in various societies. Significantly, scholars in many disciplines—including sociology, anthropology, biology, economy, history, law, literature, philosophy, political science, psychology, and theology—have contributed to the burgeoning and diversifying of contemporary feminist theories.

Much feminist work argues for a distinctive materialistic perspective, one that locates the heart of sexism and patriarchy in the tangible and material inequalities of everyday life. One approach is sometimes called *radical feminist theory*. For example, the sociologically oriented legal scholar Catharine MacKinnon suggests that at the heart of a feminist analysis should be the material reality of reproduction and sexuality—the tangible reproductive and sexual relationships that exist between men and women. Analysis of the identities and symbols of gender must be grounded in these everyday realities. In the core of a sexist society like the United States is the alienating reality of a dehumanized sexuality forced onto women. A woman's sexuality is that which should be most her own, but in fact is that which is most taken away from her in a highly sexist society. Who she is sexually is defined principally within the still-dominant patriarchal system, which shapes men's treatment of and orientation toward women across many generations. Dehumanization of women, today as in the past, is sexism's psychological dynamic.[40]

More than half a century after the Universal Declaration of Human Rights (see Chapter 1) defined what a human being is and is entitled to, MacKinnon has recently asked,

Are women human yet? If women were regarded as human, would they be sold into sexual slavery worldwide; veiled, silenced, and imprisoned in homes; bred, and worked as menials for little or no pay; stoned for sex outside marriage or burned within it; mutilated genitally, impoverished economically, and mired in illiteracy—all as a matter of course and without effective recourse?[41]

MacKinnon continues to expose the consequences and magnitude of the systematic mistreatment of women in the United States and globally, and she emphasizes the transforming possibilities of human rights efforts. For example, in her latest work she examines rape as a type of genocide in Bosnia–Herzegovina and asks why the international community rallies against terrorism but fails to take a committed and effective stand against violence against women.[42]

One of the influential sociological theorists of our era is Dorothy Smith, who has helped to develop an important sociological perspective known as standpoint theory. Smith proposes a sociology done from the standpoint of women, a distinctive viewpoint not unlike that of the proletariat's perspective in Marxist theory. She writes, "At the line of fault along which women's experience breaks away from the discourses mediated by texts that are integral to the relations of ruling in contemporary society, a critical standpoint emerges."[43] For some time, Smith has critically explored and questioned the discipline of sociology, which she has described as a "means of knowing about the shape of my world beyond the immediately known."[44] However, she calls into question the objectified ways of knowing in which the usual patriarchal "relations of ruling" become manifest. Taken-for-granted mainstream sociology, and its conventional methods and conceptual theories, are "built up within the male social universe, even when women have participated in its doing."[45] She discovered in her life, especially at a dramatic moment in her graduate education, that there was a distinctive standpoint from which women often experience and thus know the world differently than those men who create most of the established knowledge of academia and other public discourse. From this distinctive place, women can "speak to and of the society at large, moving into a terrain of public discourse that somewhere along the line had been appropriated by and ceded to men."[46]

In one biographical sketch, Smith explains that her critical social theory derives from everyday life as a woman, especially as a woman living between the male-dominated academic world and the female-centered life of a single mother.[47] From these experiences, she has drawn the concept of "bifurcation," or disjuncture, which plays an important part in her theorizing. This refers to the separation between people's lived experiences and social scientific descriptions, between women's lives and the often-patriarchal ideal types used by mainstream social science to describe such everyday experience. Her most recent books, including *Mothering for Schooling* and *Institutional Ethnography: A Sociology for People,* demonstrate her continued centrality to a feminist liberation sociology.[48]

For liberation sociologists, Smith's work is important for several reasons, including her focus on the diversity of human experiences and standpoints. If they are to be sustainable in the long run, all human societies must be restructured to be much less oppressive and to be meaningfully democratic—in the sense of full participation by all in the society, including its female majority, in decision-making about all critical facets of social and personal lives. The diversity of people and views must be recognized structurally and culturally. Monocultures are not healthy, and they tend to deteriorate. In her contemporary feminist theory, Smith tracks the earlier insights of the feminist pragmatists and provides numerous important insights into the character of the social domination and oppression of women. As she sees it, oppressors are not simply individual actors making rational decisions based on self-interest. In making sense of societal oppression, she contextualizes it. She thereby integrates Marx's concerns with the structures of domination with insights into a variety of subjective and microsocial life worlds. As with Habermas, these everyday life worlds are shaped by the larger macrostructures, which are in turn shaped by specific historical demands.

Numerous feminist social scientists have accented these and other elements of a feminist research methodology. These include a focus on gender and gender inequality with constant reflectivity and a goal of giving voice to the everyday experiences and realities of women. There is usually an emphasis, too, on the importance of social action being linked to feminist research. Moreover, central to the research effort is a focus on breaking down the traditional distancing relationship between the researcher and those researched. In one revealing account of this feminist methodology, Claire Renzetti, a former president of the Society for the Study of Social Problems and editor of the important journal *Violence Against Women,* has discussed her shift to a "reformed positivist" now doing pioneering qualitative research on domestic violence among women. Discussing the feminist participatory model used in this field project, she notes how social scientists have too often undertaken such field research as "outside experts" who make little effort to look at the world from the point of view of those they are studying or to listen carefully to their voices. In her view, feminist participatory research involves researchers being learners as well as teachers. She summarizes well the ways in which the participation of those researched in a project can sharply improve its quality: "They help to ensure that (a) the most significant issues—from the perspective not only of the researcher but also of the researched—get identified and studied; (b) meaningful (in terms of their lived experience) and nonalienating research instruments are developed; (c) the data collected are analyzed in the realistic context of their everyday lives; and (d) the project has a practical effect in terms of personal and social change."[49]

In this way, she argues, research is much more than some academic exercise and can have a positive impact on societal change. Continuing in this liberation sociology tradition, Renzetti's recent ethnographic work concerns faith-based organizations involved in antitrafficking work, a survey of organizations that offer services to trafficking victims, and a national study of the relationship between intimate partner violence and religiosity. For this important work, she was named the recipient of the Saltzman Award for Contributions to Practice, awarded by the Women and Crime Division of the American Society of Criminology, and was the recipient of the Lee Founders Award, from the Society for the Study of Social Problems.[50]

In recent years, one of the important contributions of feminist thinking and research is its growing recognition of racial diversity. For example, in pioneering social science analyses, bell hooks (Gloria Jean Watkins) and Patricia Hill Collins have accented the importance of the thought and action of African American women in making feminist thought in the United States and elsewhere more nuanced, inclusive, and liberationist. Though technically a humanities scholar and activist, bell hooks is sociological in much of her societal analysis. For example, she has examined the deep structures of racist imaging that portray black women as ugly, deviant, and criminal. The omnipresent standard of white-female beauty, seen in the mainstream media and other places, is consistent with a continuing ideology of white superiority. African American women, who depart from the common white-beauty norm, suffer much painful humiliation and everyday discrimination. In addition, hooks has pointed out the ways in which a white perspective on society constantly gets precedence in regard to prevailing views of women.[51] In one probing article, hooks discusses the omnipresent misogyny sometimes found in the rap music of certain black male musicians. Ironically, these negative views of women in rap music are often condemned by white commentators and politicians, even as white executives are central to their propagation and as young whites purchase the majority of songs by these rap artists. The black male misogyny present in much commercial rap music is seen as a severe social malignancy by numerous white analysts. Yet, the widespread misogyny of white men, seen in many movies and other areas, gets much less public commentary and criticism. Indeed, hypermasculinity and misogyny are old creations of European Americans and are even glorified in the larger white-dominated culture, especially in times of overseas invasions and wars.[52]

As a pioneering analyst in feminist thought, hooks has constantly raised serious sociological questions about the patriarchal and racist structures of US society. She indicates that she has been influenced by the writings of the US writer James Baldwin, the South American Paulo Freire, the German American psychologist Erich Fromm, and the Vietnamese monk Thicht Nhat Hanh, among numerous others active in human rights movements. Standing on the shoulders of these activist-intellectual giants, she merges emancipatory politics, postmodern theory, and cultural studies. As with many other social researchers and analysts discussed throughout this book, her views on racial, gender, and educational issues have periodically courted controversy. In 2002, for example, she gave a speech at Southwestern University in Texas, telling the graduating class that if they were complacent in the face of injustice, they implicitly supported government violence and oppression. Some graduates tried to drown her out as she spoke, but afterward many went out of their way to shake her hand or embrace her. She has also been the target of reactionary backlash from influential white conservatives, yet another thing she has in common with many liberation sociologists profiled in this book. The public criticisms and hostility that she has faced are the shared fate of liberation social scientists and others who confront the hierarchies of societal power.[53]

Moreover, as in Chapter 4, the influential sociologist Patricia Hill Collins has argued that a black-feminist theoretical framework must critique the negative stereotypes of black women: "Portraying African American women as stereotypical mammies, matriarchs, welfare recipients, and hot mommas has been essential to the political economy of domination fostering Black women's oppression."[54] These images are webbed deeply into the social fabric of the United States and—thanks to the US mass media—many other societies, and they frequently precipitate and rationalize antiblack discrimination. Collins insists that one must also look at resistance to discrimination. Thus, she has shown how black women were a constant and integral part of the civil rights movement of the 1960s.

In her book *Fighting Words*, Collins takes her arguments ever deeper in regard to the character of critical social theory and the condition of African Americans. "Social theory in particular can serve either to reproduce existing power relations or to foster social and economic justice."[55] Elites do not produce more socially oriented thought than others; they simply have the great ability—such as through the control of the mainstream media and major think tanks—to make their thought central and accepted as the only legitimate framework in society. Given the white dominance of US sociology from the 1890s to the 1960s, there was virtually no treatment of black women from an emancipatory viewpoint in any of the major sociology journals during that time.[56] After developing a critique of sociology and of critical theory, Collins moves to a level of analysis that accents the moral foundations of all social theory: "Because the search for justice has been central in African American women's history, I emphasize an ethical framework grounded in notions of justice as specific cultural material for exploring this more general question of moral authority for struggle."[57]

Collins's current sociology of knowledge projects include the epistemology of intersectionality, whereby she expressly analyzes how racial, class, gender, sexual, and/or age characteristics and hierarchies interact, reinforce each other, and differentially affect people's lives. She also examines critical race theory, nationalism, and feminism as examples of epistemologies of emancipatory knowledge. Further still, her sociology of knowledge projects today include an examination of how African American female and male youth's experiences with education, unemployment, popular culture, and activism are related to global capitalist development and transnationalism.[58] Repeatedly, we see the centrality of ideas of human freedom and social justice for these liberation sociologists and for their critical social theories about systems of gender and other oppressions.

QUESTIONING HETEROSEXUAL THEORIES

One of the areas of critical social theory that has expanded impressively in recent decades is sometimes known as *queer theory*. Much of this theorizing is located in the humanities and is influenced by feminist and postmodern thinkers. Within sociology, this theoretical work has developed as a critique of the way in which this social science discipline has ignored the heterosexual assumptions often shaping its methods and knowledge accrual. Major issues dealt with in this theory framework have to do with how categories such as "gay," "lesbian," and "straight" are socially constructed and how these categories serve to define positive and negative identities and to include and exclude people within communities. The conventional heterosexual-homosexual boundary places some inside and some outside a given human community.[59]

Some critical sociologists have tackled the issue of the hegemony of heterosexuality and the part that it plays in distorting research on gender and sexuality. Chrys Ingraham, for example, writes about an ideological construct, termed the *heterosexual imaginary*, a framing that "conceals the operation of heterosexuality in structuring gender and [closing off] any critical analysis of heterosexuality as an organizing institution."[60] She calls for a feminist sociology that develops a critique of the often hidden, fully institutionalized heterosexuality, a critical sociology that does not participate in heterosexual framing. A crucial step in developing such a liberated sociology is the reframing of conventional gender norms and structures as "heterogender" to emphasize the asymmetrical stratification of the sexes within the conventional system of patriarchal heterosexuality. This concept "de-naturalizes the 'sexual' as the starting point for understanding heterosexuality with the gender division of labor and the patriarchal relations of production."[61]

In addition, Dorothy Smith's idea of bifurcation is applicable since much mainstream sociology uses, however implicitly, many ideas developed within and exclusive to a heterosexual "male universe."[62] In this way, sociology is "heteronormative," inasmuch as heterosexuality is generally the conceptual starting point for analysis. Indeed, in this society heterosexuality is still routinely institutionalized and mostly reinforced generation after generation. Chrys Ingraham's questioning of heterosexual theories is central to liberation sociology. Her research contributions are numerous and include these important books: *White Weddings: Romancing Heterosexuality in Popular Culture*; *Thinking Straight: The Power, the Promise, and the Paradox of Heterosexuality*; and *Materialist Feminism*. In this recent research she uses the methodological approach of institutional ethnography to get at the everyday lived experiences of women and men.[63]

This social science theorizing about sexuality and heterogender issues has contributed significantly to the liberation sociology tradition by accenting again the importance of societal domination as a distorting centrality in the United States. These analysts also suggest that human diversity, not just along racial, class, and gender lines but also in regard to a variety of LGBT orientations, is essential to the healthy development and evolution of human societies. As a case in point, prior to his HIV diagnosis in 2002, social scientist Andrew Jolivétte focused mostly on racial and class issues, never fully considering certain important intersectionality issues until it impacted him personally. Today Jolivétte's scholarship and activism include LGBT community of color identity issues, gay marriage, AIDS disparities within racial-ethnic communities, and cultural representations among Native Americans.[64] In 2005, Jolivétte gave a keynote address for World AIDS Day where he disclosed his HIV/AIDS positive status, encouraging those listening to cross the artificial lines that shape who they are:

> I wasn't sure if I should disclose my status in this way here today. . . . I thought to myself, as a gay man of color, I have a responsibility to

disclose. This is a very personal decision, but in communities of color we lack faces to make this pandemic real. If you've never known someone living with AIDS, now you do. You know my story and in sharing it I hope that others will know that they can live with this. . . .[65]

Critical social theorists like Jolivétte focus on the negative realities and effects of oppression and regularly target issues of and strategies for human liberation from such recurring oppression. In the tradition of other critical social thinkers, Jolivétte supports the action of human beings in their own liberation. Much social creativity comes from contemporary societal diversity and the interpersonal and intergroup communication generated by it.

ANTIRACIST SOCIAL THEORY

Another type of critical social theory with deep roots in US sociology is antiracist theory. The early sociologists W. E. B. Du Bois and Anna Julia Cooper, among others, began the development of a conceptual framework probing US racism as more than a matter of racial prejudice or fringe extremism. Both saw it instead as a centuries-long, deep-lying institutionalized system of white racial exclusion and violence. Cooper wrote in the 1890s of violent racist practices targeting black men and women across the country; she noted "instances of personal violence to colored women traveling in the less civilized sections of our country, where women have been forcibly ejected from cars, thrown from their seats, their garments rudely torn, their person wantonly and cruelly injured."[66] She described the "jungles of barbarism" created by white Americans. Moreover, by the early 1900s, Du Bois was working from a conceptual perspective that all major US institutions were structured in racial terms. He viewed this racist order in global terms, one of the first theorists to do so.[67] Du Bois continued to develop his ideas about white supremacy and an institutionalized racist order until his death in 1963.

Writing extensively on racism and capitalism in a number of books published between the 1940s and his death in 1974, Oliver C. Cox deviated from the ideas of his University of Chicago teachers (see Chapter 2). He contributed much to the development of antiracist theory with his well-substantiated investigation of how the labor exploitation of African Americans created a structure of racialized classes. He showed that the white ruling elite had worked hard to subordinate African Americans, "to proletarianize a whole people—that is to say, the whole people is looked upon as a class—whereas white proletarianization involves only a section of the white people."[68] Moreover, since the 1960s, social science analysts like Kwame Ture (formerly known as Stokely Carmichael) and Charles Hamilton have developed similar ideas and accented the centrality of institutionalized racism for contemporary US society—those patterns of racism built into all this society's major institutions.[69]

Working on racist hierarchies and other structures of racial oppression, critical social theorists have rejected older concepts like "race relations," the phrase often used by social scientists concerned with portraying all racially defined groups as more or less responsible for the so-called race problems in countries like the United States. Such terminology is often conservative in impact, for it takes the focus off those powerful whites who have created, maintained, and benefited from the hierarchical and exploitative system of racism since the seventeenth century.[70]

The reader should recall previous discussions of the theoretical work of Patricia Hill Collins and bell hooks on the racist construction of black women within a larger structure and culture of contemporary racism. They, too, examine closely and empirically the larger contextual and historical aspects of racism in the United States. Drawing on the analyses of Du Bois and Cooper, as well as on Kwame Ture, Frantz Fanon, bell hooks, and Patricia Hill Collins, the first two authors have contributed to this development of antiracist theory in our own work.[71] We have developed the concept of *systemic racism*, a far-reaching framework of oppression that encompasses an array of important dimensions—the unjustly gained economic and political power of whites (e.g., under slavery and Jim Crow segregation), the continuing resource inequalities across the color line, and the prevailing white racial frame with its racist ideologies, attitudes, images, emotions, and inclinations to discriminate. This societal system of white-imposed racism has now persisted in the North American case over nearly four centuries. An important aspect of this approach is an accent on the United States as a "total-racist society," one in which most social arenas are shaped to some degree by the systemic racist realities. The macrostructure of racial oppression is reinforced by, and creates, racist ideologies and attitudes that play out at the micro level of everyday interaction.[72]

We have also explored the ways in which a range of "sincere fictions" created by white Americans are part of a broad white racial framing of this society and are regularly used to reinforce racial discrimination on an everyday basis. Critical to the maintenance of systemic racism are the persisting stereotypes and prejudices—the negative ways in which whites see racialized "others"—and the pervasive white views of whiteness, the ways in which whites positively see themselves as superior and virtuous. Traditional theories of prejudice involve little reference to white sentiments about the white self, yet racist actions require not only a representation of the racialized other but also a conception of the white self as virtuous. The latter entails the creation of an array of sincere fictions, those white-framed myths and ideological constructions that make up and reproduce the broad racial framing of society that is held in some form by all individual whites. Thus, white men and women often view themselves as "not racist," as "good people," even while they racially frame or discriminate against African Americans and other Americans of color.[73]

The use of these systemic-racism concepts can aid scholars and activists to probe beneath the contemporary white denials of racism and the many contemporary myths about "race." A social theory critical of systemic racism can help people understand the racially manipulated dimensions of their lives. Today, more antiracist theory needs to be developed not only to lay bare the system of racial oppression but also to help in the collective struggles to overcome it. Antiracist theory generally attempts to facilitate human action against racist attitudes and practices. For example, in their work on racism, Patricia Hill Collins and bell hooks have analyzed the methods by which black men and women have historically resisted oppression. Numerous scholars of color have also examined the ways in which oppression is sometimes internalized when people of color adopt the white-racist attitudes or other white racial framing propagated within their environments—such as by the mainstream media—in regard to themselves. People of color have had to constantly create innovative strategies to resist both external racial oppression and the internalized oppression often fostered within themselves.[74]

Moreover, some antiracist sociologists, such as Eileen O'Brien, have developed empirical research and conceptual ideas directed at helping whites move toward assertive action against everyday racism. Using field interviews and participant observation, she has researched the strategies of two major antiracist organizations, the People's Institute for Survival and Beyond (PI) and Anti-Racist Action (ARA), which are attempting to move whites toward antiracist actions. The mostly white ARA groups include many young people and are organizing in a variety of ways against white racist activities in cities in the United States and Canada. For example, they have actively protested against neo-Nazi and Klan organizations and their numerous white supremacist rallies.[75]

The PI group, founded by people of color, has focused significant work on getting liberal whites to see their own racism. Various groups of whites who work with mostly poor people of color, such as social workers and other government employees, come to their Undoing Racism workshops, where they are pressed to come to terms with their own class and racial prejudices and stereotypes. In her work, O'Brien has emphasized the importance of this PI teaching about the US system of racial oppression. As she has put it, "Nearly all of us work in institutions that have historically and currently operated in racist ways. We need to acknowledge that in not actively challenging that racism, we are perpetuating it. This group is explicitly led by people of color, because it is their contention that the nature of white privilege is to unconsciously veer into that racist direction even as whites are trying to be antiracist."[76] In groups like PI, there is a conscious effort to deal with the many racial fictions of white Americans. "It is important that even when whites affiliate with an 'antiracist' label/agenda, that they have no sincere fictions about themselves, and that they are constantly self-reflective about their own role in the movement."[77]

POSTMODERN SOCIAL THEORY

The term *postmodernism* has been used for a diverse array of social phenomena—a contemporary architectural movement, a new way of writing about contemporary life that no longer relies on "metanarratives," the historical social transformations that followed World War II, and the new conditions of a capitalism centered in information technologies. It has also been used for the supposed aftermath of the "modern" industrial age—what others have called the *consumer society*, the *postindustrial society*, or the *media society*. Those writers and scholars who use these terms "are attempting to describe fields of political, cultural, aesthetic, scientific, and moral experiences which are distinctly different from those which were taken for granted in an earlier historical, commonly called modern or Enlightenment, phase of world history."[78]

In one way or another, postmodernism is defined in contrast to *modernism*, a term for the rationalist and technological culture that has expanded since the Enlightenment era of the eighteenth century. The modernist assumptions encompass the individual as the agent and creative force of society and history, the superiority of Western civilization, science as source of much truth, and a belief in social progress—views that have been basic to the development of Europe and the United States.[79] On the one hand, postmodernism often involves a radical break with this dominant modernist culture and aesthetic, which makes it important for a sociology of liberation. On the other hand, some postmodernist writers have strongly criticized the images of social liberation in the work of some social scientists for being too much a part of the modernist intellectual framework, for being tied to supposed "essentialist concepts" of human subjects that presuppose "a notion of humanity as having a fixed, unchanging identity and dynamic regardless of historical variation and social considerations such as gender, race, ethnicity, class or sexual orientation."[80]

The diversified character of postmodern critical theory makes it difficult to assess without some selectivity and, indeed, ambiguity. Postmodernism is a complex of social theories of an interdisciplinary nature. Nevertheless, there are common threads among many postmodernist writers, one of which is their challenge to what some call "foundationism"—the philosophical approach arguing that the rational, independent human subject is the foundation of ontology (being) and epistemology (how we know). This foundationism views the free-thinking individual as the source of moral and political action. Postmodernists, instead, argue that human subjects are not autonomous creators of themselves or the worlds in which they live. Rather, they are subjects produced within a complex set of relations and are constituted within and through the moral and political arrangements around them. For postmodernists, human subjects are the effects of specific social logics.[81]

As we see it, this is a false dichotomy. Liberation-oriented sociologists want to achieve a world where human beings can endeavor creatively and move autonomously; in that sense, liberation sociologists are modernist in their ultimate aims. Yet, they are often postmodernist in their diagnoses of the troubled social worlds in which all people live. Liberation social science, like all good social science, recognizes enormous differences in the capacity for agency of different social actors. Power differentials structured across racial, gender, class, and other hierarchical orders mean differences in effective social agency. A good social science recognizes the diversity within all broader social categories. Moreover, human actors are essential to a liberation analysis. No matter how determining the sociocultural order appears to be, only human beings, acting reflectively and collectively, can be the inventors of social worlds. And only human beings acting reflectively and in concert can reinvent them.

We have space here to consider only a few challenges that postmodern theorizing poses to the social sciences. Some postmodern theory is important for liberation projects because these theorists take seriously the fact that experience with reality is mediated by socially shared representations—by symbols and intersubjectivity. Human beings apprehend the reality of their own experiences, and one must take the nuanced and varying character of these experiences seriously. It is not the same thing to understand the roundness of the Earth as it is to experience the death of a loved one. We do not want to engage in a philosophical discussion on the nature of human experience here but suggest that intersubjective and empathetic understanding of other human beings is critical to the human liberation project. For this, understanding human empathy is decisive, for empathy is a critical human trait. That empathy has long been indispensable for survival and evolution is undeniable. Working to develop empathy across all lines within human groups, including the many lines of oppression, is necessary to human advancement in the future.

Among sociological theorists, Steven Seidman sees much that is useful for social science in postmodern thought, but also some pitfalls. Much postmodern thinking, he warns, "carries no promise of liberation—of a society free of domination. Postmodernism gives up the modernist idol of human emancipation."[82] This does not mean that all postmodernism gives up on ethical action to counter oppression. In fact, some postmodern thinkers make a strong appeal for an "ethically engaged intellectual life and pluralistic values."[83] For some, the hope of a great emancipatory transformation is replaced by the more modest aspiration of immediate and individual or localized struggles for more limited goals of social justice. At its best, postmodern thought "offers the possibility of a social analysis that takes seriously the history of cruelty and constraint in Western Modernity without surrendering to the retreat from criticalness that characterizes much current conservative and liberal social thought."[84] Seidman's contributions to theory continue today, as he currently focuses on sexuality and the study of empire and nation. He draws extensively on critical gender studies in his overall approach to societal analysis. As of late, LGBT gender scholars such as Judith Butler and Judith Halberstam have also reportedly informed his thinking about compulsory heterosexuality and sexual/gender identities.[85]

Even relatively conservative postmodern theorists have developed ideas that can be adapted effectively by liberation sociologists. The French philosopher Jean-François Lyotard has underscored the intertwining of community and individual in thinking about human actions of major ethical consequence: "Thou shalt not kill thy fellow human being: To kill a human being is not to kill an animal of the species Homo Sapiens, but to kill the human community present in him as both capacity and promise. And you also kill it in yourself. To banish the stranger is to banish the community, and you banish yourself from the community thereby."[86] What is common to human beings is the image each carries in herself or himself of other people. Moreover, the human community is in the individual, and the individual is in the community. This is an important insight for understanding all types of oppression of human beings. Oppressions such as racism, classism, sexism, and heterosexism not only destroy individuals, but also destroy the social communities of which they are part.

Some feminist theorists have made effective use of postmodern insights. Donna Haraway, a materialist postmodernist analyst, has written a much-cited article titled "A Manifesto for Cyborgs: Science,

Technology and Socialist Feminism in the 1980s."[87] In this seminal work, which models its title on a call to action from Karl Marx and Friedrich Engels's *Communist Manifesto*, Haraway uses the metaphor of the cyborg to offer an innovative argument against the assumptions of identity theory and mainstream feminism: "There is nothing about being female that naturally binds women. There is not even such a state as 'being' female, itself a highly complex category constructed in contested sexual scientific discourses and other social practices."[88] She also compares the cyborg to the socio-political identity of "women of color," which "marks out a self-consciously constructed space that cannot affirm the capacity to act on the basis of natural identification, but only on the basis of conscious coalition, of affinity, of political kinship."[89] Haraway thus draws on discourse analysis to call attention to the complexities of the category of "female" as constructed in social science writings. She has helped to clarify the epistemological dimensions, the ways of knowing, involved in the feminist standpoints discussed in the standpoint theory examined earlier in the chapter. The distinguished European Graduate School, where Haraway once taught as a professor, recently summed up her influential work:

> Donna Haraway argues that "one important route for reconstructing socialist-feminist politics is through theory and practice addressed to the social relations of science and technology, including crucially the systems of myth and meanings structuring our imagination." ... The relations between science and technology are "rearranging" categories of race, sex and class; Donna Haraway insists that feminism needs to take this into account.[90]

Unquestionably, one must go beyond the postmodern concern with individual subjects, dyadic relationships, and interpersonal discourse to the much larger, imposed frameworks of social oppression. Larger-scale emancipatory visions must be articulated and pursued, beyond the individual and local level, whatever the intellectual and practical difficulties of such action. Given the life-threatening problems created by a globalizing capitalist system on planet Earth—such as global climate change and its increasing threats to the atmosphere, biosphere, and sociosphere—the larger-scale emancipatory theory and research projects cannot be abandoned to a postmodern malaise and waffling on ancient philosophical issues.

Like some interpretive and ethnomethodological theory in social science, much postmodern analysis can be paralyzing, especially when it presses in the direction of making the world only into "texts" used mainly for linguistic deconstruction. For some postmodernists, the basic reality of human life is said to be language and text. Yet, there is a very substantial material world beyond all language texts, one in which people hope and empathize with others, find themselves in great pain, manage to thrive or starve, and love and die—which they experience and describe with or without words. It is these omnipresent worlds of human pain and interhuman oppression, as well as the pain and oppression of nonhuman animals discussed in Chapter 8, that liberation sociologists seek both to understand and alleviate or eradicate.

We should add that contemporary interpretive theories, such as theories of symbolic interactionism, can also be critical of existing society, depending on which aspects of the societal context are emphasized and how those aspects are conceptualized. However, they must always go beyond "micro" descriptions and analysis. "Interpretive theorists in the more critical tradition believe that it is useful to link people's activities in everyday life to the large-scale social structures that their action creates (and that necessarily constrain action in capitalist, sexist, and racist societies)."[91]

PUTTING LIBERATION THEORY INTO ACTION

Using a brief survey of a few more liberation-oriented sociologists who have been active over the past half century, we will now show how *critical* theory becomes part of lives and careers of sociologists who commit themselves to making the social world a better place. Like others discussed throughout this book, these lives and careers show how critical social theory can be webbed together with liberatory actions. We also want to emphasize that the sociologists in our admittedly limited sample here do not stand alone, for there are a great many others just like them.

The Humanist Sociology of Alfred McClung Lee

A central figure in the liberation sociology tradition over many decades was Alfred McClung Lee (1908–1992). Recall from Chapter 3 that in 1951 the progressive Society for the Study of Social Problems (SSSP) was set up with his active assistance. Lee and his associates, including his partner and talented fellow sociologist Elizabeth Briant Lee, were resisting the move to instrumental positivism in US sociology and stressed the importance of dealing with serious problems facing the society, including the problems of McCarthyism and academic freedom. In 1974, the membership of the American Sociological Association elected Lee as its president in a write-in campaign promoted by sociologists involved in the 1960s and early 1970s Liberation Sociology Movement. The election of antiestablishment Lee was a watershed event signaling the resurgence of social-liberation ideas in US sociology. These ideas were getting more recognition among some sociologists, bringing to the fore once again the activist and radical goals of those in the alternative sociological tradition going back to Harriet Martineau, Jane Addams, and W. E. B. Du Bois.

Growing up in western Pennsylvania, Lee saw discriminatory distinctions being drawn there between the Scotch Irish and Catholic Irish, which led him to participate in struggles of socially oppressed groups. (He was of Scotch-Irish background.) In his view, critical social theory should be tied to the morality of liberating those who are thus oppressed. Lee called himself an "existential humanist" and probed in his work the nature of human freedom and enslavement. He linked his humanist theory with action. Thus, he was influential in the establishment of the Association for Humanist Sociology in 1976.[92]

Writing alone or with coauthors, Lee left behind an important body of conceptual and empirical work illustrative of a career that constantly sought the emancipation of humanity. He and his associates usually chose important political and economic topics, often those neglected by other social scientists. Recall that during the 1930s most US social scientists did not research issues connected with the growing fascism in the United States and other countries.[93] However, Alfred McClung Lee and Elizabeth Briant Lee were concerned with the global rise of fascist movements and governments and helped to organize the Institute for Propaganda Analysis. "To understand propaganda, to know how it is used in the struggles for our mind, one must constantly study propaganda of all kinds," Lee wrote in his pioneering 1952 book, *How to Understand Propaganda*.[94]

Like many other liberation sociologists, the Lees paid a price for their views and activism. In the late 1930s the Lees championed an antiwar student group that was mockingly called the Veterans of Future Wars (VOFW). Some Kansans called Alfred the "socialist professor" and campaigned for his dismissal from the University of Kansas.[95] If this was not enough, there were other penalties for them to face. Elizabeth Briant Lee completed her Yale doctorate in 1938. Her dissertation, *Eminent Women: A Cultural Study*, examined the social aspects leading to the achievements of more than 600 women recorded in the *Dictionary of American Biography*. Only the second woman to receive a PhD from Yale, her dissertation was not published. This was significant because during this period nearly every Yale dissertation was published. Indignant about this, Elizabeth Briant Lee refused to allow her dissertation to be placed in the interlibrary loan program. Inaccessible, her groundbreaking feminist work would be overlooked by women's studies researchers for years to come. All her life, Elizabeth Briant Lee sorely resented the derisive devaluing of her work by Yale's mostly male faculty.[96]

Working in the era before and after World War II, Al Lee recognized that the knowledge the social sciences developed in response to the demands of government agencies, including the military, could be useful beyond the often autocratic goals of typically undemocratic established institutions. This knowledge could also be used in conceptualizing, and working for, a more egalitarian society. Lee pressed for a theoretical and research perspective in sociology that did not take oppressive social hierarchies at face value. He was interested in how traditionally oppressive customs and mentalities could be changed by social science work. For example, as ordinary people become better educated and gain critical knowledge, they often come to understand that all people, whatever their backgrounds, are equally human.[97]

In his important book on customs and human mentality, Lee argued that there was a time in Western history when speaking of changing societal customs meant socializing "backward" peoples into "the proper ways of life ... to make them over into reasonable subjects or less effective enemies. More idealistically, our panacea took the form of transforming them through education into typical middle class Europeans."[98] In the course of his work, Lee tackled these related social questions: For what purposes are customs and mentality to be changed? What about the unplanned or unintended consequences of social change? What methods are most effective and acceptable in changing customs or mentality? Lee rejected the growing propaganda machines of his day, whether governmental or corporate, for such machines often aimed at reducing humanity to some type of political or social enslavement, however subtle. In his view, there was a great need for a new research ethic in the social sciences, one attuned to improving the lives of all human beings.[99]

Lee held that sociologists should do empirical fieldwork, such as he did on racial riots and governmental propaganda, but that they must move away from the common positivistic framework that pretends to exclude human values from scientific inquiry. A *critical social theory* is essential, if it is one whose ultimate aim is to empower people to act. He rejected the common discursive currency of sociology—the language of social roles, statuses, and functions—for one accenting hierarchy, conflict, manipulation, and exploitation. The eradication of oppression was central to his research, theory, and, indeed, life. In his many writings, Al Lee articulated the analytical and activist implications of critical theory. In one commentary just before his death in 1992, Lee wrote, "Only those who choose to serve humanity rather than to get caught up in the scramble for all the immediate rewards of finance and status can know the pleasures and lasting rewards of such a pursuit."[100]

Annually since 1981, the Society for the Study of Social Problems has conferred the Lee Founders Award to a member whose career achievements embody the standards and principles of the Society's founders, specifically in the humanist tradition of Alfred McClung Lee and Elizabeth Briant Lee. Perhaps best capturing Alfred's legacy, in 2001 the Alfred McClung Lee Sociology Professorship and the Library Resource Collection were endowed at the University of Kansas by a student whom Alfred McClung Lee had taught back in 1934 for one class. The endowed chair's goal is "to promote tolerance and fight anti-Semitism and prejudice."[101]

The Critical Sociology of Robert G. Newby

We now turn to another liberation sociologist, Robert G. Newby, who has integrated his progressive research and action with critical Marxist and black nationalist theories. Over the course of a long and productive career, Newby has been an activist sociologist and has contributed especially to our sociological understanding of the role of race and class in US society.

Born in the Great Depression of the 1930s, Newby grew up in Kansas. At home, his parents taught him a critical framing of US racism, and he grew up with an active political education in the meaning of being black in the United States. Traveling a lot during his youth, Newby learned from personal experience how racially segregated the United States was.[102] Wichita, Kansas, was then segregated in many social activities, constantly inflicting the indignities of racism on its black residents. Newby attended segregated elementary schools. Since there were not enough African Americans for a separate black high school, he attended an integrated high school. As a young man, he participated in sit-in protests against restaurant segregation, which took place in Wichita in 1958. He has noted that this had a "profound impact on me personally. It was in these demonstrations that I was first told by a white woman that I should return to Africa."[103]

After graduation from the University of Wichita, Newby took a position as teacher in the Pontiac, Michigan, public schools. In March 1964, he joined with other NAACP members and other citizens in a march on school district offices and in a rally at city hall protesting school segregation. Going to Detroit to hear Malcolm X speak was a revelation for him: "His message was revolutionary—he exposed so many truths about how and why a system of white racism kept blacks in their subordinated position.... The major theme of the speech was its revelations of how blacks were being deceived by white organizations of political power—the Republicans, the Democratic Party, and its southern wing, the Dixiecrats."[104] When Newby and other young, more radical, members of the Pontiac NAACP were defeated in elections and replaced by more conservative members, they formed another group called the Progressive Action Committee for Equality. Newby became active in the local teachers union, in regard to the cause of local civil rights. In 1966 he was offered the position as the first regional director of the Battle Creek office of the Michigan Civil Rights Commission, where he worked on issues of discrimination in housing and education. In July 1967, he attended the Black Power Conference in Newark, New Jersey, at which leading black activists were present.[105]

Soon, Newby decided to go back to school, did some graduate work at Wayne State University, and then moved to Stanford University in 1970, where he earned his PhD. There he became active in campus protests and got interested in debates over the Marxist and black nationalist theories used to analyze the situation of African Americans. Returning to Wayne State as a professor in 1974, Newby joined a faculty Marxist study group. He faced a protracted battle for tenure there, during which one key member of the promotion and tenure committee said that Marxists should not get tenure.[106] He also got involved in Michigan politics, and in 1984 worked for Jesse Jackson's successful Rainbow Coalition. Drawing on his significant experiences in various political movements, Newby wrote a number of penetrating sociological analyses in journals and books dealing with African American issues.

In his evolving conceptual understanding of US society, Newby was increasingly blending both racial and class ideas in his broad theoretical perspective. He was coming to see that there are "no 'race-only' solutions to the situation of black people."[107] He learned that the economic, health, and other troubling conditions of African Americans, especially those in the working class, could only be improved if the elitist capitalistic domination of US society was directly confronted and the conditions for all Americans were improved. In his sociological work, Newby increasingly emphasized racial and class issues. He criticized orthodox Marxist analysts for failing to understand the role of racism in breaking down solidarity between white and black workers, and he criticized some black sociologists for failing to recognize the role of class oppression in the conditions faced by African Americans.[108] He argues that so long as we have a capitalist system, we are likely to have a racist system as well.[109]

Newby was president of the Association of Black Sociologists and the North Central Sociological Association. In both organizations, he was "able to set forth progressive themes for the meetings."[110] He has been active on key committees of the American Sociological Association. In his many years on the faculty of Central Michigan University, he worked to improve the climate for students and faculty of color and stressed the importance of racial and ethnic diversity for higher education. Thus, when a college athletic coach told his team they "should play like niggers," Newby worked for his dismissal. Newby was one of the founders of the university's important Association of Faculty and Staff of Color.[111] Throughout his career, Newby's academic and professional work has been shaped by questions asked by other liberation sociologists before him: "Sociology for whom?" and "Sociology for what?" Dubbed a "must read for scholars, students, pundits, political leaders, and activists," Newby's recent edited book, *What Has This Got to Do with the Liberation of Black People?*, is further evidence of his continuing and indispensable contributions to liberation sociology, African American intellectual history, and the history of the civil rights and black power movements.[112]

The Critical Sociology of T. R. Young

Another contemporary sociologist, the activist T. R. Young, integrated his research as a sociologist with sophisticated critical theories. Over a long career as an activist sociologist, Young contributed to changing the way sociology is done and taught. In discussion with the authors, Young noted not long before his death that numerous events in his biography relate to the development of liberation sociology. Young long had difficulties fitting into conventional norms of educational institutions, norms that are, as he told us directly, "fashioned such that affirmative and effective social action is very difficult, in such a way that effectively depoliticizes and dismisses even small attempts at 'liberating' sociology."[113]

As in the cases of Lee and Newby, Young tried to live a life according to principles of social justice. Significantly, Young was dismissed from his first five academic jobs because of his social justice activism. In the 1950s, his first job as a teacher at a high school in Michigan ended when at a committee meeting he proposed the gradual reduction in differences between male and female teachers' salaries. The school superintendent declared that the committee had exceeded its mandate, and at the end of the academic year, Young's contract was not renewed. Later, after serving time as an army draftee, he was admitted to the master's program at the University of Michigan. After getting the degree, he secured a teaching position at a college in Iowa. In conversation with the authors before his death, he explained:

> I fit in a bit too well with students—with Black students in particular. One day in April, a trio of Black students came to my office, told me that they were on their way to see the Dean about racism on campus and wanted me to go along for moral support. I did. The meeting went well. The students were respectful and persuasive, the Dean attentive and sympathetic.

He added, "I was surprised to hear that the Dean was furious that I had led students to his office to make trouble." Again his contract was terminated. This time his impulse was to bridge the color line, but even this moderate action got him into trouble. After getting into similar difficulties at two other colleges, in 1960 Young moved to the University of Colorado, where he got his PhD. He took a job at Colorado State University, just as the radical politics of the 1960s were heating up. Soon he became involved in the civil rights movement, the women's liberation movement, and the antiwar movement. Young noted that these were "heady times and I found both intellectual and academic support for the liberation sociology that emerged by the late '60s." By 1968 students of color were organizing their own protest groups, and some black, Latino, and Anglo students occupied the president's office. Working with the vice president, Young developed a plan by which the student demands might be heard. The university's governing board and the protesting students accepted a plan under which new racial-ethnic courses would be added, more aggressive recruiting of students of color would be funded, and more black and Latino faculty and staff would be recruited.

On the day after the assassination of Dr. Martin Luther King Jr. in 1968, Young organized a King Fellowship fund and got faculty to contribute. However, two months later, Young was notified that he would not be rehired. He wrote to us: "There were several reasons: First, I had set up an underground college to give minority students academic credit for their work in confronting the University. Second, I had lectured on the Student-as-Nigger in the faculty lounge. Third, I had told members of the Governing Board that I intended to monitor progress on the implementation of their agreement with the Black Student Association and MECHA (a Latino organization)." At the time, Young had more refereed scholarly articles than all the full professors in his department combined, was among the best teachers, and had done important service to the community. Young told his chair that he had thirty days in which to reverse the decision or "all hell would break loose." The vice president with whom Young had worked in dealing with protesting students helped to reverse the decision. Over the next two decades, Young's life in academia stabilized somewhat. He further wrote to us, "I did not fit in so much as the university changed to tolerate sociologists who added emancipatory knowledge and 'praxical' dimensions to their work."

As the 1960s passed, Young became more involved in developing critical theories to accelerate his and others' activities for social justice. He had no difficulty fitting into professional sociology as long as he held conventional liberal views. However, he soon became "attracted to Marxist and Critical Marxist scholarship. Conventional sociology simply did not explain either racism, sexism or class struggle in terms sensible to me." The Sociology Liberation Movement and similar groups "put together at the edges of Sociology Conferences provided an elegant theoretical perspective with which to understand racist violence in the deep South; nationalist violence in Vietnam as well as exclusionary politics in both academic and scholarly realms."

By the early 1970s, Young was a tenured faculty member at Colorado State University. As his work became more radical, it was rejected more often by mainstream social science journals. His work found a better reception in journals such as *Sociological Inquiry, Qualitative Sociology,* and the *American Sociologist.* Young decided to make an end run around the established journals and founded the Red Feather Institute to promote critical sociological publications and conferences. Seeking to reach a broad range of sociologists, especially those just coming out of graduate school, Young began the Transforming Sociology Series of the Red Feather Institute. He wrote that "by 1980, there were over 100 papers in the Series. Those ten years were filled with hard work and great satisfaction. My wife and I built the Red Feather Lodge and in the mid-1970s held conferences three or four times a year bringing Marxists, feminists, and activists together—all patterned after the West Coast Conference." He was also facilitating conferences on critical social theories.

The spreading influence of the Internet soon attracted Young's attention, and he was one of the first social scientists to begin publishing significant articles, journals, and books there. He developed an innovative website for postmodern criminology, an online lecture series for graduate students, websites for progressive women in sociology and Cuban sociology, and a website for the Red Feather Institute.[114] Young was a pioneer in the use of the Internet in spreading new critical-sociological ideas, and he contributed significantly to the development of critical social theories. He was one of the first US sociologists to explore the missions and methods of postmodern thought in regard to their implications for reinventing sociology.[115]

Pushing from the Margin: The Career of Maxine Baca Zinn

A leading analyst of Latino and Latina issues in US society, sociologist Maxine Baca Zinn has contributed significantly to the development of US sociology in regard to issues concerning women of color. In the late 1960s, Baca Zinn began graduate work at the University of New Mexico, where she received a master's degree in sociology and then proceeded to the University of Oregon, where she secured her PhD. She began teaching at the University of Michigan–Flint in 1975 and later held posts as a visiting professor at a number of other universities, including the innovative Center for Research on Women at the University of Memphis.[116]

In her college courses, Baca Zinn notes, "they didn't describe social life as I experienced it."[117] So she decided to do her own research on Mexican American women and families to show how their lives were lived. Inspired by her life experiences, Baca Zinn has published extensively on family and gender issues, especially in regard to Latino groups. For example, she has shown that white stereotypes of Latinas as passive and dependent are wrong, for these women are usually at the very center of decision-making in their families. Drawing on field research, Baca Zinn has criticized the commonplace blaming-the-victim perspective in regard to families of color and pressed for a new conceptual model that is structural and takes in "the whole global picture," a model that includes explanations of the benefits to whites from subordinating people of color.[118]

In her research, Baca Zinn has developed a challenge to traditional feminist thought, which has too often accented the interests of white women. In her book *Women of Color in US Society*, edited with African American sociologist Bonnie Thornton Dill, Baca Zinn has contributed to building a new tradition of Latina feminism, a perspective that begins from the life situations of Latinas and builds on their experiences.[119] One conceptual problem of much social science and humanities research, including feminist research, is the positioning of white women as the gold standard for other women, especially for Latinas and other women of color.[120] In Baca Zinn's view, a liberatory sociology must assess, criticize, and resist the role of conventional scholarly analysis, including much social science, in societal domination. Thus, by pressing for a full consideration in the social sciences of the interests and concerns of people of color, and for a full analysis of racial and gender systems of oppression, the social scientist is in fact engaged in acts of resistance. As Baca Zinn has noted, "integrating women of color into the mainstream of sociological work in a way that includes power relations between dominant and subordinate racial and class groups, as well as power relations between women and men, requires many forms of political and intellectual work."[121]

Like the other liberation sociologists considered throughout this book, Baca Zinn combines intellectual work with activism and service to society. She prefers the term "activist scholarship" for the "transformational efforts in social analysis as well as in the institutional structures where academics carry out their work."[122] In her view, educational institutions are important arenas in which to struggle for social justice. In these arenas, liberation social scientists can challenge the restrictive perspectives of older racialized and gendered scholarship, add new knowledge from their research, and engage in political activity to make educational institutions much more representative of the racial and gender diversity of US society.

Baca Zinn has been active in integrating the interests, knowledge, and perspectives of Latino Americans into higher education in the United States. She has played an important part in building the field of Chicano Studies and was the first Latina president of a regional social science association, the Western Social Science Association. As president, she worked to increase the presence of scholars of color in that organization. She has also worked to integrate this new knowledge and perspective into textbooks on family diversity, social problems, and introductory sociology. With coauthor D. Stanley Eitzen, she has argued that "textbooks need not be limited to the synthesis of dominant perspectives. Instead, texts have possibilities for constructing and transmitting liberatory knowledge."[123]

Moving to Michigan State University in 1990, where today she is professor emerita, Baca Zinn has continued her activist scholarship. In the 1990s, she was codirector of a Michigan State University summer institute of the American Sociological Association's MOST (Minority Opportunity through School Transformation), an important project designed to recruit promising students of color at the undergraduate level in sociology and to improve the recruitment of students of color in PhD programs. An active scholar in the Julian Samora Research Institute at Michigan State, which was created to study Latinos in the Midwest, she has worked to break down college structures of exclusion by recruiting graduate students from underrepresented racial-ethnic and working-class communities and by including these students, as well as progressive white students, in her research projects. As she told us, "mentoring graduate students, making them skilled, independent, and networked is activist work in settings where nondominant students have had few opportunities to become part of the networks that produce and monitor knowledge."[124] Significantly, Baca Zinn received the Charles Horton Cooley Award for Distinguished Scholarship from the Michigan Sociological Association in 2013, and in 2010 she received the American Sociological Association's Jessie Bernard Award for developing the scope of sociology to include the study of women and women of color.[125]

Recovering the Feminist Past of US Sociology: The Career of Mary Jo Deegan

Mary Jo Deegan, a pioneering feminist sociologist whose work we have already cited, has worked for decades to challenge discrimination against women both in US society and in sociology. She has done much to bring the ideas and research work of numerous forgotten women sociologists back into mainstream discussions and research in sociology.

In the late 1960s, Deegan began graduate work at Western Michigan University with a focus on disability issues, but soon transferred to the University of Chicago. At the university's Center for Hospital Administration, she worked with Odin Anderson and Ronald M. Anderson. The only graduate student interested in qualitative research at a center doing mostly quantitative research, Deegan became interested in theory and studied with sociological theorist Talcott Parsons, cultural anthropologist Victor Turner, and religious theorist Mircea Eliade. Early on, she decided that she "wanted to be a feminist, activist, and change agent ... while the men [she studied with] wanted to be great thinkers and power brokers in academia and some of them have done so."[126] In her career, Deegan has devoted herself to the areas of disability studies, popular culture, feminist theory, and the history of sociology.

In the late 1960s, Deegan started searching for materials on the forgotten women sociologists whom she was convinced had been very important in the early development of the field of sociology. Finding very little published material, she undertook what became a long-term research project, which included searching many libraries and archives, compiling lists of women sociologists' names and bibliographies, and writing about these women sociologists and their research. As she told us, "I discovered to my amazement the enormous early sociological literature by women scholars on women and labor markets, women and unions, women and wages, and so on. I immediately asked myself two questions: (1) who were these early female sociologists, and (2) why didn't anyone ever mention them or their writings in my so-called 'best' and advanced training?"[127]

Clearly, one of the key tasks undertaken by some liberation sociologists has been to recover the critical history of the discipline, for that history has been forgotten or suppressed when it has been in the interests of those influential white men who have historically dominated the discipline. Deegan uncovered and described the history of women sociologists and resurrected their important theoretical ideas and empirical research.

For several decades, Deegan has answered these questions in many important articles and books. Perhaps most influential is Deegan's major book, *Jane Addams and the Men of the Chicago School, 1892–1918*. This book is pathbreaking and is beginning to make US sociologists aware of the early and influential women sociologists and their pioneering conceptual perspective of feminist pragmatism. Deegan shows that central among these early sociologists was Jane Addams, a founder of US sociology. Recall from earlier chapters that Addams was head resident at Chicago's influential Hull House settlement complex and was an active sociological researcher and theorist and a founding member of the American Sociological Society.[128]

In the process of researching this early history of sociological radicalism, Deegan developed a penetrating sociology-of-knowledge approach to this history: "Sociologists who specialized in criticizing the economic structure of society and women's limitations within it were particularly subject to neglect or damning interpretations.... The early passion, political forays, and verve were abstracted from accounts of 'scientific' sociology."[129] This was also true for some of the early male sociologists, but especially true for the early women. As noted previously, by the 1930s the male leadership of sociology, increasingly centered in academic departments, was moving rapidly away from the more radical and activist roots of the discipline. As Deegan has shown, "these later men therefore condemned political action for sociologists, while the ideas of the elite, in fact, permeated their work. Society as based on competition and conflict over scarce goods was a patriarchal and capitalist model of social action."[130]

Deegan has done important research on the conceptual framework called *feminist pragmatism*. Recall from Chapter 3 our discussion of the women sociologists and a few associated male sociologists in Chicago who developed feminist pragmatism. Pragmatism was an intellectual movement whose central idea was that the test of a concept lay in its practical significance. The feminist pragmatism of Addams and her associates emphasized a cooperative ethic, coupled with the values of liberal education and democracy. As noted earlier, these feminist pragmatists played a very important role in efforts to develop welfare-state programs supportive of families and individuals in the United States.[131]

Some of these early sociologists, like Addams, contributed to the development of symbolic interactionism, the distinctively US perspective that rejects social determinism and views human beings as controlling their behavior interactively by means of socially constructed meanings.[132] Addams was an early symbolic interactionist who understood that "female" and "woman" were clearly social constructions. She researched and analyzed the division of private and public places for women, their struggles between family claims and public-sphere claims. Building on the work of these early women sociologists, Deegan has shown that symbolic interactionism is one of the few social theories that asserts that people can create and re-create their own lives. Thus, in its more radical form that recognizes the importance of "macro" structures of oppression, it offers a liberatory framework for considering the present and future of women in society. Efforts at liberating women will meet resistance, but "it is people who create human behavior, and it is people who can change it.... Women can do this, but only if a large enough number want to do it, agree on definitions of what is desirable, and have access to the means to obtain these goals."[133]

Given the pathbreaking character of Deegan's work, it is perhaps not surprising that some sociologists have had negative reactions to her research. For example, she tells of going to an American Sociological Association meeting in 1987 and hearing several groups of sociologists comment negatively on her book on Jane Addams, even though it had not yet been published! She is not alone in this experience. Other liberation sociology books and research efforts have suffered similar negative attacks, which, as Deegan notes, reduce the likelihood that such scholarship will "cross the barriers protecting mainstream ideology, gatekeeping, and practices."[134] Deegan has also noted that liberation sociologists sometimes suffer greatly but that they also have interesting lives "defined and expressed very differently than those bounded by traditional and narrowly defined careers in the discipline."[135] One of the satisfactions of doing liberation sociology is getting other people to see ideas and histories that they have never seen before and to read books and materials they have not read before.

Recovering the Southern Black Woman's Role in Civil Rights: Bernice McNair Barnett

Like Deegan, Bernice McNair Barnett has shown that the pen is a powerful tool for liberation sociologists. She, too, has gotten people to see ideas about and histories of women in society that they have rarely seen before. In challenging patricentric civil rights scholarship, her work has shed light on the hugely valuable roles Southern black women—such as Septima Poinsette Clark, McCree Harris, Shirley Sherrod, Diane Nash, Johnnie Carr, Thelma Glass, Georgia Gilmore, and Jo Ann Robinson—played in the long civil rights movement, especially from the 1950s to the 1960s. African American women have seldom been recognized as leaders even though they often were the ones who initiated protest, formulated strategies and tactics, and mobilized other community resources necessary for successful civil rights protests. Without the work of Barnett and a few other scholars, such efforts of African American women would likely have remained largely invisible.[136]

CONCLUSION

In presenting the lives and work of a few critical sociologists like Alfred McClung Lee, Elizabeth Briant Lee, Robert G. Newby, T. R. Young, Maxine Baca Zinn, Mary Jo Deegan, and Bernice McNair Barnett, we do not intend to suggest that these are the only sociologists who have worked on liberation theory and activist sociology over the past few decades. Numerous other countersystem sociologists mentioned in this and previous chapters are part of that important list, as are many sociologists we have not had the space to discuss. However, these cases do suggest how, over the decades since instrumental positivism became established in US sociology, the lives of particular sociologists interact with the development of liberation sociology and with the academic and other important social settings surrounding them. In their careers, these sociologists illustrate a central point of liberation sociology—that lives, research projects, and theories unavoidably intersect and co-reproduce each another.

However presented, critical social theories supply liberation sociologists with ideas that are indispensable for thinking through contemporary human problems and possibilities. As all the critical theorists show, the mainstream of sociology and the other social sciences is drenched with unexamined assumptions, distorting beliefs, and even self-aggrandizing claims designed to reproduce a still-oppressive status quo. Critical social theorists often focus on the social histories and contexts of oppressive structures limiting human achievement and progress. They reject the idea of inevitable, permanent, and natural laws of society—for societies are historically shaped and ever in the process of change. Critical social theories are grounded in the idea of science as a "thoroughly historical, philosophical, and political activity."[137] Thus, as we have seen, critical social theory and instrumental-positivistic theory are generally different in their key domain assumptions and their general outlooks.

The ideas of the critical social theorists reviewed in this and previous chapters may sometimes appear rather abstract and thus irrelevant for the task of transforming the world into a more just and freer place. Yet the presumption of the irrelevance of anything this theoretical is usually misguided. We must not conceive of the relation between theory and action in a simplistic or mechanical way, as if there were a one-to-one correspondence between theory and practical activity—a correspondence in which the social scientist plays no part. For the authors of this book, this has not turned out to be the case. Often when we have been confronted by relatively abstract critical theory, we have been forced to rethink and modify our concrete and practical ideas. Critical social theories are reservoirs of important ideas, and the creativity of the actor is what accounts for their application to interpretations of specific empirical phenomena or to collective action. Indeed, much critical theory has its roots, as we have often noted, in the thinking of "ordinary" citizens, the organic intellectuals whose thinking is shaped by everyday experience with social oppressions and resistance and that can be revealed to all by social science research at its best.

We have noted throughout this book the importance of interdisciplinary perspectives in the development of critical social theories and consequent research. This interdisciplinary work, together with the growing diversity of research perspectives in sociology, bodes well for the future of the field. Patricia Hill Collins has optimistically noted that "sociology's unique social location as a contested space of knowledge construction allows us to think through new ways of doing science."[138] This is a good position to be in, as a science. Clearly, the increasing intellectual diversity in sociology and the diversity of its practitioners are virtues to be embraced. Such diversity puts sociology in a good position to deal effectively with the present and future complexities and crises of both US society and global society.

CHAPTER 8

Sociology, Present and Future

Two Sociologies

In the twenty-first century, sociology continues to ignite the imagination of countless citizens who read its books in private or in groups, as well as those who take its courses in colleges and universities around the globe. Many people continue to be drawn to sociological ideas, research, and teachings to help them make sense of the complex and difficult worlds within which they live. Indeed, since its beginning, the ideas and research of sociologists have provided excitement and insights for people in all walks of life, the world over.

Sociology is often used in a narrowly instrumental way to generate findings, such as in the statistically framed survey and demographic research that conventionally serves as a basis for some government and other official decision-making. In this book we have accented a broader and alternative tradition, one that accepts an array of methodological approaches and a range of critical and contending ideas. As we see it, the persisting questions are, "Sociology for what?" and "Sociology for whom?"

In this book, we have emphasized, and proposed the further extension of, the critical sociological tradition that has clear-cut answers to these two questions: Sociology for making a better world and sociology for those who struggle for their emancipation and liberation from

243

numerous social miseries. We believe it is time for mainstream sociology to correct its skewed course so that the important knowledge its practitioners generate can be placed at the service not only of government and corporate policymakers but also of those social groups and community organizations that seek to change the troubling and oppressive conditions in which they live. We realize that this goal is not easy to achieve, but it is essential for social justice, and perhaps for human survival beyond this century.

From its beginnings, sociology has had internal contradictions. On the one hand, there is a deep-lying conventional and relatively conservative tradition of sociologists involved in theoretical and empirical work that generally undergirds the existing social order. On the other hand, there are progressive-reformist and revolutionary traditions of sociologists involved in theoretical and empirical work aimed at substantial social change. The classical theorists examined in Chapter 2 illustrate how these two traditions can exist even in a single sociological theorist, and how what is liberating for some can be oppressive for others. Auguste Comte, for example, proposed to change the world radically by substituting positivist-scientific thinking for theological and metaphysical thinking. Politically, however, he was a conservative who yearned for the security and social order similar to that provided earlier by the authoritarian Catholic Church, which, ironically enough, he wished to defeat. Over several generations now, the tradition of "positive science," which he had proposed to change the social world, has become one of the important instruments for maintenance of the status quo.

As we have demonstrated previously, much of the work connected with the social science mainstream reflects some type of instrumental positivism. Contemporary sociologists have their own versions of these age-old contradictions. For example, the great exemplar of US sociologists, Émile Durkheim, was reconstructed a few decades after his death by Talcott Parsons and other sociologists as a positivistic theoretician of social order and consensus. However, as we have noted previously, Durkheim actually advocated a broad array of sociological methods and approaches and was a staunch supporter of France's Third Republic, which in his time was a rather radical force in the struggle against monarchists and the clerical establishment. As we have demonstrated, Durkheim was also a *moral* philosopher and saw that expanding social justice was essential to the future of healthy societies.

As used in this book, *liberation sociology* is a contemporary term for the old progressive and radical tradition in sociology, the approach deeply critical of existing society and its oppressive institutions and oriented to the significant reduction or elimination of social oppressions. In fact, it represents the real sociology, the sociology that can help bring a more just social world. In Europe, this tradition goes back to early sociologist-intellectuals like Harriet Martineau, and in the United States, it goes back to Jane Addams and the women (and men) of Hull House, as well as to the work of pathbreaking black sociologists like W. E. B. Du Bois and Anna Julia Cooper. Most were organic intellectuals representing the concerns and interests of those communities—women, African Americans, and the poor—who had mostly been excluded from the political interests of elites and from the interests of most mainstream academics. Significantly, too, included in this progressive group were numerous white male sociologists like George Herbert Mead. And we have seen elements of this orientation to building better societies in the "classical" sociologists such as Émile Durkheim and Max Weber.

This countersystem tradition has been kept alive by many people and groups over more than a century. It was manifested in the creation of the Society for the Study of Social Problems (SSSP) in the 1950s and the creation of the Women's Caucus, the Association of Black Sociologists, and the Sociology Liberation Movement in the 1960s and 1970s. This tradition has its global dimension. During the 1960s, many activist students, including student leaders, in protest movements in France, Germany, and the United States were sociology undergraduate or graduate students. They developed a tradition, which continues to the present, of progressive student activists often being sociology majors in college. These youthful activities and movements have helped keep the countersystem tradition alive within the field of sociology across the globe.

NEW VOICES, NEW SOCIOLOGIES

Sociology, like everything human, is always in flux. At some points in its history changes have been revolutionary and at other times evolutionary. In the twenty-first century we see that all social sciences are pressed hard by new voices and participants, many of whom were previously excluded or suppressed. As in the past, sociology frequently leads other sciences in incorporating these progressive changes. During the 1960s, men, most of whom were white, made up some 85 percent of the sociology PhD recipients and sociology faculty members in the country. The percentage of degrees awarded to men dropped steadily from the mid-1960s to 2000s. This gender difference tapered off for a while after 2007 when the number of PhD recipients dropped overall, but has increased then as the number of new PhDs has grown yet again.[1] Even with the decline after 2007, over half of sociology doctoral degrees continue to be awarded to women.[2] The percentage of women PhDs is higher in sociology than in economics and political science.[3] In addition, the number of sociology

PhDs earned by sociologists of color has grown over this period, from a very modest percentage in the 1960s to a significant proportion of all sociology PhDs today. For example, in 2006, among the social science disciplines, sociology had the highest percentage of African Americans receiving PhDs. Today, these trends appear to be continuing.[4]

As noted previously, membership in the American Sociological Association declined from the early 1970s to the mid-1980s but then grew to 13,708 in 2010. A 2013 American Sociological Association (ASA) national meeting set the all-time attendance record. In addition, a record-breaking 4,664 submissions of scholarly papers for presentation were received for the 2014 ASA annual national meeting.[5] Today, we see that more than half of those in the field of sociology are white women and people of color, and this proportion seems to be growing. These sociologists are not simply new voices—for younger generations have always replaced earlier generations—but often represent the voices of those who were once studied as social problems in need of official government attention. They were once the silent objects of sociological study. Many thus represent the views of those suppressed and oppressed over many generations—in society generally and within the social sciences themselves.

As a result of these changes in the ranks, sociology today is a field of much deeper, broader, and more multivoiced contributions to the understanding and improvement of society. These new voices, at the same time, are feared by some sociologists who have worked to enhance sociology's influence and prestige by developing a more conventional professional and "pure science" status. For these conventional sociologists, the new multivoiced theory and research are sometimes seen as a huge shift away from "scientific" sociology into a much weaker sociology, one allegedly concerned mainly with particularistic matters and lifestyle issues. Yet, these critics often exaggerate the speed and impact of this change. For one thing, these professional changes have happened only gradually, over several decades.

Still, the gradual changes are often significant. Many of these relatively new sociologists are bringing important changes in the direction of a more emancipatory sociology. First, the continuing growth means a great range of new people in the field of sociology, making it more representative of the country and the world and thus more democratic. Second, this expansion of a liberation sociology generally means more intellectual power for the field. Many novel and original ideas have arisen and been pursued in field research, ideas once excluded because of the conventional understandings of the sociologists who once dominated the field. As these new voices achieve national audiences in sociology, and more generally, the expanded dialogue will greatly strengthen intellectual pluralism.

We can note briefly a contemporary example of this new intellectual contribution to an emancipatory sociology: Duke University Professor Eduardo Bonilla-Silva, a winner of the American Sociological Association Lewis Coser Agenda Setter Award. The author of influential books on US racism, Bonilla-Silva submitted to the Sociologists Without Borders (a liberation sociology international group) LISTSERV a brief essay about his personal experiences entitled "Eréndira in American Sociology." In the essay he tells his social science colleagues that recent months have been hard for him, because he has been working with and counseling junior faculty of color as they attempt to secure tenure in their colleges and universities. Bonilla-Silva built his essay around the powerful metaphor of the innocent Eréndira, a character in a famous novel by the late Gabriel García Márquez. The young Eréndira—who Bonilla-Silva equates to faculty of color in US sociology departments—accidentally burns down her *abuela's* (grandmother's) house. In his account this *abuela* represents white sociology. The *abuela* tells Eréndira not to worry because she will be able to pay for her damage working as a prostitute. This story has been widely interpreted as an allegory for the people of Latin America represented by Eréndira and their exploitative governments represented by the *abuela*. In his essay, Bonilla-Silva draws on his years of experience in historically white universities and on numerous accounts from faculty of color in the many sociology departments he has visited to call attention to the "collective pain endured by sociologists of color." Among those painful experiences is the realization among many young sociologists of color that, after having been recruited to join a historically white department of sociology, the interest in their presence is often substantially or mostly symbolic on the part of the majority of white sociologists there. There is the accompanying pain of isolation, disenfranchisement, and discriminatory treatment. Bonilla-Silva concludes his essay by urging "young members of Eréndira not to let Abuela get your heart.... You must not accept insults, disrespect, and white sociological nonsense. You must fight back."[6] Clearly, the demographic changes that have come in recent years to sociology and other social sciences mark only the beginning of the changes necessary for these disciplines to be considered fair and open social sciences.

We saw significant evidence of the impact of new demographic pluralism in Chapters 5 through 7, in such important areas as feminist theory and antiracist theory, teaching, and research. Feminist scholars and antiracist scholars of color have raised many new issues about the structure and character of US society, and changes therein, that have been ignored or neglected by traditional research and analysis. And it is clear that the progressive tradition in US sociology has been populated not only by women and people of color but also by a considerable number of farsighted white male sociologists. From the early case of George Herbert Mead to the later examples of C. Wright Mills and Albert Lee in the 1950s and 1960s, to T. R. Young and Carl Jensen more recently, we see numerous white men playing important roles in developing the progressive and radical traditions within contemporary sociology, a sociology committed to the emancipation of groups traditionally oppressed and, indeed, to a society where "liberty and justice for all" is much more than conventional rhetoric.

RESEARCH CHALLENGES AND THE FUTURE OF SOCIOLOGY

In spite of the expansion in sociology's voices, and the changes in research and theory noted above, too much social science research remains a type of top-down research that does not recognize social domination, exploitation, and oppression as critical social issues. Too often, the critical experiences of those suffering from such forms of oppression as racism, classism, sexism, and heterosexism are not assessed in a thoroughgoing way within the conventional outlets of mainstream sociology, such as the *American Sociological Review*. Because they typically have little access to social research or social scientists, those at or near the bottom of this society's resource and power hierarchies generally have a modest impact on what becomes the dominant knowledge of this society, knowledge that is used to make mainstream public policy. Clearly, the oppressing classes and the bureaucratic organizations they control often try to conceal or disguise their operations for the general public and do not seek or desire social science or other critical research on the everyday practices of social oppression. This can be seen clearly in the historical cases of genocide in dictatorial societies such as Nazi Germany, Joseph Stalin's Soviet Union, or Augusto Pinochet's Chile, where probing social researchers did face a significant possibility of imprisonment or death.

Another example of what happens to those probing too deeply into systems of domination and exploitation is the case of Shirin Ahmadnia, a faculty member in Allameh Tabatabai University's sociology department in Iran. She was fired in 2013 just for discussing homosexuality in her classes. Sadr-Aldin Shariati, a radical Shiite clergyman who was then president of university, upheld the decision to discharge a large number of professors, condemning them as "morally corrupt." Speaking specifically on Ahmadnia's case, he said, "One of those professors went to the class and told her students that homosexuality is a good thing ... She is a sociologist ... [W]hat should I do with her ... ? The Quran tells me [that homosexuality] is a moral decay ... is Satanism.... Now, are you telling me that I should let this professor stay on faculty? No way."[7] He sounded like some religiously oriented administrators and faculty members at certain US universities. Today, in numerous Western countries, those researchers probing too deeply into systems of antigay discrimination and other societal discrimination often are punished in one way or another, whether by exclusion from major research funding or by failing to receive earned tenure, promotions, or salary raises in the academic system or other organizational settings. Moreover, in some countries such as El Salvador and Argentina, liberation-oriented academics and theologians have in the past been murdered by police or military forces.

Liberation sociology is a major irritant for power elites in all countries, for it seeks to render visible the oppressive structures and processes of a society. This is an indispensable step in the eradication of social oppressions. For that reason, even in a society where "freedom of speech" and "academic freedom" are acclaimed, critically examining the problems created by existing governments and by major national or international corporations typically requires some courage and boldness. In fact, this is the likely reason that relatively little in-depth critical research has been done on the ruling elites of countries like the United States.

One important goal for liberation sociology is the collection of data that is not distorted by or closely bound to established and usually conservative sociopolitical forces. There is no more significant bias in much of the sciences than the researchers' need or desire to please the rulers of the society, especially when the latter provide the funding for much research. Today much of the data produced by established organizations, as studies previously cited have shown, is manipulated or distorted to fit with the major political-economic and bureaucratic goals of those organizations. Indeed, we need more research on how the current "official data" produced by social scientists are distorted or misleading as guides for interpreting and understanding US society.

There are also deeper concerns of values and morality often ignored by mainstream researchers such as the instrumental positivists. Social scientists whose vision is grounded in a concern for human liberation and human rights go beyond the research that social elites at the helm of the nation-state or multinational corporations can use to formulate major societal policies. They are concerned with implementing the long-standing ideals of liberty and justice in the larger society by means of reliable, innovative, and action-oriented social research.

LIBERATION PSYCHOLOGY AND ANTHROPOLOGY

Of course, sociology does not stand alone. Some psychologists and anthropologists have developed a liberation orientation for their disciplines. In a 1969 keynote speech, George Miller, president of the American Psychological Association, advocated an instrumental-positivistic psychology and distinguished between the promotion of human welfare by psychologists who are social activists and the work of the positivistic psychologists.[8] In contrast, liberation psychologists have proposed a much different role for psychology.

For example, Ignacio Martín-Baró, a creative social psychologist who was murdered in El Salvador in 1989, proposed a liberation psychology that would demonstrate and critique the common and institutionalized misrepresentations of the poor and their poverty. He asserted that psychologists, as scientists of human behavior, should seek the welfare of the discipline of psychology and shape psychology into a major instrument of conscientization and of debunking dominant-group myths of the poor. Martín-Baró supported activism that, buttressed by solid research data, attempts to change oppressive sociopolitical and economic structures that trespass on human welfare.[9] An example of Martín-Baró's liberation psychology is his critical analysis of the common arguments about the conformism and resignation of the Latin American poor. He argued that this social psychological image of Latin American fatalism "accurately detects the symptom but it misses in the diagnosis."[10] It misses the oppressive structures that generate most fatalism, for most Latin American societies have historically been structured so that an elite owning class routinely oppresses the ordinary workers and the poor.

Some anthropologists have proposed a liberation anthropology. In 1994 the American Anthropological Association selected the theme of human rights for its annual meeting, and more sessions were dedicated to that theme than to traditional anthropological topics. Among the anthropologists who have embraced this human rights orientation is Leigh Binford. Binford has proposed a liberation anthropology that works closely with grassroots and community organizations, such as in the documentation and investigation of human rights abuses. An example can be seen in Binford's *The El Mozote Massacre*, a study of a mass murder of Salvadorans by a battalion of El Salvador's army.[11] In addition to providing an exhaustive description of events, Binford examines the political climate, the ruling oligarchy's ideology, and the military objectives that accounted for this crime against humanity. He also examines how this crime was covered up or justified by the US government and by the media and international commissions that investigated it. Binford also describes the history and the social structure of El

Mozote, the community where the massacre occurred. Here a liberation anthropologist rescues the collective memory of the men, women, and children whose lives were ended by this military operation. This work of liberation anthropology was generated by a liberation anthropologist's commitment to human rights.

LIBERATION THEOLOGY: AN ANALOGOUS SITUATION

Recall "liberation theology," the powerful movement of Catholic activism for progressive change in postcolonial countries, particularly in Central and South America. In the 1960s, major efforts toward making liberation theology central in Catholic religious commitments came to the world's attention as a result of a Latin American Bishop's Council in Colombia, where Catholic priests pressed for new initiatives to meet social justice needs in Latin America. Many priests, some other clergy, and many laypeople associated with this movement have dedicated their lives to working hard for the social liberation of the poor and oppressed, which has meant being a strong voice for real political and economic change and for reforming church theology. However, in the early 2000s, John Paul II, then the pope of the Catholic Church, spoke out against the liberation theology movement and acted to subvert its spread by replacing activist bishops with more conventional bishops. Nevertheless, even he was influenced by liberation theology pressures to issue strong condemnations of poverty and economic oppression around the globe and to encourage Catholics to work for social reforms.

In 2013, a *New York Times* reporter suggested that Pope Francis has "an affinity for liberation theology" and that his "speeches draw clearly on the themes of liberation theology." It was also reported that Francis had been a student of an Argentine Jesuit priest "who was a proponent of liberation theology."[12] However, Pope Francis has so far been an inconsistent actor in regard to liberation theology's principles. Indeed, serious concerns remain about his cowardly role during Argentina's brutal military dictatorship. Pope Francis was then in charge of the Jesuit order when the Catholic Church backed the military government in Argentina and called for super-patriotism. Catholic priests and bishops who spoke out against the dictatorship subsequently disappeared, and the Church hierarchy seemed to close its eyes to the murders of progressive clerics. Pope Francis twice refused to testify in court about his role then as head of the Jesuit order. When he ultimately appeared in front of a judge in 2010, he was accused by lawyers of being elusive. Yet, in 2000, the Argentine Catholic Church had made a public apology for its failure to take a stand against the generals.[13]

Nonetheless, Pope Francis's verbal support for liberation theology principles in regard to the world's poor workers and families has inflamed conservatives in numerous countries. In December 2013, the US arch-conservative radio talk show host, Rush Limbaugh referred to the Pope's recent comments about the world economy as "pure Marxism." In the November 2013 document referenced by Limbaugh, and perceived as a platform for Pope Francis's papacy, the pontiff criticized unregulated capitalism as "a new tyranny" and suggested that an "economy of exclusion and inequality" has proven to be deadly for many people around the world. In response to his critics, the Pope—the first Latin American pontiff—said he was not speaking "as a technician but according to the social doctrine of the Roman Catholic Church, and this does not mean being Marxist.... But in my life I have known many Marxists who are good people, so I don't feel offended." Despite his critics, the Pope continued to make statements about unregulated capitalism as morally problematic—for example, arguing that huge corporate executive salaries are symptoms of an economy based on greediness and calling on national leaders to narrow the huge wealth gaps.[14]

Significantly, in many postcolonial countries the Catholic laity have supported liberation theology strongly and insisted on having activist priests committed to real social change. For instance, Ismael Moreno Coto is a Honduran priest and activist who worked on civil rights in El Salvador after other Jesuits were murdered in 1989. In 2014, Coto was director of Radio Progreso, a national leader in investigative reporting that was shut down by the new Honduran government at the time of the 2009 military coup d'état and has subsequently endured military occupations.[15] Coto and other journalists there work with organizations and communities struggling to shield themselves from corporate exploitation—from mining companies to hydroelectric dams to large landowners.[16] Coto travels internationally, bringing attention to human rights abuses occurring throughout Honduran society—particularly inside the journalistic world and within farmworkers' and indigenous communities. He offers comprehensive analysis into the systemic causes for the ongoing injustices and explains the innumerable effects of the international "drug war."[17]

The US government has not escaped his censure. In 2012, in his testimony before the US House's human rights committee, he asked committee members, "How can freedom of expression be defended in a country like Honduras where the biggest violators of this fundamental freedom are the friends and partners of a 'democracy' backed by policies and agencies of the US government?" A dedicated public lecturer, he encourages the many US students to whom he speaks to read about Honduras. He also urges them to write to influential politicians about their concern for Honduras and the rest of Latin America, ensuring their Congressional officials know their concerns about the US government's security policy in Honduras. He tells them, "You could get involved with groups like Witness for Peace or School of the Americas Watch."[18]

In recent years, there has been significant cross-fertilization between liberation theology and the social sciences. For example, Ignacio Ellacuría, a Latin American liberation theologian who was murdered in 1989 in El Salvador, once wrote:

> There are social and historical structures that are the objectification of the power of sin and, also, carriers of that power against human beings, human life. And there are social and historical structures that are the objectification of grace and are carriers of power in favor of human life. The former constitute structural sin, the latter, structural grace.[19]

This comment shows how the social sciences have penetrated the thought of liberation theologians. Although the concept of sin is theological, the ideas of objectification and of social and historical structures are drawn directly from the social sciences. Central here is a rejection of the dualism between the inner experience of faith and the experience of actual participation in a given culture and society.[20]

Similarly, liberation theologians in South Africa have rejected the dualism between the religious experience and the societal experience. These liberation theologians participated actively in the long black African struggle for freedom from white domination (apartheid) in South Africa and other African countries. Pan-Africanism, the century-old political and ideological framework that accents the oneness of all people of African descent and a commitment to African liberation everywhere, is the historical context for the development of African theologians who have taken a strong stand against traditional racial colonialism, as well as against its successor, economic neocolonialism, today.[21]

The liberation sociology we propose shares with liberation theology its commitment to social justice and human rights and its taking sides with the socially oppressed. It also shares with it the rejection of the dualism that segregates the professional scientific and civic lives of its practitioners. However, liberation sociology does not seek to convert anyone to a religious or political set of beliefs.

Today, within US sociology, there are still the old "priests" of mainstream sociology, such as those who assertively represent the tired doctrines of instrumental positivism. They still dominate many established institutions, including major funding agencies and mainstream journals. However, these social science priests are constantly being challenged by the forces of change, especially those sociologists committed to a progressive sociology. Many of the new entrants into the field of sociology are overt or covert supporters of liberation sociology ideas and research strategies. They lead in calling for a new understanding of sociology's history and for a recognition that some of the earliest founders and thinkers in the field were themselves white women and African Americans. Indeed, during the first decade of sociology's development in the United States, numerous sociologists of various class, racial, and gender backgrounds were committed, albeit to varying degrees, to societal reforms, including eradicating the exploitation of workers, building unions, expanding social programs for the poor and immigrants, fighting militarism, and making political and socioeconomic democracy a reality in the United States.

LIBERATION CRIMINOLOGY: A DECOLONIZATION PARADIGM

Onwubiko Agozino, professor of sociology and Africana studies at Virginia Polytechnic Institute and State University, understands well what happens to those whose research penetrates systems of domination and exploitation. He told us:

> My first book, *Black Women and the Criminal Justice System: Towards the Decolonisation of Victimisation* was rejected left, right, and center by publishers. Eventually a perceptive commissioning editor at Ashgate Publishers saw the proposal and contacted me with the offer of launching a new Ashgate Publishers Interdisciplinary Research Series in Ethnic, Gender and Class relations, with me as the series editor....[22]

Citing such intellectual and activist giants as Chinua Achebe, Angela Davis, Cheikh Anta Diop, W. E. B. Du Bois, Frantz Fanon, among others, Agozino considers his research, teaching, and advocacy to be informed by their racial, class, and gender analyses. As a critical criminologist, he views himself, and these role models, as responding to the "white-supremacist imperialist patriarchy—the domination of the world system by racism, sexism and finance capital—which tends to neglect human beings and the environment in the search for more glory, profits, and power."[23]

In this tradition, his critically acclaimed book *Counter-Colonial Criminology* includes analyses of the Enlightenment and later Euro-American theories of the judicial process, feminist perspectives and critical criminology, executive lawlessness, and the struggle for democracy in Africa. It has tried to revolutionize the study of criminology, promoted a critical criminology discipline internationally, and continued to provoke scholars entrenched in European canons and white approaches to criminological discourse.[24] Agozino warns former colonial countries against the "mother" countries' criminology apparatuses that are saturated with imperialistic philosophy and practice. He is unapologetic in his critique of western imperialism as it has traversed and defined much of the so-called Third World's judicial systems. He writes: "Criminology was developed primarily as a tool for imperialist domination and it continues to operate largely as a repressive technology. Other technologies of domination crafted by imperialism, such as the army, the police and the prison, have been generally appropriated by neocolonial regimes around the world."[25]

Currently, as editor in chief of the *African Journal of Criminology and Justice Studies* (AJCJS), the official organ of the African Criminology and Justice Association, Agozino uses his editorial essays to advance the arguments about a countercolonial criminology—a perspective that could be termed *liberation criminology*. Agozino has said this about AJCJS:

> Given the fact that criminological technologies have been used to control people of African descent disproportionately for centuries, it is not surprising that Africans and Africanist scholars have a lot to say that is relevant to both the discipline of criminology and to criminologists. From the Trans-Saharan slavery by Arabs to the Trans-Atlantic slavery by Europeans, Africans have borne the brunt of the most unimaginable crimes ever known to humanity . . . Add to those, the crimes of colonialism and apartheid, a total of wrongs which have been recognized as crimes against humanity by the United Nations, and you will wonder how criminology could have gone on for so long without a significant African perspective.[26]

As a product of a childhood marked by the Nigerian Civil War, Agozino advocates for democratic means of settling disputes. As the chair of the Social Policy Committee of the Association of Black Sociologists, he initiated a program of collaborating with community organizations in the host cities of the annual meetings to support social justice campaigns there. As he explains, "scholar-activism against patriarchy, military dictatorship, and the control-freak state shapes my liberation sociology." As for the costs associated with doing liberation sociology work, Agozino takes an interesting position not unlike Mary Jo Deegan (Chapter 7), who noted that liberation sociologists sometimes suffer greatly but have interesting lives. As he puts it, "W. E. B. Du Bois was never tenured and was nearly jailed during the McCarthy era for trying to start a peace organization. We remember him, but few remember the cowards who got tenure and sold their sociological souls to the metaphorical devil."[27]

Animal Liberation Sociology:
Critical Species-ism Studies

Renowned within animal rights movements as the author of *Animal Rights/Human Rights*, David Nibert is a sociology professor at Ohio's Wittenberg University. He contends that human oppression and the oppression of animals are intricately connected and compound each other.[28] In so doing, he expands a theory on the origins of racial-ethnic conflict created by sociologist Don Noel. Nibert explains:

> Racism is an ideology that rationalizes and explains why humans of color should be treated unequally. Sexism is an ideology that rationalizes the oppression of women. And speciesism is an ideology that defends the oppression of other animals. So, speciesism by itself is not the problem. Challenging speciesist beliefs is important, but challenges also have to be made to the system that drives the singled-minded quest for profits—some of which are used to control the political processes necessary to legalize and support such an oppressive system.[29]

Further illustrating how the exploitation of "other animals" is interconnected with the most pressing problems facing today's world, in *Animal Oppression and Human Violence* Nibert links animal domestication and consumption to environmental catastrophe and some political violence.[30]

Like other liberation sociologists, Nibert understands well what happens to those whose research penetrates existing societal systems of domination and exploitation:

> Advocates for other animals, especially advocacy beyond those labeled as "pets," are treated with considerable reproach. Certainly, I've experienced it on an individual level, facing jeers and worse during demonstrations and marches and more subtle hostility even in academic settings in presentations or when raising issues about other animals in faculty meetings and the like. Other animals are at the bottom of a socially constructed hierarchy of worth and humans are taught to devalue them and disregard their interests. This profound devaluation is necessary for terrible and systemic—but profitable—oppression to occur.[31]

John Sorenson, a Canadian sociologist, has described Nibert as "one of the most important scholars writing in the field of critical animal studies today."[32] Like Nibert, Sorenson promotes an abolitionist agenda and endorses veganism as a political and personal commitment. In his research he sheds light on the economic, environmental, and health costs of animal exploitation and emphasizes animal rights as a social justice issue. Sorenson embraces Mahatma Gandhi's belief that "the greatness of a nation and its moral progress can be judged by the way its animals are treated." His research and activism focus on the status of animals in Canada, with a concentration on institutional exploitation in agriculture, entertainment, and fashion—including the fur trade, puppy mills, and the country's practically unregulated vivisection industry.[33] In the spirit of liberation sociology, Nibert's and Sorenson's research and activism shed light on the connections between various types of animal species's subjugation and the social construction of inequality.

As illustrated throughout this book, liberation sociology can be practiced by sociologists wearing many different ideological labels. One of the great satisfactions of doing liberation sociology is getting other people to see ideas that they have never encountered and to read materials they have not read before. Nibert and Sorenson embody well these facets of liberation sociology.

LIBERATION HISTORY: A PEOPLE'S HISTORY

Much history has been written from the point of view of those powerful people (mostly white men) in charge of running other people's lives, but little from the actual experiences of "we, the people." The late US historian Howard Zinn was long committed to a people-focused history. As he writes in *A People's History of the United States,*

> In that inevitable taking of sides which comes from selection and emphasis in history, I prefer to try to tell the story of the discovery of America from the viewpoint of the Arawaks, of the Constitution from the standpoint of the slaves, of Andrew Jackson as seen by the Cherokees, of the Civil War as seen by the New York Irish, of the Mexican war as seen by the deserting soldiers of Scott's army, of the rise of industrialism as seen by the young women in the Lowell textile mills, of the Spanish-American war as seen by the Cubans, the conquest of the Philippines as seen by black soldiers on Luzon, the Gilded Age as seen by southern farmers, the First World War as seen by socialists, the Second World War as seen by pacifists, the New Deal as seen by blacks in Harlem, the postwar American empire as seen by peons in Latin America.[34]

The broad and deep vision of social history that Zinn sought to present testifies to the importance of sociological ideas in his scholarship and activism. For Zinn, an accurate people's history was a weapon that could be used to resist classism, racism, violent conflict, and other societal oppressions.

Near the end of his life, Zinn movingly captured the central point of this liberation history, focusing on opposition to US imperialism and war, an issue that remained important to the historian, a World War II veteran, throughout his long life. "We cannot depend on the governments of the world to abolish war because they and the economic interests they represent benefit from war. Therefore, we, the people of the world, must take up the challenge," Zinn wrote. "The governments of the world cannot wage war without the participation of the people. Albert Einstein understood this simple fact. Horrified by the carnage of World War I ... [he] said: 'Wars will stop when men refuse to fight.' This is our challenge."[35]

Zinn's message predictably aligns with the organization that now bears Einstein's name. Today, the Albert Einstein Institution is a nonprofit organization that promotes research, policy studies, and education on the strategic uses of nonviolent struggles and protests. Founded by Gene Sharp, this progressive Institution has translated and distributed some of the most prominent writings on nonviolent action, many of which have been studied by resistance movements worldwide. For example, Sharp's own *From Dictatorship to Democracy* has been translated into at least thirty-four languages. The book has been used by nonviolent movements worldwide, including Serbia's Otpor, Georgia's Kmara, Ukraine's PORA, and Kyrgyzstan's KelKel.[36] Michael True has recently summed up the joint message of Zinn and the Einstein Institute: "More essential than public and academic discourse on peacemaking are the men and women who often risk their lives in confronting tyrants and repressive regimes. As with feminists, abolitionists and workers in the mid-19th century, as well as students in the US, China and the Middle East, they worked to redirect the priorities of their own governments."[37]

THE IMPORTANCE OF A BROAD HUMAN RIGHTS STANCE

The Moral Stance

As we have demonstrated throughout this book, all social research has an underlying moral stance, whether openly expressed or kept undercover. All analyses of the social world carry the assumptions and values of those doing that work. However, for many social scientists engaged uncritically in conventional research techniques, it is obligatory to conceal most or all of their metasociological assumptions and values. In addition to the goal of a deeper understanding of social oppression, liberation sociologists seek to take an overt moral stance toward the research process from the first formative steps. As we see it, there is great need for a renewal of the alternative social science tradition that openly embraces the moral dimensions of all human life, including that of all social research.

One problem for many contemporary sociologists, as for most classical sociologists, is that they do not develop a moral perspective that goes substantially beyond the confines of the nation-state in which they work. Fortunately, there are growing numbers of sociologists who are openly concerned with moral issues in sociological analysis and in the larger society. For example, "communitarian" sociologists like the late Robert Bellah and Amitai Etzioni have tried to bring questions of ethics and morality back into social science and public debates.[38] Generally speaking, the communitarians reject a positivistic social science that tries to ignore moral issues. In this regard, their contribution is healthy for developing both a better sociology and a better society. They are, however, opposed to a too-heavy accent on human rights and prefer instead to emphasize the importance of civic duties and obligations within an existing nation-state like the United States. They stress the importance of the contemporary family and of each individual's responsibility to it and to larger communities.[39] Although they accent civic responsibilities, they see the world mostly from the vantage point of those who are white and affluent, while neglecting the antioppression perspectives of the poor or people of color. The poor and oppressed in the United States cannot carry out the requisite civic responsibilities in a system that systematically exploits and discriminates against them. Moreover, most communitarian analysts do not work aggressively to challenge the institutional discrimination and oppressive socioeconomic dominance of the governing elites in the United States or across the globe.

In contrast, liberation sociologists assert the importance of openly proclaiming a human morality that supports the liberation of the socially oppressed. As we see it, an overt moral perspective is essential to a viable liberation sociology, and that perspective must go beyond the confines of the existing nation-state to draw heavily on the burgeoning human rights tradition at the international level. Probing serious problems in current powerful nation-states and corporations requires a bold moral position that asserts the human rights of all citizens of the planet. Those researchers who are well supported by funding from nation-state agencies are not very likely to collect data on, or analyze critically, extant state-fostered oppression overseas. A broad international human rights perspective can enable a social scientist to examine government manipulation or oppression more critically, and even to choose elites' manipulation or oppression as major research topics.

Unfortunately, the repeated emphasis on certain types of state-funded, quantitative-positivistic methods as the main or only way to do serious social science and the insistent teaching of these techniques and orientations to sociology undergraduates and graduate students have broad consequences for the field of sociology. A heavy stress on such procedures shapes the way that these students view the social world and thus frequently limits their minds and imaginations.[40]

What Human Rights Perspective?

The idea that basic human rights transcend the boundaries and authority of a particular society or government was articulated by Thomas Jefferson and his fellow revolutionaries. Drawing mostly on European thinkers, Jefferson in 1776 wrote, "We hold these truths to be self-evident, that all men are created equal and are endowed by their creator with certain unalienable rights … Life, Liberty, and the pursuit of Happiness." Envisioned here are not only legal rights but also basic and broad human rights. Jefferson and his fellow white male revolutionaries declared that the North American minority of the British Empire had rights that derive from the natural law that transcends the authority of the British nation-state. However, later on, in the debates leading to the US Constitution, many of these same members of the North American elite coupled this "rights" talk to their strong concerns for protecting mainly the interests and property (including many enslaved African Americans) of well-off Americans against less-privileged Americans.

In contrast, some non-European traditions do not view private property as the primary bedrock for human rights. Very important in expanding our conception of human rights traditions are the dissident rights perspectives of Native, African, and Latino Americans and the perspectives of women and other oppressed peoples across the globe. There are much stronger human rights arguments in these traditions than in many of the elitist perspectives of theorists such as the Europeans John Locke and John Stuart Mill. For example, there is the community-centered human rights tradition of Native American groups. Moreover, over the past several decades, an ever-larger body of international agreements and laws has grown up to buttress the reality of expanding human rights on the global scene. An international perspective on human rights was clearly strengthened by the Nuremberg trials of former German Nazi government officials after World War II. The trials established the principle that "crimes against humanity" are condemned by principles higher than the laws of any given nation-state. Thus, human rights are much broader than "civil rights," since the latter are only those legal rights guaranteed by a particular nation-state. In this broader framework, each person is entitled to equal concern and treatment because they are human beings, not because they are members of a particular society.[41]

The struggle to deal with German Nazi oppression and Western imperialist oppression in many countries led to the creation of the United Nations' Universal Declaration of Human Rights right after World War II. We noted earlier that this international agreement stipulates that "all human beings are born free and equal in dignity and rights" and "all are equal before the law and are entitled without any discrimination to equal protection of the law." The declaration extends these rights to everyday life: "Everyone has the right to a standard of living adequate for the health and well-being of himself and his family, including food, clothing, housing."[42]

This extraordinarily important international declaration affirms that human beings have rights independent of the particular governmental conditions in which they live and presses governments to incorporate human rights into their societies. This international rights tradition has been buttressed by a long series of subsequent international agreements, international court decisions, and court decisions within individual nations based on these agreements. Although this human rights impetus may initially have been substantially Western in its orientation, today a broad human rights perspective has been shaped and asserted by many citizen and political groups around the globe and, increasingly, by established nongovernmental agencies and by political and legal agencies in many nation-states.

At its best, this international human rights vision requires more than the integration of the formerly oppressed into a modestly adjusted societal framework. The oppressed may not be "seen" in most societies, but they have always been there. As they rise up periodically in liberation movements, they make evident their centrality to their societies. As this happens, it becomes clear that simply integrating them into adjusted structures that continue much of the oppression in less overt forms will not be sufficient. The ultimate goal will have to be to replace the oppressive structures and processes with totally new democratic structures grounded in a full respect for all fundamental human rights—including civic, political, family, and economic rights.

LIBERATION SOCIOLOGY: RECALLING KEY DIMENSIONS

The Countersystem Perspective

Recall that the countersystem approach in social science involves social scientists stepping outside the thought patterns and practices of a conventional instrumental-positivistic paradigm to look very critically at their own society. One good example of this can be seen in the work of Stephen Lyng, a countersystem sociologist working in the Gideon Sjoberg tradition. Lyng has pioneered in a critical analysis of alternative health care systems and what they mean practically, philosophically, and politically for a country facing continuing and large-scale health care crises, yet unwilling to discuss critically its mainstream (e.g., drug-oriented) approaches to health care. Generally, those adopting a countersystem approach question existing social structures and sometimes propose a counter set of societal arrangements. A newly envisaged countersystem can include elements of an existing society, or it can involve entirely new arrangements. Some countersystem analysts accent the importance of an external standard to judge existing societal arrangements, such as the standard in the aforementioned international vision of human rights. Other countersystem analysts accent the idea of alternative societal futures and suggest thinking about the possible range of such societal futures. Both approaches can generate important discussions about the ways to create new and more just social structures and arrangements.[43]

We view liberation sociology as a countersystem approach, one that aggressively seeks the goal of human emancipation from exploitative and dominative structures. This perspective foresees a better society where most people have real compassion for human suffering and a commitment to eliminate all major forms of socially generated misery and oppression. It seeks research relevant to dealing with social miseries and oppressions as they are manifested in everyday life. A liberation sociology perspective envisions a society where people are reflective, develop empathetic compassion for human suffering, and commit themselves to changing that suffering. It creates research and analysis relevant to everyday social problems. An adequate standard for assessing existing social institutions includes a vision of more humane social arrangements, one that includes the best elements of past and present societies.

Recognizing Crises in "Normal" Systems

One of the key insights of Karl Marx was that fully human action is possible only when people are substantially liberated from economic oppression. What type of person one can become, Marx showed, is significantly shaped by the social structures in which we find ourselves. The structures of contemporary capitalism are frequently destructive of a person's humanity. This includes both the capitalists and their exploited workers.

One of the tragedies of any society is the failure of its people and leaders to understand the deep-lying social crises and dilemmas confronting them. Much empirical data reveal that the United States is on a path of accentuated economic and social inequalities and probably of increasing social conflict. Thus, the social and economic contradictions of modern capitalism are becoming quite evident. Income inequality has reached a record level in recent years. Wealth inequality has increased significantly in recent decades. According to economists Emmanuel Saez and Thomas Piketty, in 2012 the top 10 percent of US earners took home more than half of the country's overall income. This was the highest percentage recorded since the government started amassing such data a century ago. The top 1 percent took home more than one-fifth of the income earned, one of the peak levels on record since 1913 when the government introduced an income tax.[44] *New York Times* reporter Annie Lowrey writes:

> The figures underscore that even after the recession the country remains in a new Gilded Age, with income as concentrated as it was in the years that preceded the Depression of the 1930s, if not more so. High stock prices, rising home values and surging corporate profits have buoyed the recovery-era incomes of the most affluent Americans, with the incomes of the rest still weighed down by high unemployment and stagnant wages for many blue- and white-collar workers.[45]

The US political elites and media seem relatively unconcerned. One has to turn to the alternative media, especially on the Internet, to get serious and sustained analysis of the crises of capitalism. Only occasionally in mainstream social science journals does one find serious discussion of the deep-lying contradictions of contemporary capitalism.

In the last few decades the failures of other political-economic systems—for example, the demise of state communism in Eastern Europe—have received more attention in the mainstream media than the present political-economic contradictions and crises of modern capitalism. Increasing economic inequalities in the United States and other Western societies do get some media coverage, but typically in scattered presentations with little sustained critical analysis. Moreover, they are sometimes even accompanied by attacks on the principles of equality and pluralism that supposedly underlie the political institutions of the United States.

For example, in the area of racial matters, many policymakers, media commentators, and mainstream social scientists have abandoned analyses of the widespread racial oppression that persists in US society, adopting instead thinly disguised racial code words created by influential whites, such as *law and order, quotas, welfare (or food stamp) recipients, inner city, street crime,* and *illegal aliens.* Claims that African Americans, Native Americans, Latinos, Latin American immigrants, and other people of color are unintelligent, lazy, welfare-preferring, or criminal—which marked an era in US history said to have passed decades ago—have regularly resurfaced in recent decades in the sound bites, books, articles, and political programs of numerous influential media pundits and conservative academics.

There is also a reluctance to face the central and continuing role of US corporations in environmental degradation, both in the United States and across the planet. In recent decades, the levels of greenhouse gases in the Earth's atmosphere have grown significantly—mainly because of fossil fuel use, deforestation, technological agriculture, and transport pollution. The processes have often been triggered by, or generated by, large US-based corporations, many of them transnational corporations. This global warming melts ice packs, increases coastal flooding, generates severe weather, spreads disease, and reshapes agriculture across the globe.[46]

Numerous leading politicians in the West, as well as a great many corporate leaders, have been unwilling to take more than modest steps to deal with this accelerating and increasingly obvious environmental destruction. Indeed, they produce speeches suggesting that the environmental crises are exaggerated—or are someone else's fault (such as of China and India). However, some respected environmental experts are discussing the possibility that most plant and animal species, including possibly the human species, will be sharply decreased by the year 2100 or shortly thereafter. A few principled political leaders and numerous physical scientists are now speaking out on the substantial scientific evidence on ongoing and future environmental catastrophes. The only question now is whether the ultimate civilization-threatening crises are likely to "strike our children or our grandchildren, and whether we choose to adopt now the many obvious countermeasures."[47] The data on ongoing crises suggest that intellectual defenses of the status quo inside and outside contemporary social science are yet one more way to "fiddle while Rome burns."

Working for a Global Civil Society

Liberation social science includes a focus on global organization, cooperation, and action on egalitarian and democratic policies of broad concern. Alternative policy groups (APGs) such as the Third World Institute, the Centre de recherche et d'information pour le développement (Research Center and Information for Development, Paris), the

Transnational Institute (Amsterdam), and Focus on the Global South (Bangkok) regularly generate knowledge that challenges prevailing corporate-capitalistic priorities and state policies, while championing alternative methods of organizing economic, political, and cultural life. Such internationally oriented groups disseminate knowledge by means of mainstream media venues, alternative media, and activist networks. They regularly collaborate with social movements in implementing more egalitarian and democratic ideas. Accordingly, such groups play a significant role in dealing with social conflicts that transcend national borders and pose political challenges to established undemocratic authorities. There has been little comprehensive investigation of how these APGs function, and with what tangible effect upon global civil society—until now.[48]

An international group of social scientists is working to fill the void. They include William K. Carroll (University of Victoria, Canada), Elaine Coburn (Ecole des Hautes Etudes en Sciences Sociales, France), Christopher Chase-Dunn (University of California–Riverside), Vishwas Satgar (University of Witwatersrand, South Africa), and Yahilo Unno (Kanazawa State University, Japan). These internationally oriented researchers have explored the networks, research, discourses, and practices through which these alternative policy groups exert political and cultural influence, while also examining challenges faced by the transnational change agents. For liberation social science, the contribution is one of examining the role that these transnational alternative policy groups play in producing knowledge for truly democratizing types of societal social change.[49]

These concerned researchers typically employ a mixed-methods approach. In 2011 to 2012, using the *Yearbook of International Organizations* as a source, an initial set of several dozen alternative policy groups was snowballed into a census of these APG organizations. Analysis of APG websites and of documents and media issued by APGs provided an overview of each organization, global networks, and related cultural production. Proceeding on the knowledge gained through this census, the social scientists focused on the Canadian Centre for Policy Alternatives, ten key transnational APGs, and the World Social Forum. The latter is an important open space bringing together many peoples' movements, progressive nongovernment organizations, and APGs into an alternative public sphere away from conventional corporate and nation-state control. The researchers did comparative case studies of these APGs through field observation and in-depth interviewing, focusing on each group's practices and networking with other APGs. The project had a participatory component. This research culminated in a series of dialogues and a workshop involving researchers and participating groups. These efforts have helped to locate the important work of the APGs within a global context.[50]

As the first comprehensive study of its kind, the project offers an unprecedented understanding of the role of APGs in the struggle for real democratic and egalitarian globalization. These social science researchers have developed important knowledge of value to social scientists, policy-makers and analysts, and those active in such organizations within the global civil society. The project delivers empirically based knowledge that enriches sociological understanding and democratic practice and moves well beyond the main interests and goals of the nation-state and corporate elites.[51]

Note, too, that liberation sociology at its best accents this type of interdisciplinary and holistic thinking, and this includes social theory and research about social developments at both the national and the international levels. Originally, sociology became a separate discipline at a time when the sciences were being divided into an array of specialties. Compartmentalization of ideas and methodology was useful in early struggles to establish sociology and the other social sciences as distinctive disciplines, but such efforts were political, not scientific. Marcel Mauss, Émile Durkheim's leading disciple, thus advised his students that at their best, human beings do not give themselves to observation in separate compartments fitting each discipline, but actually live all at once.[52] Thus, liberation sociologists frequently insist on a holistic approach to the social worlds.

Breaking with the Nation-State Perspective

The nation-state bias in much US social science means that global issues are not researched as much as they need to be. The globalization of the capitalist system is engulfing all societies and most areas of organization within these societies. Global organizations oriented to world capitalism, such as the Western-controlled World Bank and the International Monetary Fund, as well as huge transnational supercorporations like Exxon-Mobil and IBM, are to some degree autonomous of any particular society or government. In the social sciences, much more attention needs to be given in research and analysis to these major bureaucratic actors in the global frameworks that have dramatically reshaped much of the world in recent decades.

One challenge to building more humane societies that recognize the full range of human rights lies in the way in which large bureaucratized organizations perpetuate the "iron cages" of social oppression. Gideon Sjoberg has underscored the way in which political liberals tend to support government action and to be critical of corporate action, whereas neoconservatives tend to have a positive view of corporate bureaucracies and to be skeptical of government action except where they benefit. Yet, the global scene is increasingly dominated by large, highly bureaucratized corporations that function, to a varying degree, without the substantial control of any nation-state, including the United States. Such bureaucratic capitalism is a dominant, worldwide force constantly creating major problems for the world's inhabitants, especially increasing economic inequalities and ecological problems. Sjoberg notes that "as transnational organizations control agro-food systems, farmers in many developing nations are being encouraged to produce cash crops that can be sold to those who hold positions of privilege in global bureaucratic structures. ... These cash crops, in turn, are replacing the production of staples for the local populace."[53] Working in their own economic interests, these large transnational corporations often remake or destroy regions, countries, peoples, and environments around the globe.

As we conceive it, liberation sociology should be fundamentally opposed to the many nationalisms that divide human beings. Sandra Harding notes that "Western sciences clearly have been and continue to be complicit with racist, colonial, and imperial projects."[54] Scientists of all types should examine their role in societal exploitation, domination, and oppression. Today, there are many people's movements around the globe that are fighting against colonialist, racist, classist, sexist, and heterosexist structures within societies. In these efforts, social science can be helpful, as it is a place where inherited social views can be carefully examined and debated, and revolutionary new ideas asserted and promoted.[55] If liberation sociology involves a weakening of conventional sociology within a given nation-state, that is often of positive consequence, especially if that weakening means an expansion of sociology's meaningful development across the globe.

As liberation sociologists view these matters, if human beings are to have a voice in changing the conditions that exploit and oppress them, then they should have great access to the generation of the knowledge about those conditions and to the strategies for changing them.

Ongoing Reflectivity and Empathy

A potentially liberating aspect of sociology is its omnivorous observational curiosity. Sociology relies on field observations, surveys, interviews, experimentation, and historical comparisons to reach general conclusions. Sociology can liberate when it applies humanistic concern and empathetic reason to solving serious problems afflicting human beings.

Early in the history of social science, the application of reason through scientific method was once thought to bring progress; reason would make us free once we rid ourselves of ancient prejudices. Yet this promise was never delivered. Although the reason of science can be used to liberate, it has also been used to oppress.

A number of contemporary sociologists, from Jürgen Habermas and Pierre Bourdieu in Europe to Gideon Sjoberg in the United States, have argued aggressively for the importance of reflectivity—of thinking critically and deeply about the self and about the self in relation to others—in providing a basis for expanded ideas of human rights. One key theme of this book is that liberation sociology should be self-reflective. The idea that a human being can arrive at knowledge that is independent of all particular selves has been an assumption of intellectual activity since the time of the Ancient Greeks. Historically, the various sciences have made valiant efforts at producing this type of knowledge. Yet, for all the demonstrated ability of science to produce such knowledge, it has not been possible, even in physics, chemistry, or biology, to discount the impact of particular human biases and social group interests in the form and content of knowledge. The understandings of bias that sociologists and other social scientists generate can be applied to their own situations and disciplines.

Moreover, reflectivity, broadly conceived, is at the heart of what it means to be human; it is integral to the ability to understand, and to empathize with, the social other. As Sjoberg notes, "reflectivity cannot be sustained without physical security and basic subsistence" and that "by recognizing reflectivity as an essential feature of human nature, one must ultimately consider just how persons often are able, or can be enabled, to take the roles of multiple divergent Others."[56]

Conclusion

Progressive social scientists have long asked whether social things really are what they seem to be. Human societies are, of course, created by many people, who make frequent errors in arrangements, beliefs, and choices. Yet the current arrangements need not be allowed to stand when they destroy the lives of many people caught within them. Liberation sociology seeks to stimulate debate in the field of sociology, the other social sciences, and the larger society over what humane and fully democratic societal arrangements would look like and how they could be fully implemented.

Liberation sociologists have been rowing against the mainstream currents since sociology found its strong disciplinary identity in the late

1800s. Indeed, the conventional cultural expectations about what is "good social science" can become "a form of symbolic violence that relies on a relationship of constrained communication to extort submission."[57] That is, department chairs, deans, and other college administrators, as well as many established colleagues, often generate this internalized symbolic violence in young, and older, sociologists by ruthlessly claiming that in their academic decision-making they are only applying timeless rationality and depersonalized rules, when in fact they are imposing a narrow status-quo framing of both the college setting and the larger society.

Sociology can help to liberate when humanistic concern, critical reflectivity, and empathetic reason are applied to the everyday social problems that create much misery for human beings. Throughout this book we have accented a broad human rights perspective and the value of expanded humanization. This means a maximizing of human potential, self-realization, and achievement. More specifically, the aim of liberation sociology is to make sure that in classrooms more ideas are created than are brought to the classrooms by means of the assigned readings. Moreover, it is rather easy to demonstrate empirically that all social scientists mix research and moral concerns. And too often their morality is that of the status quo—and is thus taken for granted. Only a modest number of social scientists have so far explicitly coupled their research interests with a broad human rights perspective that reaches beyond the borders of conventional nation-states. Today, the early human rights tradition of US sociology needs to be strongly recalled and fully reinstituted—this time in the context of the internationally recognized human rights, rights not only to life and liberty but also to a decent standard of living and a safe environment in which to raise families. The main purpose of liberation sociology is to research the social world and to change it. And to change it in the direction of greater fairness, social justice, and equality.

A just and democratic society, at both national and global levels, should be devoid of all forms of institutionalized exploitation and oppression. As we see it, this just society is not only a desirable goal for humanity but is also likely a requirement for human survival over the next century. The destructive mentality of modern capitalism, now the world's dominant economic force, is gradually destroying the planet's atmosphere, flora, and fauna; by the year 2100, if current trends continue, much of the planet will likely be uninhabitable.

Place this ongoing environmental crisis in the set of all social crises facing the world's peoples—growing economic inequality, continuing racial and ethnic oppression, high levels of patriarchal and heterosexual oppression in most countries—and you have a planet where a detached and amoral social science makes no human rights sense. In envisioning a better human future, a sociology of liberation sides with those seeking liberation from oppression. It works with people who are trying to bring changes and it attempts to voice those who are oppressed. It envisions a better future for all humanity.

CHAPTER 9

Epilogue

The Challenges of Teaching
Liberation Sociology

Karl Marx and Frederick Engels once famously proposed that "the ideas of the ruling class are in every epoch the ruling ideas, that is, the class which is the ruling material force of society is at the same time its ruling intellectual force."[1] Sociologists who wish to teach from the liberation sociology perspective need a critical awareness of this elementary fact about society, or otherwise they will end up teaching a social science that substantially derives from, and significantly supports, the conventional ruling ideas of society. Savvy liberation sociologists are aware that "hidden exploitation is the form taken by man's exploitation of man whenever overt, brutal exploitation is impossible," as Pierre Bourdieu once put it.[2] He used the term *symbolic violence* for the violence that people in less powerful groups do to *themselves* by accepting the dominant social and cultural framing of those who dominate them. Thus, teachers of liberation sociology can assist their students in escaping much internalized violence by keeping their emancipatory mission in mind. The teaching of human emancipation begins with teaching students the essential role that the dominant sociocultural framing of society plays in the maintenance by dominant groups of society's established hierarchies of power and privilege.

This dominant cultural framing of society, and its array of conventional beliefs that protect these social hierarchies of power and privilege,

271

are often disguised by a variety of strategies that Pierre Bourdieu termed strategies of "misrecognition." To communicate to college students this sociological concept of misrecognition, one of the authors devised a series of discussion questions that college students are asked to respond to in order for them to develop some awareness of how misrecognition works in everyday life.

One such discussion question asks students what they talk about with potential marriage partners. Though both partners clearly have a vested economic interest in each other's economic futures, in classroom discussions of misrecognition *very few* college students in fact acknowledge discussing with their partners (i.e., recognizing) these crucial economic interests. Another classroom discussion explores advertising. One needs only to open a recent newspaper or mainstream website to realize that most "sale" advertisements emphasize savings for buyers, when the truth is that the advertising merchants actually seek to increase their never-acknowledged profits. In our use of videos and movies in the classroom, most students do not "see" the underlying realities of social hierarchy and discrimination. Consider the famous and still viewed Disney movie *The Lion King* (1994). Only a few students initially recognize that the central plot of that movie teaches that a society's rulers (the lions) are the born rulers and that the followers (hyenas, elephants, and so forth) are born followers. If one adds to the critical analysis of the movie the important consideration of actors' voices and the colors (of fur) of the central animals, one can then recognize just how the movie makes use of standard US racial stereotypes. Course discussions about this movie have unearthed just how strongly many students feel about lions being the "kings" of the jungle and how strong they argue that the movie is just telling an accepted truth about the natural hierarchy of the "circle of life," what Western philosophers have for centuries called the "great chain of being." Such classroom exercises make very clear to students just how much of social reality is hidden from or misrepresented to them, and how they in turn come to misrecognize what is so plainly in front of them.

The task of the liberation sociology teacher is *not* to tell students what to think but to suggest to them the social "what" that they should think critically about. This change from the aim of most conventional educational practice necessitates a significant change in many current relationships between teachers and students. The authors have discovered, in different settings, that numerous social science concepts can have an emancipatory effect when used to help students see what is culturally arbitrary or hidden in society. For example, to emphasize the importance of everyday life settings, one of us has asked college students to examine the actual physical and social layout of the room in which the class—say, an introductory sociology class—is actually taking place. Students quickly realize that there is a recurring and conventional seating arrangement. Most often, the teacher is at the front, and students are in rows of chairs or desks facing the teacher. Students have learned to take this arrangement as the "natural" way for them to be educated. In such classroom discussions, questions then proliferate from usually unreflective college youths: "How else can one learn from a teacher?" "Are you proposing that we return to the round tables of our kindergarten days?" "Are you suggesting that all classrooms be set up with chairs in a circular shape so that students can see each others' faces and learn from each other as well as the teacher?"

Indeed, consider what might happen to educational impacts, to students, and to society if the single change of roundtable-seating for classroom arrangements were to be implemented on a large-scale in US classrooms. In the overwhelming majority of classrooms, chairs or desks are neatly arranged in ways that allow the teacher to dominate physically. Pressing a class for such a critical examination of what is taken for granted and submissively accepted as the normal way of doing education creates a rich lode for self-discovery and can lead students to taking the initiative to discuss important concepts learned in yet other classes. In one class a reflective student once asked us why sociology majors are taught about the social construction of reality, yet are not taught that even their sociological concepts are social constructions. In the dialogue that followed, various students came up with a long list of conventionally constructed social science dichotomies: order versus anarchy, social system versus randomness, secular versus sacred, democracy versus totalitarianism. Soon they became reflective about the artificiality and arbitrariness of many conceptual dichotomies.

Another exciting example of progressive sociology teaching involves the instructional methods known as *service learning* and *case teaching*, approaches passionately adopted by sociologists like Joe Bandy. In the early 2000s, before he became assistant director at Vanderbilt University's Center for Teaching, Bandy used such service learning in courses at Bowdoin College. Over 200 Bowdoin students worked on more than thirty different community projects under Bandy's guidance. In the process, they matched needs or problems of community partners with knowledge and skills developed in the sociology classroom.[3]

Presently, at Vanderbilt, service learning remains central to his liberation sociology teaching. He tries to actively engage students in the process of critical thinking so that they may become empowered national and global citizens.[4] Recently, he explained the potential benefits of service learning:

Service learning is what educators often call "high-impact pedagogy," because it tends to lead students to experiential learning in the community.... It often asks them to engage in interdisciplinary thinking, critical problem-solving and sometimes group learning processes that are prime for leadership development. And that can be good across the disciplines—from the humanities to the social sciences to the natural sciences.... It can lead to more engaged students and a more vigorous intellectual culture.[5]

Case teaching, also central to Bandy's progressive sociology approach, is characteristically about a particular social problem or crisis. Drawing on a case study—that is, a written and detailed account of a social situation—students role-play while examining possible origins of and resolutions to a problem or crisis. While cases often include usefully fabricated components, most describe actual historical or contemporary situations. Students act as participants not just as disinterested observers, and in the process they have the potential to improve their analytical and leadership skills, while enhancing their understanding of the multifaceted intersection of practical and theoretical community concerns.[6]

A recent example of a liberation sociology approach in college teaching is that of one of the authors (Ducey) at the University of Winnipeg in Canada. She has used this book since its initial publication. In 2005, Ducey sent the first two authors a large box of creative class projects submitted by her students, who were often influenced by liberation sociology ideas. These projects included multifaceted methods for getting at and presenting sociological ideas and empirical findings: paintings, artisan artifacts, music, videos, and pieces of cloth for a quilt made up of themes describing the highlights of a sociological career. These student class projects, then as now, fill us with much hope for the future of sociology. The projects reveal a great enthusiasm not only for data collection and analysis but also for the sociological informed pursuit of social justice, equality, and democracy. Of great interest in Ducey's social science courses is how, when allowed to express sociological ideas and findings in the media of their choice, students develop significant knowledge and release much creativity and originality, thereby exhibiting much more learning and insight than commonplace multiple-choice examinations and similar conventional evaluations allow them to express.

Moreover, Ducey has also organized an annual Liberation Sociology Tribute Day, giving her sociology students the opportunity to research the career of a liberation sociologist of their choosing, and in the process to highlight social justice issues important to them. Students are asked to select a social scientist who has been doing liberation sociology work in the last few years, with interesting new methodologies or really sharp new conceptual ideas. She has encouraged her students to contact the individual to gain more information about their activism and research.

As an illustration, one of her students, Joey Lywak, chose to research the life and work of the African-born sociologist we discussed previously, Onwubiko "Biko" Agozino. Lywak sums up the journey:

> My search for a liberation sociologist began with slight trepidation. After quickly deciding upon highlighting Biko's work, I came to realize, to my dismay, that few public writings documented his contributions to fighting oppression. With little else to go on, and in hopes of resolving my predicament, I decided to contact Biko.... Not only was my request met promptly, but great effort, thought, and humility went into the detailed responses which followed every question I posed. Equally significant were the added benefits which came from our conversations. These, I believe, are a testament to the character of Biko. Because of his commitment to my learning, I was able to gain valuable experiences I otherwise would not have had.... The PowerPoint presentation I created for Liberation Sociology Day was met with great enthusiasm on the part of my fellow students and others present.... I find my experiences to have been immensely valuable.... One of Biko's mantras is that 'learning is fun essentially,' which he refers to as LIFE. The liberation sociology project certainly proved LIFE.[7]

Another exciting example of liberation-sociology teaching involves Scott Myers-Lipton, a sociologist at San Jose State University (SJSU), whose dedication to social justice and to students has reportedly proved transformative. In a recent conversation with the authors, he explained what educators might do to encourage more liberation sociology research and teaching:

> The single greatest thing that we can do to encourage liberation sociology is to get folks (both students and community members) out into the world doing community work, and then integrate this action with an analysis of sociological theory and concepts. This dialectical movement between action (i.e., praxis) and theory/concepts is what sociologists need to focus on in the twenty-first century. Without it, liberation is not possible.[8]

His own path to liberation sociology began when he was a high school teacher. A watershed moment for the young teacher came when one of his students asked him to explain the origins of the Holocaust.

The question led him to examine other major societal questions and to seek out the writings of Mohandas Gandhi and Dr. Martin Luther King Jr. As a direct result of that seminal moment, he would eventually pursue a master's degree in the humanities and a doctorate in sociology.[9]

For some years now, Myers-Lipton's students have been thinking critically about such issues as sweatshop labor, equal access to education, Hurricane Katrina and its aftermath, immigrant rights, and the minimum wage. He believes that leadership is more than critically thinking about such issues, as it is also about applying that knowledge and developing actual solutions. In conversation with the authors, he shared a few of his students' successes. In 2007, they led a campaign that convinced (then) SJSU president Don W. Kassing to sign an executive order to join the Worker Rights Consortium (WRC), making SJSU the 160th university to become a "sweatshop-free" institution of higher education. In 2008, students led a successful campaign to get Kassing to sign another executive order, this time to fully restore the equal opportunity program. Currently serving over 2,000 students, who are the first in their family to attend college, the program provides support services so students can achieve their goals at SJSU and beyond. From 2006 to 2009, Myers-Lipton's students actively partook in an effort to rebuild the Gulf Coast after Hurricane Katrina by means of a massive public works program and by advocating for the introduction of congressional legislation. His students have also led a successful effort to allow undocumented students the ability to check out computers on the campus and to make available scholarships to undocumented students. And finally, his students initiated and helped to lead a minimum wage campaign. The creation and eventual passing of Measure D increased the minimum wage in the city of San José to $10 an hour.[10]

For more than two decades now, Myers-Lipton has encouraged his students to seek resolutions to poverty and its associated problems. They regard him as not only a liberation sociologist, but also as a top-notch teacher who connects the sociology of the classroom to the community and gets them to do the same. For a teacher who "never took a sociology class up to that point of having a master's degree," Myers-Lipton's transition to liberation sociology teacher is both revealing and inspiring.[11]

These examples of social science students coupling significant self-analysis with socio-analysis in and outside the classroom might be multiplied endlessly from the experiences of the many social science teachers who do accent critical thinking in the classroom. Many sociologists practice a critical and reflexive approach to teaching and research and know they are part of the teaching and research observations in which they engage. This significant feature of the sociology discipline opens the possibility of increased and more highly participatory teaching and research. In the examples mentioned, the complexity of classroom interaction is learned by students as they concentrate their attention on the here-and-now world in which they live. Concepts such as social class, institutional racism, gender, heterosexuality, privilege, ideology, and subjectivity can all be studied and illuminated within the boundaries of the institutional arrangements of classrooms, in which a savvy teacher can derive much sociologically relevant data from students about social interactions and meaning. The data thus derived can then be examined for representativeness and compared critically with similar data from other such settings or from other research sources.

In our capitalistic society, with its pressure to judge everything in profitability terms, higher education is more and more being "run like a business," a cliché one hears from many college administrators. Indeed, researchers in a book edited by Dennis Hayes and Robin Wynward explore in some depth the "McDonaldization of higher education," which refers to the ways in which the business values of efficiency and control by authorities are often accented over creativity, critical thinking, and democratic exchange in the classroom.[12]

Moreover, in recent decades ever more undergraduate courses, especially those in colleges and universities accenting research and grants, have been taught by graduate students, who are usually poorly remunerated for their efforts. The pressures of graduate school—or for junior faculty in similar situations, of getting tenure—encourage these instructors to use introductory textbooks that are sold with manuals, collections of multiple-choice questions, and PowerPoint databases to facilitate the tasks of instructors. These convenient devices encourage a pedagogy that is relatively unidirectional and requires rather modest commitments of students to deep learning. In addition, most teachers in social science departments and programs—including the authors—have agreed to teach courses within the confining limits of the preestablished, conventional sociology curriculum. The standard sociology curriculum for undergraduate and graduate students is, for the most part, centered around a predefined range of topical areas, such as crime and deviance, family, demography, complex organizations, stratification, racial-ethnic relations, theory, and standard research methods.

Yet, contemporary social life is richer than what is indicated by the usual presentation of social facts within conventional sociology courses, as well as other conventional social science courses. Progressive sociologists often suggest new courses for the social science curriculum. Indeed, over the last century sociologists have been at the forefront in creating new academic areas of study, such as more critical racial and ethnic studies, gay and lesbian studies, women's studies, and the study of aging. Moreover, instead of mostly encouraging students to memorize facts, we should teach them how to study the world sociologically for themselves, to get out of the classroom and into communities to see what contemporary social life actually is like, and to be deeply critical and self-reflective in the process.

Consider the Transformative Studies Institute (TSI), founded in 2007 by scholar-activists John Asimakopoulos, a sociologist, and Ali Zaidi. This institute was born out of their disillusionment with what they see as the betrayal of the working class by institutions of higher learning. As Asimakopoulos told us,

> Beacons, such as the City University of New York, that were tuition free are now tuition dependent putting education out of reach for many of the working poor. It is no coincidence that social injustice and inequality are on the rise, while political power is diminishing for the bottom ninety-nine percent of society. True change begins with ideas that challenge elite ideology and education that exposes exploitation, corruption, and violations of human rights.[13]

TSI is a social justice think tank managed and operated by a global team of scholar-activists, grassroots activists, and other concerned members of the public. TSI holds that universal free education is a fundamental right upon which democratic societies must be founded. As such, its goal is to establish a tuition-free accredited graduate school for working-class students. This will be an innovative university that will foster interdisciplinary research, bridge theory with activism, and encourage community involvement to solve major societal problems. As a participatory space designed to foster critical and imaginative dimensions of learning, TSI will offer degrees closely aligned with its mission. All programs will include concentrations in different areas of innovative knowledge and transformative learning that emphasize community and global responsibility and service. "To this end," explains Asimakopoulos, "we announced our endowment drive to counter the well-funded rightwing think tanks and corporatist universities that are eroding human rights. We seek no less than the transformation of social institutions to achieve direct political and economic democracy.... We encourage readers of *Liberation Sociology* to visit our website at transformativestudies.org."[14]

And everyday life, as we see it, is the most important of all individual and social processes. In Spanish, the word *vivencia* refers to an event—one that is necessarily subjective—in a person's everyday life and is intimately tied to a related term *convivencia*, sometimes poorly translated as "the act of living together." From this nuanced perspective, an individual can only be thought of as living collectively and in connection with significant others. Thus, to change the quality of our lives, we need to change the quality of our interrelations. Liberation and emancipation ideals carry the connotation that the end of oppression brings into being a new collective life, a new type of living together justly and democratically. In this way the future emancipation that liberation sociology promises is not eschatological, such as the otherworldly emancipation promised by much religious revelation, but is a new way of thinking in the present and future, a new collective life that liberation social scientists often seek to bring into being.

One of the flaws in many social science methods courses for undergraduate and graduate students—as well as in much traditional research by social science faculty—is the recurring accent on analysis of previously collected survey or demographic data. We believe that this emphasis on other people's data, which are usually framed by other people's assumptions and language, should often be replaced by encouraging students and faculty to get out of the college setting and research the societal worlds for themselves. Sociology's great promise is to discover, imagine, and interpret the interrelationships of human beings in everyday settings—to study carefully the intricacies, pains, and wonders of the human experience.

As we suggested previously, the educational process is typically one-way and hierarchical, if not authoritarian. Paulo Freire notes the prevalence of the "banking" concept of education, in which "knowledge is a gift bestowed by those who consider themselves knowledgeable upon those whom they consider to know nothing. Projecting an absolute ignorance onto others, a characteristic of the ideology of oppression, negates education and knowledge as a process of inquiry."[15] The banking concept tries to alter the mentality of students so that they will fit into the rigid Procrustean bed of an existing society. The major alternative is liberatory education, which is, at base, a process of mutual education with mutual respect. Freire envisions enlightened education—much like the research procedures in the best participatory action research—where the teachers are taught by the students and the students are taught by the teachers.[16] Freire offers a clear statement about the mutual education vision of liberation sociology.

Furthermore, in the conventional social science curricula, there are too few courses concerned substantially and centrally with the oppressive structures and processes that a human rights reading of society would highlight. We noted in Chapter 5 the intense debate that just one such course created at one of the country's premier universities, the University of Connecticut. There, major attempts were made by outsiders to derail a sociology professor's creative attempt to teach a scholarly course that was explicitly focused on "white racism." Just the attempt to teach such a well-framed and innovative course made news in the national media, and it was attacked by other faculty members and politicians.

Indeed, those teaching about society from a strong critical perspective should be prepared to deal with the substantial energy and emotional labor that is required, inside and outside the classroom. Such teaching requires significant preparation for the challenges that come within the classroom in getting a good hearing for ideas and evidence on issues regarded as controversial by the typically uncritical or uninformed students. The good news is that the issues and data discussed in many sociology classrooms currently force average students to engage, often in a critical way, in material they have never had to think much about—and thus to become thoughtful participants in the surrounding society. A central and continuing difficulty is that most students come to sociology classes with a conventional and uncritical view of societal realities, one that has been drilled into their heads for years by parents, peers, and mainstream media. This ideological "common sense" is usually individualistic and unencumbered with a critical bent, a viewpoint that inclines many of them to challenge or reject even the most data-filled and substantiated analysis of important societal matters such as class, racial, and gender inequality and oppression.

Many social science teachers have found their carefully documented arguments challenged by students who think that their homegrown "common sense" is equivalent in substance to the social science evidence presented in detail. For this reason, some liberation sociology instructors begin their sociology classes with a forthright discussion of certain ground rules for class discussion and interpretations. These ground rules include getting students to suspend certain common-sense assumptions, to understand that interactive educational settings are different from conventional teaching settings, and to develop a more thoughtful and critical view of what counts as substantial evidence for arguments about society.[17]

Teaching and researching from a strong liberation sociology perspective also may mean that such a social scientist has to seek out "less prestigious," in conventional terms, publication outlets and academic careers. There are many alternatives to the mainstream journals for such critical research and writing, such as major book publishers that we discussed earlier. Interestingly, these publishers are usually more interested in substantial social science writing that is readable, that has narrative, and that is interesting for the general reader than are the mainstream social science journals, whose editors assert they are interested in this broader audience but continue to publish articles that are inaccessible to all but a small group of social scientists. In addition, over the last few decades, numerous pathbreaking social scientists have found that smaller colleges and "less prestigious" universities are more hospitable to research that deviates from the instrumental positivism and narrow topics of mainstream social science. An example is Stephen Lyng (see Chapter 8), a small college sociologist whose research on alternative medicine has been pioneering and internationally well known. Ben Agger, a brilliant sociological thinker at a "less prestigious" university, has sagely summarized the contemporary social science career situation: "If you publish work that other people want to reread, work that does not disclose itself fully upon first reading but, through its craft and sensibility, entices the reader back for a second, deeper meditation upon it, you will find a job somewhere, especially if you bring the same excitement to your teaching as to your writing.... There are many sociologists who share my view of sociology as a literary activity, to be pursued in order to make good ideas about social change accessible."[18]

Given the level of public resistance to critical sociology courses like that of Connecticut professor Noel Cazenave, it is no wonder that there are only a modest number of courses in academia, including in sociology, that are centrally and critically focused on the various social oppressions in US society or other societies across the globe. Although societal oppression is dealt with as part of some social science courses—depending on the courage of instructors—there are relatively few courses dealing systematically with such topics as white racism, institutional sexism, capitalist class oppression, and antigay oppression under those specific titles. Liberation sociology seeks to expand the range of courses offered to include courses on all forms of institutionalized exploitation, domination, and marginalization. It seeks to put students in connection with the complex realities of everyday life and the full range of experiences of human beings—including those who have not yet received adequate social science attention and those who are exploited and oppressed.

Some critics may suggest that even these improved educational procedures and curricula are of limited value in the liberation project. Certainly, they do have their limitations, for educational institutions constitute but one area of a contemporary society. It would be good if all citizens of a society had great access to settings where there was full and open learning and debate about societal problems and likely social futures. Thoroughgoing liberation pedagogy and learning thus must encompass all societal institutions, including the conventional media and the Internet's social media and websites, and not just traditional educational institutions.

Moreover, for many people, especially those who are exploited and oppressed, the beginning of liberation may lie in having their voices heard, or heard more broadly, in both learning/teaching and research settings. One of the goals of countersystem research and teaching is to help voice the voiceless and thereby assist the project of large-scale human liberation in this and other societies. In our experience, a liberation sociology teacher can provide the space for a substantially interactive and discussion-oriented learning setting, which usually adds much to the education of all those present. In such uniquely reserved societal space, students from privileged class, racial, and gender backgrounds can listen to and learn from those who are the recurring targets of stereotyping and discrimination in society, those whose everyday-world knowledge is rarely encountered in typical classroom settings. Liberation sociology teachers can provide more open learning environments in which male students hear directly what it is like for female students to suffer from sexist stereotyping and gender discrimination, or in which white students can learn much about what it means for students of color to suffer from racist stereotyping and discrimination. The liberation sociology teacher can make sure that in the classroom the voices of socially oppressed groups are given a fair hearing and, where possible, are evaluated fairly in terms of data and analysis presented in the larger course. In this sense, liberation social science is centrally about real academic freedom and the equality of social discourse.

A Concluding Note: The Example of Professor Walter Chivers and Dr. Martin Luther King Jr.

Let us conclude by considering briefly a man who was both a liberation sociologist and one of the most important activists for social change in US history, Dr. Martin Luther King Jr. Graduating from Morehouse College in 1948, King was a sociology major who was significantly influenced by Professor Walter Chivers, a favorite professor with whom King took numerous sociology courses. A now mostly forgotten liberation sociologist who provided his African American students with a savvy sociological analysis of US racism, Chivers is credited with providing major input into King's institutional analyses of US racism and his racial and political realism.[19] Chivers is a major example of the way in which one teacher of liberation sociology can quietly have very significant and lasting positive effects on both individuals and society.

Inspired by his education in sociology and theology, Dr. King gave numerous lectures and speeches in which he highlighted the themes of social liberation and justice. Consider just two powerful statements from his speeches that indicate his progressive sociological insights. In one famous commentary, Dr. King connects the ideal of social justice to major structural changes in US society: "Justice for black people will not flow into society merely from court decisions nor from fountains of political oratory. Nor will a few token changes quell all the tempestuous yearnings of millions of disadvantaged black people. White America must recognize that justice for black people cannot be achieved without radical changes in the structure of our society."[20] In yet another famous speech, King discussed the need to go beyond the supposedly "peaceful relations" that some people asserted existed between white and black Americans to a positive situation of social justice: "We've never had true peace, we've never had positive peace, and what we're seeking now is to develop this positive peace. For we must come to see that peace is not merely the absence of some negative force; it is the presence of a positive force. True peace is not merely the absence of tension; it is the presence of justice and brotherhood."[21]

April 4, 1968, the day that Dr. King was murdered in Memphis, is also the anniversary of the Memphis sanitation workers' heroic fight against hazardous working conditions and dismal wages that kept the majority of them, like other low-wage workers, on some government social support programs. Leaders in the civil rights movement viewed the strike as a struggle for economic justice for all African Americans. Dr. King traveled to the city to offer support to the 1,300 predominantly African American sanitation workers who had been on strike since February 1968. In fact, the Memphis sanitation workers' strike was also a focus of Dr. King's "Poor People's Campaign" to expand the civil rights agenda to include economic oppression and inequality issues.[22]

Over many decades, across much of North America, Dr. King and countless others of diverse social backgrounds have been injured or have died demanding the fair treatment of an array of ordinary workers. Their fight continues today through student organizations such as the Student Labor Action Project (SLAP). Since its inception, SLAP has boosted student and worker power across the United States and has fought for the right to have affordable and accessible higher education, the right to unionize, the right to a living wage, and the right to fair labor contracts.[23]

SLAP is responsible for launching the Student Labor Day of Action and linking it to this critical April 4 date in North American history. Thus, April 4, 2000, marked the first Day of Action and included fifty-nine such actions in thirty-two US states. The Day of Action commemorates the assassination of King and celebrates his commitment to the struggle for economic and social justice. On the very first Day of Action, students from Indiana's Earlham College, Indiana University at Bloomington, and Purdue University joined over 400 people in a march to support a group of Indiana sanitation workers seeking to join the American Federation of State, County and Municipal Employees

(AFSCME), the fastest-growing public services employees union in the United States.[24]

More recently, in 2012, the SLAP chapters proved to have a very productive year. At the University of Massachusetts Amherst, SLAP successfully formed a coalition of student, faculty, and staff allies to prevent the loss of numerous student workers' jobs. At the University of Central Florida, SLAP students engaged in solidarity actions with the Communications Workers of America against Verizon, the giant US telecommunications company. By attending the Verizon share-holders meeting in Alabama, this chapter of SLAP visibly supported the struggles of Verizon workers to win a reasonable work contract. In addition, students at the University of California–Santa Cruz chapter of SLAP worked in a coalition to ensure affordable housing for students with families on that campus. Their efforts garnered the attention of the mainstream media on the issue of affordable housing and also of various administrative officials, thereby signaling much needed student involvement in college decisions being made. [25]

Today's student-activists across North America continue to honor King's admonitions and actions for change. Standing in solidarity with workers on April 4 each year, and through various progressive campaigns and victories, they are a living embodiment of his legacy—and in a number of direct and indirect ways what we mean by liberation sociology.

Notes

Preface

1. See Walter Isaacson, *Einstein: His Life and Universe* (New York: Simon and Schuster, 2007).

2. Fred Polak, *The Image of the Future*, trans. and abrid. E. Boulding (San Francisco: Jossey-Bass, 1973), p. 305.

Chapter 1

1. Karl Marx, *Theses on Feuerbach*, reprinted in Karl Marx and Frederick Engels, *Selected Works, vol. 2* (Moscow: Foreign Languages Publishing House, 1962), p. 405.

2. See Gideon Sjoberg and Leonard D. Cain, "Negative Values, Counter-system Models, and the Analysis of Social Systems," in *Institutions and Social Exchange: The Sociologies of Talcott Parsons and George C. Homan*, ed. Herman Turk and Richard L. Simpson (Indianapolis: Bobbs-Merrill, 1971), pp. 212–229; and Ted R. Vaughan, "The Crisis in Contemporary American Sociology: A Critique of the Discipline's Dominant Paradigm," in *A Critique of Contemporary American Sociology* (New York: General Hall, 1993), pp. 42–47.

3. Hawthorn, "Unrest in Iran Nothing New to Professor," *Globe and Mail,* www.theglobeandmail.com/news/british-columbia/unrest-in-iran-nothing-new-to -professor/article4276608/ (retrieved February 23, 2014).

4. Peyman Vahabzadeh, email communication to authors, February 2014. Used with permission.

5. Ibid.

6. Ibid.

7. Ibid.

8. Mohammad Amin Ghaneirad, "A Critical Review of the Iranian Attempts at the Development of Alternative Sociologies," www.ios.sinica.edu.tw/cna /download/proceedings/20.Ghaneirad.Iran.pdf (retrieved February 23, 2014), p. 58.

9. It is now called *Critical Sociology*.

285

10. Berch Berberoglu, "Introduction," in *Critical Perspectives in Sociology*, ed. Berch Berberoglu (Dubuque, Iowa: Kendall/Hunt, 1991), p. xiv.

11. Ben Agger, *Critical Social Theories: An Introduction* (Boulder: Westview, 1998), p. 5.

12. "Some Comments About Project Censored and Sociology," personal communication from Carl Jensen, July 13, 1996, p. 1.

13. Ibid.

14. Ibid.

15. Carl Jensen and Project Censored, eds., *Censored: The News That Didn't Make the News and Why* (New York: Seven Stories Press, 1996), p. 35.

16. Project Censored, "Signs of an Emerging Police State," Project Censored, www.projectcensored.org/1-signs-of-an-emerging-police-state (retrieved December 22, 2013).

17. Project Censored, "Fukushima Nuclear Disaster Worse than Anticipated," www.projectcensored.org/3-fukushima-nuclear-disaster-worse-than-anticipated (retrieved December 22, 2013).

18. Walter Cronkite, "Let the Chips Fall Where They May," in *Censored: The News That Didn't Make the News and Why*, p. 25.

19. Ibid., p. 27.

20. Peter Phillips, "Media Censorship and a Free Press in America," *Censored Alert* (newsletter), Director's Column, Spring 1998.

21. Quoted in Jensen and Project Censored, *Censored: The News That Didn't Make the News and Why*, p. 32.

22. Phillips, "Media Censorship and a Free Press in America."

23. Jamie Panzarella, "Kevin Bales: Using Sociology to Fight Slavery," *ASA Footnotes*, vol. 40, no. 3, published March 2012, www.asanet.org/footnotes/mar12/app_soc.html#sthash.z61MYra7.dpuf (retrieved 19 December 2013).

24. "Kevin Bales," www.kevinbales.net/books.html (retrieved December 19, 2013).

25. Panzarella, "Kevin Bales: Using Sociology to Fight Slavery."

26. "Free the Slaves," www.freetheslaves.net (retrieved December 19, 2013).

27. Kevin Bales, "How to Combat Modern Slavery," TED Talks (filmed February 2010, posted March 2010), www.ted.com/talks/kevin_bales_how_to_combat_modern_slavery.html (retrieved December 19, 2013).

28. Panzarella, "Kevin Bales: Using Sociology to Fight Slavery."

29. Quoted in Frank E. Manuel and Fritzie P. Manuel, *Utopian Thought in the Western World* (Cambridge: Harvard University Press, 1979), p. 717.

30. Robert S. Lynd, *Knowledge for What?: The Place of Social Science in American Culture* (New York: Grove Press, 1964), p. 215.

31. William J. Wilson, *When Work Disappears: The World of the New Urban Poor* (New York: Knopf, 1996).

32. See Michel Foucault, *Power/Knowledge* (New York: Pantheon, 1980), p. 98.

33. C. Wright Mills, *The Sociological Imagination* (New York: Oxford University Press, 1959), p. 7. Some liberation sociologists have paid a substantial price. C. Wright Mills, for example, never was promoted to the rank of full professor.

34. David L. Featherman and Robert M. Hauser, *Opportunity and Change* (New York: Academic Press, 1978).

35. Richard J. Herrnstein and Charles Murray, *The Bell Curve: Intelligence and Class Structure in American Life* (New York: Free Press, 1994); see Hernán

Vera, Joe R. Feagin, and Andrew Gordon, "Superior Intellect? A Sincere Fiction of the White Self," *Journal of Negro Education* 64, 3 (Summer 1995): 295–306.

36. Alvin Gouldner, *The Coming Crisis of Western Sociology* (New York: Basic Books, 1970), p. 12.

37. Dorothy Smith, *The Everyday World as Problematic: A Feminist Sociology* (Boston: Northeastern University Press, 1987), p. 56.

38. Mills, *The Sociological Imagination*, p. 99.

39. Iris M. Young, *Justice and the Politics of Difference* (Princeton: Princeton University Press, 1990), pp. 38–39.

40. Ibid., p. 38.

41. Betty Friedan, *The Feminine Mystique* (New York: Dell, 1963), p. 306.

42. Ibid., p. 40.

43. Ibid., pp. 40–42.

44. Mary R. Jackman, *The Velvet Glove: Paternalism and Conflict in Gender, Class, and Race Relations* (Berkeley: University of California Press, 1994).

45. W. E. B. Du Bois, *The World and Africa* (New York: International Publishers, 1965 [1946]), p. 37.

46. For evidence on this, see Joe R. Feagin, *Racist America: Roots, Current Realities, and Future Reparations* (New York: Routledge, 2000).

47. See Gunnar Myrdal, *Objectivity in Social Research* (New York: Pantheon Books, 1969).

48. Donatella della Porta, email communication to authors, February 2014. Used with permission.

49. Ibid.

50. Onwubiko Agozino, email communication to authors, January 2014. Used with permission.

51. Paulo Freire, *Pedagogy of the Oppressed* (New York: Continuum, 1995), p. 26.

52. Antonio Gramsci, *Letters from Prison*, trans. Lynne Lawner (New York: Harper and Row, 1973), pp. 43–44, 183–185.

53. Walda Katz-Fishman and Jerome Scott, personal communication, November 2000; and www.wideopen.igc.org/projectsouth/indexl.html (retrieved Nov. 16, 2000).

54. This paragraph draws heavily on an updating email communication from Walda Katz-Fishman, December 31, 2013. Used with permission.

55. Jerome W. Scott, personal communication, November 2000.

56. Ibid.

57. Ibid.

58. Ibid.

59. Walda Katz-Fishman, email communication to authors, November 2000.

60. Ibid.

61. Ibid.

62. This paragraph draws heavily on an updating email communication from Walda Katz-Fishman, December 31, 2013. Used with permission.

63. Philip Nyden, Anne Figert, Mark Shibley, and Darryl Burrows, "University-Community Collaborative Research: Adding Chairs at the Research Table," in *Building Community: Social Science in Action*, ed. Philip Nyden, Anne Figert, Mark Shibley, and Darryl Burrows (Thousand Oaks, CA: Pine Forge Press, 1997), p. 7.

64. Quoted in Sidney Liebes, Elisabet Sahtouris, and Brian Swimme, *A Walk Through Time: From Stardust to Us* (New York: Wiley, 1998), p. 204.

65. Translator's note in Freire, *Pedagogy of the Oppressed*, p. 17.

66. Freire, *Pedagogy of the Oppressed*, p. 19.

67. Ibid.

68. Alia R. Tyner-Mullings, "Central Park East Secondary School," *Schools: Studies in Education* 9 (September 2012): 227–245.

69. Tim Woods, email communication, February 10, 2014. Used with permission.

70. Ibid.

71. Ibid.

72. Ibid.

73. Sheldon S. Wolin, "Political Theory as a Vocation," *American Political Science Review* 63 (1969): 1080.

74. Karl Mannheim, *Ideology and Utopia* (New York: Harcourt, Brace and World, 1969), pp. 4–5.

75. W. E. B. Du Bois, "'To the World': Manifesto of the Second Pan-African Congress," in *W.E.B. Du Bois Pamphlets and Leaflets*, compiled by Herbert Aptheker (White Plains, NY: Krauss-Thompson, 1986), as quoted by Leigh Binford, *The El Mozote Massacre* (Tucson: University of Arizona Press, 1996), p. 201.

76. Sandra Harding, "Introduction," in *The "Racial" Economy of Science: Toward a Democratic Future* (Bloomington: Indiana University Press, 1993), p. 18.

77. See Charles Lemert, *Sociology after the Crisis* (Boulder: Westview, 1995), pp. 117–118.

78. Ibid., p. 118.

79. For international human rights documents, see Department of Public Information, United Nations, *The United Nations and Human Rights, 1945–1995* (New York: United Nations, 1995), pp. 33–225.

80. Stan Bailey, email communication, spring 1996.

81. Jaime Weinman, "Pope Francis: The unlikeliest liberal hero?" *Maclean's*, www2.macleans.ca/2014/01/08/cafeteria-catholics (retrieved February 7, 2014).

82. Ibid.

83. See Bertell Ollman, *Alienation: Marx's Conception of Man in Capitalist Society*, 2nd ed. (Cambridge: Cambridge University Press, 1976), pp. 227–228.

84. Ibid., p. 16.

85. Karin Kamp, "By the Numbers: The Incredibly Shrinking American Middle Class" (September 20, 2013), Moyers and Company, http://billmoyers.com/2013/09/20/by-the-numbers-the-incredibly-shrinking-american-middle-class/ (retrieved February 28, 2014).

86. Frances F. Piven and Richard A. Cloward, *Regulating the Poor* (New York: Pantheon Books, 1971).

87. Brian Stelter, "Spotlight From Glenn Beck Brings a CUNY Professor Threats," www.nytimes.com/2011/01/22/business/media/22beck.html (retrieved February 17, 2014).

88. Frances Fox Piven. *Who's Afraid of Frances Fox Piven?: The Essential Writings of the Professor Glenn Beck Loves to Hate* (New York: New Press, 2011).

89. Gunnar Myrdal, *An American Dilemma* (New York: McGraw-Hill, [1944] 1964); and Leo Grebler, Joan W. Moore, and Ralph G. Guzman, *The Mexican-American People* (New York: Free Press, 1970).

90. Cheri Jo Pascoe, *Dude, You're a Fag: Masculinity and Sexuality in High School* (Berkeley: University of California Press, 2011).

91. Gouldner, *The Coming Crisis in Western Sociology*, p. 86.

92. Dorothy Ross, *The Origins of American Social Science* (New York: Cambridge University Press, 1991); see also Donald N. Levine, *Visions of the Sociological Tradition* (Chicago: University of Chicago Press, 1995), p. 79.

93. Levine, *Visions of the Sociological Tradition*, p. 80.

94. Harding, "Introduction," p. 17.

95. Jennifer Schuessler, "Academia Occupied by Occupy," www.nytimes.com /2012/05/01/books/academia-becomes-occupied-with-occupy-movement.html ?partner=rssnyt&emc=rss (retrieved February 10, 2014).

96. Alex S. Vitale, "Rule of Law vs. the Forces of Order," *Occupied Wall Street Journal*, http://occupiedmedia.us/2011/10/rule-of-law/ (retrieved February 23, 2014).

97. Howard Becker, "Whose Side Are We On?" *Social Problems* 14 (1967): 241, 243.

98. Henry A. Giroux, *Teachers as Intellectuals: Toward a Critical Pedagogy of Learning* (Granby, MA: Bergin and Garvey, 1988), pp. 40–45 and passim; and Abigail A. Fuller, "Academics and Social Transformation: The Radical Movement in Sociology, 1967–1975," PhD dissertation, University of Colorado Boulder, 1995, pp. 10–11.

99. Christopher G. A. Bryant, *Positivism in Social Theory and Research* (New York: St. Martin's Press, 1985), p. 133; on "abstracted empiricism," see Mills, *The Sociological Imagination*, chapter 3.

100. L. L. Bernard, "The Teaching of Sociology in the U.S.," *American Journal of Sociology* 15 (October 1909): 196. His italics. The sexist phrasing of this comment is particularly important given the fact that many of the early founders were women sociologists, most of whom were also progressive activists.

101. Fuller, "Academics and Social Transformation," p. 11.

102. On misunderstandings of physical science, see Paul Feyerabend, *Against Method* (London: Verson, 1975), p. 19.

103. Bryant, *Positivism in Social Theory and Research*, p. 142.

104. Wolin, "Political Theory as a Vocation," p. 1064.

105. Thomas Kuhn, *The Structure of Scientific Revolutions* (Chicago: University of Chicago Press, 1962), pp. 165–166.

106. Gouldner, *The Coming Crisis in Western Sociology*, p. 441.

107. Ben Agger, *Public Sociology: From Social Facts to Literary Acts*, 2nd ed. (Lanham, MD: Rowman and Littlefield, 2007).

108. Michael Burawoy, "For Public Sociology," *American Sociological Review* 70 (February 2005): 4–28.

109. Ibid., pp. 9–11.

110. Agger, *Public Sociology*, p. 274. See also p. 269. Personal communication with Ben Agger, December 26, 2013. See also Ben Agger, *Critical Social Theories*, 3rd ed. (New York: Oxford University Press, 2013).

111. Burawoy, "For Public Sociology," p. 24,

112. Ibid., p. 25. See also pp. 21–24.

113. Mills, *The Sociological Imagination*, p. 187.

114. Smith, *The Everyday World as Problematic*, pp. 157–167.

115. Karl Marx, *The Eighteenth Brumaire of Louis Bonaparte*, in *Karl Marx and Frederick Engels, Selected Works* (London: Lawrence and Wishart, 1968), p. 97.

116. Mills, *The Sociological Imagination*, p. 181.

117. Quoted in Alfred M. Lee, *Sociology for the People: Toward a Caring Profession* (Syracuse: Syracuse University Press, 1988), p. 57.

CHAPTER 2

1. Peter Gay, *The Enlightenment: The Science of Freedom* (New York and London: W. W. Norton, 1977), p. 62.

2. Irving M. Zeitlin, *Ideology and the Development of Sociological Theory*, 6th ed. (Upper Saddle River, NJ: Prentice-Hall, 1997), p. 4.

3. David Hume, *Treatise of Human Nature*, as quoted in Gay, *The Enlightenment*, p. 187.

4. Irving M. Zeitlin, *Ideology and the Development of Sociological Theory*, 7th ed. (Upper Saddle River, NJ: Prentice-Hall, 2001), p. 48.

5. Max Horkheimer and Theodor W. Adorno, *Dialectic of Enlightenment* (New York: Continuum Publishing Company, 2000), p.3.

6. Gay, *The Enlightenment*, p. 555.

7. George Simpson, ed. *Auguste Comte: Sire of Sociology* (New York: Thomas Y. Crowell, 1969), p. 139.

8. Herbert Marcuse, *Reason and Revolution: Hegel and the Rise of Social Theory* (Boston: Beacon, 1968), p. 325.

9. Auguste Comte, "On the Three Stages of Social Evolution," in *Theories of Society: Foundations of Modern Sociological Theory*, ed. Talcott Parsons, Edward Shils, Kaspar D. Naegele, and Jesse R. Pitts (New York: Free Press, 1965), p. 1332; Auguste Comte, *The Positive Philosophy of Auguste Comte*, trans. and ed. Harriet Martineau (New York: AMS Press, 1974).

10. Leon Bramson, *The Political Context of Sociology* (Princeton: Princeton University Press, 1961), p. 12.

11. Ibid.

12. Zeitlin, *Ideology and the Development of Sociological Theory*, 7th ed., pp. 64–70.

13. See K. Thompson, *Auguste Comte: The Foundations of Sociology* (London: Nelson, 1976); and David Jary and Julia Jary, *Dictionary of Sociology* (New York: HarperCollins, 1991), pp. 73–75.

14. Peter Halfpenny, *Positivism and Sociology: Explaining Social Life* (London: George Allen and Unwin, 1982), p. 20.

15. See Comte, *The Positive Philosophy of Auguste Comte*.

16. Harriet Martineau, *Society in America, 3 vols.* (New York: Saunders and Otley, 1837); see also Patricia M. Lengermann and Jill Niebrugge-Brantley, "Harriet Martineau (1802–1876): The Beginnings of a Science of Society," in *The Women Founders: Sociology and Social Theory, 1830–1930*, ed. Patricia M. Lengermann and Jill Niebrugge-Brantley (Boston: McGraw-Hill, 1998), pp. 23–45.

17. Harriet Martineau, *How to Observe Morals and Manners* (New Brunswick, NJ: Transaction Publishers, [1838] 1989), p. 73; see also Michael R. Hill, "Empiricism and Reason in Harriet Martineau's Sociology," in *Harriet Martineau, How to*

Observe Morals and Manners (New Brunswick, NJ: Transaction Publishers, 1989), pp. xv–lx.

18. Talcott Parsons, *The Structure of Social Action: A Study in Social Theory with Special Reference to a Group of Recent European Writers* (New York: Free Press, [1937] 1949), pp. 591–601.

19. Wilhelm Hennis, "The Meaning of 'Werfreiheit': On the Background and Motives of Max Weber's 'Postulate,'" *Sociological Theory* 12 (1994): 113–125.

20. Max Weber, as quoted in ibid., p. 116.

21. Max Weber, *The Methodology of Social Sciences*, trans. and ed. Edward A. Shils and Henry A. Finch (Glencoe, IL: Free Press, 1949), p. 72.

22. Lewis A. Coser, *Masters of Sociological Thought: Ideas in Historical and Social Context*, 2nd ed. (New York: Harcourt Brace Jovanovich, 1977), p. 242.

23. Max Weber, as quoted in Hennis, "The Meaning of 'Werfreiheit,'" p. 119.

24. Max Weber, as quoted in Ahmad Sadri, *Max Weber's Sociology of Intellectuals* (New York: Oxford University Press, 1992), p. 14.

25. Sadri, *Max Weber's Sociology of Intellectuals*, p. 16.

26. Max Weber, as quoted in ibid.

27. Max Weber, as quoted in ibid., p. 17.

28. Ibid., p. 18.

29. Gunnar Myrdal, *An American Dilemma* (New York: McGraw-Hill, [1944] 1964), vol. 2, p. 1052.

30. Ibid., p. 1057.

31. Gunnar Myrdal, *Objectivity in Social Research* (New York: Pantheon, 1969), p. 5.

32. Robert A. Jones, "The Positive Science of Ethics in France: German Influences on De la division du travail social," *Sociological Forum* 9 (1994): 37–58.

33. Emile Durkheim, *The Elementary Forms of the Religious Life*, trans. Joseph W. Swain (London: Allen and Unwin, 1915).

34. Emile Durkheim, *Journal Sociologique* (Paris: Presses Universitaires de France, 1969), p. 161.

35. Ibid. Our italics.

36. Ibid.

37. Emile Durkheim, *The Division of Labor in Society* (New York: Free Press, 1933), p. 374.

38. Ibid., p. 379. Also, *Emile Durkheim, Professional Ethics and Civic Morals* (London: Routledge, [1957] 1992), p. 213.

39. Durkheim, *The Division of Labor in Society*, p. 384.

40. Ibid., p. 388.

41. Marcel Fournier, *Emile Durkheim* (Paris: Fayard, 2007), pp. 365–390; Lloyd P. Gartner, *History of the Jews in Modern Times* (New York: Oxford University Press, 2001), pp. 232, 234–235; H. R. Kedward, *The Dreyfus Affair: Catalyst for Tensions in French Society* (London: Longmans, 1965); Steven Lukes, *Emile Durkheim, His Life and Work: A Historical and Critical Study* (New York: Harper & Row, 1973), pp. 347–349; Ivan Strenski, *Durkheim and the Jews of France* (Chicago: University of Chicago Press, 1997); David Vital, *A People Apart: The Jews in Europe, 1789–1939.* (New York: Oxford University Press, 1999), pp. 540–566.

42. Chad Alan Goldberg, "Introduction to Emile Durkheim's 'Anti-Semitism and Social Crisis,'" *Sociological Theory* 26 (2008): 299–300.

43. Ibid., 305–306.

44. Ibid.

45. Parsons, *The Structure of Social Action*, pp. 317–322; see also Talcott Parsons, *The Social System* (Glencoe, IL: Free Press, 1951).

46. Nicholas Timasheff, *Sociological Theory: Its Nature and Growth* (New York: Random House, 1967).

47. Don Martindale, *The Nature and Types of Sociological Theory* (Boston: Houghton Mifflin, 1960).

48. Georges Gurvitch, *Dialectique et Sociologie* (Paris: Flammarion, 1962), pp. 180–181.

49. Bertell Oilman, *Alienation: Marx's Conception of Man in Capitalist Society*, 2nd ed. (Cambridge: Cambridge University Press, 1976), p. 18.

50. Ibid., pp. 16–29.

51. C. Wright Mills, *The Sociological Imagination* (New York: Oxford University Press, 1959), p. 57.

52. See Mary Jo Deegan, *Jane Addams and the Men of the Chicago School, 1892–1918* (New Brunswick, NJ: Transaction Books, 1988), pp. 106–107.

53. George Herbert Mead, *Mind, Self, and Society*, ed. Charles W. Morris (Chicago: University of Chicago Press, 1934), p. xxv.

54. Zeitlin, *Ideology and the Development of Sociological Theory*, 7th ed., pp. 427–428.

55. Ibid., p. 431.

56. Gideon Sjoberg and Ted R. Vaughan, "The Ethical Foundation of Sociology and the Necessity for a Human Rights Perspective," in *A Critique of Contemporary American Sociology*, ed. Ted R. Vaughan, Gideon Sjoberg, and Larry T. Reynolds (New York: General Hall, 1993), p. 135.

57. Deegan, *Jane Addams and the Men of the Chicago School*, pp. 107–111.

58. Ibid., pp. 110–118.

59. Barbara Finlay, "Lester Frank Ward as a Sociologist of Gender," *Gender and Society* 13 (April 1999): 251–257.

60. Lester F. Ward, *Pure Sociology*, 2nd ed. (London: Macmillan, [1903] 1914), p. 364.

61. Finlay, "Lester Frank Ward as a Sociologist of Gender," pp. 258–261.

62. Thomas Kuhn, *The Structure of Scientific Revolutions* (Chicago: University of Chicago Press, 1962).

63. George Ritzer, *Sociology: A Multiple Paradigm Science* (Boston: Allyn and Bacon, 1975), p. 7.

64. Kuhn, *The Structure of Scientific Revolutions*, pp. 165–166.

65. Niels H. D. Bohr, *Essays, 1958–1962: On Atomic Physics and Human Knowledge* (New York: Interscience Publishers, 1963), p. 1.

66. Ibid., p. 2.

67. Ibid.

68. Ibid., p. 4.

CHAPTER 3

1. Herman Schwendinger and Julia Schwendinger, *The Sociologists of the Chair: A Radical Analysis of the Formative Years of North American Sociology (1883–1922)* (New York: Basic Books, 1974), p. xix.

2. Stephen P. Turner and Jonathan H. Turner, *The Impossible Science: An Institutional Analysis of American Sociology* (Newbury Park, CA: Sage, 1990), p. 13.

3. Robert W. Friedrichs, *A Sociology of Sociology* (New York: Free Press, 1970), p. 73.

4. Ibid., pp. 72–73.

5. In criticizing capitalists' exploitation of Chinese laborers, Ross took a racist perspective on Chinese immigration to California. Schwendinger and Schwendinger, *The Sociologists of the Chair*, pp. 494–496.

6. Lester Ward, as quoted in Jay Rumney and Joseph Maier, *Sociology: The Science of Society* (New York: Henry Schuman, 1953), p. 167.

7. Lester F. Ward, as quoted in Schwendinger and Schwendinger, *The Sociologists of the Chair*, p. 420.

8. Mary Jo Deegan, "An American Dream: The Historical Connections Between Women, Humanism, and Sociology, 1890–1920," *Humanity and Society* 11 (August 1987): 353–365.

9. Mary Jo Deegan, "'Dear Love, Dear Love': Feminist Pragmatism and the Chicago Female World of Love and Ritual," *Gender and Society* 10 (October 1996): 590–591.

10. Mary Jo Deegan, "Gender at Hull House and the University of Chicago: The Origins and Influence of Feminist Pragmatism, 1889–2008," University of Nebraska, unpublished research manuscript, 2007.

11. Mary Jo Deegan, *Jane Addams and the Men of the Chicago School, 1892–1918* (New Brunswick, NJ: Transaction Books, 1988), pp. 33–35.

12. Mary Jo Deegan, "A New Conscience Against Ancient Evils: The Theory and Praxis of Race Relations in Chicago, 1892–1960," University of Nebraska–Lincoln, unpublished research manuscript, 2000, p. 66.

13. Deegan, "'Dear Love, Dear Love,'" p. 592.

14. Alfred McClung Lee, "Steps Taken Toward Liberating Sociologists," in *Radical Sociologists and the Movement: Experiences, Lessons, and Legacies* (Philadelphia: Temple University Press, 1991), pp. 28–29.

15. Schwendinger and Schwendinger, *The Sociologists of the Chair*, p. 421.

16. Mary Jo Deegan, "Early Women Sociologists and the American Sociological Society: The Patterns of Exclusion and Participation," *American Sociologist* 16 (February 1981): 14–16.

17. Patricia M. Lengermann and Jill Niebrugge-Brantley, "Jane Addams (1860–1935): Ethics and Society," in *The Women Founders: Sociology and Social Theory, 1830–1930*, ed. Patricia M. Lengermann and Jill Niebrugge-Brantley (Boston: McGraw-Hill, 1998), pp. 66–72; Deegan, Jane Addams, pp. 42–44.

18. Jane Addams, *Democracy and Social Ethics* (New York: Macmillan, 1902), p. 6.

19. Deegan, *Jane Addams and the Men of the Chicago School*, p. 304.

20. Ibid., p. 304.

21. Addams did reject a Marxist class conflict model, preferring to accent human cooperation as seen from a pragmatic-feminist point of view.

22. Southern Connecticut State University, "'Not All People Are Polluted Equally: Environmental Injustices in New England,'" http://calendar.southernct.edu/index.php?eID=98#sthash.ZSYy4leg.dpuf (retrieved January 30, 2014).

23. Rose Marie Berger, "Women Heroes of Environmental Activism," http://sojo.net/magazine/1997/07/good-housekeeping-award (retrieved February 8, 2014).

24. Residents of Hull House, *Hull House Maps and Papers, by Residents of Hull House, a Social Settlement* (New York: Arno Press, [1895] 1970); and Mary Jo Deegan, personal communication, July 21, 2000.

25. Deegan, *Jane Addams*, p. 47.

26. Ibid., pp. 44–64.

27. Jane Addams, as quoted in Schwendinger and Schwendinger, *The Sociologists of the Chair*, p. 474.

28. Ibid., p. 475.

29. William E. B. Du Bois, *The Philadelphia Negro: A Social Study* (Millwood, NY: Kraus-Thomson, [1899] 1973).

30. Turner and Turner, *The Impossible Science*, p. 15.

31. See Mary Jo Deegan, "W.E.B. Du Bois and the Women of Hull-House, 1895–1899," *American Sociologist* 19 (Winter 1988): 304–308.

32. W.E.B. Du Bois, Some Notes on Negroes in New York City (Atlanta, 1905), as quoted in Adolph L. Reed Jr., *W.E.B. Du Bois and American Political Thought: Fabianism and the Color Line* (Oxford: Oxford University Press, 1997), p. 44.

33. Reed, *W.E.B. Du Bois and American Political Thought*, p. 49. Reed describes Du Bois as a "positivist" social scientist, but he is using this term in the sense of a researcher who accents finding social laws, not in the detached instrumental-positivist sense we accent in this book.

34. W.E.B. Du Bois, *Dusk of Dawn: An Essay Toward an Autobiography of a Race Concept* (New Brunswick, NJ: Transaction Books, [1940] 1984), p. 62.

35. Ibid., p. 93; Schwendinger and Schwendinger, *The Sociologists of the Chair*, p. 506.

36. Du Bois, *The Philadelphia Negro*, p. 394.

37. W.E.B. Du Bois, *Black Reconstruction in America, 1860–1880* (New York: Atheneum, [1935] 1992), p. 30.

38. W.E.B. Du Bois, *Darkwater* (1920), as reprinted in *The Oxford W.E.B. Du Bois Reader*, ed. Eric J. Sundquist (New York: Oxford, 1996), pp. 497–498.

39. Du Bois, *Dusk of Dawn*, p. 6.

40. Du Bois, *Darkwater* (1920), as reprinted in *The Oxford W.E.B. Du Bois Reader*, p. 504.

41. W.E.B. Du Bois, *The World and Africa* (New York: International Publishers, [1946] 1965), p. 37.

42. Ibid., p. 23.

43. Du Bois, *Darkwater* (1920), as reprinted in *The Oxford W.E.B. Du Bois Reader*, p. 504.

44. Du Bois, *Black Reconstruction in America, 1860–1880*, p. 10.

45. Manning Marable, *W.E.B. Du Bois: Black Radical Democrat* (Boston: Twayne, 1986), pp. 100–102.

46. Alford A. Young Jr., Jerry G. Watts, Manning Marable, Charles Lemert, and Elizabeth Higginbotham, *The Souls of W. E. B. Du Bois* (Boulder and London: Paradigm Publishers, 2006).

47. See Patricia Madoo Lengermann and Jill Niebrugge-Brantley, *The Women Founders: Sociology and Social Theory, 1830–1930* (New York: McGraw-Hill, 1998).

48. Ida B. Wells-Barnett, as quoted in ibid., p. 163. We draw here on pp. 150–165.

49. Ibid., pp. 154–165.

50. Ida B. Wells-Barnett, *A Red Record* (Chicago: Donohue and Henneberry, 1895); Anna Julia Cooper, *A Voice from the South by a Black Woman from the South* (Xenia, Ohio: Aldine Press, 1892).

51. Earl Wright II, "Deferred Legacy! The Continued Marginalization of the Atlanta Sociological Laboratory," *Sociology Compass* (OnlineEarly Articles), www .blackwell-synergy.com/toc/soco/0/0?cookieSet=1 (retrieved December 2, 2007).

52. Ibid.

53. L. L. Bernard, "The Teaching of Sociology in the U.S.," *American Journal of Sociology* 15 (October 1909): 164–231.

54. For a listing, see Andrew Abbott, *Department and Discipline: Chicago Sociology at One Hundred* (Chicago: University of Chicago Press, 1999), p. 199.

55. Robert E. Park, quoted in Winifred Raushenbush, *Robert E. Park: Biography of a Sociologist* (Durham, NC: Duke University Press, 1979), p. 34.

56. Ibid., p. 41.

57. Robert E. Park, as quoted in ibid., p. 49.

58. Robert E. Park, as quoted in ibid., p. 50.

59. Robert E. Park, as quoted in ibid., pp. 49–50.

60. Robert E. Park, "Education in Its Relation to the Conflict and Fusion of Cultures: With Special Reference to the Problems of the Immigrant, the Negro, and Missions," *Publications of the American Sociological Society* 13: 38–63. See also Robert E. Park, *Race and Culture* (New York: Free Press, 1950), p. 387.

61. Raushenbush, *Robert E. Park*, pp. 67–84.

62. E. Franklin Frazier, as quoted in Deegan, "A New Conscience Against Ancient Evils," p. 191. We draw here on Deegan's summary of the events.

63. Ibid., pp. 188–195.

64. Valora Washington and William Harvey, *Affirmative Rhetoric, Negative Action* (Washington, DC: George Washington University, 1989), p. 6.

65. Robert E. Park and Ernest W. Burgess, *Introduction to the Science of Sociology* (Chicago: University of Chicago Press, 1921).

66. See Schwendinger and Schwendinger, *The Sociologists of the Chair*, pp. 388–410.

67. Stuart A. Queen and Delbert M. Mann, *Social Pathology* (New York: Thomas Y. Crowell, 1925).

68. Turner and Turner, *The Impossible Science*, pp. 46–51.

69. Raushenbush, *Robert E. Park*, p. 97.

70. Harold Gosnell, as quoted in Raushenbush, *Robert E. Park*, p. 98.

71. Abbott, *Department and Discipline*, p. 196.

72. See, for example, Joe R. Feagin, *Racist America: Roots, Current Realities, and Future Reparations*, 3rd ed. (New York: Routledge, 2014).

73. Oliver C. Cox, *Race Relations: Elements and Social Dynamics* (New York: Philosophical Library, 1976), p. 277.

74. Ibid., p. 474.

75. Ibid., p. xi.

76. Ibid., p. 22.

77. Oliver C. Cox, *Caste, Class, and Race* (Garden City, NY: Doubleday, 1948), p. x.

78. Ibid., p. xvi.

79. Oliver Cromwell Cox, *The Foundations of Capitalism* (New York: Philosophical Library, 1959), p. 2.

80. Cox, *Caste, Class, and Race*, p. 462.

81. Cox, *Race Relations*, p. 21.

82. Oliver Cromwell Cox, *Capitalism and American Leadership* (New York: Philosophical Library), p. 288.

83. Bernard, "The Teaching of Sociology in the U.S.," p. 196.

84. See Paul F. Lazarsfeld and Morris Rosenberg, "Introduction," to Section 5, in *The Language of Social Research*, ed. Paul F. Lazarsfeld and Morris Rosenberg (New York: Free Press, 1955), pp. 389–390.

85. Abbott, *Department and Discipline*, pp. 210–211.

86. Lazarsfeld and Rosenberg, *The Language of Social Research*, pp. 15–17.

87. Ibid., p. 111.

88. Ibid. They note that this is a "somewhat facetious" way of putting the matter.

89. Arthur J. Vidich and Stanford M. Lyman, *American Sociology: Worldly Rejections of Religion and Their Directions* (New Haven: Yale University Press, 1985), p. 138.

90. Ibid., p. 145.

91. Jennifer Platt, "Research Methods and the Second Chicago School," in *A Second Chicago School: The Development of Postwar American Sociology*, ed. Gary A. Fine (Chicago: University of Chicago Press, 1995), pp. 82–107.

92. Roger C. Bannister, "Principle, Politics, Profession: American Sociologists and Fascism," in *Sociology Responds to Fascism*, ed. Stephen P. Turner and Dirk Kasler (London: Routledge, 1992), p. 189.

93. Ibid., pp. 290–291.

94. George Lundberg, *Can Science Save Us?* (New York: Longmans, Green, 1947), pp. 47–48.

95. Bannister, "Principle, Politics, Profession: American Sociologists and Fascism," p. 175.

96. Ronald J. Berger, *The Holocaust, Religion, and the Politics of Collective Memory: Beyond Sociology*, reprint ed. (New Jersey: Transaction Publishers, 2013).

97. Bannister, "Principle, Politics, Profession: American Sociologists and Fascism," p. 205.

98. Berger, *The Holocaust, Religion, and the Politics of Collective Memory*, pp. 6–7.

99. Gardner Murphy, "The Research Task of Social Psychology," presidential address to the Society for Psychological Study of Social Issues, 1938, as cited in Robert S. Lynd, *Knowledge for What? The Place of Social Science in American Culture* (New York: Grove Press, [1939] 1964), p. 18.

100. Lynd, *Knowledge for What?* p. 18.

101. Ibid., p. 18.

102. Ibid., p. 181.

103. Ibid., p. 215.

104. Ibid., p. 19.

105. Ibid., pp. 220–221.

106. Gunnar Myrdal, *An American Dilemma* (New York: McGraw-Hill, [1944] 1964), vol. 2, p. 1052.

107. Ibid., p. 1057.

108. Turner and Turner, *The Impossible Science*, pp. 109–128.

109. Ibid., pp. 134–135.

110. "National Support for Behavioral Science," pamphlet, Washington, DC, February 1958, as reprinted in Friedrichs, *A Sociology of Sociology*, p. 88.

111. Ibid., pp. 87–89.

112. Abigail A. Fuller, "Academics and Social Transformation: The Radical Movement in Sociology, 1967–1975," PhD dissertation, University of Colorado Boulder, 1995, p. 42.

113. Turner and Turner, *The Impossible Science*, pp. 134–135.

114. See Gideon Sjoberg and Ted Vaughan, "The Bureaucratization of Sociology: Its Impact on Theory and Research," in *A Critique of Contemporary American Sociology*, ed. Ted R. Vaughan, Gideon Sjoberg, and Larry T. Reynolds (Dix Hills, NY: General Hall, 1993), pp. 60–65.

115. See David L. Featherman and Robert M. Hauser, *Opportunity and Change* (New York: Academic Press, 1978).

116. C. Wright Mills, *The Sociological Imagination* (New York: Oxford University Press, 1959), pp. 91–92.

117. T. R. Young, email communication, *Progressive Sociologists Network* (PSN), May 1996.

118. Turner and Turner, *The Impossible Science*, pp. 140–141, 184.

119. Dick Flacks, "The Sociology Liberation Movement: Some Legacies and Lessons," in *Radical Sociologists and the Movement: Experiences, Lessons, and Legacies*, ed. Martin Oppenheimer, Martin J. Murray, and Rhonda Levine (Philadelphia: Temple University Press, 1991), pp. 18–25.

120. Alan Barcan, *Sociological Theory and Educational Reality: Education and Society in Australia since 1949* (Kensington, Paddington: University of New South Wales Press, 1993), p. 150.

121. Dick Flacks, "Paul Goodman and the Old New Left," *Dissent. A Quarterly of Politics and Culture*, www.dissentmagazine.org/article/paul-goodman-and-the -old-new-left (retrieved February 8, 2014).

122. Friedrichs, *A Sociology of Sociology*, p. 108.

123. Reinhard Bendix, as quoted in Friedrichs, *A Sociology of Sociology*, p. 109.

124. Ben Agger, *Reading Science: A Literary, Political, and Sociological Analysis* (Dix Hills, NY: General Hall, 1989), pp. 182–193.

125. George Lakoff, *Women, Fire, and Dangerous Things: What Categories Reveal About the Mind* (Chicago: University of Chicago Press, 1987), pp. 383–385.

126. Naomi Quinn, "The Cultural Basis of Metaphor," in *Beyond Metaphor: The Theory of Tropes in Anthropology*, ed. James Fernandez (Stanford: Stanford University Press, 1991), pp. 65–66.

127. Ian Craib, *Modern Social Theory: From Parsons to Habermas*, 2nd ed. (New York: St. Martin's, 1992), p. 39. His italics.

128. Kingsley Davis, "The Myths of Functional Analysis in Sociology and Anthropology," *American Sociological Review* 24 (1959): 757–773.

129. Alvin Gouldner, *The Coming Crisis of Western Sociology* (New York: Basic Books, 1970), p. 373.

130. Ibid., p. 86.

131. Talcott Parsons, *The Structure of Social Action* (New York: Free Press, [1937] 1949).

132. See Joe R. Feagin and Clairece B. Feagin, *Social Problems: A Critical Power-Conflict Perspective* (Upper Saddle River, NJ: Prentice-Hall, 1997), p. 16.

133. U.S. Department of the Interior, Public Land Statistics, 1961 (Washington, DC: Government Printing Office, 1961), Appendix, Table 22.

134. Craib, *Modern Social Theory*, pp. 53–54. We are indebted to T. R. Young for some insights here.

135. Gouldner, *The Coming Crisis of Western Sociology*, p. 410.

136. Society for the Study of Social Problems, "In Pursuit of Social Justice," www.sssp1.org/index.cfm/m/480/pageID/1528/fuseAction/contentpage.main/detailID/2462 (retrieved February 8, 2014).

137. Lee, "Steps Taken Toward Liberating Sociologists," p. 36.

138. Association of Black Sociologists, "2012 Year In Review," http://associationofblacksociologists.org/news/ (retrieved February 8, 2014).

139. Lee, "Steps Taken Toward Liberating Sociologists," p. 39.

140. Association for Humanist Society, "Links to Activist Organizations," www.ccsu.edu/page.cfm?p=9329 (retrieved February 8, 2014).

141. Alfred M. Lee, *Sociology for Whom?* (New York: Oxford University Press, 1978), p. 216.

142. Ibid., p. 216.

CHAPTER 4

1. See Donald N. Levine, *Visions of the Sociological Tradition* (Chicago: University of Chicago Press, 1995), pp. 284–289.

2. See Stephen P. Turner and Jonathan H. Turner, *The Impossible Science: An Institutional Analysis of American Sociology* (Newbury Park, CA: Sage, 1990), pp. 140–141.

3. American Sociological Association, *The Health of Sociology* (Washington, DC: American Sociological Association, 2007); earlier data were calculated by American Sociological Association staff from 1992, 1995, and 1998 editions of the *Survey of Graduate Departments of Sociology* (Washington, DC: American Sociological Association) and from National Science Foundation data. We are indebted to Roberta Spalter-Roth for assistance; Introsocsite: Introduction to Sociology, "Introduction to Sociology Course," www.asanet.org/introtosociology/documents/IntroToSociologyCourse070308.htm (retrieved March 8, 2014).

4. American Sociological Association, "Number of Doctoral Degrees Awarded in Sociology Since 1966 by Gender," www.asanet.org/research/stats/gender/number_doctorate.cfm (retrieved March 8, 2014).

5. Roberta Spalter-Roth and Nicole Van Vooren, "Paying Attention to the Master's Degree in Sociology," ASA (p.43), www.asanet.org/research/MAinSociology.pdf (retrieved 8 March 2014).

6. American Sociological Association, *The Health of Sociology* (Washington, DC: American Sociological Association, 2007).

7. See Turner and Turner, *The Impossible Science*, pp. 194–196 and passim.

8. See Levine, *Visions of the Sociological Tradition*, pp. 289–290.

9. Irving L. Horowitz, "Searching for Enemies: Sociological Theories at the End of the 20th Century," *Society* (November 1995): 42.

10. *Transaction*, "Irving Louis Horowitz: Founder of Transactions Publishers, Dies at 82," www.transactionpub.com/merchant2/merchant.mvc?Screen=STORY&articleid=102 (retrieved February 9, 2014).

11. Ibid.

12. Ibid.

13. On issues of racism, see, for example, Joe R. Feagin, *Racist America: Roots, Current Realities, and Future Reparations* (New York: Routledge, 2000).

14. Monte Bute, "Unplugged. A Populist Sociology," *Contexts*, http://contexts.org/articles/spring-2013/a-populist-sociology/ (retrieved February 23, 2014).

15. Ibid.

16. Ibid.

17. Ibid.

18. Monte Bute, email communication to authors, February 2014. Used with permission.

19. Al Gedicks, "Activist Sociology: Personal Reflections," http://comm-org.wisc.edu/si/gedicks.htm (retrieved February 23, 2014).

20. Ibid.

21. Ibid.

22. Ibid.

23. Ibid.

24. Ibid.

25. Peter M. Blau, "Reflections on the Future of Social Problems Theory," *SSSP Social Problems Theory Division Newsletter* 4 (Summer 1975): 3, as quoted in Alfred M. Lee, Sociology for Whom? (New York: Oxford University Press, 1978), p. 82.

26. Lee, *Sociology for Whom?* p. 83.

27. American Sociological Association, "Percentage of Sociology Degrees Awarded to Women Awarded Since 1966," www.asanet.org/research/stats/gender/soc_degrees_women.cfm (retrieved March 8, 2014); American Sociological Association, "Trend Data on the Profession," www.asanet.org/cs/root/leftnav/research_and_stats/profession_trend_data/trend_data_on_the_profession (retrieved November 16, 2007). Earlier data are from tabulations by American Sociological Association staff and are from National Science Foundation, *Science and Engineering Degrees: 1966–1997* (Washington, DC: U.S. Government Printing Office, 1997), Tables 26, 35, and 49–54.

28. American Sociological Association, "Trend Data on the Profession," www.asanet.org/cs/root/leftnav/research_and_stats/profession_trend_data/trend_data_on_the_profession (retrieved November 16, 2007); Roberta Spalter-Roth, Felice J. Levine, and Andrew Sutter, "Research Brief: The Pipeline for Faculty of Color in Sociology," *Footnotes*, newsletter of the American Sociological Association, April 1999.

29. American Sociological Association, 2011, "Percentage of Doctoral Degrees Awarded in Sociology by Race/Ethnicity," www.asanet.org/research/stats/race_ethnicity/doctorate_degrees_1995-2006.cfm (retrieved February 12, 2014).

30. American Sociological Association, 2011, "Doctorate Recipients by Race/Ethnicity in Selected Disciplines," www.asanet.org/research/stats/race_ethnicity/doctorate_recipients_80_90_00_06.cfm) (retrieved February 12, 2014).

31. American Sociological Association, 2011, "Percentage of Doctoral Degrees Awarded in Sociology by Race/Ethnicity," www.asanet.org/research/stats/race_ethnicity/doctorate_degrees_1995-2006.cfm (retrieved February 12, 2014).

32. American Sociological Association, 2011, "Percentage of Doctoral Degrees Awarded in Sociology by Race/Ethnicity," www.asanet.org/research/stats

/race_ethnicity/doctorate_degrees_1995-2006.cfm (retrieved February 12, 2014). We are indebted to the American Sociological Association staff for these data.

33. National Science Foundation, 2012, "Doctoral Degrees by Citizenship and Race/Ethnicity: 2001–10," Table 7-4, National Center for Science and Engineering Statistics, U.S. Department of Education, National Center for Education Statistics, Integrated Postsecondary Education Data System, Completions Survey, 2001–2010, www.nsf.gov/statistics/wmpd/2013/pdf/tab7-4.pdf (retrieved February 14, 2014).

34. National Science Foundation, 2012. "Bachelor's Degrees by Race/ Ethnicity, Citizenship, Sex, and Field: 2001–10," Table 5-7, National Center for Science and Engineering Statistics. National Center for Science and Engineering Statistics, U.S. Department of Education, National Center for Education Statistics, Integrated Postsecondary Education Data System, Completions Survey, 2001–2010, www.nsf.gov/statistics/wmpd/2013/pdf/tab5-7.pdf (retrieved February 14, 2014).

35. Janene Scelza, Roberra Spalter-Roth, and Olga Mayorova, "A Decade of Change: ASA Membership from 2000–2010," American Sociological Association, Department of Research and Development, www.asanet.org/images/research /docs/pdf/2010_asa_membership_brief.pdf (retrieved February 14, 2014).

36. David Fowler, "2013 ASA Annual Meeting Breaks Attendance Record," American Sociological Association, *Footnotes*, www.asanet.org/footnotes /septoct13/am_2013.html (retrieved February 14, 2014).

37. Claire M. Renzetti, "All Things to All People or Nothing for Some: Justice, Diversity, and Democracy in Sociological Societies," *Social Problems* 54 (2007): 161–169.

38. American Sociological Association, "Section Membership Counts," www .asanet.org/sections/CountsLastFiveYears.cfm (retrieved March 8, 2014).

39. Patricia Hill Collins, *Black Feminist Thought: Knowledge, Consciousness, and the Politics of Empowerment* (Boston: Unwin Hyman, 1990), p. 67.

40. Lee, *Sociology for Whom?*

41. Michael R. Hill, "Epistemology, Axiology, and Ideology in Sociology," *Mid-American Review of Sociology* 9 (1984): 59–77; G. Radnitzky, *Contemporary Schools of Metascience*, 3rd ed. (Chicago: Henry Regnery, 1973), pp. xii–xiii.

42. See Gideon Sjoberg, "Reflective Methodology: The Foundations of Social Inquiry," introduction to *A Methodology for Social Research*, by Gideon Sjoberg and Roger Nett (Prospect Heights, IL: Waveland Press, 1997), p. xxii. We examined *Sociological Methodology* for recent years, including 2013, and discovered this pattern.

43. Jaber F. Gubrium and James A. Holstein, *The New Language of Qualitative Method* (New York: Oxford University Press, 1997), p. 5.

44. Ibid., pp. 5–6.

45. Michel Foucault, "The Discourse on Language," appendix in *The Archeology of Knowledge* (New York: Harper and Row, 1972), pp. 222–223.

46. Alvin W. Gouldner, *The Coming Crisis of Western Sociology* (New York: Basic Books, 1970), p. 41.

47. Turner and Turner, *The Impossible Science*, pp. 188–191.

48. Historically, well-funded social scientists have played a role in papering over severe problems of economic, gender, and class inequality with technical methods they proclaim to be the panaceas for social understanding. See, for example, this

well-funded book: Richard J. Herrnstein and Charles Murray, *The Bell Curve: Intelligence and Class Structure in American Life* (New York: Free Press, 1994).

49. See William Alonso and Paul Starr, eds., *The Politics of Numbers* (New York: Russell Sage, 1987); Travis Hirschi, "Administrative Criminology," *Contemporary Sociology* 22 (1993): 348–350.

50. Albert J. Meehan, "The Organizational Career of Gang Statistics: The Politics of Policing Gangs," *Sociological Quarterly* 41 (2000): 364.

51. William J. Chambliss, *Power, Politics, and Crime* (Boulder: Westview, 1999), p. 35.

52. Paul Feyerabend, *Against Method* (London: Verson, 1975), p. 19.

53. Ben Agger, *Public Sociology: From Social Facts to Literary Acts*, 2nd ed. (Lanham, MD: Rowman and Littlefield, 2007).

54. This happened to Joe Feagin when he was finally able to get a qualitative data article accepted by the *American Sociological Review* in the 1990s. The article dealt with data from in-depth interviews with African Americans on experiences with discrimination in public places. In an arduous cycle of reviews, the very quantitatively oriented *ASR* editor pressured the author to include a quantitative data table in the article as a condition for publication.

55. See Ben Agger, *Reading Science: A Literary, Political, and Sociological Analysis* (Dix Hills, NY: General Hall, 1989).

56. John J. Macionis, *Sociology*, 15th ed. (Upper Saddle River, NJ: Prentice-Hall, 2013); see also Diana Kendall, *Sociology in Our Times*, 2nd ed. (Belmont, CA: Wadsworth, 1999).

57. Levine, *Visions of the Sociological Tradition*, p. 81.

58. Edward Shils, *The Calling of Sociology and Other Essays on the Pursuit of Learning* (Chicago: University of Chicago Press, 1980), p. 15.

59. Ivan van Illich, *Disabling Professions* (London: M. Boyars Publishers, 1977).

60. Richard Cohen, "Sociological Quarterly Looks at the Occupy Movement," http://nonprofitquarterly.org/policysocial-context/22150-sociological-quarterly-looks-at-the-occupy-movement.html (retrieved February 23, 2014).

61. Jennifer Schuessler, "Academia Occupied by Occupy," www.nytimes.com/2012/05/01/books/academia-becomes-occupied-with-occupy-movement.html?partner=rssnyt&emc=rss (retrieved February 10, 2014).

62. Ibid.

63. Robert Blauner and David Wellman, "Toward the Decolonization of Social Research," in *The Death of White Sociology: Essays on Race and Culture*, ed. Joyce Ladner (Baltimore, MD: Black Classic Press, [1973] 1998), p. 315.

64. Ben Agger, *Critical Social Theories: An Introduction* (Boulder: Westview, 1998), p. 4.

65. Richard Centers, *The Psychology of Social Classes: A Study of Class Consciousness* (Princeton: Princeton University Press, 1949). This study was done on what at the time was considered a nationally "representative" sample—1,097 white men.

66. Rich Fantasia, "From Class Consciousness to Culture, Action and Social Organization," *Annual Review of Sociology* 21 (1995).

67. Ibid., p. 271.

68. Sjoberg, "Reflective Methodology," p. xxiv.

69. See George Marshall, "Some Remarks on the Study of Working Class Consciousness," *Politics and Society* 12 (1983): 263–301.

70. Fantasia, "From Class Consciousness to Culture, Action, and Social Organization," p. 270.

71. Ibid., p. 271.

72. See "Marx's Enquête Ouvrière," in *Karl Marx: Selected Writings in Sociology and Social Philosophy*, trans. and ed. Tom Bottomore and Maximillien Rubel (New York: McGraw-Hill, 1956), pp. 203–212.

73. Ibid., p. 203.

74. Ibid., p. 208.

75. Fantasia, "From Class Consciousness to Culture, Action, and Social Organization," p. 273.

76. C. Wright Mills, *The Sociological Imagination* (New York: Oxford University Press, 1959), p. 85.

77. Ted R. Vaughan, "The Crisis in Contemporary American Sociology: A Critique of the Discipline's Dominant Paradigm," in *A Critique of Contemporary American Sociology*, ed. Ted R. Vaughan, Gideon Sjoberg, and Larry Reynolds (Dix Hills, NY: General Hall, 1993), pp. 10–53.

78. Kai Erikson, "Sociology and Contemporary Events," in *Conflict and Consensus: A Festschrift in Honor of Lewis A. Coser*, ed. Walter W. Powell and Richard Robbins (New York: Free Press, 1984), p. 306. Note, too, that this critique is in a book, not a journal article!

79. Patricia Wilner, "The Main Drift of Sociology Between 1936 and 1984," *Journal of the History of Sociology* 5 (1985): 1–20.

80. Walter Powell, "From the Editor's Desk," *Contemporary Sociology* 23 (November 1994): v–vi.

81. We are indebted here to comments from Diana Kendall.

82. Macionis, *Sociology*, p. 18.

83. Ibid., p. 20.

84. Ian Craib, *Modern Social Theory: From Parsons to Habermas*, 2nd ed. (New York: St. Martin's, 1992), p. 37.

85. Macionis, *Sociology*, p. 22.

86. See, for example, Diana Kendall, *Sociology in Our Times*, 2nd ed. (Belmont, CA: Wadsworth, 1999), pp. 13–17. We also draw here on personal communication with the author. See also. Macionis, *Sociology*, pp. 19–20.

87. Sjoberg, "Reflective Methodology," p. xviii.

88. Karl Marx, "Letters from the Franco-German Yearbooks," in *Early Writings of Marx*, trans. R. Livingstone and G. Benton (London: Penguin Books, [1843] 1975), p. 209.

89. Gubrium and Holstein, *The New Language of Qualitative Method*, p. 115.

90. Michael Burawoy et al., *Ethnography Unbound: Power and Resistance in the Modern Metropolis* (Berkeley: University of California Press, 1991), pp. 271–287.

91. See W. E. B. Du Bois, *The Souls of Black Folk* (New York: Bantam Books, [1903] 1989); Jane Addams, "Charity and Social Justice," *Survey* 24 (June 11, 1910): 441–449; Jane Addams, *Newer Ideas of Peace* (New York: Macmillan, 1907); and Charlotte Perkins Gilman, *Women and Economics: A Study of the Economic Relation Between Men and Women as a Factory in Social Evolution* (Boston: Small, Maynard, 1898).

92. This was the experience of the first two authors in several research studies of African Americans, in which respondents were allowed to wander from the open-ended interview schedules used to initiate discussions. See Joe R. Feagin

and Melvin Sikes, *Living with Racism: The Black Middle-Class Experience* (Boston: Beacon, 1994); and Joe R. Feagin, Hernán Vera, and Nikitah Imani, *The Agony of Education* (New York: Routledge, 1996).

93. Charles Harrison, Acting Provost of the University of Pennsylvania, as quoted in David L. Lewis, *W. E. B. Du Bois: Biography of a Race* (New York: Henry Holt, 1993), p. 188. See also pp. 187–189.

94. Lewis, *W. E. B. Du Bois*, pp. 190–210; W. E. B. Du Bois, *The Philadelphia Negro* (Millwood, NY: Kraus-Thomson, [1899] 1973).

95. Du Bois, *The Philadelphia Negro*, p. 394. Italics added.

96. Ibid. Italics added.

97. See, for example, Amitai Etzioni, *The Moral Dimension* (New York: Free Press, 1988); Dorothy Smith, *The Conceptual Process of Power* (Boston: Northeastern University Press, 1990); and Immanuel Wallerstein, *After Liberalism* (New York: New Press, 1995).

98. Hill, "Epistemology, Axiology, and Ideology in Sociology," p. 69.

99. Gideon Sjoberg and Ted Vaughan, "The Ethical Foundations of Sociology and the Necessity for a Human Rights Perspective," in *A Critique of Contemporary American Sociology*, ed. Ted R. Vaughan, Gideon Sjoberg, and Larry Reynolds (Dix Hills, NY: General Hall, 1993), pp. 114–159.

100. See G. William Domhoff, "Who Rules America?" www2.ucsc.edu /whorulesamerica/about.html (retrieved February 9, 2014).

101. G. William Domhoff, *Who Rules America?* (Englewood Cliffs, NJ: Prentice-Hall, 1967); G. William Domhoff, *The Power Elite and the State: How Policy Is Made in America* (New York: Aldine, 1990; see also Joe R. Feagin, *Free Enterprise City: Houston in Political-Economic Perspective* (New Brunswick, NJ: Rutgers University Press, 1988).

102. Domhoff, "Who Rules America?"

Chapter 5

1. Robert Blauner and David Wellman, "Toward the Decolonization of Social Research," in *The Death of White Sociology: Essays on Race and Culture*, ed. Joyce Ladner (Baltimore, MD: Black Classic Press, [1973] 1998), p. 310.

2. "What Do We Do?" www.industrialareasfoundation.org/iafabout /aboutwhat.htm (retrieved November 16, 2007).

3. West Southwest IAF, "Executive Order Builds on IAF's Living Wage Tradition," www.swiaf.org/uncategorized/executive-order-builds-on-iafs-living -wage-tradition/ (retrieved January 31, 2014).

4. Donald C. Reitzes and Dietrich C. Reitzes, *The Alinsky Legacy: Alive and Kicking* (Greenwich, CT: JAI Press, 1987), p. 2.

5. Saul D. Alinsky, *Reveille for Radicals* (Chicago: University of Chicago Press, 1946), p. 76.

6. Quoted in Bernard Doering, *The Philosopher and the Provocateur: The Correspondence of Jacques Maritain and Saul Alinsky* (Notre Dame, IN: University of Notre Dame Press, 1994), p. 18.

7. Hernán Vera and Michael Francis, "A Totalitarianism in Latin America: Chile's New Military Messiahs," *Third World Review* 3 (Spring 1977): 20–30.

8. Charles E. Curran, *Directions in Catholic Social Ethics* (Notre Dame, IN: Notre Dame University Press, 1985), p. 155.

9. Lawrence J. Engel, "The Influence of Saul Alinsky on the Campaign for Human Development," *Theological Studies* 59 (December 1998): 636; "Breaking the Cycle of Poverty," www.usccb.org/cchd (retrieved November 18, 2007).

10. United States Conference of Catholic Bishops, "Catholic Campaign for Human Development," www.usccb.org/about/catholic-campaign-for-human -development/ (retrieved February 10, 2014).

11. John Gehring, "CCHD: Putting the Gospel into Practice," *National Catholic Review*, www.americamagazine.org/content/all-things/cchd-putting -gospel-practice (retrieved February 10, 2014).

12. Reitzes and Reitzes, *The Alinsky Legacy*, p. 207.

13. Cesar Chavez interview, June 19, 1984, as quoted in Reitzes and Reitzes, *The Alinsky Legacy*, p. 225.

14. UCTV Blog, "Cesar Chavez and the Community Service Organiza- tion," http://myuctv.tv/2012/03/29/cesar-chavez-and-the-community-service -organization/ (retrieved February 10, 2014).

15. Ernesto Cortes, "Reweaving the Social Fabric," at http://cpn.org/topics /community/reweaving.html (retrieved June 23, 2014).

16. South Bronx Churches, www.sbc-iaf.org/ (retrieved February 10, 2014).

17. See Harry C. Boyte, *Community Is Possible* (New York: Harper and Row, 1984), pp. 137–159. We draw on Stella Capek and Joe R. Feagin, "Grassroots Movements in a Class Perspective," in *Research in Political Sociology*, ed. P. C. Wasburn (Greenwich, CT: JAI Press, 1989), pp. 27–53.

18. C.O.P.S./The Metro Alliance, "Immigration," http://copsmetro.wordpress .com/immigration/ (retrieved February 10, 2014).

19. Mark R. Warren, "Creating a Multi-Racial Democratic Community: A Case Study of the Texas Industrial Areas Foundation," www.cpn.org/sections /topicskommunity/stories-studies/texas_iafl.htm, 1996, p. 3 (retrieved February 10, 2014).

20. Ibid., p. 3.

21. Ibid.

22. Stanley Ziemba, "Alinsky Rules Are Still Activist's Bible," *Chicago Tribune*, June 6, 1982, pp. 1, 5, as quoted in Reitzes and Reitzes, *The Alinsky Legacy*, p. 231.

23. We follow Reitzes and Reitzes, *The Alinsky Legacy*, closely here.

24. Robert E. Park, "The City: Suggestions for the Investigation of Human Behavior in the City Environment," *American Journal of Sociology* 20 (March 1916): 577–612.

25. See Mary Jo Deegan, *Jane Addams and the Men of the Chicago School, 1892–1918* (New Brunswick, NJ: Transaction Books, 1988), pp. 33–37.

26. John Cornwell, *Hitler's Pope: The Secret History of Pius XII* (New York: Viking, 1999).

27. Jacques Maritain, *Integral Humanism* (Notre Dame, IN: University of Notre Dame Press, 1973), p. 230.

28. Saul Alinsky as quoted in Doering, *The Philosopher and the Provocateur*, p. xxii.

29. Alinsky, *Reveille for Radicals*, p. 17.

30. Ibid., p. 22. Alinsky notes that to be radical, one does not need to be radical all of one's life or on all issues.

31. Ibid., p. 71.

32. Ibid., p. 66.

33. Ibid., p. 73.

34. Ibid., p. 79.

35. Saul D. Alinsky, *Rules for Radicals: A Practical Primer for Realistic Radicals* (New York: Random House, 1971), pp. 46–47.

36. Sanford D. Horwitt, *Let Them Call Me Rebel: Saul Alinsky—His Life and Legacy* (New York: Knopf, 1989), p. 532.

37. "A Sociological Technique in Clinical Criminology," Proceedings of the Sixty-Fourth Annual Congress of the American Prison Association, September 17–21, 1934, p. 176.

38. Horwitt, *Let Them Call Me Rebel*, p. 132.

39. Alinsky, *Reveille for Radicals*, p. 81.

40. Ibid., p. 82.

41. Ibid., p. 84.

42. Marcel Mauss, *The Gift* (London: Cohen and West, 1954), p. 1.

43. Alinsky, *Reveille for Radicals*, p. 58.

44. We draw here on Capek and Feagin, "Grassroots Movements in a Class Perspective," pp. 27–53. See also Alain Touraine, "An Introduction to the Study of Social Movements," *Social Research* 52 (Winter 1985): 749–787.

45. Harry Boyte, "Beyond Politics as Usual," in *The New Populism*, ed. Harry C. Boyte and Frank Riessman (Philadelphia: Temple University Press, 1986), pp. 3–15.

46. Robert A. Slayton, *Back of the Yards* (Chicago: University of Chicago Press, 1986), p. 196.

47. Randy Stoecker and Susan Stall, "Community Organizing or Organizing Community?" Paper presented as part of an Internet (H-Urban) Seminar on the History of Community Organizing and Community-Based Development, 1996–1997, http://comm-org.utoledo.edu/papers96/gender2.html.

48. Ibid., n.p.

49. Ibid., n.p.

50. Ibid., n.p.

51. Alinsky, *Reveille for Radicals*, p. 33.

52. Ibid., p. 40.

53. Ibid., p. 33.

54. Ibid., p. 57.

55. Ibid., p. 60.

56. Ibid., pp. 83–84.

57. Horwitt, *Let Them Call Me Rebel*, pp. 132, 529.

58. These numbers are taken from the Social Science Citation Index, Institute for Scientific Information, 2000, a Web of Science database.

59. See Martin Oppenheimer, Martin J. Murray, and Rhonda Levine, eds., *Radical Sociologists and the Movement: Experiences, Lessons, and Legacies* (Philadelphia: Temple University Press, 1991).

60. L. David Alinsky, "Son Sees Father's Handiwork in Convention," *Boston Globe*, www.boston.com/bostonglobe/editorial_opinion/letters/articles/2008/08/31/son_sees_fathers_handiwork_in_convention/ (retrieved February 10, 2014).

61. Joe R. Feagin and Hernán Vera, *White Racism: The Basics* (New York: Routledge, 1995).

62. Noel A. Cazenave, "The Militant Denial of the Existence of White Racism in Contemporary America," unpublished paper, University of Connecticut, 1996, p. 3.

63. Cazenave, "The Militant Denial of the Existence of White Racism in Contemporary America," p. 4.

64. Ibid., pp. 5–6.

65. Quoted in Katherine Farrish, "'White Racism' Course Approved," *Hartford Courant*, December 13, 1995, p. A3. See also Denise K. Magner, "'White Racism' Course Causes Skirmish at U. of Connecticut," *Chronicle of Higher Education*, January 26, 1996, p. A16.

66. Cazenave, "The Militant Denial of the Existence of White Racism in Contemporary America," p. 9.

67. Katherine Farrish, "'White Racism' Course Approved," p. A3.

68. "White Racism," *Hartford Courant*, January 12, 1996, n.p., from Xeroxed copy provided by Noel Cazenave.

69. Laurence D. Cohen, "The 'White Racism' Professor Has His Own Racial Agenda," *Hartford Courant*, February 25, 1996, p. C3.

70. Magner, "'White Racism' Course Causes Skirmish," p. A16.

71. Cazenave, "The Militant Denial of the Existence of White Racism in Contemporary America," p. 10.

72. Ibid., pp. 15, 20.

73. Noel A. Cazenave and Darlene Alvarez-Maddern, "Defending the White Race: White Male Faculty Opposition to a 'White Racism' Course," paper presented at the Annual Meeting on Race and Ethnicity in Higher Education, Memphis, Tennessee, June 1999, p. 6. This paper has been published as Noel A. Cazenave and Darlene Alvarez-Maddern, "Defending the White Race: White Male Faculty Opposition to a 'White Racism' Course," *Race and Society* 2 (2000): 25–50.

74. Ibid., p. 6.

75. Greg Smith, "Course on Racism Stalled," *Daily Campus*, Friday, December 1, 1995, pp. 1, 4; Katherine Farrish, "White Racism Course Approved: U Conn Teacher's Proposed Class Led to Controversy," *Hartford Courant*, December 13, 1995, p. 2; Jason Jakubowski, "Uphill Battle Fails to Block Approval of Racism Course," *Daily Campus*, Friday, January 26, 1996, pp. 1, 4; and Magner, "'White Racism' Course Causes Skirmish," p. A16.

76. Cazenave and Alvarez-Maddern, "Defending the White Race," p. 14.

77. Ibid., p. 15.

78. Ibid., p. 20.

79. Frances Grandy Taylor, "'White Racism' Course Magnifies, Teaches Evolution of Bigotry," *Hartford Courant*, November 19, 1996, pp. A3, A10.

80. Cazenave and Alvarez-Maddern, "Defending the White Race," p. 21.

81. Ibid., p. 25.

82. Donald Cunnigen, ed. *Teaching Race and Ethnic Relations: Syllabi and Instructional Materials*, 3rd ed. (Washington, DC: American Sociological Association, 1997).

83. ¡Vote! "The Citizenship Project/El Proyecto Ciudadanía," http://ciudadania .yaeshora.info/centers (retrieved April 15, 2014).

84. Paul Johnston, personal communication, December 7, 1999.

85. ¡Vote! "The Citizenship Project/El Proyecto Ciudadanía."

86. Paul Johnston, personal communication, December 7, 1999.

87. Ibid.

88. Ibid.

89. Ibid. Johnston's publications are divided between academic research pieces and popular pieces. See http://members.cruzio.com/-johnston.

90. Ibid.

91. University of Illinois at Chicago, "Immigrant Mobilization Project," www .uic.edu/las/latamst/research/immigrant.shtml (retrieved January 14, 2014).

92. Nilda Flores-Gonzalez, "New Destinations in an Old Gateway: The Interplay between Public and Private Actors in Shaping Local Immigration Policy," www.uic.edu/cuppa/ipce/interior/NewDestinationsExecSummary2011 .pdf (retrieved January 30, 2014).

93. University of Illinois at Chicago, "Immigrant Mobilization Project," www .uic.edu/las/latamst/research/immigrant.shtml (retrieved January 30, 2014).

94. Flores-Gonzalez, "New Destinations in an Old Gateway: The Interplay between Public and Private Actors in Shaping Local Immigration Policy."

95. Quoted in Jean Arthur, "Schmalzbauer Studies Changing State of Montaña," *Mountains and Minds Magazine,* http://web1.msu.montana.edu /mountainsandminds/fall2007/schmalzbauer/print.html (retrieved January 30, 2014).

96. Leah Schmalzbauer, *Striving and Surviving: A Daily Life Analysis of Honduran Transnational Families* (New York: Routledge, 2006).

97. Leah C. Schmalzbauer, "Gender, Migration and (Il)legality in the New West," paper presented at the annual meeting of the American Sociological Association Annual Meeting, Hilton New York and Sheraton New York, New York, NY Online (PDF) (2014), http://citation.allacademic.com/meta/p647702_index .html (retrieved February 10, 2014).

98. Leah Schmalzbauer, email communication to authors, February 2014. Used with permission.

99. Ibid.

100. Ibid.

101. Ibid.

102. Ibid.

103. The United Students Against Sweatshops, "Mission, Vision, and Organizing Philosophy," http://usas.org/about/mission-vision-organizing/ (retrieved December 19, 2013).

104. Ibid.

105. Philip Nyden, Anne Figert, Mark Shibley, and Darryl Burrows, "University-Community Collaborative Research: Adding Chairs at the Research Table," *Building Community: Social Science in Action*, ed. Philip Nyden, Anne Figert, Mark Shibley, and Darryl Burrows (Thousand Oaks, CA: Pine Forge Press, 1997), p. 3.

106. The United Students Against Sweatshops, "Mission, Vision, and Organizing Philosophy."

CHAPTER 6

1. William F. Whyte, Davydd J. Greenwood, and Peter Lazes, "Participatory Action Research: Through Practice to Science in Social Research," in *Participatory Action Research*, ed. William F. Whyte (Newbury Park, CA: Sage, 1991), p. 21.

2. William F. Whyte, "Introduction," in *Participatory Action Research*, ed. William F. Whyte (Newbury Park, CA: Sage, 1991), pp. 10–12.

3. William F. Whyte, "Conclusions," in *Participatory Action Research*, ed. William F. Whyte (Newbury Park, CA: Sage, 1991), p. 237.

4. Philip Nyden, Anne Figert, Mark Shibley, and Darryl Burrows, "Effective Models of Collaboration," in *Building Community: Social Science in Action*, ed. Philip Nyden, Anne Figert, Mark Shibley, and Darryl Burrows (Thousand Oaks, CA: Pine Forge Press, 1997), p. 17.

5. See Paulo Freire, *Pedagogy of the Oppressed* (New York: Continuum, 1995).

6. Robert Blauner and David Wellman, "Toward the Decolonization of Social Research," in *The Death of White Sociology: Essays on Race and Culture*, ed. Joyce Ladner (Baltimore: Black Classic Press, [1973] 1998), p. 315.

7. Ibid.

8. John Gaventa, "Preface," to "Research for Social Justice: Some North-South Convergences," by Orlando Fals-Borda, *Sociological Imagination, Part II, Special Issue of Sociology and Social Action* 33 (1996): 1.

9. Orlando Fals-Borda, *Peasant Society in the Colombian Andes: A Sociological Study of Saucío* (Gainesville: University of Florida Press, 1955).

10. Orlando Fals-Borda, *Acción Comunal en Una Vereda Colombiana: Su Applicación, Sus Resultados y Su Interpretatión* (Bogota: Universidad Nacional de Colombia, Departamento de Sociología, 1960), p. 5. The quotes that follow are our translations.

11. Ibid., pp. 5, 51–52.

12. Ibid., pp. 51–52.

13. Orlando Fals-Borda, *Conocimiento y Poder Popular: Lecciones con Campesinos de Nicaragua, Mexico, Colombia* (Bogota: Siglo Veintiuno, Editores, 1985).

14. Orlando Fals-Borda and Carlos Rodriguez Brandão, *Investigación Participativa* (Montevideo: Instituto del Hombre, Ediciones de la Banda Oriental, 1987). For example, this work is quoted in M. Eugenia Sanchez and G. H. Eduardo Almeida, "Synergistic Development and Participatory Action Research," *American Sociologist* 23 (Winter 1992): 83–99.

15. Fals-Borda, "Research for Social Justice: Some North-South Convergences," 1, 5.

16. Dedication in Orlando Fals-Borda, *Historia Doble de la Costa, Tomo IV: Retorno a la Tierra* (Bogota: Carlos Valencia Editores, 1986); see also Orlando Fals-Borda, *Historia Doble de la Costa, Tomo I: Mom pox y Loba* (Bogota: Carlos Valencia Editores, 1979); Orlando Fals-Borda, *Historia Doble de la Costa, Tomo II: El President Nieto* (Bogota: Carlos Valencia Editores, 1981); Orlando Fals-Borda, *Historia Doble de la Costa, Tomo III: Resistencia en el San Jorge* (Bogota: Carlos Valencia Editores, 1984).

17. Fals-Borda, *Historia Doble de la Costa, Tomo I*.

18. Fals-Borda and Brandão, *Investigación Participativa*, p. 16.

19. Ibid., p. 17.

20. Ibid., p. 12.

21. Fals-Borda, "Research for Social Justice: Some North-South Convergences," p. 5.

22. Ibid., p. 5.

23. Davydd J. Greenwood and Morten Levin, *Introduction to Action Research: Social Research for Social Change* (Thousand Oaks, CA: Sage, 1998), p. 180.

24. Hernán Vera, "On Being Treated Like a Person: The Client's View on High-Quality Care in Santiago, Chile," *Studies in Family Planning* 24 (1993): 1–10.

25. Maria Eugenia Sanchez and F. H. Eduardo Almeida, "Synergistic Development and Participatory Action Research in a Nahuat Community," *American Sociologist* 23 (Winter 1992): 83–99.

26. Ibid., p. 91.

27. Blas Soto Islas, Felipe Gutierrez Sandoval, and Aguilar Lopez Anastacio, "A Global Experience of Self Promotion (voluntary association): The Case of San Miguel de Tzincapan," *Wisconsin Sociologist* 22 (1985): 129–132, as quoted in Sanchez and Almeida, "Synergistic Development and Participatory Action Research in a Nahuat Community," p. 96.

28. Sanchez and Almeida, "Synergistic Development and Participatory Action Research in a Nahuat Community," p. 97.

29. Rakesh Rajani and Mustafa Kudrati, "The Varieties of Sexual Experience of the Street Children of Mwanza, Tanzania," in *Learning About Sexuality: A Practical Beginning*, ed. Sondra Zeidenstein and Kirsten Moore (New York: Population Council International Women's Health Coalitions, 1996), pp. 301–323.

30. Ibid., p. 303.

31. Ibid., pp. 304–306.

32. Ibid., p. 315.

33. Peter H. Mettler and Thomas Baumgartner, "Large-Scale Participatory Co-Shaping of Technological Developments," *Futures* 30 (1998): 535–554.

34. Ibid., pp. 546–547.

35. Richard E. Walton and Michael E. Gaffney, "Research, Action, and Participation: The Merchant Shipping Case," in *Participatory Action Research*, ed. William F. Whyte (Newbury Park, CA: Sage, 1991), p. 99.

36. Ibid., p. 102.

37. Ibid., pp. 103–104.

38. Statistics Canada, "2006 Aboriginal Population Profile for Winnipeg," *Ottawa: Statistics Canada* (February 26, 2010), www.statcan.gc.ca/pub/89-638-x/2010003/article/11082-eng.htm (retrieved December 19, 2013).

39. Shauna MacKinnon and Sara Stephens, "Is Participation Having an Impact? Measuring Progress in Winnipeg's Inner City Through the Voices of Community-Based Program Participants," *Journal of Social Work* 10 (2010): 32.

40. Elizabeth Comack, John Loxley, and Jim Silver, email communication to authors, July 2013. Used with permission.

41. Ibid.

42. Ibid.

43. Ibid.

44. Ibid.

45. Bronwyn Dobchuk-Land, Owen Toews, and Jim Silver, "Neighbourhood Level Responses to Safety Concerns in Four Winnipeg Inner-City Neighbourhoods: Reflections on Collective Efficacy," *Canadian Journal of Urban Research* 19

(2010): 18–33; Elizabeth Comack and Jim Silver, "A Canadian Exception to the Punitive Turn? Community Reponses to Policing Practices in Winnipeg's Inner City," *Canadian Journal of Sociology* 33 (2008): 815–844.

46. Maya Seshia, "Naming Systemic Violence in Winnipeg's Street Sex Trade," *Journal of Urban Research* 19 (2010): 1–17.

47. Elizabeth Comack, Lawrence Deane, Larry Morrissette and Jim Silver, *Indians Wear Red: Colonialism, Resistance and Aboriginal Street Gangs* (Halifax and Winnipeg: Fernwood Publishing, 2013).

48. Jim Silver, *In Their Own Voices: Building Urban Aboriginal Communities* (Halifax and Winnipeg: Fernwood Publishing, 2006).

49. Jim Silver, *Good Places to Live: Poverty and Public Housing in Canada* (Halifax and Winnipeg: Fernwood Publishing, 2011).

50. Shauna MacKinnon, "The Effectiveness of Neo-Liberal Labour Market Policy as a Response to the Poverty and Social Exclusion of Aboriginal Second-Chance Learners," PhD dissertation, University of Manitoba (2012); Jim Silver, ed. *Moving Forward, Giving Back: Transformative Aboriginal Adult Education* (Halifax and Winnipeg: Fernwood Publishing, 2013).

51. MacKinnon and Stephens, "Is Participation Having an Impact? Measuring Progress in Winnipeg's Inner City Through the Voices of Community-Based Program Participants."

52. Agnieszka Pawlowska, "Using the Global to Support the Local: Community Development at Poplar River and the Establishment of a UNESCO World Heritage Site in Northern Manitoba," MA Thesis, University of Manitoba (2009); Rosa Sanchez, "Critical Institutions Governing Hollow Water First Nation Economic Gendered Activity," MA Thesis, University of Manitoba (2013).

53. Elizabeth Comack, John Loxley, and Jim Silver, email communication to authors, July 2013. Used with permission.

54. Ibid.

55. Ibid.

56. Roberta Stout and Sheryl Peters, *Kiskinohamâtôtâpânâsk: Intergenerational Effects on Professional First Nations Women Whose Mothers are Residential School Survivors* (Winnipeg: Prairie Women's Health Centre of Excellence, 2011), www.pwhce.ca/kiskino.htm (retrieved February 10, 2014).

57. Ibid.

58. Ibid.

59. Ibid.

60. Gregory D. Squires and Dan Willett, "The Fair Lending Coalition: Organizing Access to Capital in Milwaukee," in *Building Community: Social Science in Action*, ed. Philip Nyden, Anne Figert, Mark Shibley, and Darryl Burrows (Thousand Oaks, CA: Pine Forge Press, 1997), pp. 52–54.

61. Ibid., p. 56.

62. Gianpaolo Baiocchi, Personal website, http://gianpaolobaiocchi.net/2013/10/ (retrieved January 30, 2014).

63. Ibid.

64. Participatory Budgeting Project, "Mission and Approach," www.participatorybudgeting.org/who-we-are/mission-approach/ (retrieved January 30, 2014).

65. Ibid.

66. Philip Nyden, Joanne Adams, and Kim Zalent, "Creating and Sustaining Racially and Ethnically Diverse Communities," in *Building Community: Social Science in Action*, ed. Philip Nyden, Anne Figert, Mark Shibley, and Darryl Burrows (Thousand Oaks, CA: Pine Forge Press, 1997), pp. 32–35.

67. Ibid; ONE, "Victories," www.onechicago.org/victories.htm (retrieved November 19, 2007).

68. ONE, "News," http://onechicago.org/2013/11/16-one-northside-leaders-go-to-springfield-for-corporate-tax-transparency/#sthash.leYIG8uC.dpuf (retrieved February 9, 2014).

69. Ibid.

70. Nyden, Adams, and Zalent, "Creating and Sustaining Racially and Ethnically Diverse Communities," pp. 33–36.

71. Gregory D. Squires, "Do Subprime Loans Create Subprime Cities? Inequality and Access to Financial Services," *Briefing Paper*, Economic Policy Institute, 2007.

72. Association of Community Organizations for Reform Now, "History of ACORN," www.acorn.org/ (retrieved February 9, 2014).

73. Ibid.

74. National Community Reinvestment Coalition, "NCRC Reacts to President Obama's 2014 State of the Union Address," www.ncrc.org/media-center/press-releases/item/915-ncrc-reacts-to-president-obama%E2%80%99s-2014-state-of-the-union-address (retrieved February 9, 2014).

75. National Fair Housing Alliance, "NFHA Urges Utah Senate to Consider, Not Kill, LGBT Anti-Discrimination Bill for a Fair Vote," www.nationalfairhousing.org/ (retrieved February 9, 2014).

76. Robert D. Bullard, "Dismantling Environmental Racism in the Policy Arena: The Role of Collaborative Social Research," in *Building Community: Social Science in Action*, ed. Philip Nyden, Anne Figert, Mark Shibley, and Darryl Burrows (Thousand Oaks, CA: Pine Forge Press, 1997), pp. 67–68; see also Robert D. Bullard, *Dumping in Dixie: Race, Class, and Environmental Quality* (Boulder: Westview, 1990).

77. Bullard, "Dismantling Environmental Racism in the Policy Arena," pp. 67–68.

78. Robert D. Bullard, Glenn S. Johnson, Denae W. King, and Angel O. Torres, "Environmental Justice Timeline and Milestones: 1964–2014," *Texas Southern University* (2014), http://tsu.edu/academics/colleges__schools/publicaffairs/files/pdf/EJMilestoneExecutiveSummary.pdf (retrieved February 22, 2014).

79. Ibid., p. 72; see also Robert D. Bullard, *Growing Smarter: Achieving Livable Communities, Environmental Justice, and Regional Equity* (Cambridge: MIT Press, 2007); and Robert D. Bullard, *The Black Metropolis in the Twenty-First Century: Race, Power, and the Politics of Place* (New York: Rowman and Littlefield, 2007).

80. Bullard, Johnson, King, and Torres, "Environmental Justice Timeline and Milestones."

81. Clark Atlanta University News Brief, "*Newsweek* Names CAU Scholar One of 13 Environmental Leaders of Century," (September 17, 2008), www.cau.edu/p_releases/BullardNewsBrief.pdf (retrieved December 19, 2013).

82. MELDI, University of Michigan, "David Pellow," http://meldi.snre.umich.edu/node/12475 (retrieved January 30, 2014).

83. Ibid.

84. David Naguib Pellow and Lisa Sun-Hee Park, *The Silicon Valley of Dreams: Environmental Injustice, Immigrant Workers, and the High-Tech Global Economy* (New York: New York University Press, 2002).

85. MELDI, University of Michigan, "David Pellow."

86. David Naguib Pellow and Lisa Sun-Hee Park, *The Slums of Aspen. Immigrants vs. the Environment in America's Eden* (New York: New York University Press, 2013).

87. Lisa Sun-Hee Park and David Naguib Pellow, "The Slums of Aspen," *Denver Post*, www.denverpost.com/ci_19642218 (retrieved January 30, 2014).

88. MELDI, University of Michigan, "David Pellow."

89. University of California Television, "Interview with David Pellow and Jorge Mariscal," www.uctv.tv/RelatedContent.aspx?RelatedID=20 (retrieved January 30, 2014).

90. Daniel Faber, email communication to authors, February 2014. Used with permission.

91. Daniel Faber, *Capitalizing on Environmental Injustice: The Polluter-Industrial Complex in the Age of Globalization* (Lanham, MD: Rowman and Littlefield Publishers, 2008).

92. Community Farm Alliance, http://communityfarmalliance.org/sample -page/mission/ (retrieved January 30, 2014). This paragraph draws heavily on an email communication from Daniel Faber, January 26, 2014. Used by permission.

93. Nancy A. Matthews and Anne Parry, "Grassroots Approaches to Violence Prevention: Rainbow House's Choosing Non-Violence Institute," in *Building Community: Social Science in Action*, ed. Philip Nyden, Anne Figert, Mark Shibley, and Darryl Burrows (Thousand Oaks, CA: Pine Forge Press, 1997), pp. 190–192.

94. Ibid., p. 194.

95. See, for example, the special issue: "Feminism, Restorative Justice, and Violence against Women," *Violence Against Women* 11 (May 2005): 563–730.

96. Nyden, Figert, Shibley, and Burrows, "Effective Models of Collaboration," pp. 16–17.

97. Ibid., pp. 25–26.

98. Greenwood and Levin, *Introduction to Action Research: Social Research for Social Change*, p. 181.

99. Philip Nyden, Anne Figert, Mark Shibley, and Darryl Burrows, "Conclusion: Collaboration Gives Hope and Voice in an Age of Disillusionment," in *Building Community: Social Science in Action*, ed. Philip Nyden, Anne Figert, Mark Shibley, and Darryl Burrows (Thousand Oaks, CA: Pine Forge Press, 1997), p. 240.

CHAPTER 7

1. C. Wright Mills, *The Sociological Imagination* (New York: Oxford University Press, 1959), p. 63.

2. Alfred McClung Lee, *Sociology for Whom?* (New York: Oxford University Press, 1978), p. 80.

3. Talcott Parsons and Edward A. Shils, "Values, Motives, and Systems of Action," in *Toward a General Theory of Action: Theoretical Foundations for the Social*

Sciences, ed. Talcott Parsons and Edward A. Shils (New York: Harper Torchbooks, 1965), p. 54.

4. Talcott Parsons, Edward A. Shils, Gordon W. Allport, Clyde Kluckhohn, Henry A. Murray, Robert R. Sears, Richard C. Sheldon, Samuel A. T. Stouffer, and Edward C. Tolmon, "Some Fundamental Categories of the Theory of Action: A General Statement," in *Toward a General Theory of Action*, ed. Talcott Parsons and Edward A. Shils (New York: Harper Torchbooks, 1965), p. 3.

5. Talcott Parsons, *The Structure of Social Action: A Study in Social Theory with Special Reference to a Group of Recent European Writers* (New York: Free Press, [1937] 1949), pp. 720–730.

6. Mills, *The Sociological Imagination*, p. 49.

7. bell hooks, "Intellectual Life: In and Beyond the Academy," *Z Magazine*, November 1995, p. 28.

8. Richard and Gerald T. Flacks, "Radical Sociology: The Emergence of Neo-Marxian Perspectives in U.S. Sociology," *Annual Review of Sociology* 4 (1978): 193–233.

9. Mills, *The Sociological Imagination*, p. 7.

10. Here we are using composite examples from a number of cases we have personally seen, as well as some we have read about.

11. See Michael Lerner, *Jewish Renewal: A Path to Healing and Transformation* (New York: Harper Perennial, 1994), p. xviii.

12. Robert W. Friedrichs, *A Sociology of Sociology* (New York: Free Press, 1970), p. 65.

13. Donald E. Comstock, "A Method for Critical Research: Investigating the World to Change It," in *Archives of the Transforming Sociology Series of the Red Feather Institute for Advanced Studies in Sociology* (1980), www.tryoung.com (retrieved September 1, 1999).

14. Martin Jay, *The Dialectical Imagination: A History of the Frankfurt School and the Institute of Social Research, 1923–1950* (Boston: Little, Brown, 1973), p. 253; see also Calvin J. Larson, *Sociological Theory: From the Enlightenment to the Present* (Bayside, NY: General Hall, 1986).

15. Tom Bottomore, "Marxism and Sociology," in *A History of Sociological Analysis*, ed. Tom Bottomore and Robert Nisbet (New York: Basic Books, 1978), p. 133. Bottomore cites a series of articles by Horkheimer.

16. Max Horkheimer and Theodor W. Adorno, *Dialectic of Enlightenment* (New York: Continuum Publishing Company, 2000), p. 3; see also p. xiiiff.

17. Jurgen Habermas, *Knowledge and Human Interests* (Boston: Beacon Press, 1971), p. 356.

18. Jurgen Habermas, "The Analytical Theory of Science and Dialectics," in *The Positivist Dispute in German Sociology*, as cited in Larson, *Sociological Theory*, p. 187.

19. Ibid., p. 189.

20. Jurgen Habermas, "Modernity Versus Postmodernity," in *Culture and Society: Contemporary Debates*, ed. Jeffrey C. Alexander and Steven Seidman (Cambridge, UK: Cambridge University Press, 1990), p. 353.

21. Ibid.

22. Ibid.

23. Daniel Bell, *The Coming of Post-Industrial Society* (New York: Basic Books, 1973), p. 453.

24. Bottomore, "Marxism and Sociology," p. 134.

25. Larson, *Sociological Theory*, p. 189.

26. See Bertell Oilman, *Dialectical Investigations* (New York: Routledge, 1993), pp. 42–45.

27. Jurgen Habermas, *The Philosophical Discourse of Modernity: Twelve Lectures*, trans. Frederick Lawrence (Cambridge: MIT Press, 1987), pp. vii–xvii and passim.

28. Jurgen Habermas, *The Theory of Communicative Action, vol. 1, Reason and the Rationalization of Society* (Boston: Beacon Press, 1984), pp. 305–387.

29. Richard Munch, *Sociological Theory: Developments Since the 1960s* (Chicago: Nelson Hall, 1993), pp. 240–241.

30. Habermas, *The Theory of Communicative Action*, p. 10.

31. Larson, *Sociological Theory*, p. 186.

32. David M. Rasmussen, *Reading Habermas* (Cambridge, UK: Basil Blackwell, 1990), p. 34.

33. Habermas, *The Theory of Communicative Action*, p. 398.

34. Erving Goffman, "The Nature of Deference and Demeanor," *American Anthropologist* 58 (1956): 477.

35. See Erving Goffman, *The Presentation of Self in Everyday Life* (Garden City, N.Y.: Anchor Books, 1959); Erving Goffman, *Behavior in Public Places: Notes on the Social Organization of Gatherings* (New York: Free Press, 1963).

36. Patricia M. Lengerman and Jill Niebrugge-Brantley, "Feminist Sociological Theory: The Near-Future Prospects," in *Frontiers in Social Theory*, ed. George Ritzer (New York: Columbia University Press, 1990), p. 317.

37. Judith Stacey and Barrie Thorne, "Is Sociology Still Missing Its Feminist Revolution?" *Perspectives: The ASA Theory Section Newsletter* 18 (Summer 1996): 1.

38. University of California, "Press Release. Social Problems Special Issue: The Missing Feminist Revolution in Sociology," (2006), http://ucpressjournals.com/assets/SP534PR.pdf (retrieved February 10, 2014).

39. Christine Williams, "Still missing? Comments on the twentieth anniversary of 'The Missing Feminist Revolution in Sociology,'" *Social Problems*, 53 (2006): 454–458.

40. See Catharine A. MacKinnon, *Toward a Feminist Theory of the State* (Cambridge: Harvard University Press, 1989), pp. 2–10.

41. Harvard University Press, "Catharine A. MacKinnon. Are Women Human? And Other International Dialogues," www.hup.harvard.edu/catalog.php?isbn=9780674025554 (retrieved February 10, 2014).

42. Catharine A. MacKinnon, *Are Women Human? And Other International Dialogues* (Boston: Harvard University Press, 2007).

43. Dorothy Smith, *The Conceptual Practices of Power* (Boston: Northeastern University Press, 1990), p. 11.

44. Ibid., p. 12.

45. Ibid., p. 13.

46. Ibid., p. 199.

47. See George Ritzer, *Modern Social Theory* (New York: McGraw-Hill, 1996), pp. 328–329.

48. Dorothy Smith, *Mothering for Schooling* (New York: Routledge, 2005) and *Institutional Ethnography: A Sociology for People* (Lanham, MD: Rowman & Littlefield, 2005).

49. Claire M. Renzetti, "Confessions of a Reformed Positivist: Feminist Participatory Research as Good Social Science," in *Researching Sexual Violence against Women: Methodological and Personal Perspectives* (Thousand Oaks, CA: Sage, 1997), p. 142.

50. SAGE, "Claire Renzetti," www.sagepub.com/authorDetails.nav?contribId =588888 (retrieved February 10, 2014).

51. bell hooks, *Outlaw Culture* (New York: Routledge, 1994); see also bell hooks, *Feminist Theory: From Margin to Center* (Boston: South End Press, 1984), pp. 6–51.

52. bell hooks, "Sexism and Misogyny: Who Takes the Rap?" *Z Magazine*, February 1994, pp. 26–29.

53. The European Graduate School, "bell hooks—Biography," www.egs.edu /library/bell-hooks/biography/ (retrieved February 10, 2014).

54. Patricia Hill Collins, *Black Feminist Thought: Knowledge, Consciousness, and the Politics of Empowerment* (Boston: Unwin Hyman, 1990), p. 67.

55. Patricia Hill Collins, *Fighting Words: Black Women and the Search for Justice* (Minneapolis: University of Minnesota Press, 1998), pp. xi–xii.

56. Ibid., p. 96.

57. Ibid., p. 199.

58. University of Maryland, Department of Sociology, "Patricia Hill Collins," www.socy.umd.edu/facultyprofile/Collins/Patricia%20Hill (retrieved February 10, 2014). Collins' books include, *Black Feminist Thought: Knowledge, Consciousness, and the Politics of Empowerment* (New York: Routledge, 1990), with a revised tenth-year anniversary edition published in 2000; *Black Sexual Politics: African Americans, Gender, and the New Racism* (New York: Routledge, 2004); *Another Kind of Public Education: Race, Schools, the Media and Democratic Possibilities* (Boston: Beacon Press, 2009).

59. Ki Namaste, "The Politics of Inside/Out: Queer Theory, Poststructuralism, and a Sociological Approach to Sexuality," *Sociological Theory* 12 (July 1994): 220–231.

60. Chrys Ingraham, "The Heterosexual Imaginary: Feminist Sociology and Theories of Gender," *Sociological Theory* 12 (July 1994): 203–219.

61. Ibid., p. 204.

62. See Smith, *The Conceptual Practices of Power*, p. 13.

63. Purchase College, State University of New York, "Dr. Chrys Ingraham," https://openscholar.purchase.edu/chrys_ingraham/ (retrieved February 10, 2014).

64. Ava Roesslein, "Andrew Jolivétte, Tribal Historian, Speaks to Students About His Research on Native People and HIV/AIDS," *The Journal* (2012), http://websterjournal.com/2012/12/05/andrew-Jolivétte-tribal-historian-speaks-to -students-about-his-research-on-native-people-and-hivaids/ (retrieved February 10, 2014); Speak Out, "Andrew Jolivétte," www.speakoutnow.org/userdata_display .php?modin=50&uid=424 (retrieved February 10, 2014).

65. Speak Out, "Andrew Jolivétte."

66. Charles Lemert and Esme Bhan, *The Voice of Anna Julia Cooper* (Lanham, MD: Rowman and Littlefield, 1998), p. 93.

67. W. E. B. Du Bois, *Darkwater* (1920), as reprinted in *The Oxford W. E. B. Du Bois Reader*, ed. Eric J. Sundquist (New York: Oxford, 1996), p. 504.

68. Oliver C. Cox, *Caste, Class, and Race* (Garden City, NY: Doubleday, 1948), p. 344. We draw on Joe R. Feagin, *Racist America: Roots, Current Realities, and Future Reparations* (New York: Routledge, 2000), chapters 1–2.

69. Stokely Carmichael [Kwame Ture] and Charles V. Hamilton, *Black Power: The Politics of Liberation in America* (New York: Vintage, 1967).

70. See Joe R. Feagin and Hernán Vera, *White Racism: The Basics* (New York: Routledge, 1995).

71. See Feagin, *Racist America*, chapters 1–2; and Feagin and Vera, *White Racism*, chapter 1.

72. See, for example, Joe Feagin, *The White Racial Frame*, 2nd ed. (New York: Routledge, 2013); Joe Feagin, *Systemic Racism* (New York: Routledge, 2006).

73. See Feagin and Vera, *White Racism*, chapter 7.

74. See bell hooks, *Killing Rage* (New York: Henry Holt, 1995), p. 201.

75. Eileen O'Brien, "Whites Doing Antiracism: Discourse, Practice, Emotion, and Organizations," doctoral dissertation, University of Florida, 1999; Feagin, *Racist America*, pp. 255–257.

76. Eileen O'Brien, personal communication, November 11, 2000.

77. Ibid.

78. Norman K. Denzin, *Images of Postmodern Society: Social Theory and Contemporary Cinema* (Newbury Park, CA: Sage, 1991), p. 180.

79. Steven Seidman, "Introduction," in *The Postmodern Turn: New Perspective on Social Theory*, ed. Steven Seidman (Cambridge: Cambridge University Press, 1994), p. 1.

80. Steven Seidman, "The End of Sociological Theory," *Sociological Theory* 9 (Fall 1991): 140.

81. See George Ritzer, *Postmodern Social Theory* (New York: McGraw-Hill, 1997), p. xvii.

82. Seidman, "The End of Sociological Theory," p. 131.

83. Robert J. Antonio, "Postmodern Storytelling Versus Pragmatic Truth-Seeking: The Discursive Bases of Social Theory," *Sociological Theory* 9 (Fall 1991): 161.

84. Seidman, "The End of Sociological Theory," p. 131.

85. College of Arts and Science, the University of Albany, "Steven Seidman," www.albany.edu/sociology/fac_profile_Seidman.shtml (retrieved February 10, 2014).

86. Jean-François Lyotard, "The Other's Rights," in *On Human Rights: The Oxford Amnesty Lectures*, ed. Stephen Shute and Susan Hurley (New York: Basic Books, 1993), p. 136.

87. Donna Haraway, "A Manifesto for Cyborgs: Science, Technology and Socialist Feminism in the 1980s," in *Feminism/Postmodernism*, ed. Linda J. Nicholson (London: Routledge, 1990), pp. 190–234.

88. The European Graduate School, "Donna Haraway–Biography," www.egs.edu/faculty/donna-haraway/biography/ (retrieved February 9, 2014), p. 55.

89. Ibid.

90. Ibid.

91. See Ben Agger, *Critical Social Theories: An Introduction* (Boulder: Westview, 1998), p. 31.

92. Alfred McClung Lee, "Steps Taken Toward Liberating Sociologists," in *Radical Sociologists and the Movement: Experiences, Lessons, and Legacies*, ed. Martin

Oppenheimer, Martin J. Murray, and Rhonda Levine (Philadelphia: Temple University Press, 1991), p. 39. We draw here on the article.

93. See Roger C. Bannister, "Principle, Politics, Profession: American Sociologists and Fascism," in *Sociology Responds to Fascism*, ed. Stephen P. Turner and Dirk Kasler (London: Routledge, 1992), p. 189.

94. Alfred M. Lee, *How to Understand Propaganda* (New York: Rinehart, 1952), p. viii.

95. "Elizabeth Briant Lee and Alfred McClung Lee," *Dictionary of Unitarian & Universalist Biography*, http://uudb.org/articles/alfredmcclunglee.html (retrieved February 9, 2014).

96. Ibid.

97. Alfred M. Lee, *How Customs and Mentality Can Be Changed* (The Hague: Uitgeverij Van Keulen N.V., 1958), pp. 1–2.

98. Ibid., p. 1.

99. Ibid., p. 3.

100. Lee, *Sociology for Whom?* pp. 16–17.

101. "Elizabeth Briant Lee and Alfred McClung Lee," *Dictionary of Unitarian & Universalist Biography*.

102. Robert G. Newby, "The Making of a Class-Conscious 'Race Man': Reflections on Thirty Years of Struggle," in *Radical Sociologists and the Movement: Experiences, Lessons, and Legacies*, ed. Martin Oppenheimer, Martin J. Murray, and Rhonda Levine (Philadelphia: Temple University Press, 1991), pp. 159–163. This section on Newby draws heavily on this article.

103. Ibid., p. 161.

104. Ibid., pp. 168–169.

105. Ibid., pp. 70–72.

106. Ibid., p. 176.

107. Ibid., p. 177.

108. Ibid., p. 178.

109. Ibid., p. 178.

110. Robert Newby, email communication, December 4, 2000.

111. Ibid.

112. SUNY Press, "What Has This Got to Do with the Liberation of Black People? The Impact of Ronald W. Walters on African American Thought and Leadership," www.sunypress.edu/p-5848-what-has-this-got-to-do-with-th.aspx (retrieved February 9, 2014).

113. T. R. Young, personal communication, January 2000. In this section all quotes from Young and all information on his life are from this communication, unless otherwise indicated.

114. See www.tryoung.com.

115. See T. R. Young, "Marx and the Postmodern: Compatibilities and Contrarities," *Archives of the Transforming Sociology Series of the Red Feather Institute* (1991), www.tryoung.com; and T. R. Young, "Reinventing Sociology: Missions and Methods for Postmodern Sociologists," *Archives of the Transforming Sociology Series of the Red Feather Institute* (1993), www.tryoung.com (retrieved September 1, 1999).

116. Yleana Martinez, "Maxine Baca Zinn," in *Latinas: Women of Achievement*, ed. Diane Telgen and Jim Kamp (Detroit: Visible Ink Press, 1996), p. 33.

117. Ibid., p. 31.

118. Ibid., p. 34.

119. Maxine Baca Zinn and Bonnie Thornton Dill, eds., *Women of Color in U.S. Society* (Philadelphia: Temple University Press, 1994).

120. This is from a biographical statement at www.chicanas.com/chingonas .html.

121. Maxine Baca Zinn, email communication, December 3, 2000.

122. Ibid.

123. Ibid.

124. Ibid.

125. Sociology Global Transformations, "Maxine Baca Zinn," http://sociology .msu.edu/faculty/profile/dr.-maxine-baca-zinn/ (retrieved February 9, 2014).

126. Mary Jo Deegan, personal communication, July 18, 2000.

127. Ibid.

128. Mary Jo Deegan, *Jane Addams and the Men of the Chicago School, 1892–1918* (New Brunswick, NJ: Transaction Books, 1988).

129. Ibid., p. 2.

130. Ibid., p. 304.

131. Mary Jo Deegan, "'Dear Love, Dear Love': Feminist Pragmatism and the Chicago Female World of Love and Ritual," *Gender and Society* 10 (October 1996): 590–607.

132. Mary Jo Deegan, "Symbolic Interaction and the Study of Women: An Introduction," in *Women and Symbolic Interaction*, ed. Mary Jo Deegan and Michael R. Hill (Boston: Allen and Unwin, 1987), pp. 3–15.

133. Ibid., p. 13.

134. Mary Jo Deegan, personal communication, July 18, 2000.

135. Ibid.

136. Bernice McNair Barnett, "Invisible Southern Black Women Leaders in the Civil Rights Movement: The Triple Constraints of Gender, Race, and Class," *Gender & Society* 7 (1993): 162–82; Bernice McNair Barnett, *Sisters in Struggle: Invisible Black Women in the Civil Rights Movement 1945–1970* (New York: Routledge, 1999).

137. Agger, *Critical Social Theories*, p. 6.

138. Patricia Hill Collins, "On Book Exhibits and New Complexities: Reflections on Sociology as Science," *Contemporary Sociology* 27 (January 1998): 10.

CHAPTER 8

1. U.S. Department of Education, National Center for Education Statistics (NCES), *Integrated Post-Secondary Education Data System (IPEDS) Completions, 1996–2010* (Washington, DC: NCES, 2011), https://webcaspar.nsf.gov (retrieved February 10, 2014).

2. U.S. Department of Education, National Center for Education Statistics (NCES), *Integrated Post-Secondary Education Data System (IPEDS) Completions, 1996–2012* (Washington, DC: NCES, 2012), https://webcaspar.nsf.gov (retrieved February 10, 2014).

3. Ibid.

4. National Science Foundation, Division of Science Resources Statistics. *Survey of Earned Doctorates/Doctorate Records File.* (Arlington, VA: NSF, 2011), http://caspar.nsf.gov (retrieved February 10, 2014).

5. American Sociological Association, "109th ASA Annual Meeting," www.asanet.org/AM2014/am2014.cfm (retrieved February 10, 2014).

6. Eduardo Bonilla-Silva, "Eréndira in American Sociology," SSF LISTSERV, November 2, 2007 (retrieved November 2, 2007).

7. Hossein Alizadeh, "Sociology Professor Fired in Iran for Discussing Homosexuality?" *Huffington Post* (September 16, 2013), www.huffingtonpost.com/hossein-alizadeh/sociology-professor-fired-in-iran-for-discussing-homosexuality_b_3916652.html (retrieved January 30, 2014).

8. George Miller, "Psychology as an Instrument at the Service of Human Welfare," *American Psychologist* 21 (1969): 1063–1075.

9. Ignacio Martín-Baró, *Writings for a Liberation Psychology*, ed. Adrianne Aron, Shawn Come, and Elliot Mishler (Cambridge: Harvard University Press, 1994).

10. Ignacio Martín-Baró, "El Latino Indolente," in *Ignacio Martín-Baró, Psicología de la Liberatión*, ed. Amalio Blanco (Madrid: Editorial Trotta, 1998), p. 91. See also pp. 73–101.

11. Leigh Binford, *The El Mozote Massacre: Anthropology and Human Rights* (Tucson: University of Arizona Press, 1996), pp. 199–203.

12. Rachel Donaduo, "Francis' Humility and Emphasis on the Poor Strike a New Tone at the Vatican," *New York Times*, May 25, 2013, www.nytimes.com/2013/05/26/world/europe/pope-francis-changes-tone-at-the-vatican.html?partner=rss&emc=rss&smid=tw-nytimes&_r=3& (retrieved December 19, 2013).

13. Uki Goni and Jonzthon Watts, "Pope Francis: Questions Remain over His Role during Argentina's Dictatorship," *Guardian* (March 14, 2013), www.theguardian.com/world/2013/mar/14/pope-francis-argentina-military-junta (retrieved December 19, 2013).

14. Philip Pullella, "'I'm no Marxist,' Pope Francis Tells Conservative Critics," *Reuters* (December 15, 2013), http://ca.news.yahoo.com/39-39-m-no-marxist-39-pope-francis-130636200.html (retrieved December 19, 2013).

15. "Padre Melo to Visit Ashland," *Mail Tribune* (March 26, 2013), www.mailtribune.com/apps/pbcs.dll/article?AID=/20130326/NEWS/303260326 (retrieved December 19, 2013).

16. Alexandra Puffer, "Social Justice League Hosts Honduran Activist," *Comment* (October 17, 2013), http://thecommentnewspaper.wordpress.com/2013/10/17/social-justice-league-hosts-honduran-activist/ (retrieved December 19, 2013).

17. Ibid.

18. Doreen, "Padre Melo Speaking Dates in New England," *New Hampshire Peace Action* (20 September 2013), http://nhpeaceaction.org/padre-melo-speaking-dates-in-new-england/ (retrieved December 19, 2013).

19. Ignacio Ellacuría, quoted in *Ignacio Martín-Baró, Psicología de la Liberación*, ed. Amalio Blanco (Madrid: Editorial Trotta, 1998), p. 27. Our translation.

20. Amalio Blanco, "Introduction," in *Ignacio Martín-Baró, Psicología de la Liberación*, ed. Amalio Blanco (Madrid: Editorial Trotta, 1998), p. 27.

21. Emmanuel Martey, *African Theology: Inculturation and Liberation* (Maryknoll, NY: Orbis, 1993), p. 11.

22. Onwubiko Agozino, email communication to authors, January 2014. Used with permission.

23. Ibid.

24. Onwubiko Agozino, *Counter-Colonial Criminology: A Critique of Imperialist Reason* (London: Pluto Press, 2003).

25. Ibid., p. 228.

26. Onwubiko Agoznio, "Editorial," *African Journal of Criminology and Justice Studies*, 1 (2005), http://umes.edu/cms300uploadedFiles/AJCJS/acjavol1no1 Editorial.pdf (retrieved January 30, 2014).

27. Onwubiko Agozino, email communication to authors, January 2014. Used with permission.

28. David Nibert, *Animal Rights/Human Rights: Entanglements of Oppression and Liberation* (Lanham, MD: Rowman & Littlefield, 2002).

29. Animal Rights Zone, "Transcript of Prof. David Nibert's Live ARZone Guest Chat," http://arzone.ning.com/profiles/blogs/transcript-of-prof-david-niber #sthash.efVyxc1d.dpuf (retrieved January 30, 2014).

30. David Nibert, *Animal Oppression and Human Violence: Domesecration, Capitalism, and Global Conflict* (New York: Columbia University Press, 2013).

31. Animal Rights Zone, "Transcript of Prof. David Nibert's Live ARZone Guest Chat," http://arzone.ning.com/profiles/blogs/transcript-of-prof-david -niber#sthash.efVyxc1d.dpuf (retrieved January 30, 2014).

32. Columbia University Press, "Animal Oppression and Human Violence: Domesecration, Capitalism, and Global Conflict," http://cup.columbia.edu/book/978-0-231-15188-7/animal-oppression-and-human -violence/reviews (retrieved January 30, 2014).

33. Fernwood Publishing, "About Canada: Animal Rights," http://fernwood-publishing.ca/About-Canada-Animal-Rights-John-Sorenson/ (retrieved January 30, 2014).

34. Howard Zinn, "Chapter 1: Columbus, the Indians, and Human Progress," www.historyisaweapon.com/defcon1/zinncol1.html (retrieved January 30, 2014).

35. Howard Zinn, *Just War* (San Giovanni, Italy: Edizioni Charta, 2005), p. 14.

36. The Albert Einstein Institute, "About Us," www.aeinstein.org/ (retrieved January 31, 2014).

37. Michael True, "The Invention of Peacemaking. As I See It," 2013, www .telegram.com/article/20130326/NEWS/103269891/0 (retrieved January 30, 2014).

38. See Robert N. Bellah et al., *The Good Society* (New York: Knopf, 1991); Amitai Etzioni, *The Spirit of Community: The Reinvention of American Society* (New York: Simon and Schuster, 1993).

39. See Etzioni, *The Spirit of Community*.

40. Sheldon S. Wolin, "Political Theory as a Vocation," *American Political Science Review* 63 (1969): 1064.

41. See Gideon Sjoberg, Elizabeth Gill, Norma Williams, and Kathryn E. Kuhn, "Ethics, Human Rights, and Sociological Inquiry: Genocide, Politicide, and Other Issues of Organizational Power," *American Sociologist* 26 (Spring 1995): 11–13.

42. For international human rights documents, see Department of Public Information, United Nations, *The United Nations and Human Rights, 1945–1995* (New York: United Nations, 1995), pp. 33–225.

43. Stephen Lyng, *Holistic Health and Biomedical Medicine: A Countersystem Analysis* (Albany, NY: SUNY Press, 1990); and Ted R. Vaughan, "The Crisis in Contemporary American Sociology: A Critique of the Discipline's Dominant Paradigm," in *A Critique of Contemporary American Sociology* (New York: General Hall, 1993), p. 47.

44. Emmanuel Saez and Thomas Piketty, "Striking It Richer: The Evolution of Top Incomes in the United States (updated with 2012 preliminary estimates)," 2013, http://elsa.berkeley.edu/~saez/saez-UStopincomes-2012.pdf (retrieved March 8, 2014).

45. Annie Lowrey, "The Rich Get Richer Through the Recovery," *New York Times*, September 10, 2013, http://economix.blogs.nytimes.com/2013/09/10/the-rich-get-richer-through-the-recovery/?_php=true&_type=blogs&_php=true&_type=blogs&_r=1 (retrieved March 8, 2014).

46. See Michael M. Bell, *An Invitation to Environmental Sociology* (Thousand Oaks, CA: Pine Forge Press, 1998).

47. Jared Diamond, *The Third Chimpanzee: The Evolution and Future of the Human Animal* (New York: HarperCollins, 1992), p. 362.

48. William K. Carroll, email communication to authors, June 2013. Used with permission.

49. Ibid.

50. Ibid.

51. Ibid.

52. See Marcel Mauss, *The Gift* (London: Cohen and West, 1954).

53. Gideon Sjoberg, "The Human Rights Challenge to Communitarianism: Formal Organizations and Race and Ethnicity," in *Macro Socio-Economics: From Theory to Activism*, ed. David Sciulli (Armonk, NY: M. E. Sharpe, 1996), p. 287.

54. Sandra Harding, "Introduction," in *The 'Racial' Economy of Science: Toward a Democratic Future* (Bloomington: Indiana University Press, 1993), p. 3.

55. Ibid., pp. 12–16.

56. Sjoberg, "The Human Rights Challenge to Communitarianism," pp. 281–282.

57. Pierre Bourdieu and Loic Wacquant, "New Liberal Speak: Notes on the New Planetary Vulgate," trans. David Macy, *Radical Philosophy* (Jan–Feb 2001), www.radicalphilosophy.com/default.asp?channel_id=2187&editorial_id=9956 (retrieved December 2, 2007).

Chapter 9

1. Karl Marx and Frederick Engels, "The German Ideology," in Robert C. Tucker, ed. *The Marx and Engels Reader* (New York: W. W. Norton, 1978), p.154.

2. Pierre Bourdieu, *Outline of Theory of Practice* (Cambridge: Cambridge University Press, 1977), p. 192.

3. "Campus Compact Honors Joe Bandy for Service Learning," *Bowdoin Campus News*, March 13, 2006, www.bowdoin.edu/news/archives/1bowdoincampus/002894.shtml (retrieved December 19, 2013).

4. Vanderbilt University, Center for Teaching, "Joe Bandy," http://cft.vanderbilt.edu/about/staff/joebandy/ (retrieved December 29, 2013).

5. Kara Furlong, "The Vanderbilt Center for Nashville Studies Connects Needs with Campus Research," *Vanderbilt View* (January 1, 2011), http://sitemason.vanderbilt.edu/vanderbiltview/articles/2011/01/01/town-and-gown.129113 (retrieved December 19, 2013).

6. John Foran, University of California, Santa Barbara, "The Case Study Method," June 2002, www.soc.ucsb.edu/projects/casemethod/ (retrieved December 19, 2013).

7. Joey Lywak, email communication to authors, December 2013. Used with permission.

8. Scott Myers-Lipton, email communication to authors, December 2013. Used with permission.

9. Tyler Huffman and Andrea Blackwell, "Do Something. Do Anything," *Spartan Daily* (March 5, 2013), http://spartandaily.com/99535/do-something-do-anything (retrieved December 19, 2013).

10. Scott Myers-Lipton, email communication to authors, December 2013. Used with permission.

11. Huffman and Blackwell, "Do Something. Do Anything."

12. Dennis Hayes and Robin Wynward, eds. *The McDonaldization of Higher Education* (Westport, CT: Greenwood Press, 2002).

13. John Asimakopoulos, email communication to authors, February 2014. Used with permission.

14. Ibid.

15. Paulo Freire, *Pedagogy of the Oppressed* (New York: Continuum, 1995), p. 53.

16. Ibid., p. 55.

17. We are indebted here to critical comments by Jennifer Mueller.

18. Ben Agger, *Public Sociology: From Social Facts to Literary Acts* (Lanham, MD: Rowman and Littlefield, 2000), p. 266.

19. Michael G. Long, *Against Us, But for Us: Martin Luther King, Jr. and the State* (Macon, GA: Mercer University Press, 2002), pp. 29–30.

20. James M. Washington, ed. *A Testament of Hope: The Essential Writings and Speeches of Martin Luther King* (New York: HarperCollins, 1991), p. 314.

21. Ibid., pp. 50–51.

22. Ella Hereth, "Boot the Bell Campaign University of Chicago Case Study," www.sfalliance.org/resources/UofC%20case-study.pdf (retrieved December 19, 2013).

23. Student Labor Action Project, "History," www.studentlabor.org/history/ (retrieved December 19, 2013).

24. Ibid.

25. Ibid.

Index

About the Authors

Joe Feagin, the Ella C. McFadden Professor of Liberal Arts at Texas A & M University, has written or cowritten sixty-four scholarly books and many scholarly articles in his areas of sociology of racism, sexism, and urban life. He is the recipient of the 2013 American Association for Affirmative Action's Arthur Fletcher Lifetime Achievement Award and the American Sociological Association's 2013 W. E. B. Du Bois Career of Distinguished Scholarship Award. He was the 1999 to 2000 president of the American Sociological Association.

Hernán Vera is professor emeritus of sociology at the University of Florida–Gainesville and a leading scholar in US racial and ethnic relations. His books include *Screen Saviors: Hollywood Fictions of Whiteness*.

Kimberley Ducey is an assistant professor in sociology at the University of Winnipeg, Manitoba, Canada. She is a recipient of Québec's Forces AVENIR Award for her efforts in promoting liberation sociology. She has published articles on liberation sociology, genocide, and pedagogical strategies.